SOMETHING ABOUT THE AUTHOR®

ALA
RUSA

Something about
the Author *was named
an "Outstanding
Reference Source,"
the highest honor given
by the American
Library Association
Reference and Adult
Services Division.*

ISSN 0276-816X

SOMETHING ABOUT THE AUTHOR®

**Facts and Pictures about Authors
and Illustrators of Books for Young People**

volume 224

GALE
CENGAGE Learning™

Detroit • New York • San Francisco • New Haven, Conn • Waterville, Maine • London

GALE
CENGAGE Learning

Something about the Author, Volume 224

Project Editor: Lisa Kumar

Permissions: Leitha Etheridge-Sims

Imaging and Multimedia: Leitha
    Etheridge-Sims, John Watkins

Composition and Electronic Capture:
    Amy Darga

Manufacturing: Rhonda Dover

Product Manager: Mary Onorato

Gale, Cengage Learning
27500 Drake Rd.
Farmington Hills, MI, 48331-3535

LIBRARY OF CONGRESS CATALOG CARD NUMBER 62-52046

ISBN-13: 978-1-4144-6127-4
ISBN-10: 1-4144-6127-5

ISSN 0276-816X

This title is also available as an e-book.
ISBN-13: 978-1-4144-6456-5
ISBN-10: 1-4144-6456-8
Contact your Gale, Cengage Learning sales representative for ordering
information.

Printed in Mexico
1 2 3 4 5 6 7 15 14 13 12 11

Contents

Authors in Forthcoming Volumes

Below are some of the authors and illustrators that will be featured in upcoming volumes of *SATA*. These include new entries on the swiftly rising stars of the field, as well as completely revised and updated entries (indicated with *) on some of the most notable and best-loved creators of books for children.

*John Burningham ▌ During his long career, British author/illustrator Burningham has created such memorable picture-book characters as a goose with no feathers in *Borka,* an eccentric rustic in *Mr. Gumpy's Outing* and its sequel, *Mr. Gumpy's Motor Car,* a little girl whose parents desperately want her to stay out of trouble in *Come away from the Water, Shirley,* a balalaika-playing mouse in *Trubloff,* and a cat with a wild nightlife in *It's a Secret.* Honored with numerous awards that include a pair of Kate Greenaway medals, he has also shared his inspirations, his art, and his life in *John Burningham's England* and *John Burningham's France* as well as in the illustrated autobiography *John Burningham.*

*R. Gregory Christie ▌ A three-time recipient of the prestigious Coretta Scott King Honor Book designation, Christie is praised for creating bold, evocative illustrations—primarily in acrylics and gouache—for a number of highly regarded children's books. His intensely colored paintings, which have also been featured in the *New Yorker, Village Voice, Rolling Stone,* and other periodicals, depict the elongated, stylized figures that are a hallmark of Christie's work. His work for Rukhsana Khan's *Ruler of the Courtyard* exhibits his versatility by drawing on images from a Middle Eastern aesthetic; other cultural traditions are reflected in the art he contributes to stories by Anne F. Rockwell, Nikki Grimes, and Vaunda Micheaux Nelson.

*Candace Fleming ▌ In her engaging picture books for young children, Fleming often weaves together elements of history and tradition, while other titles pair the author's whimsical humor with likeable animal characters. A girl sailing down the bayou finds her tiny boat full to brimming after several critters climb aboard in the counting book *Who Invited You?,* while in *Seven Hungry Babies* a mother bird becomes overwhelmed while caring for seven insistent young hatchlings. *Muncha! Muncha! Muncha!* echoes Beatrix Potter's classic childhood story *Peter Rabbit* in its tale of three rabbits. Fleming's tales are particularly notable for their illustrations, which feature work by G. Brian Karas, Yumi Heo, Anne Wilsdorf, and David Catrow, among others.

*Diane Goode ▌ Goode is a celebrated author and illustrator who is noted for her whimsical picture books as well as for anthologies of folk tales and songs. Her original tales, such as *Where's Our Mama?, Mind Your Manners!,* and *The Most Perfect Spot,* have earned praise for their sly narratives and expressive artwork, while *Cinderella: The Dog and Her Little Glass Slipper* and *The Dinosaur's New Clothes,* recast old stories in a fresh and humorous setting. The versatile Goode has also paired her illustrations with the writings of other authors to create works such as the Cal-

decott honor book *When I Was Young in the Mountains, Alligator Boy,* and *My Mom Is Trying to Ruin My Life,* as well as beautifully illustrated renditions of such classics as *Peter Pan* and *A Child's Garden of Verses.*

Kim Dong-hwa ▌ Well known in his native Korea, Kim is an acclaimed author and illustrator in the field of "manhwa," or comics. The unique perspective he brings to the genre through his thoughtful and evocative story arcs, as well as his brilliantly colored art, have been known to Korean readers for over three decades. That changed when Kim's highly acclaimed "Story of Life on the Golden Plains" series was translated into English and published as the graphic-novel trilogy that includes *The Color of Earth, The Color of Water,* and *The Color of Heaven.*

Malagy Morales ▌ The sister of award-winning Mexican artist Yuyi Morales, Morales is a teacher and designer whose colorful acrylic paintings reflect the colorful, stylized art of her native traditions, but with a twist. Her illustrations are showcased in several picture books, among them Pat Mora's *A Piñata in a Pine Tree: A Latino Twelve Days of Christmas, What Can You Do with a Paleta?/¡Qué puedes hacer con una paleta?* by Carmen Tafolla, and Monica Brown's *Chavela and the Magic Bubble.*

Sujean Rim ▌ Rim's watercolor images, with their elongated figures and retro feel, can be seen in advertisements for Almay, Target, Tiffany & Company, and Barney's as well as on the popular Daily-Candy Web site. Beginning in the mid-2000s Rim has also created art for several children's books, among them Lisa Barham's multi-volume "Fashion-forward Adventures of Imogene" series, Laura Schaefer's middle-grade novel *The Teashop Girls,* and her own picture-book story, *Birdie's Big-Girl Shoes.*

*Tony Ross ▌ The work of Ross, an award-winning British author and illustrator, has been well known to both young children and their parents since he began his career in the mid-1970s. As exhibited in the books *I'm Coming to Get You!, Centipede's 100 Shoes,* and *I Want Two Birthdays!,* Ross's whimsical watercolor and pen-and-ink art appeals to bookworms from infancy to the pre-teen years, and his original self-illustrated "Little Princess" stories have even inspired an animated television series broadcast in his native England.

Philip Christian Stead ▌ Stead is the author and illustrator of the whimsically titled original picture books *Creamed Tuna Fish and Peas on Toast* and *Jonathan and the Big Blue Boat,* both of which capture a child's fascination with absurdity and fun. His writing projects also include a collaboration with his wife, artist Erin E. Stead, which resulted in the 2010 Caldecott Medal-winning *A Sick Day for Amos McGee.*

David Whitley ▌ Whitley began earning plaudits for his writing as a student at Oxford University, where one of his children's stories was awarded the Cheshire Prize for Literature. Fame did not sideline Whitley's efforts to pursue an education; he returned to writing full time only after graduation with a degree in English. Published in 2009 as the beginning of his "Agora Trilogy", his

middle-grade fantasy *The Midnight Charter* appeared on the long list for both the Carnegie and Bradford Boase awards in his native England, and was followed by *The Children of the Lost*.

Introduction

Something about the Author (*SATA*) is an ongoing reference series that examines the lives and works of authors and illustrators of books for children. *SATA* includes not only well-known writers and artists but also less prominent individuals whose works are just coming to be recognized. This series is often the only readily available information source on emerging authors and illustrators. You'll find *SATA* informative and entertaining, whether you are a student, a librarian, an English teacher, a parent, or simply an adult who enjoys children's literature.

What's Inside *SATA*

SATA provides detailed information about authors and illustrators who span the full time range of children's literature, from early figures like John Newbery and L. Frank Baum to contemporary figures like Judy Blume and Richard Peck. Authors in the series represent primarily English-speaking countries, particularly the United States, Canada, and the United Kingdom. Also included, however, are authors from around the world whose works are available in English translation. The writings represented in *SATA* include those created intentionally for children and young adults as well as those written for a general audience and known to interest younger readers. These writings cover the entire spectrum of children's literature, including picture books, humor, folk and fairy tales, animal stories, mystery and adventure, science fiction and fantasy, historical fiction, poetry and nonsense verse, drama, biography, and nonfiction. Obituaries are also included in many volumes of *SATA* and are intended not only as death notices but also as concise overviews of people's lives and work. Additionally, each edition features newly revised and updated entries for a selection of *SATA* listees who remain of interest to today's readers and who have been active enough to require extensive revisions of their earlier biographies.

Autobiography Feature

Beginning with Volume 103, many volumes of *SATA* feature one or more specially commissioned autobiographical essays. These unique essays, averaging about ten thousand words in length and illustrated with an abundance of personal photos, present an entertaining and informative first-person perspective on the lives and careers of prominent authors and illustrators profiled in *SATA*.

Two Convenient Indexes

In response to suggestions from librarians, *SATA* indexes no longer appear in every volume but are included in alternate (odd-numbered) volumes of the series, beginning with Volume 57.

SATA continues to include two indexes that cumulate with each alternate volume: the Illustrations Index, arranged by the name of the illustrator, gives the number of the volume and page where the illustrator's work appears in the current volume as well as all preceding volumes in the series; the Author Index gives the number of the volume in which a person's biographical sketch, autobiographical essay, or obituary appears in the current volume as well as all preceding volumes in the series.

These indexes also include references to authors and illustrators who appear in *Gale's Yesterday's Authors of Books for Children, Children's Literature Review,* and *Something about the Author Autobiography Series.*

Easy-to-Use Entry Format

Whether you're already familiar with the *SATA* series or just getting acquainted, you will want to be aware of the kind of information that an entry provides. In every *SATA* entry the editors attempt to give as complete a picture of the person's life and work as possible. A typical entry in *SATA* includes the following clearly labeled information sections:

PERSONAL: date and place of birth and death, parents' names and occupations, name of spouse, date of marriage, names of children, educational institutions attended, degrees received, religious and political affiliations, hobbies and other interests.

ADDRESSES: complete home, office, electronic mail, and agent addresses, whenever available.

CAREER: name of employer, position, and dates for each career post; art exhibitions; military service; memberships and offices held in professional and civic organizations.

MEMBER: professional, civic, and other association memberships and any official posts held.

AWARDS, HONORS: literary and professional awards received.

WRITINGS: title-by-title chronological bibliography of books written and/or illustrated, listed by genre when known; lists of other notable publications, such as plays, screenplays, and periodical contributions.

ADAPTATIONS: a list of films, television programs, plays, CD-ROMs, recordings, and other media presentations that have been adapted from the author's work.

WORK IN PROGRESS: description of projects in progress.

SIDELIGHTS: a biographical portrait of the author or illustrator's development, either directly from the biographee— and often written specifically for the *SATA* entry—or gathered from diaries, letters, interviews, or other published sources.

BIOGRAPHICAL AND CRITICAL SOURCES: cites sources quoted in "Sidelights" along with references for further reading.

EXTENSIVE ILLUSTRATIONS: photographs, movie stills, book illustrations, and other interesting visual materials supplement the text.

How a *SATA* Entry Is Compiled

SATA editors examine a wide variety of published sources to gather information for an entry. Biographical and bibliographic sources are consulted, as are book reviews, feature articles, published interviews, and material sometimes obtained from the biographee's family, publishers, agent, or other associates. Whenever possible, the author or illustrator is sent a copy of the entry to check for accuracy and completeness.

Entries that have not been verified by the biographees or their representatives are marked with an asterisk (*).

Contact the Editor

We encourage our readers to examine the entire *SATA* series. Please write and tell us if we can make *SATA* even more helpful to you. Give your comments and suggestions to the editor:

Editor
Something about the Author
Gale, Cengage Learning
27500 Drake Rd.
Farmington Hills MI 48331-3535

Toll-free: 800-877-GALE
Fax: 248-699-8070

Something about the Author Product Advisory Board

The editors of *Something about the Author* are dedicated to maintaining a high standard of excellence by publishing comprehensive, accurate, and highly readable entries on a wide array of writers for children and young adults. In addition to the quality of the content, the editors take pride in the graphic design of the series, which is intended to be orderly yet inviting, allowing readers to utilize the pages of *SATA* easily and with efficiency. Despite the longevity of the *SATA* print series, and the success of its format, we are mindful that the vitality of a literary reference product is dependent on its ability to serve its users over time. As literature, and attitudes about literature, constantly evolve, so do the reference needs of students, teachers, scholars, journalists, researchers, and book club members. To be certain that we continue to keep pace with the expectations of our customers, the editors of *SATA* listen carefully to their comments regarding the value, utility, and quality of the series. Librarians, who have firsthand knowledge of the needs of library users, are a valuable resource for us. The *Something about the Author* Product Advisory Board, made up of school, public, and academic librarians, is a forum to promote focused feedback about *SATA* on a regular basis. The nine-member advisory board includes the following individuals, whom the editors wish to thank for sharing their expertise:

Eva M. Davis
Director,
Canton Public Library,
Canton, Michigan

Joan B. Eisenberg
Lower School Librarian,
Milton Academy,
Milton, Massachusetts

Francisca Goldsmith
Teen Services Librarian,
Berkeley Public Library,
Berkeley, California

Susan Dove Lempke
Children's Services Supervisor,
Niles Public Library District,
Niles, Illinois

Robyn Lupa
Head of Children's Services,
Jefferson County Public Library,
Lakewood, Colorado

Victor L. Schill
Assistant Branch Librarian/Children's Librarian,
Harris County Public Library/Fairbanks Branch,
Houston, Texas

Caryn Sipos
Community Librarian,
Three Creeks Community Library,
Vancouver, Washington

Steven Weiner
Director,
Maynard Public Library,
Maynard, Massachusetts

SOMETHING ABOUT THE AUTHOR

ADAMS, Kathryn

Personal

Born in United States; immigrated to Canada; father an industrial designer, mother an art teacher. *Education:* Attended Ontario College of Art (now Ontario College of Art and Design); Sheridan College, diploma (illustration); attended Reigate School of Art and Design.

Addresses

Home—Toronto, Ontario, Canada. *E-mail*—info@ kathrynadams.com.

Career

Illustrator, calligrapher, and educator. Freelance illustrator, beginning 1986; former co-owner of illustration representation agency. Instructor in illustration business skills at Sheridan College, beginning 2001, and Ontario College of Art and Design, beginning 2005.

Awards, Honors

Silver Award, Advertising and Design Club of Canada, 1994; CAPIC Awards Merit selection, 1994; *Applied Arts* magazine merit selection, 1994, and two awards, 2003; *3X3* magazine award, 2006; American Illustration Award, 2006, 2009.

Illustrator

Kenneth Hewitt-White, *Night Sky Navigator: Observer's Guide to the Stars, Constellations, and Planets,* Somerville House (Toronto, Ontario, Canada), 1999.

Mark Abley, *Camp Fossil Eyes: Digging for the Origins of Words,* Annick Press (Toronto, Ontario, Canada), 2009.

Also illustrator of foreign-language dictionaries for Rényi Publishers.

Sidelights

Kathryn Adams is a Canadian illustrator whose color-splashed, black-line drawings are a feature of Mark Abley's *Camp Fossil Eyes: Digging for the Origins of Words* as well as of *Night Sky Navigator: Observer's Guide to the Stars, Constellations, and Planets,* an astronomy-themed book by Kenneth Hewitt-White.

Kathryn Adams' line drawings are a feature of Mark Abley's linguistic-themed chapter book Camp Fossil Eyes. (Annick Press Ltd., 2009. Illustration copyright © 2009 by Kathryn Adams. All rights reserved. Reproduced by permission.)

Now a resident of Toronto, Adams teaches on the college and university level, sharing her technical expertise as well as her knowledge of the business side of being an artist.

Although Adams was born in the United States, she grew up in Ottawa, Ontario. She developed a talent for drawing and eventually earned a diploma in illustration from Sheridan College. Adams spent a year in England, pursuing her interest in heraldry and calligraphy, before returning to Canada and beginning her illustration career. While much of her work is used in advertising and other commercial applications, Adams moved into book publishing by creating small spot illustrations for foreign-language dictionaries.

Camp Fossil Eyes tells a story of siblings Jill and Alex and the summer they spent at a camp in the western prairie. Expecting to hunt for dinosaur bones at Camp Fossil Eyes, the young teens find themselves on a different sort of hunt: a hunt for the roots of the English language. In places mapped out as Old English Hill and the Greek Mountains, Jill and Alex dig down and discover the ancient words that have added to the patchwork that is modern English. While noting that Albey's story moves slowly, a *Kirkus Reviews* writer added that Adams' "cartoonish color illustrations . . . break up the text and add a light touch." Calling *Camp Fossil Eyes* "a clever idea," *Resource Links* contributor Carolyn Cutt also noted the appeal of the story's "whimsical, coloured illustrations" and predicted that the book "should be a popular addition to both an Elementary and Secondary School Library Resource Centre."

Biographical and Critical Sources

PERIODICALS

Kirkus Reviews, October 1, 2009, review of *Camp Fossil Eyes: Digging for the Origins of Words.*
Resource Links, December, 2009, Carolyn Cutt, review of *Camp Fossil Eyes,* p. 12.
School Library Journal, February, 2010, Kim Dare, review of *Camp Fossil Eyes,* p. 104.

ONLINE

Annick Press Web site, http://www.annickpress.com (December 15, 2010), "Kathryn Adams."
Kathryn Adams Home Page, http://www.kathrynadams. com (November 29, 2010).

*   *   *

ANDERSON, Jessica Lee 1980-

Personal

Born 1980, in Phoenix, AZ; married; husband's name Michael. *Education:* Hollins University, M.A. (children's literature). *Hobbies and other interests:* Travel, visiting national parks.

Addresses

Home—Austin, TX.

Career

Author. Institute of Children's Literature, West Redding, CT, writing instructor. Also worked as computer salesperson and vision therapy clinic coordinator. Presenter at schools.

Awards, Honors

Milkweed Prize for Children's Literature, 2005, and International Reading Association Notable Children's Book designation, both for *Trudy;* CYBILS Young-Adult Fiction Award nomination, 2009, for *Border Crossing.*

Writings

Trudy, Milkweed Editions (Minneapolis, MN), 2005.
Border Crossing, Milkweed Editions (Minneapolis, MN), 2009.

Contributor to periodicals, including *Highlights for Children, Holiday Crafts 4 Kids,* and *Wee Ones.*

Sidelights

Like many authors of children's books, Jessica Lee Anderson transformed a childhood love of reading and writing into a second career as a writer. "When I was about eight years old, my parents got me a writing program for our Commodore 64 [computer]," Anderson recalled on her home page. "I learned all the keys on the keyboard so that I could touch them and make the words come to life on the screen. . . . I was so determined to write that I went to Hollins University to study what I'm passionate about—children's and young adult literature." Anderson's first novel, *Trudy,* won the Milkweed Prize for Children's Literature in 2005, and her follow up, *Border Crossing,* has also earned praise from critics and readers alike.

In *Trudy* a sixth grader faces challenges in several aspects of her life all at once. For one thing, middle-school math is challenging; besides that, her best friend forever now spends more time with other girls. Trudy also worries about life at home, where her loving but elderly parents have always created a secure environment. Her dad's forgetfulness has been diagnosed as Alzheimer's, which means that her mom faces new challenges and some difficult choices. Trudy's efforts to deal with these changes are aided by a new friendship and the sensitive advice of an English teacher that gains her confidence. Noting the "matter-of-fact, yet unique look" at the "changing dynamics" of an unusual family that the novel allows, Alison Grant added in her *School Library Journal* review of *Trudy* that Anderson's "quiet story is well paced."

Anderson turns to older readers in *Border Crossing,* a novel for teens that is set in the author's home state of Texas. Living in a rural small town, Manz Martinez feels trapped by his family—his undocumented and schizophrenic Mexican dad died years ago and his alcoholic Anglo mom barely makes a living as a migrant farm worker—and the jumbled thoughts in his head constantly veer between his love of his home place and the need to escape. While teaming up with best friend Jed to mend fences for a nearby cattle rancher, the fifteen year old becomes interested in a young woman who cooks for the ranch hands. Any thought of romance takes a back seat to Manz's increasingly chaotic visions and the soundless voice of the Messenger speaking inside his head. The teen also harbors growing fears that a sixty-year-old program to forcibly return illegals back to Mexico may be back in operation. Reviewing *Border Crossing* in *Kirkus Reviews,* a contributor praised Anderson's "poignant" novel as "a sad and thought-provoking exploration of mental illness," and Lynn Rutan noted in *Booklist* that her "descriptions of Manz's escalating symptoms are compelling." Referencing the unusual themes in *Border Crossing, School Library Journal* contributor Roxanne Myers Spencer

wrote that the author's decision to relate Manz's story in a first-person narration "gives readers a poignant close-up of the teen's gradual loss of control to paranoid schizophrenia."

Biographical and Critical Sources

PERIODICALS

Booklist, October 1, 2009, Lynn Rutan, review of *Border Crossing,* p. 33.

Kirkus Reviews, October 1, 2009, review of *Border Crossing.*

School Library Journal, December, 2005, Alison Grant, review of *Trudy,* p. 136; November, 2009, Roxanne Myers Spencer, review of *Border Crossing,* p. 99.

Voice of Youth Advocates, April, 2006, Catherine Gilmore-Clough, review of *Trudy,* p. 37.

ONLINE

Cynsations Web site, http://cynthialeitichsmith.blogspot.com/ (October 14, 2009), joint interview with Anderson and P.J. Hoover.

Jessica Anderson Home Page, http://www.jessicaleeanderson.com (November 29, 2010).*

*   *   *

ARMSTRONG, Shelagh 1961-
(Shelagh Armstrong-Hodgson)

Personal

Born 1961, in Owen Sound, Ontario, Canada; married; children: Caden. *Education:* University of Toronto, B.F. A.; Ontario College of Art, degree (communications and design).

Addresses

Home—Toronto, Ontario, Canada. *E-mail*—shelagh@shelagharmstrong.com.

Career

Illustrator and artist. Worked as a courtroom illustrator and commercial designer. Commissioned to create artwork for Canadian postage stamps; designer of Canadian Olympic coins. Presenter at schools. *Exhibitions:* Works exhibited in solo and group shows in galleries in Ontario, Canada.

Awards, Honors

Will Davies Award for Illustration, 1985; International Reading Association (IRA) Children's Book Award, IRA/Children's Book Council Children's Choice selec-

Cover of Jessica Lee Anderson's young-adult novel **Border Crossing,** *which focuses on a teen dealing with a troubled home life.* (Milkweed Editions, 2009. Reproduced by permission.)

tion, Gold Award, National Parenting Publications Awards, and *Smithsonian* magazine Notable Book designation, all 2003, all for *If the World Were a Village* by David J. Smith; several art awards.

Illustrator

David J. Smith, *If the World Were a Village: A Book about the World's People,* Kids Can Press (Toronto, Ontario, Canada), 2002, second edition, 2011.

Mairi Cowan, *Going to the Park,* Scholastic Canada (Markham, Ontario, Canada), 2005.

David J. Smith, *If America Were a Village: A Book about the People of the United States,* Kids Can Press (Toronto, Ontario, Canada), 2009.

David J. Smith, *This Child, Every Child,* Kids Can Press (Toronto, Ontario, Canada), 2011.

Books featuring Armstrong's art have been translated into several languages, including Arabic, Braille, Catalan, Chinese, Danish, Dutch, German, Greek, Italian, Japanese, Korean, Portuguese, Spanish, Thai, Turkish, and Vietnamese.

Adaptations

If the World Were a Village: A Book about the World's People was adapted for film by Kate Barris, Visual Education Center, 2006.

Sidelights

Shelagh Armstrong is an artist and illustrator who is based in Toronto, Ontario. Her first book-illustration project, *If the World Were a Village: A Book about the World's People,* teamed Armstrong up with fellow Canadian David J. Smith. Since producing their first award-winning effort, Armstrong and Smith have gone on to create the companion picture book *If America Were a Village: A Book about the People of the United States,* as well as *This Child, Every Child,* an illustrated children's book based on the United Nations' Convention on the Rights of the Child.

In *If the World Were a Village* Smith shrinks the population of Earth (6.2 billion people) down to a size that children can relate to, comparing the planet to a village of one hundred residents, along with assorted livestock that includes fifteen pigs and 189 chickens. Within that village, every man, woman, and child represents their share of humankind, and statistics take on a human face. From languages spoken and religious beliefs to literacy, health, affluence and home life, computer usage, and foods eaten, the village population is revealed in all its diversity—and its extremes—in fact-based text and colorful art. In *Booklist* Lauren Peterson likened Armstrong's acrylic paintings to "stained glass windows" that serve as "nice complements to the text," while *School Library Journal* contributor Anne Chapman Callaghan dubbed them "colorful and, of course, multicultural." "Thought-provoking and highly effec-

tive, this world-in-miniature will open eyes to a wider view of our planet and its human inhabitants," concluded Jennifer M. Brabander in her *Horn Book* review of *If the World Were a Village.*

Armstrong and Smith refocus their statistical lens on just one nation in *If America Were a Village,* compressing the U.S. population down from 306 million to one hundred. By Smith's calculations, there are twenty two-parent families in the village, along with seven single parent families and twenty-four one-person or non-family households. In addition to capturing the ranges in American life, Smith also includes information placing the United States into a global context. "The facts are accompanied throughout the book by beautiful illustrations in acrylic," wrote Claire Hazzard in *Resource Links,* the critic dubbing the collaborative picture book "an excellent tool for starting a discussion" of population that will be "both accessible and understandable, even by the youngest student." The "warm acrylic paintings" featured in *If America Were a Village* help readers understand "a whole new way to think about our country," concluded *Booklist* contributor Ilene Cooper, while a *Kirkus Reviews* writer praised the "impressionistic street and crowd scenes" Armstrong crafts for the book. While noting that statistical analysis can sometimes be misleading, Lucinda Snyder Whitehurst recommended the picture book to "provoke discussion" and analysis, and the artist's "lively, cheerful acrylic paintings depict the diversity of our country in a somewhat idealized manner that suits the all-inclusive tone" of Smith's text. "Armstrong's cheerful, smudgy paintings" keep the tone light despite the serious themes in *If America Were a*

Shelagh Armstrong's illustration projects include David J. Smith's multicultural picture book **If American Were a Village.** (Illustration copyright © 2009 by Shelagh Armstrong. All rights reserved. Reproduced by permission.)

Village, according to a *Publishers Weekly* contributor, the critic citing the book's "important but complex message."

Biographical and Critical Sources

PERIODICALS

Booklist, March 1, 2002, Lauren Peterson, review of *If the World Were a Village: A Book about the World's People,* p. 1135; September 1, 2009, Ilene Cooper, review of *If America Were a Village: A Book about the People of the United States,* p. 88.

Horn Book, May-June, 2002, Jennifer M. Brabander, review of *If the World Were a Village,* p. 351.

Kirkus Reviews, July 1, 2009, review of *If America Were a Village.*

Publishers Weekly, June 22, 2009, review of *If America Were a Village,* p. 44.

Resource Links, April, 2002, Victoria Pennell, review of *If the World Were a Village,* p. 37; December, 2009, Claire Hazzard, review of *If America Were a Village,* p. 26.

School Library Journal, May, 2002, Anne Chapman Callaghan, review of *If the World Were a Village,* p. 144; September, 2009, Lucinda Snyder Whitehurst, review of *If America Were a Village,* p. 148.

ONLINE

Canadian Children's Book Centre Web site, http://www. bookcentre.ca/ (December 29, 2010), "Shelagh Armstrong-Hodgson."

Shelagh Armstrong Home Page, http://www.shelagh armstrong.com (December 29, 2010).

Shelagh Armstrong Web log, http://shelagharmstrongillustra tor.blogspot.com (December 29, 2010).*

*   *   *

ARMSTRONG-HODGSON, Shelagh
See ARMSTRONG, Shelagh

B

BANSCH, Helga 1957-

Personal
Born February 23, 1957, in Leoben, Austria. *Education:*
Attended Pädagogik Akademie (Graz).

Addresses
Home—Vienna, Austria. *E-mail*—mail@helga-bansch.
com.

Career
Illustrator and educator. Elementary-grade teacher in
Styria, 1978-2003. *Exhibitions:* Works exhibited at Bologna Illustration Exhibition, 2002, 2003; Bratislava Bi-
enale, 2005; and in Croatia, Italy, Japan, and Slovakia.

Awards, Honors
Österreich Kinder-und Jugendbuchpreis, 2000; Vienna
Kinder-under Jugendbuchpreis, 2001, 2008;
Kritikerjury-Design prize (Austria), and International
Board on Books for Young People Honour List inclu-
sion, both 2004; Vienna Illustrationspreis, 2006; other
illustration awards.

Writings

SELF-ILLUSTRATED

Frau Bund und Hund, Verlag Jungbrunnen (Vienna, Aus-
tria), 2004.
Ein schräger Vogel, Beltz & Gelberg (Weinheim, Ger-
many), 2007, translated as *Odd Bird Out,* 2009.
Petra, Verlag OQO Editora (Galacia, Spain), 2007.
Mäuseplage, Verlag Jungbrunnen (Vienna, Austria), 2008.
Mein lieber Papa, Verlag Jungbrunnen (Vienna, Austria),
2009.
Drei Katzen, Residenz Verlag, 2009.

Lisa will einen Hund, NordSüd (Zurich, Switzerland),
2009, translated as *I Want a Dog!,* NorthSouth (New
York, NY), 2009.

Author's work has been translated into French.

ILLUSTRATOR

Heinz Janisch, *Zack Bumm!,* Jungbrunnen (Vienna, Aus-
tria), 2000.
Heinz Janisch, *Es gibt so Tage,* Jungbrunnen (Vienna,
Austria), 2001.
Heinz Janisch, *Zu Haus,* Jungbrunnen (Vienna, Austria),
2002.
Heinz Janisch, *Bärenhunger,* Jungbrunnen (Vienna, Aus-
tria), 2002.
Karl Ferdinand Kratzl, *Schlappi,* Verlag Georg Hoanzl (Vi-
enna, Austria), 2003.
Karl Ferdinand Kratzl, *Schlappi am anfang war dar Hase,*
Verlag Georg Hoanzl (Vienna, Austria), 2003.
Heinz Janisch, *Katzensprung,* Jungbrunnen (Vienna, Aus-
tria), 2004.
Antonie Schneider, *Die Verwandlung,* Bloomsbury Verlag
(Berlin, Germany), 2005, translated by Alyson Cole as
Leo's Dream, Bloomsbury (New York, NY), 2006.
Mirjam Pressler, *Guten Morgen, gute Nacht,* Beltz Verlag
(Weinheim, Germany), 2005.
Antonie Schneider, *Fuchs und Gans,* Verlag Bajazzo (Zur-
ich, Switzerland), 2006.
Heinz Janisch, *Krone sucht König,* Jungbrunnen (Vienna,
Austria), 2006.
Marisa Nunez, *Chocolata,* Verlag OQO Editora (Galacia,
Spain), 2006.
Marisa Nunez, *Cocorico,* Verlag OQO Editora (Galacia,
Spain), 2006.
Heinz Janisch, *Ein Haus am Meer,* Verlag Jungbrunnen
(Vienna, Austria), 2006.
Heinz Janisch, *Wenn ich nachts nicht schlafen kann,* Jung-
brunnen (Vienna, Austria), 2007.
Antonie Schneider, *Montags Engelchen,* Berlin Verlag
(Berlin, German), 2007.
Roberto Aliaga, *El sueño del osito rosa,* Verlag OQO Edi-
tora (Galacia, Spain), 2007.

Heinz Janisch, *Frau Friederich,* Verlag Jungbrunnen (Vienna, Austria), 2008.
Raquel Mendez, *Os tres proquiños,* Verlag OQO Editoria (Galacia, Spain), 2008.
Heinz Janisch, *Bärensache,* Verlag Jungbrunnen (Vienna, Austria), 2008.
Michaela Herzog, *Ene mene mu, und Rechte hast du,* 2009.
Michaela Herzog, *Anton, das Umweltschweinchen,* 2009.
Heinz Janisch, *Und du darfest rein,* Verlag Jungbrunnen (Vienna, Austria), 2010.
Heinz Janisch, *Die Brücke,* Verlag Jungbrunnen (Vienna, Austria), 2010.

Biographical and Critical Sources

PERIODICALS

Kirkus Reviews, August 15, 2009, review of *I Want a Dog!.*
Publishers Weekly, November 6, 2006, review of *Leo's Dream,* p. 60.
School Library Journal, December, 2009, Linda Ludke, review of *I Want a Dog!,* p. 78; May, 2010, Ana Rodriguez, review of *En haus am meer,* p. 103.

ONLINE

Helga Bansch Home Page, http://www.helga-bansch.com (November 29, 2010).*

*   *   *

BARRATT, Mark 1954-

Personal
Born 1954, in London, England; married; children: Luke, Adam, Jessica. *Hobbies and other interests:* Fishing.

Addresses
Home—London, England.

Career
Actor, writer, and educator. Actor in television series, c. 1980s, including *When the Boat Comes In, Blakes 7,* and *The Dark Side of the Sun.* Formerly worked as a theatre director.

Awards, Honors
Best Entertainment Award, New York Festival, 1994, for *The Wizard's Spell.*

Writings

FOR CHILDREN

Joe Rat, Red Fox (London, England), 2008, Eerdmans Books for Young Readers (Grand Rapids, MI), 2009.

The Wild Man, Red Fox (London, England), 2009, Eerdmans Books for Young Readers (Grand Rapids, MI), 2010.

OTHER

The Wizard's Spell (audioplay), produced 1994.
Ian McKellan: An Unauthorised Biography, Virgin (London, England), 2005.

Sidelights
Mark Barratt was born and raised in London, England, and has worked as an actor and stage director as well as a teacher. Barratt has also gained a reputation as a writer, crafting radio plays and a biography of noted British actor Sir Ian McKellan before turning to middle-grade adventure novels. His "Joe Rat" novels, which are set in Victorian London, include *Joe Rat* and *The Wild Man.*

In *Joe Rat* Barratt introduces Joe Rat, a preteen runaway who has learned his way through the maze of sewer tunnels that beneath London. Through the direction of an obese criminal mastermind known only as "Mother," who controls the impoverished Pounds Field

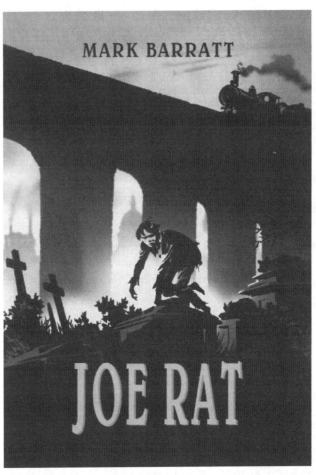

Cover of Mark Barratt's young-adult novel **Joe Rat,** *featuring cover art by David Frankland.* (Eerdmans Books for Young Readers, 2008. Reproduced by permission.)

neighborhood, Joe retrieves the small but precious coins and other metal articles that have been lost down the city's drains. Unfortunately, his take as a "tosher" is rarely enough to please her and his indebtedness increases. When Joe meets Bess, a fellow runaway, he escapes Mother and hides out in the crumbling home of a local madman whose true identity is a mystery but who aids them in their quest for freedom. In capturing Joe and Bess's separate and then intertwined stories, Barratt's narrative "is also a tale steeped in the sights, sounds, and smells of 19th-century London," according to *School Library Journal* contributor Emma Burkhart, the critic adding that the author "does not shy away from the gritty realism" of the era. Reviewing *Joe Rat* for *Booklist,* Daniel Kraus cited Barratt's "perfectly tuned [depiction] . . . of Victorian social mores and grotesqueries" and deemed the novel "leisurely and convincing historical fiction." "A chilling mystery that will haunt readers long after the final page," according to a *Kirkus Reviews* writer, *Joe Rat* will draw fans on the strength of its "gritty, flawed characters, propulsive plot and brooding atmosphere."

Joe returns in *The Wild Man,* which finds him above ground working as a street sweeper in Lomesbury Square. After he spots a burglar and sounds the alarm, the teen is befriended by the intended victim, a banker named Mr. Harvey, who repays Joe by tracking down the boy's father, an army deserter who has fled to Canada. The man's generosity extends to returning Joe's father to England and finding father and son better jobs. Complications arise when Mr. Harvey's son Alec becomes jealous and the true identity of Joe's father is called into question. "Barratt writes as if he is keeping an adjacent berth to [Charles] Dickens," noted Kraus in his favorable *Booklist* review of *The Wild Man.*

Biographical and Critical Sources

PERIODICALS

Booklist, October 15, 2009, Daniel Kraus, review of *Joe Rat,* p. 43; November 1, 2010, Daniel Kraus, review of *The Wild Man,* p. 62.
Horn Book, January-February, 2010, Roger Sutton, review of *Joe Rat,* p. 80.
Kirkus Reviews, September 15, 2009, review of *Joe Rat.*
School Library Journal, October, 2009, Emma Burkhart, review of *Joe Rat,* p. 119.*

*   *   *

BARTON, Chris

Personal

Born in TX; father an optometrist, mother a high-school teacher; married; wife's name Casey; children: Sage, Fletcher (sons). *Education:* University of Texas, degree. *Hobbies and other interests:* Raising hens, music.

Addresses

Home—Austin, TX. *Office*—P.O. Box 170151, Austin, TX 78717. *Agent*—Erin Murphy Literary Agency, 2700 Woodlands Village, No. 300-458, Flagstaff, AZ 86001-7127. *E-mail*—chris@chrisbarton.info.

Career

Writer.

Member

Society of Children's Book Writers and Illustrators.

Awards, Honors

100 Titles for Reading and Sharing selection, New York Public Library, and Best Children's Books of the Year selection, Bank Street College of Education, both 2009, and Notable Children's Books for Middle Readers selection, Association for Library Service to Children, Children's Choices selection, International Reading Association/Children's Book Council, and Robert F. Sibert Informational Book Medal Honor Book designation, American Library Association, all 2010, all for *The Day-Glo Brothers;* Parent's Choice Silver honor, and Best of the Best selection, Chicago Public Library, both 2010, both for *Shark vs. Train.*

Writings

The Day-Glo Brothers: The True Story of Bob and Joe Switzer's Bright Ideas and Brand-new Colors, illustrated by Tony Persiani, Charlesbridge (Watertown, MA), 2009.
Shark vs. Train, illustrated by Tom Lichtenheld, Little, Brown (New York, NY), 2010.
Can I See Your I.D.?: True Stories of False Identities, illustrated by Paul Hoppe, Dial Books (New York, NY), 2011.

Sidelights

Austin, Texas-based writer Chris Barton looks at a pair of unheralded inventors in his debut work for children, *The Day-Glo Brothers: The True Story of Bob and Joe Switzer's Bright Ideas and Brand-new Colors,* a Robert F. Sibert Informational Book Medal honor book. Barton followed that critically acclaimed title with *Shark vs. Train,* which humorously depicts the fierce rivalry between two unlikely combatants. "I alternate between writing fiction and nonfiction . . . ," the author remarked to *Cynsations* online interviewer Cynthia Leitich Smith. "When doing the former, I often long for the certainty and structure that come with established fact, and when doing the latter, I sometimes wish for the freedom to just make stuff up."

Raised in Sulphur Springs, Texas, a small town east of Dallas, Barton developed an early interest in the literary arts, penning his first tale for public consumption, "The

Chris Barton's Shark vs. Train *comes to life in quirky cartoon art by* *Tom Lichtenheld.* (Illustration copyright © 2010 by Tom Lichtenheld. All rights reserved. Reproduced by permission of Little, Brown & Company.)

Ozzie Bros. Meet the Monsters," while in elementary school. Barton's interest in storytelling continued into his teen years; as he noted on his home page: "I loved writing with my friends, whether it was making up parodies of superheroes and soap operas or putting out an award-winning student newspaper." After moving to Austin to attend the University of Texas, he joined the staff of the *Daily Texan* and eventually earned a degree in history. Although he dabbled in writing for a few years, Barton began seriously exploring the world of children's literature after his description of a home improvement project—installing a smoke detector—garnered an enthusiastic response from his young son. "One day," the author recalled to Smith, "it hit me that if I could make him happy with that story, there were probably other stories I could tell, and more kids that I could share them with."

The idea for *The Day-Glo Brothers* came to Barton after he spotted an obituary for Robert Switzer, one of the creators of fluorescent paints. "Up until that moment, I had never wondered where those fluorescent oranges, yellows, and greens came from, even though I had seen them my entire life," Barton told Smith. "It hadn't occurred to me that those colors had been invented or that there had been a time when they didn't exist or that there was a particular name for the glow they give off: daylight fluorescence." In his extensively researched picture-book biography, featuring brightly colored illustrations by Tony Persiani, Barton chronicles the tale of brothers Bob and Joe Switzer, whose experiments with chemical dyes and ultraviolet light—originally intended to enliven Joe's magic act—led to the development of the Day-Glo paints used during World War II to help airplanes land safely at night. "The story is one of quint-

essentially American ingenuity," a *Publishers Weekly* critic asserted. In *Booklist* Carolyn Phelan noted that Barton "writ[es] with a sure sense of what will interest children," and a contributor to *Kirkus Reviews* remarked that the author "brings two unknown inventors into the brilliant light they deserve."

A bragging session between two imaginative playmates leads to a series of far-fetched battles between their favorite toys in *Shark vs. Train*. The contests range from the familiar to the absurd: a;though Shark outperforms his competitor at diving and Train scores big during marshmallow roasting, neither fares well at balancing on a tightrope. "This is a genius concept," declared a *Publishers Weekly* reviewer, and Steven Engelfried observed in *School Library Journal* that "this inspired pairing, executed with ingenuity and packed with action and humor, is a sure winner."

Barton is also the author of *Can I See Your I.D.?: True Stories of False Identities*. "I love the fact that *Shark vs. Train* is sandwiched between that book and the recognition that *The Day-Glo Brothers* has received, because I've always loved doing both types of writing— the thoroughly-researched and the extremely silly," he remarked in a *Seven Impossible Things before Breakfast* online interview. "Now readers can see that for themselves before they get the notion that . . . they might be expected to limit the kinds of writing they do."

Biographical and Critical Sources

PERIODICALS

Booklist, June 1, 2009, Carolyn Phelan, review of *The Day-Glo Brothers: The True Story of Bob and Joe Switzer's Bright Ideas and Brand-new Colors,* p. 85; April 15, 2010, Ian Chipman, review of *Shark vs. Train,* p. 53.
Horn Book, July-August, 2010, Chelsey G.H. Philpot, review of *Shark vs. Train,* p. 85.
Kirkus Reviews, June 15, 2009, review of *The Day-Glo Brothers.*
New York Times Book Review, December 20, 2009, Rich Cohen, December 20, 2009, review of *The Day-Glo Brothers,* p. 12.
Publishers Weekly, June 29, 2009, review of *The Day-Glo Brothers,* p. 129; February 15, 2010, review of *Shark vs. Train,* p. 127.
School Library Journal, August, 2009, Arme Chapman Callaghan, review of *The Day-Glo Brothers,* p. 118; April, 2010, Steven Engelfried, review of *Shark vs. Train,* p. 120.
Science and Children, October, 2009, Ann Rubino, review of *The Day-Glo Brothers,* p. 65.

ONLINE

Chris Barton Home Page, http://www.chrisbarton.info (January 15, 2011).

Cynsations Web log, http://cynthialeitichsmith.blogspot.
com/ (July 2, 2009), Cynthia Leitich Smith, interview
with Barton; (May 11, 2010) Cynthia Leitich Smith,
"Writing across Formats: Chris Barton."

Seven Impossible Things before Breakfast Web log, http://
blaine.org/sevenimpossiblethings/ (March 15, 2010),
interview with Barton and Tom Lichtenheld.*

* * *

BAXTER, Andy
See DAKIN, Glenn

* * *

BEDFORD, David 1969-
(David J. Bedford)

Personal

Born 1969, in England; married Kate (formerly Deborah) Jackson; children: Isobel, Tom. *Education:* Attended University of East Anglia and Santa Barbara
University; Ph.D. (science).

Addresses

Home—Norfolk, England. *E-mail*—david@davidbed
ford.co.uk.

Career

Writer, beginning 1997. Worked as a genetic scientist,
1991-97. Presenter at schools and libraries.

Awards, Honors

Portsmouth (England) Book Award shortlist, 2004, for
The Copy Crocks; British Booktrust Early Years Award
shortlist, 2008, for *It's a George Thing!*

Writings

It's My Turn, illustrated by Elaine Field, Little Tiger Press
(London, England), 2000, Tiger Tales (Wilton, CT),
2001.
Big Bears Can!, illustrated by Gaby Hansen, Tiger Tales
(Wilton, CT), 2001.
Big Bear, Little Bear, illustrated by Jane Chapman, Little
Tiger Press (London, England), 2001, published as
Touch the Sky, My Little Bear, Handprint Books
(Brooklyn, NY), 2001.
Shaggy Dog and the Terrible Itch, Barron's Educational
Series (Hauppauge, NY), 2001, published in *Shaggy
Dog and Titus: Two Troublesome Tales,* Little Tiger
(London, England), 2007.
The Long Journey Home, illustrated by Penny Ives, Little
Tiger Press (London, England), 2001.

(With wife, Deborah Jackson) *Hairy Monkey: A Touch-
and-Feel Storybook,* illustrated by Joanne Stone,
Tango Books (London, England), 2002.
Tiger Eats Pizza: A Touch-and-Feel Storybook, illustrated
by Jan Lewis, Tango Books (London, England), 2002.
Ella's Games, illustrated by Peter Kavanagh, Barron's
Educational Series (Hauppauge, NY), 2002.
What Are You Doing in My Bed?, illustrated by Daniel
Howarth, Little Tiger Press (London, England), 2003.
Mo's Smelly Jumper, illustrated by Edward Eaves, Little
Tiger Press (London, England), 2003, published as
Mo's Stinky Sweater, Hyperion (New York, NY), 2004.
Let's Play Colours, illustrated by Leonie Worthington,
Little Hare (Surry Hills, New South Wales, Australia),
2003.
The Copy Crocs, illustrated by Emily Bolam, Peachtree
(Atlanta, GA), 2004.
Big and Small, illustrated by Leonie Worthington, Little
Hare (Surry Hills, New South Wales, Australia), 2004.
Bums, illustrated by Leonie Worthington, Little Hare
(Surry Hills, New South Wales, Australia), 2004.
Tums, illustrated by Leonie Worthington, Little Hare (Surry
Hills, New South Wales, Australia), 2004.
In-o-saur, Out-o-saur, illustrated by Leonie Worthington,
Little Hare (Surry Hills, New South Wales, Australia),
2005.
One-o-saur, Two-o-saur, illustrated by Leonie Worthing-
ton, Little Hare (Surry Hills, New South Wales, Aus-
tralia), 2005.
Knock, Knock!, illustrated by Bridget Strevens-Marzo,
Little Hare (Surry Hills, New South Wales, Australia),
2005.
The Way I Love You, illustrated by Ann James, Simon &
Schuster Books for Young Readers (New York, NY),
2005.
Hound Dog, illustrated by Melanie Williamson, Oxford
University Press (Oxford, England), 2005, Tiger Tales
(Wilton, CT), 2006.
Max and Sadie, illustrated by Steve Lavis, Oxford Univer-
sity Press (Oxford, England), 2005.
I've Seen Santa!, illustrated by Tim Warnes, Little Tiger
Press (London, England), 2005, Tiger Tales (Wilton,
CT), 2006.
Little Otter's Big Journey, illustrated by Susan Winter,
Good Books (Intercourse, PA), 2006.
Time for Bed, Isobel, illustrated by Keith Brumpton, Little
Hare (Surry Hills, New South Wales, Australia), 2006.
Bedtime for Little Bears!, illustrated by Caroline Pedler,
Good Books (Intercourse, PA), 2007.
Leon Bites, illustrated by Eleanor Taylor, Bloomsbury
Children's (London, England), 2007.
Tails, illustrated by Leonie Worthington, Little Hare (Surry
Hills, New South Wales, Australia), 2007.
Toes, illustrated by Leonie Worthington, Little Hare (Surry
Hills, New South Wales, Australia), 2007.
It's a George Thing!, illustrated by Russell Julian, Egmont
(London, England), 2008.
Daddy Does the Cha Cha Cha!, illustrated by Bridget
Strevens-Marzo, Little Hare (Surry Hills, New South
Wales, Australia), 2008.
Little Bear's Big Sweater, illustrated by Caroline Pedlar,
Good Books (Intercourse, PA), 2009.
Mole's in Love, illustrated by Rosalind Beardshaw, Eg-
mont (London, England), 2009.

Babies, illustrated by Leonie Worthington, Trafalgar (New York, NY), 2009.

Who's Yawning?, illustrated by Leonie Worthington, Trafalgar (New York, NY), 2009.

Mole's Babies, illustrated by Rosalind Beardshaw, Egmont (London, England), 2010.

Josh and the Whoo Whoo, illustrated by Daniel Howarth, QEB (Mankato, MN), 2010.

The Polar Bear Paddle, illustrated by Karen Sapp, QEB (Mankato, MN), 2010.

Ed's Egg, QEB (Mankato, MN), 2011.

Contributor to scientific journals under name David J. Bedford, including *Chemistry and Biology, FEMS Microbiology Letters, Gene,* and *Journal of Bacteriology.*

Author's works have been translated into numerous languages, including Chinese, Danish, Dutch, French, German, Icelandic, Italian, Korean, Polish, Spanish, and Taiwanese.

"THE TEAM" JUNIOR NOVEL SERIES; ILLUSTRATED BY KEITH BRUMPTON

The Football Machine, Little Hare (Surry Hills, New South Wales, Australia), 2003.

Top of the League, Little Hare (Surry Hills, New South Wales, Australia), 2003.

Soccer Camp, Little Hare (Surry Hills, New South Wales, Australia), 2004, Kane/Miller (La Jolla, CA), 2006.

Banned!, Little Hare (Surry Hills, New South Wales, Australia), 2005.

Superteam,, Little Hare (Surry Hills, New South Wales, Australia), 2004, Kane/Miller (La Jolla, CA), 2006.

Football Rules, Little Hare (Surry Hills, New South Wales, Australia), 2006.

The Team (series omnibus), Little Hare (Surry Hills, New South Wales, Australia), 2007.

The Team Strikes Again (collection), Little Hare (Surry Hills, New South Wales, Australia), 2009.

Big Bear mimicks the child-sized Little Bear with unfortunate results in David Bedford's Big Bears Can!, **illustrated by Gaby Hansen.** (Tiger Tales, 2001.

Masters of Soccer, Little Hare (Surry Hills, New South Wales, Australia), 2010.

Soccer Superstars, Little Hare (Surry Hills, New South Wales, Australia), 2010.

World Cup Heroes, Little Hare (Surry Hills, New South Wales, Australia), 2010.

Sidelights

British writer David Bedford casts animals in his many humorous stories for young children. A young monkey is the star of *Mo's Stinky Sweater,* while bears act out the part of human children in *Big Bears Can! Mole's in Love* features a particularly unusual hero in the lowly Morris the mole, *It's a George Thing* focuses on a zebra that loves to dance, and *Time for Bed, Isobel* captures the classic bedtime battle between parents and children through the actions of a young panda. Reflecting his long-held interest in soccer—"football" to the British—Bedford is also the author of the middle-grade "Team" novels, a humorous series about a youth soccer team that climbs up the rankings with the help of gadgets invented by the imaginative Professor Gertie.

Bedford came to writing along a very unusual path. While growing up, he had little interest in school or reading until his early teens, when his efforts to catch up on his studies after a long holiday gave him a taste for learning. Bedford's newfound drive, along with his interest in biology and chemistry, eventually led him to a Ph.D. and a career in microbiology and genetic engineering that involved exploring the possibilities of new pharmaceuticals in scientific laboratories. In his spare time, he began writing stories as a balance to long workdays at the lab, and soon the stories became more interesting to Bedford than his lab work. "As a scientist I used my imagination, solved problems, and discovered

Bedford teams up with noted illustrator Rosalind Beardshaw to create the picture book Mole's in Love. (Tiger Tales, 2009. Illustration copyright © 2009 by Rosalind Beardshaw. All rights reserved. Reproduced by permission.)

new things," the author noted on his home page. "As a writer, and particularly as a children's writer, I now let my imagination wander far more widely, solve far more problems, and there is still plenty to discover (like what my characters are going to say next. . .!). And, most important of all for me, as a writer I'm allowed to spend a lot of my time Making Things Up. Which is a joy, I can tell you."

First published in England as *Big Bear, Little Bear, Touch the Sky, My Little Bear* focuses on a mother polar bear and her baby exploring the world together. As captured in detailed paintings by Jane Chapman, Bedford's affectionate characters work on their den, swim in icy water, and play in the snow. According to *Booklist* contributor Linda M. Kenton, the author's prose in *Touch the Sky, My Little Bear* "has a gentle tone, yet it is simultaneously enthusiastic about the prospect of adventuring in the grown-up world."

Bedford also casts bears in starring roles in *Big Bears Can!, Little Bear's Big Sweater,* and *Bedtime for Little Bears!* A babysitting job goes awry in *Big Bears Can!,* as Big Bear is left to watch over his younger brother while Mother Bear runs an errand. Little Bear soon takes control of the situation, however, challenging his sibling to a series of dares that turns the house into a disaster area. Illustrator Caroline Pedlar captures the humor of *Little Bear's Big Sweater,* Bedford's story about two bear brothers, an unraveling sweater, and a fun day of play, while *Bedtime for Little Bears!* finds a mother polar bear taking her young cub on a tour of nature that leads to sleep. Youngsters will appreciate the "no-you-can't/yes-I-can repetitive dialogue," observed John Sigwald in his *School Library Journal* review of *Big Bears Can!,* while fellow contributor Martha Simpson called *Little Bear's Big Sweater* "a cozy book that will appeal to young children, especially those dealing with sibling issues." Praising *Bedtime for Little Bears!* as "lovely and soothing," a *Kirkus Reviews* contributor added that Bedford's unusual just-before-bed tale will appeal to both "rambunctious and more tranquil preschoolers."

Like *Big Bears Can!, Ella's Games* also concerns sibling rivalry. Ella, a tiny mouse, would like nothing better than to be included in her older brothers' activities. The older mice are quick with objections, however, noting that Ella is too small and too timid for their liking. The imaginative Ella concocts a number of fantastic scenarios to prove her worth, including her successful attempt to rescue an elephant that is stuck in the mud, and she ultimately wins her brothers' approval. "The book ends on a rousing note, with Ella firmly in charge of a pretend pirate adventure aboard a pot of honeysuckle," wrote a critic in *Publishers Weekly.*

A reptile that seeks a little privacy is the subject of *The Copy Crocs.* When Crocodile tires of the overcrowded conditions at his home, he searches for a new place to call his own. Wherever he lands, though, be it in a muddy puddle or on a floating log, his friends are sure

Bedford's quirky story in* Mo's Stinky Sweater *is captured in Edward Eaves' entertaining art. (Illustration copyright © 2003 by Edward Eaves. Reproduced by permission of Hyperion Books for Children.)

to follow. Crocodile decides to return to his pool, which is now empty, but he soon misses his friends and learns to appreciate their camaraderie once they rejoin him. "The rhythmic pacing and effective use of dialogue make this an ideal book for reading aloud," noted Shawn Brommer in *School Library Journal.*

Spring is in the air in *Mole's in Love,* as a lonely mole named Morris is hoping to find his true love. Although

Morris cannot see very well above ground, he knows that his beloved will have a pink nose and big feet. At a farmyard several creatures fit at least one of the mole's criteria. Something is not quite right with each one, but love finds Morris when he goes back underground. A sequel, *Mole's Babies,* follows Morris and his growing family and again captures the warmth of BEDFORD's story here is captured in brightly colored artwork by illustrator Rosalind Beardshaw. Young readers "will relate to

Morris . . . and will cheer for him as he keeps trying," predicted *School Library Journal* contributor Margaret R. Tassia in her review of *Mole's Babies*.

Bedford introduces a human character in his picture book *The Way I Love You*, focusing on the strong and loving bond between children and their pets. In the work, a preschooler lists the many ways she cherishes her frisky, spirited pup, praising her pet's ability to run, jump, wag its tail, snuggle, and even smile. Describing *The Way I Love You* as a "gentle poem," a critic in *Publishers Weekly* faulted the sentimentality of Bedford's text, but also noted that "it never intrudes on . . . the feeling that, for this pair, the world is their oyster." *Booklist* critic Jennifer Mattson observed that the story's "cozy, satisfying refrain 'And that's the way I love you'" will have particular appeal to youngsters.

Biographical and Critical Sources

PERIODICALS

Booklist, April 15, 2001, Amy Brandt, review of *Touch the Sky, My Little Bear,* p. 1563; December 15, 2004, Jennifer Mattson, review of *The Way I Love You,* p. 746; April 15, 2009, Connie Fletcher, review of *Little Bear's Big Sweater,* p. 47.

Kirkus Reviews, September 1, 2007, review of *Bedtime for Little Bears!*; December 15, 2007, review of *Time for Bed, Isobel*; February 15, 2009, review of *Mole's in Love*; June 1, 2009, review of *Who's Yawning?*

Publishers Weekly, August 19, 2002, review of *Ella's Games,* p. 88; July 26, 2004, review of *Mo's Stinky Sweater,* p. 53; December 6, 2004, review of *The Way I Love You,* p. 59; June 29, 2009, review of *Babies,* p. 128.

School Library Journal, May, 2001, Linda M. Kenton, review of *Touch the Sky, My Little Bear,* p. 109; August, 2001, John Sigwald, review of *Big Bears Can!,* p. 142; January, 2002, Linda Ludke, review of *Shaggy Dog and the Terrible Itch,* p. 95; December, 2002, Meghan R. Malone, review of *Ella's Games,* p. 84; March, 2004, Shawn Brommer, review of *The Copy Crocs,* p. 152; October, 2004, Be Astengo, review of *Mo's Stinky Sweater,* p. 109; July, 2005, Joy Fleishhacker, review of *The Way I Love You,* p. 64; March, 2008, Linda Staskus, review of *Time for Bed, Isobel,* p. 154; March, 2009, Margaret R. Tassia, review of *Mole's in Love,* p. 106; May, 2009, Martha Simpson, review of *Little Bear's Big Sweater,* p. 70.

ONLINE

David Bedford Home Page, http://www.childrensauthor. co.uk (December 15, 2010).

*   *   *

BEDFORD, David J.
See BEDFORD, David

BISHOP, Rudine Sims
(Rudine Sims)

Personal

Married James J. Bishop (an educational administrator). *Education:* West Chester University, B.S.; University of Pennsylvania, M.S.; Wayne State University, Ed.D.

Addresses

Home—Columbus, OH. *E-mail*—bishop.77@osu.edu.

Career

Educator and author. University of Massachusetts, Amherst, associate professor, then professor of education, 1973-86; Ohio State University, Columbus, professor of education, 1986-2002, professor emeritus, beginning 2002. Member, Ohioana Library Board of Trustees; member of advisory board for Reading Is Fundamental and CDF Langston Hughes Library.

Member

International Reading Association, International Board on Books for Young People (president of U.S. section, 1998), American Library Association (former member of Caldecott Medal and Newbery Medal selection committees), National Council of Teachers of English (former member of editorial board and executive committee).

Awards, Honors

Arbuthnot Award, International Reading Association, 1996; Distinguished Service Award, National Council of Teachers of English, 2000; Reading Hall of Fame inductee, 2001; Outstanding Educator in the English Language Arts Award, 2007. The Dr. Rudine Sims Bishop Scholarship Fund in Children's Literature was established at Ohio State University in 2004.

Writings

(As Rudine Sims) *Shadow and Substance: Afro-American Experience in Contemporary Children's Fiction,* National Council of Teachers of English (Urbana, IL), 1982.

Presenting Walter Dean Myers, Twayne (Boston, MA), 1991.

(Editor) *Kaleidoscope: A Multicultural Booklist for Grades K-8,* National Council of Teachers of English (Urbana, IL), 1994.

(Author of introduction) *I Am the Darker Brother: An Anthology of Modern Poems by African Americans,* edited by Arnold Adoff, Simon & Schuster (New York, NY), 1997.

(Compiler and author of introduction) *Wonders: The Best Children's Poems of Effie Lee Newsome,* illustrated by Lois Mailou Jones, Wordsong/Boyds Mills Press (Honesdale, PA), 1999.

Rudine Sims Bishop (Reproduced by permission.)

Free within Ourselves: The Development of African American Children's Literature, Greenwood Press (Westport, CT), 2007.

Bishop Daniel Alexander Payne: Great Black Leader, Just Us Books (East Orange, NJ), 2009.

Contributor of articles in professional journals and edited volumes; contributor of book reviews and columns to *Horn Book.*

Sidelights

A highly respected scholar, Rudine Sims Bishop has both authored and edited several notable works of nonfiction, including *Shadow and Substance: Afro-American Experience in Contemporary Children's Fiction* and *Free within Ourselves: The Development of African American Children's Literature.* A professor emeritus of education at Ohio State University, Bishop has received a number of honors during her long and distinguished career, among them the Arbuthnot Award from the International Reading Association and the Distinguished Service Award from the National Council of Teachers of English.

Shadow and Substance, Bishop's groundbreaking 1982 work, "identified and addressed key issues that have become touchstones in the study of multicultural literature," in the words of *Horn Book* reviewer Kathleen T. Horning. In *Free within Ourselves,* published more than two decades later, the author expands on those themes, chronicling the development of children's literature created by African-American authors and illustrators from the nineteenth century to date. The author looks at key figures in the emergence of this distinct genre, from W.E.B. DuBois, a seminal critic, editor, and activist, to John Steptoe, an innovative author and illustrator, to Christopher Paul Curtis, a Newbery Medal winner. In her interview with Horning, Bishop stated, "I argue in my book that African American children's literature grew in part out of a sense of necessity, a sense that African American history and heritage were being omitted from children's literature and textbooks, and a sense

that children—all American children, but especially Black children—need to learn the story of African Americans' struggle on the journey across what Virginia Hamilton called the American hopescape." According to Lisa Von Drasek in *School Library Journal,* Bishop's "writing is precise and engaging, and it really comes alive when presenting primary-source material."

In addition to her scholarly work, Bishop has also written works for young readers, among them *Presenting Walter Dean Myers,* a biography of the celebrated African-American novelist, and *Bishop Daniel Alexander Payne: Great Black Leader,* which examines the life of a noted nineteenth-century educator, author, and theologian. Born in 1811, Payne became a driving force in the African Methodist Episcopal Church and later served as president of Wilberforce University, the first black-owned college in the United States. A *Kirkus Reviews* critic described *Bishop Daniel Alexander Payne* as "a solid introduction to an historical figure who deserves to be better known."

In editing *Wonders: The Best Children's Poems of Effie Lee Newsome* Bishop compiles work by a prolific and pioneering African-American writer. According to *School Library Journal* contributor Betty Teague, Newsome's "poetry succeeds in reflecting childlike wonder in images from everyday life."

Asked by Horning how she would change the U.S. publishing industry to improve the status of African-American literature, Bishop responded: "It would be to increase the quantity, the availability, and the marketing of books by African American writers and artists. We have perennially been underrepresented in the field, and that underrepresentation continues." Despite that underrepresentation, Bishop notes that the future of African-American children's books is in good hands, thanks to a new wave of African Americans whose parents were successful in the field. "That's a very interesting phenomenon," she remarked to Horning. "It's wonderful to see Christopher Myers and Jaime Adoff and Javaka Steptoe producing books for children. And, obviously, there's the Pinkney family, where you've got Jerry and Gloria Jean Pinkney, and then the next generation, Brian and Andrea Davis Pinkney, and Myles and Sandra. And, if you consider the grandchildren who are modeling for the illustrations, you've got three generations! That is certainly the first African American family that has made children's literature their family business."

"When I was growing up there were very few children's books that presented life-like African American characters," Bishop told *SATA.* "African American children's literature began to blossom about the time I was in graduate school, and it has been my calling to follow its considerable progress over the last few decades. Today I am pleased to note that the void I experienced as a child has been filled by a substantial body of literature created by talented African-American writers and artists. Although most of my writing has been addressed to literature professionals, I hope that my recent modest efforts to create books for a young audience have added something of value to this important body of work."

Biographical and Critical Sources

PERIODICALS

Booklist, March 1, 1995, review of *Kaleidoscope: A Multicultural Booklist for Grades K-8,* p. 1271.

Horn Book, May-June, 2008, Kathleen T. Horning, interview with Bishop, p. 247.

Kirkus Reviews, September 1, 2009, review of *Bishop Daniel Alexander Payne: Great Black Leader.*

Language Arts, January, 2009, transcript of acceptance speech for Outstanding Educator in the English Language Arts award.

School Library Journal, April, 2000, Betty Teague, review of *Wonders: The Best Children's Poems of Effie Lee Newsome,* p. 118; December, 2007, Lisa Von Drasek, review of *Free within Ourselves: The Development of African American Children's Literature,* p. 164.

*   *   *

BLACK, Joe 1959-
(Rabbi Joe Black)

Personal

Born 1959; married; wife's name Susan; children: Elana, Ethan. *Religion:* Jewish.

Addresses

Home—Albuquerque, NM.

Career

Rabbi and musician. Temple Israel, Minneapolis, MN, assistant then associate rabbi, 1987-96; Congregation Albert, Albuquerque, NM, senior rabbi, 1996-2010. *The Magic Door* (television program), WBBM-TV, Chicago, IL, former host. Recordings include *Aleph Bet Boogie,* 1992, *Everybody's Got a Little Music,* 1993, *Now That Sounds Kosher!,* 2005, *Eight Nights of Joy* (with Maxwell Street Klezmer Band), *Leave a Little Bit Undone,* and *Sabbatical.* Performer in films, including *Sing Me a Story: Rabbi Joe Black in Concert,* 1993, and *Enough Already!,* 1997; performer at conferences and in concerts around the world.

Writings

FOR CHILDREN

Boker Tov!: Good Morning! (with CD), illustrated by Rick Brown, Kar-Ben Pub. (Minneapolis, MN), 2009.

Afikomen Mambo, illustrated by Linda Prater, Kar-Ben Pub. (Minneapolis, MN), 2011.

OTHER

The New Rabbi Joe Black Songbook: Selected Songs from the Recordings Aleph Bet Boogie, Everybody's Got a Little Music, Leave a Little Bit Undone, Sabbatical, Sounds Write Productions (New York, NY), 2004.

Author of songs recorded in albums, including *Aleph Bet Boogie,* 1992, *Everybody's Got a Little Music,* 1993, *Now That Sounds Kosher!,* 2005, *Eight Nights of Joy, Leave a Little Bit Undone,* and *Sabbatical.*

Sidelights

In addition to leading others in his community through his work as a congregational rabbi, Joe Black has also touched the lives of many others—both Jewish and Gentile—through his work as a storyteller and musician. Considered among the most popular contemporary Jewish performers in North America, Black has appeared onstage throughout the United States and Canada, sharing his original songs, his skill in playing the acoustic guitar, and his uplifting message of faith in a way that entertains, inspires, and teaches. In addition to live performances, Black has also recorded songs for both children and adults, appeared in films, and also written books for young children. Reviewing his performance

Rabbi Joe Black entertains young children with the upbeat story **Boker Tov!,** *featuring colorful artwork by Rick Brown.* (Illustration copyright © 2009 by Lerner Publishing Group, Inc. Reproduced by permission of Kar-Ben, a division of Lerner Publishing Group. No part of this excerpt may be used or reproduced in any manner whatsoever without the prior written permission of Lerner Publishing Group, Inc.)

in the film *Enough Already!,* Ellen Mandel noted in *Booklist* that Black brings to life a traditional Jewish folk character with his "zestful songs," "joyful instrumentation and robust, Yiddish-accented characterizations."

Illustrated by Rick Brown and containing a musical CD, Black's first picture book, *Boker Tov!: Good Morning!,* is designed to help parents and children start each day with affirmation and optimism. His rhythmic text—the lyrics of a song—combines simple English words with Yiddish expressions, such as that of the title. As with Black's second book, the Passover-themed *Afikomen Mambo, Boker Tov!* serves as a gentle introduction to the Hebrew language that is suitable for very young children.

Biographical and Critical Sources

PERIODICALS

Booklist, December 15, 1992, Ellen Mandel, review of *Aleph Bet Boogie,* p. 775; November 1, 1993, Ellen Mandel, review of *Sing Me a Story: Rabbi Joe Black in Concert,* p. 542; December 15, 1993, Laurie Hartshorn, review of *Everybody's Got a Little Music,* p. 771.
School Library Journal, January, 1993, Renee Rabinowitz, review of *Aleph Bet Boogie,* p. 67; October, 1993, Susan Pine, review of *Sing Me a Story,* p. 70, and Sandra Morton, review of *Everbody's Got a Little Music,* p. 76.

ONLINE

Rabbi Joe Black Home Page, http://www.rabbijoeblack. com (December 29, 2010).*

*   *   *

BLACK, Rabbi Joe
See BLACK, Joe

*   *   *

BROWN, Craig 1947-
(Craig McFarland Brown)

Personal

Born September 4, 1947, in Fairfield, IA; son of Carl (in sales) and Jane (a teacher) Brown; married (divorced); children: Heather Jean, Cory McFarland. *Education:* Layton School of Art, B.F.A., 1969; attended University of Wisconsin-Milwaukee, 1971-73, and Uri Shulevitz Workshop on writing and illustrating children's books, 1985.

Addresses

Home and office—1615 S. Tejon, No. 3, Colorado Springs, CO 80906.

Career

Author and illustrator. American Greetings Corporation, Cleveland, OH, artist, 1969-71; *Astronomy* magazine, Milwaukee, WI, art director, 1973-75; Koss Corporation, Milwaukee, packaging designer, 1975-77; W.C. Brown Publishing Co., Dubuque, IA, art director, 1977-81; Current, Inc., Colorado Springs, CO, artist, 1981-87; author and illustrator, beginning 1987. Teacher at Taos Institute of Arts; hospice volunteer. Presenter at schools. *Exhibitions:* Work exhibited at Children's Book of Art, Boston, 1989, by Society of Illustrators, New York, NY, 1990, 1991, and in Japan, 1990. Mural installations include Pueblo, CO, Children's Museum, 2000.

Awards, Honors

Design award for best juvenile book, Rocky Mountain Book Publishers Association, 1990; Children's Books of the Year citation, Bank Street College, 1991, for *The Ornery Morning.*

Writings

FOR CHILDREN

The Patchwork Farmer, Greenwillow Books (New York, NY), 1988.
My Barn, Greenwillow Books (New York, NY), 1991.
City Sounds, Greenwillow Books (New York, NY), 1992.
The Bandshell, Greenwillow Books (New York, NY), 1993.
In the Spring, Greenwillow Books (New York, NY), 1993.
Tractor, Greenwillow Books (New York, NY), 1995.
Animals at Home, Roberts Rinehart Publishers (Boulder, CO), 1996.
Barn Raising, Greenwillow Books (New York, NY), 2001.
Mule Train Mail, Charlesbridge (Watertown MA), 2009.

ILLUSTRATOR

Amy Lawson, *The Talking Bird and the Storypouch,* Harper (New York, NY), 1988.
Toni Knapp, *The Gossamer Tree,* Rockrimmon Press, 1988.
Peter and Connie Roop, *Snips the Tinker,* edited by Patricia and Fredrick McKissack, Milliken, 1989.
(As Craig McFarland Brown) Toni Knapp, *The Six Bridges of Humphrey the Whale,* Rockrimmon Press, 1989.
Craig Kee Strete, *Big Thunder Magic,* Greenwillow Books (New York, NY), 1990.
Lael Littke, *Storm Monster,* Silver Burdett, 1990.
Tom Raabe, *Biblioholism,* Fulcrum Publishing (Golden, CO), 1990.

Patricia Brennan Demuth, *The Ornery Morning,* Dutton (New York, NY), 1991.

Maura Elizabeth Keleher McKinley, *The Secret of the Eagle Feathers,* Raintree Steck-Vaughn (Austin, TX), 1997.

(As Craig McFarland Brown) Vickie Leigh Krudwig, *Cucumber Soup,* Fulcrum Kids (Golden, CO), 1998.

Pam Muñoz Ryan, *How Do You Raise a Raisin?,* Charlesbridge (Watertown, MA), 2003.

Sidelights

Craig Brown is an author and artist whose original picture books feature many stories inspired by his childhood and his love of nature. A painter who uses the impressionistic technique of stippling to create tiny points of color that blend in the eye of the viewer to create delicate nuances of light, shadow, and shade, Brown started as an illustrator for writers such as Toni Knapp, Peter and Connie Roop, and Pam Muñoz Ryan. His original picture books include *Barn Raising, Tractor, In the Spring,* and *Mule Train Mail.*

Raised in a rural farming Iowa community, Brown had many opportunities to develop his drawing talent. As he once recalled to *SATA,* he would rise early and ride his bike out into the country where he could draw and paint the countryside, including its barns, animals, fields, and flowers. Fishing was another favored morning activity that allowed him time to sketch and draw; free afternoons were devoted to baseball or swimming until it was time to head home for dinner.

Brown showed his talent for drawing in the third grade when he created caricatures of his classmates and teachers. Years later, as a student at the Layton School

Craig Brown takes readers in a trip into the Western frontier in his self-illustrated picture book Mule Train Mail. (Illustration copyright © 2009 by Craig Brown. All rights reserved. Used by permission by Charlesbridge Publishing, Inc.)

of Art, he developed an interest in children's books that "later turned into a love affair," as he admitted. He began to explore stippling during this time, and when visiting the Chicago Art Institute his visits would start and end at the paintings of noted French impressionist George Seurat. Grant Wood, Maurice Sendak, and Uri Schulevitz were other artists that inspired his work. After sixteen years spent working in the field of advertising, Brown returned to his first love and steered his career into the field of book illustration.

Brown's childhood memories inspired his first two original picture books. As he explained to *SATA, The Patchwork Farmer* is based on his "feelings for farmers," the respect he has for "how hard they work—their perseverance and willingness to come back day after day." The book's title recalls "the patchwork look of the fields" that can be seen when traveling through farm country. *My Barn* "was written to give children the authentic sound animals make and a look at a barn's architecture," as well as create a noisy moment or two as children repeat the sounds that each animal makes. In Brown's realistic text, a rooster goes "Er Er Er Er Er Errrrrr Errrrr" instead of Cock-a-Doodle-Do. Another early work by Brown that introduces readers to rural life, *In the Spring* "makes a virtue of simplicity with this refreshing look at farm animals and their offspring," according to a *Publishers Weekly* contributor.

In *Tractor* readers meet one of the most important machines on the farm. As the seasons pass, the farmer in Brown's book plows, plants, cultivates, and harvests his crop of corn, using one of the tractor's many attachments. As the seasons change from spring to fall, so does life around the field, as both wild and farm animals raise their young and the farmer's son works and plays to the steady hum of the tractor engine. Citing Brown's "simple text," *Horn Book* contributor Elizabeth S. Watson predicted of *Tractor* that children "who love to follow a process full circle" will request that "this satisfying deceptively simple book [be] read again and again."

The Amish community near his Iowa home town inspired Brown's self-illustrated *Barn Raising,* which captures the energy of this community effort as men, women, and children team up to construct a farmer's new barn in the aftermath of a tragic fire. A *Kirkus Reviews* writer noted the "finely detailed illustrations" that follow the project from foundation to framing to roofing and siding, all over the course of a single day. In ink and muted, earthy pastels, *Barn Raising* "spotlights a community of people who are willing and able to help their neighbors," wrote Carolyn Phelan in *Booklist,* while *School Library Journal* contributor Wendy Lukehart remarked on Brown's use of varying aerial perspectives to add interest and detail to his visual chronicle. The artist's "sweeping, visible brush strokes comprising the periwinkle sky are particularly effective," Lukehart noted, adding that Brown's author's note provides interested readers with further information about Iowa's Amish community.

Brown divides his time between writing, illustrating, and, as he explained, "working with students at schools and workshops, helping to promote their own creativity and self worth." In addition to writing, illustrating, and working with young children, Brown has also created a mural installation that greets visitors to the children's museum in Pueblo, Colorado.

Biographical and Critical Sources

PERIODICALS

Booklist, April 15, 1994, Mary Harris Veeder, review of *In the Spring*, p. 1538; September 1, 1995, Mary Harris Veeder, review of *Tractor*, p. 82; August, 2002, Carolyn Phelan, review of *Barn Raising*, p. 1969.

Horn Book, November-December, 1995, Elizabeth S. Watson, review of *Tractor*, p. 731.

Kirkus Reviews, July 1, 2002, review of *Barn Raising*, p. 949.

Publishers Weekly, February 28, 1994, review of *In the Spring*, p. 86.

School Library Journal, December, 2002, Wendy Lukehart, review of *Barn Raising*, p. 85.

ONLINE

Craig Brown Home Page, http://www.craig-brown.com (December 29, 2010).*

*   *   *

BROWN, Craig McFarland
See BROWN, Craig

*   *   *

BUTLER, M. Christina 1934-

Personal
Born December 11, 1934, in Scarborough, North Yorkshire, England; daughter of Harold Cautley (a hotel proprietor and engineer) and Mabel Tutill; married William Anthony Butler (a political agent), August 23, 1958; children: Katharyn Charlotte, Frances Emma. *Education:* Attended St. Joseph's Convent. *Politics:* Conservative. *Religion:* Church of England (Anglican). *Hobbies and other interests:* Music, swimming, walking, travel, reading.

Addresses
Home—Driffield, East Riding, Yorkshire, England.

Career
Writer. Leeds General Infirmary, Leeds, England, state-registered nurse, 1953-57; Halifax Infirmary, Sheffield, England, worked in Outpatient's Casualty Department,

1958-60, district nursing sister, 1960-65. Playgroup supervisor, 1973-76; preschool nursery supervisor, 1977-84, 1987. Served on various village committees; governor of local primary school, 1973-77, and beginning 1989; local church warden.

Member
Fine Arts Society.

Writings

Can I Live with You?, illustrated by Meg Rutherford, Macdonald Picture Books (Hove, England), 1988, published as *Can I Stay with You?*, Dial (New York, NY), 1988.

Too Many Eggs, illustrated by Meg Rutherford, David Godine (London, England), 1988.

Where Are My Bananas?, Macdonald Picture Books (Hove, England), 1989.

Stanley in the Dark, illustrated by Meg Rutherford, Simon & Schuster (Hemel Hempstead, England), 1990.

Picnic Pandemonium, illustrated by Margaret Rutherford, George Stevens, 1991.

The Dinosaur's Egg, illustrated by Val Biro, Simon & Schuster (Hemel Hempstead, England), 1992.

Mole in a Hole (and Bear in a Lair), illustrated by Meg Rutherford, Simon & Schuster (Hemel Hempstead, England), 1993.

Archie the Ugly Dinosaur, illustrated by Val Biro, Barron's (Hauppauge, NY), 1996.

The Dinosaurs' Dinner, illustrated by Val Biro, Macdonald Young (Hove, England), 1997.

Big Bad Rex, illustrated by Val Biro, Macdonald Young (Hove, England), 1999.

Who's Been Eating My Porridge?, illustrated by Daniel Howarth, Little Tiger Press (Wilton, CT), 2004.

One Snowy Night, illustrated by Tina Macnaughton, Good Books (Intercourse, PA), 2004.

Snow Friends, illustrated by Tina Macnaughton, Good Books (Intercourse, PA), 2005.

One Winter's Day, illustrated by Tina Macnaughton, Good Books (Intercourse, PA), 2006.

Don't Be Afraid, Little Ones, illustrated by Caroline Pedler, Little Tiger Press (London, England), 2007.

A Star So Bright: A Christmas Tale, illustrated by Caroline Pedler, Good Books (Intercourse, PA), 2007.

The Wishing Star, illustrated by Frank Endersby, Little Tiger Press (London, England), 2008.

The Dark, Dark Night, illustrated by Jane Chapman, Good Books (Intercourse, PA), 2008.

One Rainy Day, illustrated by Tina Macnaughton, Little Tiger Press (London, England), 2008, Good Books (Intercourse, PA), 2009.

Who's Been Eating My Porridge?, illustrated by Daniel Howarth, Little Tiger Press (London, England), 2009.

Babbity's Big Bad Mood, illustrated by Frank Endersby, Little Tiger Press (London, England), 2009.

The Smiley Snowman, illustrated by Tina Macnaughton, Good Books (Intercourse, PA), 2010.

The Special Blankie, illustrated by Tina Macnaughton, Good Books (Intercourse, PA), 2010.

Also author of children's serials and short stories for local radio.

Sidelights

British writer M. Christina Butler draws from her love of nature and her fond memories of farm life in many of her books for younger readers. In *One Snowy Night* a young hedgehog worries that he has no gifts for his many best friends; *Snow Friends* features a cast of animal characters—Little Bear, Otter, and Rabbit—as they band together to make the best snowman ever; and *Can I Stay with You?* follows a tiny bird after he falls out of his safe nest and must make his way home. Praising *Who's Been Eating My Porridge?,* which finds a young bear struggling at the dinner table, Andrea Tarr wrote in *School Library Journal* that Butler spins "a pleasant tale, complete with a mild surprise" as the finale. A former educator, Butler firmly believes in the importance of picture books, stating on the Little Tiger Press Web site that "an imaginative story, colourful art and, most importantly, [the opportunity] to understand and absorb at their own pace, has to be a huge plus in the development of a child's reading ability."

Butler was born in Scarborough, a seaside resort in North Yorkshire. While she was still young, her family moved to a small village, and these rural surroundings provided the memories she would later draw upon in writing her books for young children. "At a time when farming embraced a rich variety of activities that young people could take part in, I was fortunate enough to have a farmer's daughter as my best friend," Butler once recalled to *SATA.* "From the age of about eight years old, weekends and holidays were spent on the farm. There was so much to do. We devised our own games—had secret codes, maps, and dens. Our constant companions were dogs and horses."

Spending most of her time out of doors did not leave Butler much time for reading when she was young, although she recalls being read to by her mother. The stories of Hans Christian Andersen were among her favorites: "*The Little Match Girl . . .* never failed to have us both in tears long before the end," recalled the writer.

"I loved art but was never drawn to long essay writing," Butler admitted, adding that she "was, however, extremely happy at school." When she turned eighteen, she enrolled at Leeds General Infirmary in West Yorkshire, where she obtained her state registration as a nurse after four years of study. Following graduation, she married William Anthony Butler, and it was her spouse's busy career in politics that prompted Butler to begin her own career as a children's book author. "As my husband was often attending evening meetings, [I] began writing children's stories. For years I wrote for local radio; short stories and serials, but always cherished the hope of being published," Butler once explained.

The many hours she spent reading aloud after the birth of her two daughters were followed by several years spent working with other children as the supervisor of a nursery school. Here she became familiar with the wide variety of books available for young children and grew interested in the idea of writing children's picture books. In 1987 *Can I Stay with You?*, her first book, was published, featuring artwork by Meg Rutherford. Designed as a novelty picture book, it is the story of a little bird who tries to find a new home after he accidentally falls out of the family nest. Other books by Butler include *Too Many Nests, Stanley in the Dark,* and *Big Bad Rex,* the last illustrated by Val Biro.

Several of Butler's characters are based on people she recalls from her childhood spent on the farm. "Mrs. Bear in *Too Many Eggs* is my farming friend's mother—the best cook in the world who never used a recipe in her life," she explained. "The mouse in *Stanley in the Dark* is a memory of long walks over the field in the dark to fasten the poultry houses, surrounded by the sounds and shadows of the night, some rather scary."

A number of Butler's titles center on the exploits of Little Hedgehog, one her most popular characters, and are engagingly illustrated by Tina Macnaughton. In *One Winter's Day,* for example, the diminutive protagonist is forced to relocate after his nest blows away during a fierce storm. Bundling up in his hat, scarf, and mittens, Little Hedgehog begins making his way to Badger's house, donating his articles of clothing to the host of shivering creatures he meets along the way. After the storm passes and Hedgehog returns home to rebuild, he finds a delightful surprise awaiting him. In the words of a *Kirkus Reviews* contributor, "this sweet story becomes a testament to kindness." Little Hedgehog's opportunity to try out a new raincoat and umbrella turns into a se-

M. Christina Butler's picture book **Who's Been Eating My Porridge?** *features endearing watercolor art by Daniel Howarth.* (Tiger Tales, 2004. Illustration copyright © 2004 by Daniel Howarth. Reproduced by permission.)

ries of soggy misadventures in *One Rainy Day,* a story that "has a cozy, snuggly tone," as Adrienne Wilson noted in *School Library Journal.* In *The Special Blankie* Little Hedgehog offers to babysit his cousin with the assistance of several animal friends. When Baby Hedgehog gets tangled in his fuzzy red blanket and rolls down a hill, his caretakers give chase, in the process discovering a mouse that needs rescuing from a deep hole. According to a critic in *Publishers Weekly,* "the light-hearted conundrums" in Butler's tale "are engaging."

Little Bear, another of Butler's favorite protagonists, appears in works such as *Who's Been Eating My Porridge?* and *Snow Friends,* all brought to life in Daniel Howarth's art. In the former title, Little Bear refuses to dine on porridge, much to the consternation of his parents who warn their child that his portion will be given to Scary Old Bear, a denizen of the woods. Although Little Bear is not convinced that Scary Old Bear is real, he decides not to tempt fate after having a nightmare involving the creature. In *Snow Friends* Little Bear and his companions devise a clever plan to keep their newly constructed snowman company while they are away. A contributor in *Kirkus Reviews* applauded the latter tale, calling it a "simple, cheery outing."

Butler offers her version of Jesus's birth in *A Star So Bright: A Christmas Tale,* which features a shiny foil star surrounded by flickering lights on the final page of Caroline Pedlar's illustrations. "The rhythmic text flows easily," observed Diane Olivo-Posner in her review of the holiday story for *School Library Journal.* In *The Dark, Dark Night* a group of woodland creatures lets their imaginations run wild. While carrying a lantern as he returns home one evening, Frog spots a black "pond monster" and, terrified, rushes away to find his friends. The monster (in reality, a shadow cast by the lamp) grows larger and larger as Badger, Hedgehog, Rabbit, and Mouse each relate the story and join the search. "Preschoolers who fear the dark will relate to Frog's feelings," Gay Lynn Van Vleck commented in *School Library Journal.*

"The picture-book format is my ideal medium," Butler once explained. "With an interest in art—and not being particularly disposed to writing long tracts of text—I find the combination of moving the story on in the pictures and with a minimum of words fascinating." "To be able to write stories for young children that captivate, stimulate, entertain, and inform in an humorous way and leave them wanting more is my overriding ambition," the author continued. "There is something very special about a group of wide-eyed four year olds listening intently to a story."

Biographical and Critical Sources

PERIODICALS

Kirkus Reviews, August 1, 2004, review of *Who's Been Eating My Porridge?,* p. 738; October 1, 2005, review of *Snow Friends,* p. 1077; September 15, 2006, review of *One Winter's Day,* p. 948; May 15, 2008, review of *The Dark, Dark Night.*
Publishers Weekly, October 22, 2007, review of *A Star So Bright: A Christmas Tale,* p. 54; February 22, 2010, review of *The Special Blankie,* p. 66.
School Library Journal, January, 2005, Andrea Tarr, review of *Who's Been Eating My Porridge?,* p. 88; November, 2005, Amelia Jenkins, review of *Snow Friends,* p. 83; November, 2006, Rachel G. Payne, review of *One Winter's Day,* p. 86; October, 2007, Diane Olivo-Posner, review of *A Star So Bright,* p. 96; July, 2008, Gay Lynn Van Vleck, review of *The Dark, Dark Night,* p. 67; May, 2009, Adrienne Wilson, review of *One Rainy Day,* p. 71; April, 2010, Linda Staskus, review of *The Special Blankie,* p. 121.

PERIODICALS

Little Tiger Press Web site, http://www.littletigerpress.com/ (January 15, 2011), "M. Christina Butler."*

C

CARTER, Timothy 1972-

Personal

Born December 13, 1972, in Farnham, England; immigrated to Canada; married, 1995; wife's name Violet. *Hobbies and other interests:* Collecting toy transformers, movies.

Addresses

Home—Toronto, Ontario, Canada. *E-mail*—tim@timothycarterworld.com.

Career

Novelist and screenwriter. Panelist at science-fiction and anime conventions.

Writings

Attack of the Intergalactic Soul Hunters, Llewellyn Publications (Woodbury, MN), 2005.
Closets, SynergEbooks, 2006.
Epoch, Flux (Woodbury, MN), 2007.
Section K, Burningeffigy Press (Toronto, Ontario, Canada), 2008.
Evil?, Flux (Woodbury, MN), 2009.
Cupid Wars, Flux (Woodbury, MN), 2011.

Author's work has been translated into French and German.

Sidelights

British-born author and science-fiction fan Timothy Carter now lives in Toronto, Ontario, Canada, where he sets his entertaining stories for young readers. In addition to his imaginative elementary-grade novels *Attack of the Intergalactic Soul Hunters* and *Closets,* Carter has also written the teen novels *Epoch* and *Evil?* as well as the adult-themed *Section K,* all of which mix otherworldly elements with a thoughtful examination of contemporary social issues. "My stories are far-fetched, often humorous, and have a fantastical element to them (like aliens, monsters, demons or angels)," Carter explained in discussing his writing on his home page. "I like to poke fun at things. Occasionally I try to SAY SOMETHING. Basically, though, I just like to have fun. That, to me, is what storytelling is all about."

Geared for elementary-grade readers, *Attack of the Ingergalactic Soul Hunters* introduces two ten year olds with a shared passion for the science-fiction television program *Infinite Destiny.* Conrad Viscous and Knowlton Cabbage also have something else in common: they were both soldiers in an alien army in a past life. Haunted by flashes of this past in their dreams, the boys are also hunted by Cyscope, an admiral of the Deltran galactic empire who is sent to Earth to hunt down Conrad and acquire the powerful Shadow Matrix, which Conrad's former self stole. Carter shifts the story's narrative in a unique way, weaving Cyscope's reaction to living in a human form with the boys' efforts to untap their dream memories and locate the missing Shadow Matrix. Writing that the plot of *Attack of the Intergalactic Soul Hunters* "moves briskly," Tim Wadham added in his *School Library Journal* review that Carter's novel will find fans among "reluctant readers who are sci-fi geeks themselves."

Closets targets the same middle-grade readership and pits brothers Robbie and Sam Portal against the monsters that emerge from their closets. Fortunately, Robbie discovers that monsters cannot bite through blankets and that light of any kind will destroy them. Armed with flashlights and wrapped in their bedspreads, the boys soon venture into the secret world beyond the closet walls and take the fight to the beasts.

When readers meet fourteen-year-old Vincent Drear in *Epoch,* the teen outsider is pondering the end of the world. In fact, the demise of Earth is a trendy concept, and Vincent's school has even selected it as the theme of their annual science fair. While Vincent is typically skeptical, his parents believe strongly in the imminent end of days, and it comes as no great surprise when he finds himself talking to elves and pixies and learning that, while there is an end coming, it is not the apocalypse that Christians anticipate. With the help of his neighbor, Chanteuse, the teen learns that the time of humans is over, but that Earth will be restored for another dominant creatures to inherit. When Vincent's parents will not listen to his warnings, the teen teams up with others to find the hidden space-travel portals that will save his family and the rest of humanity. He must also battle the army of demons that is being marshaled to cleanse the planet from any humans who do not leave voluntarily. Reviewing *Epoch* in *Kliatt,* Ivy Miller called Carter's plot "interesting" and praised the "humorous edge" of his dialogue-heavy prose. "Readers will identify with Vincent's ability to see goodness in the world," wrote Donna Rosenblum in her *School Library Journal* review, the critic predicting that they will also "root for him and his companions as they triumph over evil" in Carter's novel.

Religion is also a factor in *Evil?,* and here Carter shows one teen's way of pushing back against his deeply devout family. Stuart Bradley is gay and out, even though his orientation is viewed as sinful by his small, religious community of Ice Lake. While the school's Biblical scripture teacher, a fallen angel in disguise, drums up hatred of Stuart as a means of uniting his flock, the teen marshals some interesting allies of his own: church leader Father Reedy and a demon named Fon Pyre. Soon, the supernatural battle between good and evil is raging in Stuart's small town, as Carter's "fantasy turns a critical and satirical eye on the evangelical fear of all things sexual," in the words of a *Kirkus Reviews* writer. The author is "never unfair or prurient" in telling his humorous story, added the *Kirkus Reviews* writer, and in *Publishers Weekly* a critic praised *Evil?* as a provocative teen read that "will leave readers with plenty to consider, as it addresses themes of morality, sexuality and faith." "Although the plotline seems dark" and the book's content might be deemed controversial by some, Diane Gallagher-Hayashi concluded in *Resource Links* that *Evil?* "is quite a funny book and mature teens will enjoy it."

In *Section K,* Carter's science-fiction novel for adults, Howard Plank and Johnny Tall are agents of Section K, a branch of the RCMP that deals with the paranormal. Johnny does not believe in the paranormal, and Howard is too drunk to be useful. When an alien invasion threatens the world, the two agents must rise to the occasion and assume the roles of unlikely heroes. "With a cast of characters including robots, ghosts, cultists, and many more, *Section K* is a good fun read if I do say so myself," quipped Carter. "Which I do!"

"For my readers: you are truly fantastic people, with excellent taste in literature," Carter continued. "I hope you enjoy reading my stuff as much as I enjoy writing it. And I do! If I have my way, there will be many more far-fetched stories to come."

Biographical and Critical Sources

PERIODICALS

Globe & Mail (Toronto, Ontario, Canada), September 8, 2007, Shawn Benjamin, review of *Epoch,* p. D19.
Kirkus Reviews, June 15, 2009, review of *Evil?*
Kliatt, July, 2007, Ivy Miller, review of *Epoch,* p. 30.
Publishers Weekly, August 10, 2009, review of *Evil?,* p. 58.
Resource Links, October, 2009, Diane Gallagher-Hayashi, review of *Evil?,* p. 23.
School Library Journal, April, 2006, Tim Wadham, review of *Attack of the Intergalactic Soul Hunters,* p. 136; December, 2007, Donna Rosenblum, review of *Epoch,* p. 120; January, 2010, Sarah K. Allen, review of *Evil?,* p. 97.
Voice of Youth Advocates, June, 2007, Timothy Capehart, review of *Epoch,* p. 157.

ONLINE

Timothy Carter Home Page, http://www.timothycarter world.com (November 29, 2010).
Timothy Carter Web log, http://worldsoftim.blogspot.com (December 15, 2010).

Cover of Timothy Carter's provocative young-adult novel **Evil?,** *featuring cover art by Ken Wong.* (Flux, 2009. Reproduced by permission.)

CHADDA, Sarwat

Personal

Born in England; married; wife's name Claire; children: daughters. *Education:* Imperial College London, degree (engineering).

Addresses

Home—London, England. *Agent*—Sarah Davies, Greenhouse Literary Agency, Washington, DC, and London, England; submissions@greenhouseliterary.com.

Career

Author. Civil engineer, 1989-2008; freelance novelist. Presenter at schools.

Member

Society of Children's Book Writers and Illustrators British Isles.

Awards, Honors

"Undiscovered Voices" award, Society of Children's Book Writers and Illustrators British Isles, 2007; Branford Boase Award shortlist, 2010, for *Devil's Kiss.*

Writings

Devil's Kiss, Disney/Hyperion (New York, NY), 2009.
Dark Goddess, Disney/Hyperion (New York, NY), 2011.

Adaptations

Devil's Kiss was adapted as an audiobook narrated by Anna Flosnick, Brilliance Audio, 2009.

Sidelights

After working for over fifteen years as a civil engineer, Sarwat Chadda decided to unleash his imagination and embark on a new career as a writer. His young-adult novels *Devil's Kiss* and *Dark Goddess* are inspired by Chadda's interest in the Knights Templar, an organization established during the Middle Ages. After a period of copious research and writing, Chadda worked with an editor in his native London, honing his manuscript to the point where its fast-moving, high-energy, and horror-filled plot attracted an agent, a publisher, and also critical and reader acclaim.

After fighting in the Crusades as Christ's army, the real-world Knights Templar were forced into hiding; King Philip IV of France even ordered member knights to be arrested and burned at the stake. Myths surrounding the Knights Templar grew after the 1300s, and it was rumored that the knights still worked secretly to combat evil in the name of the Church of Rome. Chadda based

Devil's Kiss on these legends of the Templars, casting his story in the present day but filling it with the elements of ageless nightmare. Billi SanGreal, Chadda's fifteen-year-old heroine, is the daughter of Master Knight Arthur SanGreal and his Muslim wife. A trained warrior, Billi is also well schooled in demonology and the history of the occult. Although her work as a knight binds her in friendship to the psychic knight Kay, the teen wants something different. As the first woman member of the Knights Templar, her constant battles against the Unholy leave her tired and bruised and they also interfere with her schoolwork and social life. Ultimately, the feisty teen finds herself facing an even-more-powerful rebel when the fallen angel Michael unleashes a scourge of evil creatures and a countdown starts that will bring about the Tenth Plague: the death of every first-born human on earth.

Billi returns in *Dark Goddess,* as Chadda weaves the ancient Russian legend of evil witch Baba Yaga into his adventurous plot. In the novel, Billi travels to eastern Europe, her mission to rescue a girl who is under the Knights' protection. This time the unholy threat comes

Cover of Sarwat Chadda's young-adult fantasy Devil's Kiss, *which draws on the history of the Knights Templar.* (Illustration © 2009 by David Eustace. Reproduced by permission of Hyperion Books for Children.)

from the angry hag Baba Yaga, who marshals an army of vicious werewolves and plots to avenge mankind's destruction of earth and its creatures.

In *Devil's Kiss* Chadda serves up "an old-fashioned high-octane horror tale" that features an "embittered heroine" and a "looming Apocalypse," according to a *Kirkus Reviews* writer, while in *Booklist* Ilene Cooper maintained that the author's "story . . . is at its best when it's exploring [teen] relationships." The novel's "scenes of spiritual warfare are gripping, . . . as is the undercurrent of supernatural romance," wrote a *Publishers Weekly* critic, the reviewer also complimenting Chadda for his "original take on familiar creatures like vampires." Reviewing *Devil's Kiss* in *School Library Journal*, Alana Joli Abbott noted that "Chadda does an excellent job of drawing on Christian, Jewish, and Muslim folk stories" while weaving together his "history-drenched horror tale."

Biographical and Critical Sources

PERIODICALS

Booklist, October 16, 2009, Ilene Cooper, review of *Devil's Kiss,* p. 59.
Guardian (London, England), July 18, 2009, review of *Devil's Kiss.*
Kirkus Reviews, August 15, 2009, review of *Devil's Kiss.*
Publishers Weekly, September 7, 2009, review of *Devil's Kiss,* p. 48.
School Library Journal, November, 2009, Alana Joli Abbott, review of *Devil's Kiss,* p. 101.

ONLINE

Sarwat Chadda Home Page, http://www.sarwatchadda.com (December 29, 2010).
Sarwat Chadda Web log, http://sarwatchadda.blogspot.com (December 29, 2010).*

*   *   *

CHERNETT, Dan

Personal

Male. *Education:* Lincoln University, degree, 2006.

Addresses

Agent—Vicki Willden-Lebrecht, The Bright Agency, Studio 102, 250 York Rd., Battersea, London SW11 3SJ, England. *E-mail*—dan@danchernett.com.

Career

Illustrator, 2006—. *Exhibitions:* Work exhibited at Colston Hall, Bristol, England, 2010.

Awards, Honors

Leeds Book Fair Graphic Novel Award, 2010, and Popular Paperbacks for Young Adults designation, American Library Association, 2011, both for *Malice* by Chris Wooding.

Illustrator

On the Ball, Pearson (Harlow, England), 2007.
Energy Boost, Pearson (Harlow, England), 2007.
The Yuck Factor, Pearson (Harlow, England), 2007.
Music Makers, Pearson (Harlow, England), 2007.
Chris Wooding, *Malice,* Scholastic (New York, NY), 2009.

"THE CREW" NOVEL SERIES

Sam Carter, *Car Wash,* Franklin Watts (London, England), 2009.
Sam Carter, *Day of the Dog,* Franklin Watts (London, England), 2009.
Sam Carter, *Geek of the Week,* Franklin Watts (London, England), 2009.
Sam Carter, *Good Luck, Bad Luck,* Franklin Watts (London, England), 2009.
Sam Carter, *Hot or Not?,* Franklin Watts (London, England), 2009.
Sam Carter, *The Real Deal,* Franklin Watts (London, England), 2009.

Sidelights

A British illustrator known for his imaginative and dynamic designs, Dan Chernett has provided the artwork for several works of fiction, including *Malice,* a hybrid work that combines a traditional prose narrative with elements from a graphic novel. Written by Chris Wooding, *Malice* centers on three friends who become fascinated by a cult comic book that, according to urban legend, depicts the often horrific—but very real—adventures of teenagers who have been transported to a fantastical but menacing otherworld. When their pal Luke goes missing and, a few days later, appears in the pages of *Malice,* Seth and Kady enact a mysterious ritual that opens a portal to the comic's dark and sinister world. There they encounter a host of malevolent creatures, including sharp-clawed, mechanical monsters known as Chitters as well as Tall Jake, a shadowy figure who rules over the unimaginable realm.

Chernett's contributions to *Malice* earned praise from several critics. "It's nice to see comics actually play a role in a half-comic, half-prose work," Ian Chipman stated in *Booklist,* and Mal Peet noted in the London *Guardian* that the interplay between text and graphics "obliges the reader to switch between two modes of reading. Reading the prose, we picture things in our heads. Reading the pictures, we supply most of the words. Shifting back and forth between the two is demanding, which is fine. It's also fun." *School Library Journal* reviewer Heather M. Campbell noted that the work features "erratic comic-book panels in which heavily slashed lines enhance the chaotic violence of the novel," and a *Publishers Weekly* critic described *Malice* as "a memorable multimedia experience."

Biographical and Critical Sources

PERIODICALS

Booklist, October 1, 2009, Ian Chipman, review of *Malice,* p. 36.

Bulletin of the Center for Children's Books, November, 2009, Kate Quealy-Gainer, review of *Malice,* p. 134.

Guardian (London, England), May 16, 2009, Mal Peet, review of *Malice.*

Kirkus Reviews, September 15, 2009, review of *Malice.*

Publishers Weekly, October 19, 2009, review of *Malice,* p. 54.

School Library Journal, November, 2009, Heather M. Campbell, review of *Malice,* p. 125.

ONLINE

Cargo Collective Web site, http://cargocollective.com/ (January 1, 2011), "Dan Chernett."

*   *   *

COLLINS, Suzanne 1963(?)-

Personal

Born c. 1963, in NJ; father a soldier in the U.S. Air Force; married Cap Pryor; children: two.

Addresses

Home and office—CT.

Career

Novelist and screenwriter. Television scriptwriter, beginning 1991. Cambridge Health Authority, Cambridge, MA, former clinical director of services for adults with learning disabilities.

Member

Authors Guild.

Awards, Honors

New York Public Library 100 Books for Reading and Sharing selection, 2003, for *Gregor the Overlander;* Oppenheim Toy Portfolio Gold Award, 2006, for *Gregor and the Curse of the Warmbloods;* Cooperative Children's Book Center (CCBC) Choices selection, 2008, for *Gregor and the Code of Claw;* Amelia Bloomer Project listee, Top Ten Best Books for Young Adults selection, and Notable Children's Book selection, all American Library Association (ALA), and Notable Children's Book selection, *New York Times,* all 2008, and CCBC Choices selection, and Stuff for the Teen Age listee, New York Public Library, both 2009, all for *The Hunger Games;* Best Books for Young Adults selection, ALA, and Top Ten Fiction Books inclusion, *Time* magazine, both 2009, and Best Children's Book selection, *Los Angeles Times,* and Stuff for the Teen Age listee, both 2010, all for *Catching Fire;* Notable Children's Book selection, *New York Times,* 2010, for *Mockingjay.*

Writings

"UNDERLAND CHRONICLES"; MIDDLE-GRADE NOVELS

Gregor the Overlander, Scholastic (New York, NY), 2003.
Gregor and the Prophecy of Bane, Scholastic (New York, NY), 2004.
Gregor and the Curse of the Warmbloods, Scholastic (New York, NY), 2005.
Gregor and the Marks of Secret, Scholastic (New York, NY), 2006.
Gregor and the Code of Claw, Scholastic (New York, NY), 2007.

"HUNGER GAMES" TRILOGY

The Hunger Games, Scholastic (New York, NY), 2008.
Catching Fire, Scholastic (New York, NY), 2009.
Mockingjay, Scholastic (New York, NY), 2010.

OTHER

When Charlie McButton Lost Power (picture book), illustrated by Mike Lester, Putnam (New York, NY), 2005.

Author of numerous scripts for television programs, including *Clarissa Explains It All,* Nickelodeon, *The Mystery Files of Shelby Woo,* Nickelodeon, *Little Bear, Oswald, Santa, Baby!,* Rankin/Bass Productions, *Clifford's Puppy Days,* Scholastic Entertainment, *Generation O!,* Kids WB, and *Wow! Wow! Wubbzy!,* Nick, Jr.

Adaptations

Collins' script for the *Oswald* television program was adapted by Dan Yaccarino as the picture book *Oswald's Camping Trip.* The "Underland Chronicles" and "Hunger Games" trilogy were adapted as audiobooks. The "Hunger Games" trilogy has been optioned for film.

Sidelights

Suzanne Collins is the author of the "Underland Chronicles," a fantasy sequence aimed at a middle-grade audience, as well as the "Hunger Games" trilogy, which is geared for young-adult readers. Additionally, she has worked as a screenwriter for several children's shows, including *Clarissa Explains It All, Little Bear,* and *Oswald.* "I find there isn't a great deal of difference technically in how you approach a story, no matter what age it's for," Collins remarked to a Scholastic Web site interviewer. "I started out as a playwright for adult audiences. When television work came along, it was primarily for children. But whatever age you're writing for, the same rules of plot, character, and theme apply. You just set up a world and try to remain true to it."

Gregor the Overlander, the first installment in Collins' "Underland Chronicles," introduces readers to her *Alice in Wonderland*-esque world, wherein Gregor must traverse an urban environment. Collins, who lived in New York City for sixteen years, wanted to gear her fantasy toward cosmopolitan young readers who are more familiar with city streets that sunlit meadows.

Gregor's adventures begin in *Gregor the Overlander* as he pursues his two-year-old sister, Boots, through an air duct and into the strange new world below. What he finds in the Underland is not only a hidden human society, but also a world in which giant-sized rats, cockroaches, and spiders are able to communicate in human language. When Gregor arrives, the Underland is on the brink of war—a war that threatens to spread into the Overland, first to Manhattan and then throughout the world. Gregor's first thought is to get home, but then he overhears that his father, who has gone missing, may now be in the Underland and need his son's help. Gregor makes new friends in the giant rat Ripred, Temp the cockroach, and Luxa, a mysterious human girl. Together they search for the missing man and put Gregor on track to his destiny.

As Collins told Jen Rees in an interview on her home page, she selected the Underland setting because "I liked the fact that this world was teeming under New York City and nobody was aware of it. That you could be going along preoccupied with your own problems and then whoosh! You take a wrong turn in your laundry room and suddenly a giant cockroach is right in your face. No magic, no space or time travel, there's just a ticket to another world behind your clothes dryer." She "creates a fascinating, vivid, highly original world and a superb story to go along with it," according to Ed Sullivan in a *Booklist* review of *Gregor the Overlander.* A *Kirkus Reviews* contributor described Collins' storyline as a "luminous, supremely absorbing quest," and Steven Engelfried wrote in *School Library Journal* that the novel's "plot threads unwind smoothly, and the pace of the book is just right."

As the "Underland Chronicles" series continues, Gregor becomes a leader in the Underland. Joined again by companions Ripred, Temp, and Luxa, *Gregor and the Prophecy of Bane* continues his adventures, undertaking to rescue Boots, who has been kidnapped. In her sequel Collins once again showcases her "careful attention to detail, pacing, and character development," in the opinion of *Horn Book* reviewer Kitty Flynn, while Sullivan dubbed Collins' protagonist "courageous, selfless, and ultimately triumphant."

In *Gregor and the Curse of the Warmbloods* Gregor's enemy is not an army, but a plague, one that his mother contracts. "Collins maintains the momentum, charm, and vivid settings of the original title," wrote Tasha Saecker in her *School Library Journal* review of this title. *Gregor and the Curse of the Warmbloods* "delivers the breakneck adventure and strong characters readers have come to expect," according to a contributor to

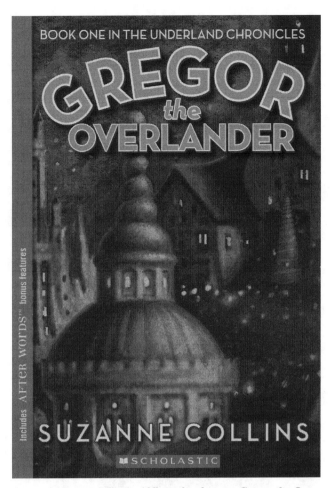

Cover of Suzanne Collins' middle-grade adventure **Gregor the Overlander,** *featuring artwork by Daniel Craig.* (Scholastic, Inc., 2003. Reproduced by permission of Scholastic, Inc.)

Kirkus Reviews, and Flynn concluded that, with this third series installment, Collins' "character development, plotting, pacing, and description all shine."

Gregor and the Marks of Secret finds some of the humans' allies in trouble. Together with Gregor, Luxa and Temp attempt to save the day, and "the breathless pace, intense drama, and extraordinary challenges" of their quest "will leave fans clamoring" for more, according to *School Library Journal* reviewer Mara Alpert. In *Horn Book* Flynn commented that "vivid description, expert pacing, and subtle character development all enhance" Collins' fourth "gripping fantasy adventure." The final entry in the series, *Gregor and the Code of Claw,* follows the action as the protagonist learns of a terrifying prophecy that foreshadows his own death. The climax of the story approaches as Gregor prepares his warriors for a great battle with the giant rats, led by the despotic Bane, in the underground city of Regalia. "Perhaps Collins's greatest achievement in these tales," according to a contributor in *Kirkus Reviews,* "is the effortless introduction of weighty geopolitical ethics into rip-roaring adventure." Flynn also offered praise for the novel, stating in her *Horn Book* review that the author "delivers more of what's made this series so compelling: vivid action scenes, detailed military machinations, and nuanced character development."

Collins' award-winning "Hunger Games" trilogy is set in a post-apocalyptic world where teenagers fight to the death for the gratification of a television audience. The author thee novels—*The Hunger Games, Catching Fire,* and *Mockingjay*—on a number of sources, among them the ancient myth of Theseus and the Minotaur, in which the citizens of Athens sacrificed their children to a terrifying beast in order to avoid the punishment of their rival, King Minos of Crete. "I appropriated the Greek mythological premise of a conquering power that bent all of its subjects to its will through violence and maintained fear and domination through a not so subtle reminder to the neighboring peoples that they are not free and autonomous," Collins told *Journal of Adolescent and Adult Literacy* interviewer James Blasingame. She also drew upon the acclaimed film *Spartacus,* in which a former slave and gladiator leads a revolt against the Roman Empire. "The very moment when the idea came to me for *The Hunger Games,* however, happened one night when I was very tired and I was lying in bed channel surfing," she remarked to Blasingame. "I happened upon a reality program, recorded live, that pitted young people against each other for money. As I sleepily watched, the lines of reality started to blur for me, and the idea for the book emerged."

Cover of The Hunger Games, *featuring cover art by Tim O'Brien.*
(Illustration copyright © 2008 by Tim O'Brien. Reproduced by permission of Scholastic, Inc.)

Series opener *The Hunger Games* focuses on Katniss Everdeen, a sixteen-year-old resident of District Twelve in Panem, a nation that has risen from the ashes of the former United States. When her younger sister is chosen to participate in the annual Hunger Games to be held in the dictatorial Capitol, Katniss volunteers to go in her stead, joining twenty-three other contestants in a bloodthirsty gladiatorial contest that will be broadcast throughout the land. A skilled hunter and tracker, Katniss is joined by childhood acquaintance Peeta Mellark, the hapless son of a baker, in her fight for survival. "Collins's characters are completely realistic and sympathetic as they form alliances and friendships in the face of overwhelming odds," Jane Henriksen Baird remarked in *School Library Journal,* and *Horn Book* reviewer Jonathan Hunt noted that Katniss "displays great compassion and vulnerability through her first-person narration."

A number of critics cited Collins' depiction of violence as a strength of *The Hunger Games.* "You might not think it would be possible, or desirable, for a young-adult writer to describe, slowly and in full focus, a teenage girl getting stung to death by a swarm of mutant hornets," Lev Grossman wrote in *Time.* "It wasn't, until Collins did it. But rather than being repellent, the violence is strangely hypnotic. It's fairy-tale violence, Brothers Grimm violence—not a cheap thrill but a symbol of something deeper." As Stephen King maintained in *Entertainment Weekly,* "Reading *The Hunger Games* is as addictive (and as violently simple) as playing one of those shoot-it-if-it-moves videogames in the lobby of the local eightplex; you know it's not real, but you keep plugging in quarters anyway."

Catching Fire centers on the aftermath of Katniss and Peeta's improbable victory in the Hunger Games. While on a public-relations tour through the districts, Katniss—whose performance was viewed as an act of rebellion by the government—learns that she will be sent back into the arena for the seventy-fifth anniversary of the games, there to face a host of former champions. "In addition to the continuing story of the girl in the ring," observed *New York Times Book Review* critic Gabrielle Zevin, "*Catching Fire* is a portrait of how a desperate government tries to hold off a revolutionary tide and as such has something of the epic feeling of [George] Orwell to it." "Again, Collins' crystalline, unadorned prose provides an open window to perfect pacing and electrifying world building," Ian Chipman noted in *Booklist,* and Hunt remarked that the author "has once again delivered a page-turning blend of plot and character with an inventive setting and provocative themes."

Collins concludes her best-selling trilogy with *Mockingjay,* a novel that "will have the same lasting resonance as William Golding's *Lord of the Flies* and Stephen King's *The Stand,*" Baird predicted. Having secured a second victory in the games, Katniss becomes a reluctant figurehead for the growing rebel movement and must lead a special mission to the Capitol for a final

Cover of Collins' young-adult novel **Mockingjay,** *featuring cover art by* ***Tim O'Brien.*** (Jacket art copyright © 2010 by Scholastic, Inc. Reproduced by permission of Scholastic, Inc.)

confrontation with the despotic President Snow. According to *New York Times Book Review* contributor Katie Roiphe, the works in the "Hunger Games" trilogy "resist our hunger for clear definitions of good and evil, our sentimental need for a worthwhile cause, our desire for happy or simple endings, or even for the characters we like not to be killed or tortured or battered or bruised in graphic ways. Like the evil Capitol that controls and shadows its world, the trilogy tends to use the things we are attached to against us."

Though the "Underland Chronicles" and the "Hunger Games" trilogy feature horrific scenes of warfare, Collins hopes the violence serves a larger purpose. "One of the reasons it's important for me to write about war is I really think that the concept of war, the specifics of war, the nature of war, the ethical ambiguities of war are introduced too late to children," she told *School Library Journal* interviewer Rick Margolis. "I think they can hear them, understand them, know about them, at a much younger age without being scared to death by the stories." The author concluded, "But I feel that if the whole concept of war were introduced to kids at an earlier age, we would have better dialogues going on about it, and we would have a fuller understanding."

Biographical and Critical Sources

PERIODICALS

Booklist, November 15, 2003, Ed Sullivan, review of *Gregor the Overlander,* p. 608; September 1, 2004, Ed Sullivan, review of *Gregor and the Prophecy of Bane,* p. 120; July, 2005, Ed Sullivan, review of *Gregor and the Curse of the Warmbloods,* p. 1924; September 1, 2008, Francisca Goldsmith, review of *The Hunger Games,* p. 97; July 1, 2009, Ian Chipman, review of *Catching Fire,* p. 62.

Bulletin of the Center for Children's Books, January, 2004, Janice Del Negro, review of *Gregor the Overlander,* p. 185; October, 2004, Timnah Card, review of *Gregor and the Prophecy of Bane,* p. 65; September, 2005, Timnah Card, review of *Gregor and the Curse of the Warmbloods,* p. 11.

Children's Bookwatch, June, 2005, review of *When Charlie McButton Lost Power.*

Entertainment Weekly, September 12, 2008, Stephen King, review of *The Hunger Games,* p. 139; September 4, 2009, Jennifer Reese, review of *Catching Fire,* p. 63.

Horn Book, September-October, 2003, Kitty Flynn, review of *Gregor the Overlander,* p. 609; September-October, 2004, Kitty Flynn, review of *Gregor and the Prophecy of Bane,* p. 578; July-August, 2005, Kitty Flynn, review of *Gregor and the Curse of the Warmbloods,* p. 467; July-August, 2006, Kitty Flynn, review of *Gregor and the Marks of Secret,* p. 437; July-August, 2007, Kitty Flynn, review of *Gregor and the Code of Claw,* p. 391; September-October, 2008, Jonathan Hunt, review of *The Hunger Games,* p. 580; September-October, 2009, Jonathan Hunt, review of *Catching Fire,* p. 555; November-December, 2010, Jonathan Hunt, review of *Mockingjay,* p. 86.

Instructor, September-October, 2010, interview with Collins, p. 51.

Journal of Adolescent and Adult Literacy, May, 2009, James Blasingame, review of *The Hunger Games,* p. 724, and interview with Collins, p. 726.

Kirkus Reviews, August 1, 2003, review of *Gregor the Overlander,* p. 1014; August 1, 2004, review of *Gregor and the Prophecy of Bane,* p. 739; May 1, 2005, review of *When Charlie McButton Lost Power,* p. 536; June 15, 2005, review of *Gregor and the Curse of the Warmbloods,* p. 680; May 15, 2006, review of *Gregor and the Marks of Secret,* p. 515; May 1, 2007, review of *Gregor and the Code of Claw;* September 1, 2008, review of *The Hunger Games;* July 1, 2009, review of *Catching Fire.*

New York Times Book Review, October 11, 2009, Gabrielle Zevin, review of *Catching Fire,* p. 13; September 12, 2010, Katie Roiphe, review of *Mockingjay,* p. 12.

Publishers Weekly, September 8, 2003, review of *Gregor the Overlander,* p. 77; November 3, 2008, Megan Whalen Turner, review of *The Hunger Games,* p. 58; June 22, 2009, review of *Catching Fire,* p. 46.

School Library Journal, November, 2003, Steven Engelfried, review of *Gregor the Overlander,* p. 134; October, 2004, Beth Meister, review of *Gregor and the Prophecy of Bane,* p. 160; July, 2005, Tasha Saecker, review of *Gregor and the Curse of the Warmbloods,*

p. 100; July, 2005, Barbara Auerbach, review of *When Charlie McButton Lost Power,* p. 71; September, 2006, Mara Alpert, review of *Gregor and the Marks of Secret,* p. 202; July, 2007, Beth L. Meister, review of *Gregor and the Code of Claw,* p. 99; September, 2008, Rick Margolis, interview with Collins, p. 30, and Jane Henriksen Baird, review of *The Hunger Games,* p. 176; August, 2010, Rick Margolis, interview with Collins, p. 24; October, 2010, Jane Henriksen Baird, review of *Mockingjay,* p. 110.

Time, September 7, 2009, Lev Grossman, review of *The Hunger Games,* p. 65.

Voice of Youth Advocates, April, 2004, review of *Gregor and the Prophecy of Bane,* p. 21.

ONLINE

Scholastic Web site, http://www.scholastic.com/ (January 15, 2011), "Suzanne Collins."

Suzanne Collins Home Page, http://www.suzannecollins books.com (January 15, 2011).*

*   *   *

CRONN-MILLS, Kirstin 1968-

Personal

Born 1968, in VA; married; husband's name Dan; children: one son. *Education:* University of Nebraska—Lincoln, B.A. (English), M.A. (English); Iowa State University, Ph.D. (rhetorical and professional communications).

Addresses

Home—Mankato, MN. *E-mail*—kirstin.cronnmills@gmail.com.

Career

Author and educator. South Central College, southern MN, English instructor.

Awards, Honors

Instructor of the Year award, Minnesota State College Student Association, 2009; Minnesota State Book Award for Young People's Literature finalist, 2010, for *The Sky Always Hears Me, and the Hills Don't Mind.*

Writings

Collapse!: The Science of Structural Engineering Failures, Compass Point Books (Mankoto, MN), 2009.

The Sky Always Hears Me, and the Hills Don't Mind, Flux (Woodbury, MN), 2009.

Beautiful Music for Ugly Children, Flux (Woodbury, MN), 2012.

Kirstin Cronn-Mills (Photograph by Chelsea Morning Photography. Reproduced by permission.)

Contributor to anthology *Millennial Mythmaking: Essays on the Power of Science Fiction and Fantasy Literature, Films, and Games,* McFarland (Jefferson, NC), 2010.

Sidelights

"I have the world's best set of jobs," Kirstin Cronn-Mills told *SATA.* "I'm a writer *and* a teacher. I love what I do!

"My careers are tied together by two things: 1) a love for stories, and 2) an awareness of how powerful words can be. In both jobs I play with language and tell stories, and I show my students/readers how to do the same. If we find the right words, we can move the world."

Biographical and Critical Sources

PERIODICALS

Bulletin of the Center for Children's Books, January, 2010, Karen Coats, review of *The Sky Always Hears Me, and the Hills Don't Mind,* p. 192.

Kirkus Reviews, August 1, 2009, review of *The Sky Always Hears Me, and the Hills Don't Mind.*

ONLINE

Kirstin Cronn-Mills Home Page, http://kirstincronn-mills.com (November 29, 2010).

D

DAKIN, Glenn 1960-
(Andy Baxter)

Personal

Born 1960, in England. *Education:* Manchester Polytechnic, B.A. (graphic design; with honours).

Addresses

Home—Cambridge, England. *E-mail*—contact@glenndakin.com.

Career

Cartoonist, comics writer, novelist, and scriptwriter for radio and television. Marvel UK, writer for comics series, including "Plasmer," "Clan-Destine," and "Spider-Man" (newspaper strip); freelance author; developer and writer of children's television programming.

Awards, Honors

Emmy Award for Best International Television Show (writer), 2008, for *Shaun the Sheep;* Great Stone Face Book Award nomination in Fantasy and Science Fiction category, 2009, for *Candle Man.*

Writings

FOR CHILDREN

The Not-Yeti, Brilliant Books (London, England), 1999.
(Adaptor) *The Contest; and, The Bongo Bob Show* (television novelization), BBC Worldwide (London, England), 1999.
How to Be Completely Rotten!: Rotten Ralph, illustrated by Colin Howard, BBC Worldwide (London, England), 1999.

Glenn Dakin (Photography by Andy Dakin. Reproduced by permission.)

Robbie the Reindeer; Hooves of Fire, illustrated by Delphine Thomas, Comic Relief (London, England), 2000.
The Ghost Train Rides Tonight, Brilliant Books (London, England), 2000.

The Frogspawn Code, Brilliant Books (London, England), 2001.

The Halloween Project, Brilliant Books (London, England) 2001.

The Impossible Dinosaur, Brilliant Books (London, England) 2001.

Finding Nemo: The Essential Guide, DK Publishing (New York, NY), 2003.

Disney Villains: The Essential Guide, DK (New York, NY), 2004.

Scooby-Doo!: The Essential Guide, DK (New York, NY), 2004.

Wallace and Gromit: Curse of the Were-Rabbit: The Essential Guide, DK (New York, NY), 2005.

Disney Animals: The Essential Guide, DK Pub. (New York, NY), 2006.

Happy Feet: The Essential Guide, DK (New York, NY), 2006.

Ice Age: The Essential Guide, DK (New York, NY), 2006.

(With Richard Platt) *Pirates of the Caribbean: The Complete Visual Guide,* new edition, DK Pub. (New York, NY), 2007.

Ratatouille (rat-a-too-ee): The Guide to Remy's World, DK (New York, NY), 2007.

Shrek Cookbook, DK Pub. (New York, NY), 2007.

(Under name Andy Baxter) *Beastly: Snake Scare,* Egmont (London, England), 2008.

(Adaptor) *The Alliance; Secrets* (television tie-in), Egmont (London, England), 2008.

Toy Story: The Essential Guide, revised edition, DK Pub. (New York, NY), 2008.

Ice Age, Dawn of the Dinosaurs: The Essential Guide, DK Pub. (New York, NY), 2009.

Author of television scripts for series, including *Bob the Builder,* Hit Animation, *Postman Pat,* Cosgrove, Hall, and *Shaun the Sheep,* Aardman, produced for British Broadcasting Corporation.

"CANDLE MAN" NOVEL SERIES

The Society of Unrelenting Vigilance, Egmont (New York, NY), 2009.

The Society of Dread, Egmont USA (New York, NY), 2010.

COMICS

Temptation (collected comics), Penguin (New York, NY), 1991.

Abe: Wrong for the Right Reasons (collected comics), Top Shelf Productions, 2001.

(With Phil Elliot) *The Rockpool Files,* Slave Labor, 2010.

Author of comics, including "Abe" (autobiographical comics), "Paris the Man of Plaster," (with Steve Way) "Temptation," "Robot Crusoe," (with Woodrow Phoenix) "Sinister Romance," and (with Phil Elliott) "Mr Day and Mr Night," "Greenhouse Warriors," and "The Man from Cancer." Work represented in anthologies, including *Gag, Honk, Escape, Deadline,* and *Prime Cuts.*

Sidelights

Demonstrating his versatility as a writer, Glenn Dakin has created comics, authored scripts for the British television series *Shaun the Sheep,* and written a number of "Essential Guide" books that collect facts, character profiles, plot synopses, and assorted trivia about popular television series and films. He has also written sketch comedy for the television and radio, working with Nick Barber. While continuing to juggle these varied projects, Dakin also turns to fantasy fiction in his "Candle Man" adventure-novel series, which includes *The Society of Unrelenting Vigilance* and *The Society of Dread.*

Dakin created his first comic, "Abe," while at secondary school and it saw print when he attended Manchester Polytechnic in the 1980s. This autobiographical work was eventually included in *Escape* magazine. While continuing "Abe," he also contributed to other comics projects—both original and collaborative—such as "The Man of Plaster," "Temptation," "Sinister Romance," and "Greenhouse Warriors." Within a decade, Dakin's work could be found in comics anthologies as well as

Cover of Dakin's middle-grade "Candle Man" adventure novel **The Society of Unrelenting Vigilance,** *featuring cover art by Greg Swearingen.* (Egmont, 2009. Illustration copyright © 2009 by Greg Swearingen. Reproduced by permission.)

in original comic books. In 2001 his "Abe" comics were collected and published in book form as *Abe: Wrong for the Right Reasons.*

Part one of Dakin's "Candle Man" series, *The Society of Unrelenting Vigilance,* introduces a sickly preteen named Theo Wickland. Theo's condition has prompted his wealthy but aloof guardian, Dr. Saint, to confine him to a few small and sterile rooms in Empire Hall, where the boy is administered a diet of leafy green vegetables and millet. Radiation treatments are also part of Theo's daily regimen, but these end when burglars invade the hall and the boy is freed. Eventually rescued by members of the secret society of the title, Theo learns that his guardian heads a nefarious clan that goes by the name of The Society of Good Works. Now living underground and having discovered his ability to melt people into puddles of goo, the boy takes a role in stopping the work of his guardian, who has helped to create unearthly creatures such as living gargoyles and smog-like beings.

Noting the "decidedly Victorian steampunk feel" of Dakin's novel, Sue Giffard added in *School Library Journal* that *The Society of Unrelenting Vigilance* will draw readers in with its "appealing characters" and "nonstop action." "Dakin skillfully brings moral ambiguity into the narrative, giving the writing a more sophisticated flair than standard superhero fare," wrote a *Kirkus Reviews* contributor in appraising the "Candle Man" series opener, and *Booklist* critic Ilene Cooper maintained that Dakin's fantastical saga "gets off to a rousing start" in the novel. For *Horn Book* critic Sarah Ellis, *The Society of Unrelenting Vigilance* holds out the promise of good things to follow; "Dakin's sparkling action/horror writing and his cast of intriguing minor characters give this fantasy a flavor all its own," she wrote of the novel.

Biographical and Critical Sources

PERIODICALS

Booklist, October 15, 2009, Ilene Cooper, review of *The Society of Unrelenting Vigilance,* p. 65.
Bulletin of the Center for Children's Books, December, 2009, April Spisak, review of *The Society of Unrelenting Vigilance.*
Horn Book, January-February, 2010, Sarah Ellis, review of *The Society of Unrelenting Vigilance,* p. 84.
Kirkus Reviews, August 15, 2009, review of *The Society of Unrelenting Vigilance.*
School Library Journal, October, 2009, Sue Giffard, review of *The Society of Unrelenting Vigilance,* p. 124.

ONLINE

Glenn Dakin Home Page, http://www.glenndakin.com (December 7, 2010).

Glenn Dakin Web log, http://glenndakin.wordpress.com (December 15, 2010).

*   *   *

DEROM, Dirk 1980-

Personal

Born 1980, in Belgium. *Education:* Katholieke Hogeschool Leuven, B.S. (social work), 2002; Vrije Universiteit Brussel, M.A. (philosophy), 2005; Victoria University of Wellington, postgraduate study (neuropsychology).

Addresses

Home—Wellington, New Zealand. *E-mail*—dirk@pigeonandpigeonette.com.

Career

Author, scholar, and project manager. BNA-BBOT (Web site), Belgium, project manager of software development.

Writings

Pigeon and Pigeonette, illustrated by Sarah Verroken, Enchanted Lion Books (Brooklyn, NY), 2009.

Biographical and Critical Sources

PERIODICALS

Children's Bookwatch, October, 2009, review of *Pigeon and Pigeonette.*
Kirkus Reviews, September 1, 2009, review of *Pigeon and Pigeonette.*
Library Media Connection, January-February, 2010, Brenda Dales, review of *Pigeon and Pigeonette,* p. 62.
School Library Journal, November, 2009, Stacy Dillon, review of *Pigeon and Pigeonette,* p. 76.

ONLINE

Dirk Derom Home Page, http://www.pigeonandpigeonette.com (December 7, 2010).*

*   *   *

DuBURKE, Randy

Personal

Born in Washington, GA; married Olivia Wolff; children: Sakai, Matthias. *Education:* New York Technical College, graduate.

Addresses

Home—Binningen, Switzerland. *E-mail*—randy@randyduburke.com.

Randy DuBurke (Photograph by Olivia Wolff. Reproduced by permission.)

Career

Illustrator, author, and animator. Manhattan Multi Media, advertising designer; commercial illustrator; animator for M.T.V. *Exhibitions:* Work included in permanent collection at the Civil Rights Museum, Birmingham, Alabama.

Awards, Honors

Coretta Scott King/John Steptoe New Talent Award for illustration, 2003, for *The Moon Ring;* Children's Book of the Year selection, Bank Street College of Education, 2004, for *Halloween Night on Shivermore Street* by Pam Pollack and Meg Belviso; *Storytelling World* Honor Award, Children's Book of the Year selection, Bank Street College of Education, and Amelia Bloomer Project listee, American Library Association (ALA), all 2006, all for *Catching the Moon* by Crystal Hubbard; Best Book for Young Adults selection, ALA, 2006, for *Malcolm X* by Andrew Helfer; Best of the Best Books selection, Chicago Public Library, and Coretta Scott King Award Author Honor Book award, both 2010, both for *Yummy* by G. Neri.

Writings

SELF-ILLUSTRATED

Hunter's Heart, Paradox Press (New York, NY), 1995.
The Moon Ring, Chronicle Books (San Francisco, CA), 2002.
Little Mister, Chronicle Books (San Francisco, CA), 2006.

ILLUSTRATOR

Olivia George, *The Bravest Girls in the World,* Scholastic (New York, NY), 2004.
Pam Pollack and Meg Belviso, *Halloween Night on Shivermore Street,* Chronicle Books (San Francisco, CA), 2004.

Crystal Hubbard, *Catching the Moon: The Story of a Young Girl's Baseball Dream,* Lee & Low Books (New York, NY), 2005.
Andrew Helfer, *Malcolm X: A Novel Graphic Biography,* Hill & Wang (New York, NY), 2006.
Patricia C. McKissack and Fredrick L. McKissack, Jr., *The Adventures of Deadwood Dick,* Chronicle Books (San Francisco, CA), 2009.
Cynthia Jaynes Omololu, *When It's Six O'clock in San Francisco: A Trip through Time Zones,* Clarion Books (New York, NY), 2009.
G. Neri, *Yummy: The Last Days of a Southside Shorty,* Lee & Low Books (New York, NY), 2010.

Contributor to comic books for DC Comics and Marvel for twelve years; contributor to "Forbidden Zone" comic-book series, 1999.

Sidelights

The art of Randy DuBurke, a recipient of the Coretta Scott King/John Steptoe New Talent Award for illustration, has graced the pages of picture books such as Crystal Hubbard's *Catching the Moon: The Story of a Young Girl's Baseball Dream* and *Little Mister,* a self-illustrated tale. DuBurke was born in Georgia and lived in the Deep South with his grandparents until age four, when he moved north to New York City to live with his mother and father. Living with extended family, he learned to appreciate the longstanding tradition of southern storytelling, as well as a respect for nature. Although he now lives in Switzerland, DuBurke's childhood continues to influence his work, which includes the award-winning *The Moon Ring.* In addition to children's books, DuBurke creates illustrations for comic books and graphic novels and, as a professional artist, has designed trading cards, advertising art, and video animation. In 2008 six of his comic pages were reproduced and installed in a permanent exhibit at Birmingham, Alabama's Civil Rights Museum.

In *The Moon Ring* DuBurke weaves a bit of Southern magic into his story of the adventures of a young African-American girl named Maxine one hot summer night. As the girl stares up into the night sky during the second full moon of the month, Maxine's grandmother explains that the "blue moon" means that magic is in the air. As the night deepens, a ring of silver falls from the moon and carries Maxine to far-away lands that range from the African savanna to the coldest reaches of Antarctica to bustling New York City streets. During Maxine's fantastic journey several animal characters accompany her: giraffes, seals, penguins, and others. When Maxine tires from her travels, she finds herself happily and safely nestled back at home.

In *Publishers Weekly* a reviewer commented that DuBurke's "magical" pen-and-ink art for *The Moon Ring,* colored with vivid acrylic paints, "combines an almost photographic realism with cartoon exaggeration" and "exude[s] a giddy energy." Ellen Heath, writing in

School Library Journal, also enjoyed the book, stating that the author/illustrator's "unusual and appealing" characters come to life in DuBurke's "impressive illustrations." While noting that the characters' expressions are sometimes exaggerated, a *Kirkus Reviews* writer concluded of *The Moon Ring* that "the boundless energy and sheer playfulness of this debut will please young readers."

In addition to creating art for his own books, DuBurke has also illustrated stories for other writers. In *Halloween Night on Shivermore Street,* a book by Pam Pollack and Meg Belviso, a host of young partygoers attends a lively masquerade party where guests carve pumpkins, play musical chairs, and bob for apples, among other activities. DuBurke's "firelit acrylics lend a ghoulish glow to the theatrical holiday," a *Publishers Weekly* critic noted, and a contributor in *Kirkus Reviews* found the illustrations "dynamic, engaging, and full of creepy (but not too creepy) detail."

A work of historical fiction, *Catching the Moon* focuses on Marcenia Lyle, the first woman to play professionally for a men's baseball team. Hubbard's story follows young Marcenia's efforts to impress Gabby Street, the manager of the St. Louis Cardinals, at a local baseball camp. "DuBurke's balanced pen-and-ink and acrylic artwork strongly supports the mood and emotion of the text," Marilyn Taniguchi commented in her *School Library Journal* review.

When It's Six O'clock in San Francisco: A Trip through Time Zones, a concept book written by Cynthia Jaynes Omololu, follows the daily activities of several youngsters and their families across the globe. Set in some of the great cities of the world, including London, England,

and Beijing, China, the work acknowledges both the similarities and differences among the children. Writing in *Booklist,* Hazel Rochman applauded the artist's "warm, colorful, individual portraits that move beyond cultural stereotypes." "Alternating between sequential panels and full-bleed spreads," a critic in *Kirkus Reviews* stated, "DuBurke's acrylics convey both cross-cultural unity and variations."

DuBurke has also provided the artwork for a pair of stirring biographical works, Andrew Helfer's *Malcolm X: A Novel Graphic Biography* and G. Neri's *Yummy: The Last Days of a Southside Shorty.* In *Malcolm X* Helfer offers a portrait of the famed twentieth-century African-American civil rights activist, basing his text on the classic 1965 work *The Autobiography of Malcolm X.* DuBurke's "detailed [black-and-]white drawings, sharp as photographs in a newspaper," earned praise from a critic in *Publishers Weekly,* and Rochman maintained that the artwork "visualizes the political struggle as well as the inner anger and turmoil" of Helfer's subject.

Neri details the harrowing true story of an youthful killer in *Yummy,* an award-winning graphic novel. In 1994, eleven-year-old Robert Sandifer, a gangbanger nicknamed "Yummy" because of his love of sweets, murdered his fourteen-year-old neighbor and spent three days on the run from police until members of his own gang, the Black Disciples Nation, executed him. DuBurke's frequent use of close-ups "offers readers an immediacy as well as emotional connection to this tragic story," wrote Barbara M. Moon in *School Library Journal,* and *Booklist* reviewer Jesse Karp maintained that DuBurke's black-and-white art "possesses a realism that grounds the nightmare in uncompromising reality and an emotional expressiveness that strikes right to the heart." In an interview on the Lee & Low Books Web site, DuBurke stated: "*Yummy* is a book about choices and consequences. I hope some kids who may be in a similar situation, or know someone who is, can read the book and because of it make the proper choices."

Biographical and Critical Sources

PERIODICALS

Booklist, September 1, 2005, Gillian Engberg, review of *Catching the Moon: The Story of a Young Girl's Baseball Dream,* p. 119; February 1, 2007, Hazel Rochman, review of *Malcolm X: A Novel Graphic Biography,* p. 50; September 15, 2009, Hazel Rochman, review of *When It's Six O'Clock in San Francisco: A Trip through Time Zones,* p. 65; August 1, 2010, Jesse Karp, review of *Yummy: The Last Days of a Southside Shorty,* p. 55.

Kirkus Reviews, August 15, 2002, review of *The Moon Ring,* p. 1222; October 15, 2004, review of *Halloween*

DuBurke's illustration projects include Cynthia James Omololu's time-bending picture book **When It's Six O'Clock in San Francisco.** (Clarion Books, 2009. Illustration copyright © 2009 by Randy DuBurke. Reproduced by permission of Clarion Books, an imprint of Houghton Mifflin Harcourt Publishing Company. All rights reserved.)

Night on Shivermore Street, p. 1012; September 1, 2005, review of *Catching the Moon,* p. 974; June 15, 2009, review of *When It's Six O'Clock in San Francisco.*

Publishers Weekly, October 7, 2002, review of *The Moon Ring,* p. 71; August 9, 2004, review of *Halloween Night on Shivermore Street,* p. 248; December 4, 2006, review of *Malcolm X,* p. 41; July 19, 2010, review of *Yummy,* p. 119.

School Library Journal, December, 2002, Ellen Heath, review of *The Moon Ring,* p. 94; August, 2004, Rosalyn Pierini, review of *Halloween Night on Shivermore Street,* p. 92; November, 2005, Marilyn Taniguchi, review of *Catching the Moon,* p. 116; May, 2007, Heidi Dolamore, review of *Malcolm X,* p. 170; October, 2009, Lisa Crandall, review of *When It's Six O'Clock in San Francisco,* p. 100; September, 2010, Barbara M. Moon, review of *Yummy,* p. 180.

Teacher Librarian, June, 2007, Michele Gorman, review of *Malcolm X.*

ONLINE

Lee & Low Books Web site, http://www.leeandlow.com/ (January 1, 2011), "From the Evening News to Graphic Novel: G. Neri and Randy DuBurke on *Yummy: The Last Days of a Southside Shorty.*"

Randy DuBurke Home Page, http://www.randyduburke. com (January 1, 2011).

E-F

EAST, Jacqueline

Personal
Born in England. *Education:* University College Falmouth, M.A. (illustration), 2009.

Addresses
Home—Bristol, England. *E-mail*—info@jacquelineeast.com; jacqueline.east@virgin.net.

Career
Author and illustrator of books for children. Illustrator, beginning c. late 1980s.

Writings

SELF-ILLUSTRATED; "ED THE PUP" SERIES

I Won't Eat That, Ragged Bears (Andover, England), 1997.
I'm Scared of the Dark, Ragged Bears (Andover, England), 1997.
Ed's New Baby Sister, Ragged Bears (Andover, England), 1998.
I Can't, Ragged Bears (Andover, England), 1998.

SELF-ILLUSTRATED; "WIGGLE-WAGGLES" SERIES

Bunny, Barron's Educational (Hauppauge, NY), 2007.
Duckling, Barron's Educational (Hauppauge, NY), 2007.
Kitten, Barron's Educational (Hauppauge, NY), 2007.
Puppy, Barron's Educational (Hauppauge, NY), 2007.

ILLUSTRATOR

Joan Stimson, *Finnigan's Flap* (interactive book), Picture Ladybird (Loughborough, England), 1996.

Tessa Krailing, *Trouble for Alberta,* Hamish Hamilton (London, England), 1996.
Philippa Gregory, *Diggory and the Boa Conductor: Three Amazing Stories,* Hippo (London, England), 1996.
Odette Elliott, *Nightingale News: Five Stories about Our School,* Hippo (London, England), 1996.
Sue Lloyd, *The Children's Book of Manners,* Award (London, England), 1997.
Sylvia Green, *A Parsnip Called Val,* Hippo (London, England), 1997.
Margaret Ryan, *Lucky Laces* ("Springboard Flyers" reader series), Ginn (Aylesbury, England), 1998.
Pat Posner, reteller, *The Frog Prince,* World International (Handforth, England), 1998.
Jonathan Meres, *The Big Bad Rumor,* Orchard Books (New York, NY), 2000.
Yvonne Carroll, reteller, *Leprechaun Tales,* Pelican (London, England), 2001.
Jenny Fry, *Building Numbers,* Barron's (Hauppauge, NY), 2002.
Clive Gifford, *The Fair of Fear,* Letts (London, England), 2004.
Martyn Beardsley, *Five Naughty Kittens,* Franklin Watts (London, England), 2004, Sea-to-Sea (Mankato, MN), 2006.
(With others) *Hickory Dickory Dock and Other Silly-Time Rhymes* (with CD), Trudy Corp. (Norwalk, CT), 2005.
Beth Shoshan, *That's When I'm Happy!,* Meadowside Children's (London, England), 2005.
Beth Shoshan, *Cuddle,* Meadowside Children's (London, England), 2006.
Bob Hartman, *The Three Billy Goats' Stuff!,* Lion Children's (Oxford, England), 2007, Lion (New York, NY), 2009.
Susanna Davidson, reteller, *The Town Mouse and the Country Mouse* (based on a story by Aesop), Usborne (London, England), 2007.
Chae. Strathie, *My Dad,* Worthwhile (San Diego, CA), 2008.
Beth Shoshan, *My Mum!,* Meadowside Children's (London, England), 2009.

ILLUSTRATOR; "JUNGLE TALES" SERIES BY RONNE RANDALL

Tiger Tales, Bright Sparks (Bath, England), 2000.
Trunk Trouble, Bright Sparks (Bath, England), 2000.
Monkey Mayhem!, Bright Sparks (Bath, England), 2000.
Gym Giraffe, Bright Sparks (Bath, England), 2000.
Hippo's Holiday, Bright Sparks (Bath, England), 2001.
Super Snakes, Bright Sparks (Bath, England), 2001.
Snap Happy, Bright Sparks (Bath, England), 2001.
Fancy Flying, Bright Sparks (Bath, England), 2001.

ILLUSTRATOR; "FAT ALPHIE AND CHARLIE THE WIMP" READER SERIES BY MARGARET RYAN

New Kit on the Block, Scholastic Children's (London, England), 2002.
Fat Alphie in Love, Scholastic Children's (London, England), 2002.
The Disappearing Dinner, Scholastic Children's (London, England), 2002.
Fat Alphie the Famous, Scholastic Children's (London, England), 2003.

Sidelights

British artist Jacqueline East began her illustration career in the late 1980s, and her work has included advertising art, greeting-card art, and book illustration for education and trade publishers. Her bright, cheery illustrations also appear in picture-book stories by a variety

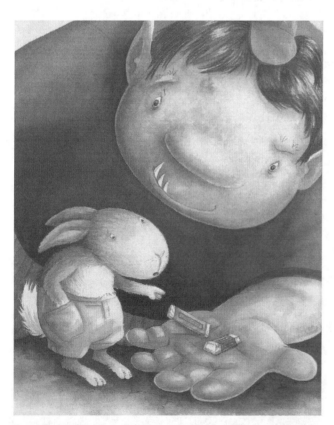

Jacqueline East's illustration projects include creating the artwork for Bob Hartman's **The Three Billy Goats' Stuff!** (Illustration copyright © 2007 by Jacqueline East. All rights reserved. Reproduced by permission of Lion Hudson plc.)

of writers that include Margaret Ryan, Beth Shoshan, Susanna Davidson, and Bob Hartman. In addition to her original "Ed the Puppy" and "Wiggle-Waggle" board books for young children, East has also created the artwork for Ronne Randall's "Jungle Tales" books and Ryan's "Fat Alphie and Charlie the Wimp" reader series.

The Big Bad Rumor, a picture book by Jonathan Meres, follows a rumor about a big bad wolf that grows more and more outlandish with each retelling by a silly farmyard goose. As the story comes to life in East's humor-filled art, her "goofy cartooning keeps the mood light," according to a *Publishers Weekly* critic. The youngest children "will enjoy the simple, expressive cartoon illustrations," predicted *School Library Journal* contributor Jody McCoy, the critic dubbing *The Big Bad Rumor* "lots of fun." Another illustration project, *The Three Billy Goats' Stuff!,* pairs East's artwork with a humorous story by Bob Hartman. In *School Library Journal* Michele Sealander cited the "clever illustrations" that capture the fun in Hartman's retelling of "The Three Billy Goats' Gruff," while a *Kirkus Reviews* writer recommended *The Three Billy Goats' Stuff!* as "a good fractured-fairy-tale read-aloud" for young readers.

Biographical and Critical Sources

PERIODICALS

Kirkus Reviews, June 15, 2009, review of *The Three Billy Goats' Stuff!*.
Publishers Weekly, July 31, 2000, review of *The Big Bad Rumor,* p. 93; October 2, 2006, review of *Hickory Dickory Dock and Other Silly-Time Rhymes,* p. 65.
School Library Journal, November, 2000, Jody McCoy, review of *The Big Bad Rumor,* p. 128; September, 2001, Alice Casey Smith, review of *Leprechaun Tales,* p. 212; August, 2009, Michele Sealander, review of *The Three Billy Goats' Stuff!,* p. 76.

ONLINE

Jacqueline East Home Page, http://www.jacquelineeast.com (December 7, 2010).*

*   *   *

FEARING, Mark 1968-

Personal

Born 1968; married; children: one daughter. *Education:* University of Wisconsin, B.F.A.; attended University of California, Los Angeles.

Addresses

Home—Portland, OR. *Agent*—Sheldon Fogelman Agency, 10 E. 40th St., Ste. 3205, New York, NY 10016. *E-mail*—mark.fearing@gmail.com; mark@markfearing.com.

Mark Fearing (Photograph by Emud Mokhberi. Reproduced by permission.)

Career

Animator, illustrator, cartoonist, and graphic designer. Hollywood Stock Exchange, graphic designer, 1995-96; Raza Digital, designer and illustrator, 1996-97; Cybermedia, senior designer, 1997; Sony Online Entertainment, San Diego, CA, art director, 1997-99; Pearson Television Entertainment, creative director, 2000-01; Fremantle Media, art director, 2000-02; freelance animator, beginning 2002; Playhut, Inc., Industry, CA, art director, 2003; Walt Disney Television Animation, Burbank, CA, production manager, 2004-05; Eduworks, Corvallis, OR, designer, 2006-08; Transamerica, Los Angeles, CA, designer and animator, 2006-09; Nickelodeon Television, character designer, 2006; Laika Entertainment, Portland, OR, story artist, 2006; G4 Television, animator and title designer, 2006; freelance illustrator, beginning 2009. *Exhibitions:* Works exhibited at galleries in Portland, OR, and by Society of Illustrators, Los Angeles.

Awards, Honors

Illustration West Show 47, certificate of merit.

Writings

Cenozoic, OPP Press (Redondo Beach, CA), 2004.
(Illustrator) John Perry, *The Book That Eats People,* Tricycle Press (Berkeley, CA), 2009.

Author of scripts for short film *The Thing With No Head,* produced for Nicktoons, 2004.

Contributor of essays and illustrations to periodicals, including *Comics Journal, Kite Tales,* and *Layers.*

Sidelights

An animator, graphic designer, and illustrator, Mark Fearing created the imaginative artwork that inhabits John Perry's unusual volume, *The Book That Eats*

People. Describing his multi-faceted career, Fearing noted on his home page: "I am most strongly motivated by opportunities to tell stories using drawings, design and words. My art is strongly narrative and I enjoy developing ideas and deciding which medium they belong—a book, a comic, a graphic novel, animation or a short story." In addition to his illustration work, Fearing has crafted the animated short film, *The Thing with No Head,* which was screened at several film festivals in addition to airing on Nicktoons in 2004.

The Book That Eats People treats readers to a darkly humorous tale as it warns about the carnivorous habits of the very work they hold in their hands, noting the sinister book's tendency to disguise itself with fake book jackets, devour literate but incautious youngsters, and—perhaps most frightening of all—escape from prison. "Fearing's Photoshopped collages and cartoon illustrations have a suitably menacing aspect," a *Kirkus Reviews* critic noted in a review of *The Book That Eats People.* Marge Loch-Wouters, writing in *School Library Journal,* complimented the artist for creating a "jazzy, jangly style that is part noir and part graphic novel," and a *Publishers Weekly* reviewer observed that the artist fills "his collage spreads with torn and crumpled papers (which take on an especially gruesome vibe in this context)."

Discussing his involvement with Perry's book project in a *Seven Impossible Things before Breakfast* online interview, Fearing recalled that after receiving Perry's

Fearing brings to life John Perry's quirky story of biblio-barbarism in his illustrations for **The Book That Eats People.** (Illustration copyright © 2009 by Mark Fearing. Used by permission of Tricycle Press, an imprint of Random House Children's Books, a division of Random House, Inc.)

Fearing's original illustrations include "Class Clown." (Reproduced by permission.)

manuscript he "realized what a treasure the story was. It offered an opportunity to jump into doing something very unique. Lots of room to have fun and very little visual repetition." He further noted, "After talking with the editor, I decided the illustrations had to feel as if they were items that had been collected in the book as it lived its life. It was a challenge—but a fun one."

Biographical and Critical Sources

PERIODICALS

Bulletin of the Center for Children's Books, November, 2009, Deborah Stevenson, review of *The Book That Eats People,* p. 124.
Kirkus Reviews, September 1, 2009, review of *The Book That Eats People.*
Publishers Weekly, October 12, 2009, review of *The Book That Eats People,* p. 47.
School Library Journal, November, 2009, Marge Loch-Wouters, review of *The Book That Eats People,* p. 86.

ONLINE

Cartoonshmartoon Web log, http://cartoonshmartoon. blogspot.com/ (January 1, 2011).

Mark Fearing Home Page, http://www.markfearing.com (January 1, 2011).
Mark Fearing Web log, http://mfearing.wordpress.com (January 1, 2011).
Seven Impossible Things before Breakfast Web log, http:// blaine.org/sevenimpossiblethings/ (October 6, 2009), interview with Fearing.

*   *   *

FITZPATRICK, Becca 1979-

Personal

Born 1979, in Ogden, UT; married; husband's name Justin; children: two sons. *Education:* Brigham Young University, B.A. (community health), 2001. *Hobbies and other interests:* Running, gardening, reading.

Addresses

Home—Fort Collins, CO. *Agent*—Catherine Drayton, InkWell Management, 521 5th Ave., 26th Fl., New York, NY 10175. *E-mail*—becca@beccafitzpatrick.com.

Career

Novelist. Formerly worked in an alternative high school in Provo, UT.

Writings

"HUSH, HUSH" YOUNG-ADULT NOVEL SERIES

Hush, Hush, Simon & Schuster Books for Young Readers (New York, NY), 2009.
Crescendo, Simon & Schuster Books for Young Readers (New York, NY), 2010.
Untitled, Simon & Schuster Books for Young Readers (New York, NY), 2011.

Author's works have been translated into several languages, including French, Italian, Polish, Spanish, and Swedish.

Sidelights

Becca Fitzpatrick had graduated from college with a degree in community health and was working as a teacher and secretary at an alternative high school when her life took a surprising twist. In February of 2003 Fitzpatrick's husband surprised her with an interesting birthday gift: a seat in an upcoming creative writing workshop. Her first novel, *Hush, Hush* grew out of that workshop and was inspired by Fitzpatrick's vivid memories of her own high-school years.

Hush, Hush taps a popular subject in young-adult fiction—angels—but approaches it in a unique manner. Fitzpatrick's hero is actually a fallen angel who travels among mankind in the guise of the handsome and laid-back teenager Patch. For Nora Grey, a sophomore hoping to earn a college scholarship at her Maine high school, Patch makes an engaging biology-class partner despite his bad-boy reputation. At first she finds him attractive and seductive, but as she falls for Patch romantically Nora also becomes aware that he knows too much about her, right down to what she is thinking. As she discovers Patch's secrets, she also learns that her birthright has enmeshed her in a battle between good and evil that is older than man. Calling *Hush, Hush* a "thrilling debut," a *Kirkus Reviews* contributor wrote that the "forbidden romance between Nora and Patch" will appeal to fans of Stephanie Meyer's "Twilight" novels. A *Publishers Weekly* also recommended Fitzpatrick's story to paranormal romance readers, noting that her "gripping chiller" treats teens to "a fast-paced, exhilarating read."

Fitzpatrick continues Nora's story in *Crescendo,* which finds Patch shifting his interest to a classmate even though he is supposed to be her guardian angel. When images of the teen's murdered father begin to haunt her dreams, Nora resolves to seek out the truth of his disappearance, with or without Patch's help.

Biographical and Critical Sources

PERIODICALS

Bulletin of the Center for Children's Books, December, 2009, Kate Quealy-Gainer, review of *Hush, Hush,* p. 152.
Kirkus Reviews, September 1, 2009, review of *Hush Hush.*
Publishers Weekly, October 12, 2009, review of *Hush, Hush,* p. 51.
School Librarian, spring, 2010, Alison A. Maxwell-Cox, review of *Hush, Hush,* p. 47.
School Library Journal, December, 2009, Sue Lloyd, review of *Hush, Hush,* p. 116; March, 2011, Rival Pollard, review of *Crescendo,* p. 160.
Voice of Youth Advocates, December, 2009, Lynne Farrell Stover, review of *Hush, Hush,* p. 419; October, 2010, Lynne Farrel Stover, review of *Crescendo,* p. 346.

ONLINE

Becca Fitzpatrick Home Page, http://beccafitzpatrick.com (December 7, 2010).

Cover of Becca Fitzpatrick's young-adult novel Hush, Hush, *which focuses on the trials of a fallen angel.*

Becca Fitzpatrick Web log, http://bec-fitzpatrick.live journal.com (December 7, 2010).

* * *

FRANCO, Tom

Personal

Born in CA; son of Douglas (director of nonprofit agency) and Betsy (an author) Franco.

Addresses

Home—CA. *E-mail*—francotho@gmail.com.

Career

Artist and illustrator. Firehouse Art Collective, Palo Alto, CA, founder, 2005, and creative director.

Writings

ILLUSTRATOR

Betsy Franco, *Metamorphosis: Junior Year,* Candlewick Press (Somerville, MA), 2009.

Contributor to books, including *Go Fish for Poetry,* Birdcage Press, 2008, and *Parts of Speech,* Really Good Stuff Publishing.

OTHER

Contributor of poetry to anthologies edited by mother, Betsy Franco, including *You Hear Me?: Poems Written by Teenage Boys,* Candlewick Press (New York, NY), 2000, and *Falling Hard: 100 Love Poems by Teenagers,* Candlewick Press, 2008.

Biographical and Critical Sources

PERIODICALS

Booklist, September 1, 2009, Hazel Rochman, review of *Metamorphosis: Junior Year,* p. 84.
Bulletin of the Center for Children's Books, April, 2010, April Spisak, review of *Metamorphosis,* p. 335.
Kirkus Reviews, September 15, 2009, review of *Metamorphosis.*
School Library Journal, December, 2009, Anthony C. Doyle, review of *Metamorphosis,* p. 118.

ONLINE

Tom Franco Web log, http://tomfranco.blogspot.com (December 7, 2010).*

G

GEAR, Kathleen M. O'Neal
See GEAR, Kathleen O'Neal

* * *

GEAR, Kathleen O'Neal 1954-
(Kathleen M. O'Neal Gear)

Personal

Born October 29, 1954, in Tulare, CA; daughter of Harold (a farmer and writer) and Wanda Lillie (a farmer and journalist) O'Neal; married W. Michael Gear (a writer), October 1, 1982. *Education:* California State University—Bakersfield, B.A. (cum laude); California State University—Chico, M.A. (summa cum laude); Ph.D. study at University of California—Los Angeles; postgraduate study at Hebrew University (Jerusalem, Israel). *Religion:* "Native American." *Hobbies and other interests:* Hunting, fishing, hiking.

Addresses

Home—P.O. Box 1329, Thermopolis, WY 82443. *Agent*—Matthew Bialer, Sanford J. Greenburger & Associates, 55 5th Ave., New York, NY 10003.

Career

Archaeologist and writer. Museum of Cultural History, Los Angeles, CA, senior museum preparator, 1979-80; City of Cheyenne, Cheyenne, WY, city historian, 1980-81; U.S. Department of the Interior, Cheyenne, state historian, 1981-82, Casper, WY, archaeologist, 1982-86; full-time writer, beginning 1986. Wind River Archaeological Consultants, Thermopolis, WY, cofounder, with W. Michael Gear, and archaeologist, beginning 1986; Timescribes, Thermopolis, writer, beginning 1986; Red Canyon Buffalo Ranch, WY, co-owner, beginning 1992.

Member

Science Fiction & Fantasy Writers of America, American Association of Physical Anthropologists, National Bison Association, Archaeological Conservancy, Nature Conservancy, Society for Historical Archaeology, Western Bison Association, Wisconsin Bison Producers Association, Western Writers of America, Center for Desert Archaeology, Wyoming Writers Incorporated.

Awards, Honors

Special Achievement Awards, U.S. Department of the Interior, 1984 and 1985, for archaeological work; Golden Spur Award for best novel of the West (with W. Michael Gear), Western Writers of America, 2005, for *People of the Raven;* inducted into Women Who Write the West Hall of Fame, 2005; (with W. Michael Gear) Golden Spur Award finalist, 2006, for *People of the Moon;* Literary Contribution Award (with W. Michael Gear), Mountain Plains Library Association, 2007.

Writings

NOVELS

Sand in the Wind, Tor (New York, NY), 1990.

This Widowed Land, Tor (New York, NY), 1993.

Thin Moon and Cold Mist, Forge (New York, NY), 1995.

(With husband, W. Michael Gear) *Dark Inheritance* (thriller), Warner Books (New York, NY), 2001.

(With W. Michael Gear) *Raising Abel* (thriller), Warner Books (New York, NY), 2002.

(With W. Michael Gear) *The Betrayal: The Lost Life of Jesus,* Forge (New York, NY), 2008.

(With W. Michael Gear) *Children of the Dawnland* (for children), Forge (New York, NY), 2009.

"POWERS OF LIGHT" NOVEL TRILOGY

An Abyss of Light, DAW Books (New York, NY), 1990.

Treasure of Light, DAW Books (New York, NY), 1990.

Redemption of Light, DAW Books (New York, NY), 1991.

"BLACK FALCON NOVEL TRILOGY"

It Sleeps in Me, Forge (New York, NY), 2005.
It Wakes in Me, Forge (New York, NY), 2006.
It Dreams in Me, Forge (New York, NY), 2007.

"FIRST NORTH AMERICANS" NOVEL SERIES; WITH W. MICHAEL GEAR

People of the Wolf, Tor Books (New York, NY), 1990.
People of the Light, DAW Books (New York, NY), 1991.
People of the Fire, Tor Books (New York, NY), 1991.
People of the Earth, Tor Books (New York, NY), 1992.
People of the River, Tor Books (New York, NY), 1992.
People of the Sea, Tor Books (New York, NY), 1993.
People of the Lakes, Tor Books (New York, NY), 1994.
People of the Lightning, Tor Books (New York, NY), 1995.
People of the Silence, Tor Books (New York, NY), 1996.
People of the Mist, Tor Books (New York, NY), 1997.
People of the Masks, Tor Books (New York, NY), 1998.
People of the Owl, Tor Books (New York, NY), 2003.
People of the Raven, Tor Books (New York, NY), 2004.
People of the Moon, Tor Books (New York, NY), 2005.
People of the Nightland, Forge (New York, NY), 2007.
People of the Weeping Eye, Forge (New York, NY), 2008.
People of the Thunder, Forge (New York, NY), 2009.
People of the Longhouse, Forge (New York, NY) 2010.
The Dawn Country, Forge (New York, NY), 2011.

"ANASAZI MYSTERY" NOVEL SERIES; WITH W. MICHAEL GEAR

The Visitant, Forge (New York, NY), 1999.
The Summoning God, Forge (New York, NY), 2000.
Bone Walker, Forge (New York, NY), 2001.

"CONTACT: THE BATTLE FOR AMERICA" SERIES; WITH W. MICHAEL GEAR

Coming of the Storm, Gallery Books (New York, NY), 2010.
Fire in the Sky, Gallery Books (New York, NY), 2011.

Adaptations

Several of the Gears's novels have been adapted as audiobooks, including *People of the Owl,* Books on Tape, 2003; and *It Sleeps in Me,* Books on Tape, 2005.

Sidelights

Kathleen O'Neal Gear and her husband, W. Michael Gear, are the coauthors of a popular series of novels that follow the tribes of prehistoric North America. Their "First North Americans" series, which includes such novels as *People of the Wolf, People of the Fire, People of the Moon,* and *People of the Thunder,* have been praised for their detailed description of an ancient way of life, descriptions enhanced by Kathleen O'Neal Gear's training as an archeologist. Praising the series in

Booklist, Brad Hooper wrote that the "First North Americans" novels "are, indeed, lessons in life past, and all the facts they marshal are well integrated into a smoothly flowing story line."

The Gears began their "First North Americans" novel series in 1990 with *People of the Wolf.* The novel centers on the power struggle between two brothers, the visionary Wolf Dreamer and the warrior Raven Hunter, as each follows his nature and ultimately divides their shared tribe. *People of the Fire* focuses on Little Dancer, a dreamer who is befriended by an outcast named Two Smokes and trained as a visionary. In *People of the River* the Gears bring to life the earth-mound-builder culture that lived in southern Illinois between 700 A.D. and 1500 A.D. The Mississippians, as they were known, cultivated corn, knew astronomy, and disappeared before European explorers reached the area. "Fast-paced and engrossing," *People of the Fire* "has the ring of authenticity as well," stated a contributor to *Publishers Weekly.*

People of the Sea is set in a coastal California Native American community around 10,000 B.C., as an Ice Age period is ending and rising water levels are wreaking havoc on the area's ecosystem. Large animals are disappearing, portending starvation for the populace. A religious leader, Sunchaser the Dreamer, worries about these changes which he cannot explain, but then a mysterious woman comes to see him and he runs away with her. Sunchaser gains understanding regarding the fate of his own community along the way. A *Publishers Weekly* contributor praised the authors for "integrating a tremendous amount of natural and anthropological research into a satisfactory narrative," and called *People of the Sea* "a vivid and fascinating portrait."

The eighth book in the "First North Americans" series, *People of the Lightning,* is set in prehistoric Florida's Windover community among a people that are not related to other Native American groups. The Standing Hollow Horn clan is led by a tyrant, Cottonmouth, who kidnaps members of a rival clan, among them Musselwhite, a warrior woman who had killed Cottonmouth's son in a previous skirmish. Musselwhite believes her husband, Diver, has been killed, and she allows herself to be married off in captivity to an albino. When she learns that Diver is in fact alive, she escapes and flees to find him. "A wealth of rich historical detail once again bolsters a pulsing narrative set in a turbulent time," noted a reviewer for *Publishers Weekly* in appraising *People of the Lightning.*

People of the Silence is set amid the Anasazi culture in New Mexico circa 1000 A.D., while *People of the Mist* focuses on a matrilineal society in the Chesapeake Bay region as a young woman named Red Knot faces an arranged marriage to Copper Thunder, chieftain of a neighboring clan. The match is a political alliance, negotiated in part by Red Knot's grandmother, and when Red Knot is slain on her wedding day more than one potential culprit surfaces. "Suffused with suspense, [the Gears'] . . . imaginative story offers a fascinating portrait of an ancient matrilineal culture," noted *Library Journal* contributor Mary Ellen Elsbernd in a review of *People of the Mist.* A *Publishers Weekly* critic recommended the same novel as a "fluid, suspenseful mix of anthropological research and character-driven mystery" that leads up to "a solid, satisfying resolution."

People of the Masks is set in long-ago New York State, where the Earth Thunderer clan—part of the Iroquois' Turtle Nation—rejoices when a dwarf is born to one of its members. According to tribal beliefs, a dwarf has the power to perform miracles, and the child, named Rumbler, is appropriately indulged and occupies a place of high honor in Paint Rock village. Neighboring villages, however, panic when they learn of his arrival, for they believe the dwarf's presence will give the Earth Thunderers an advantage. As a young child, Rumbler has a premonition of his own kidnaping, and such a thing comes to pass when a warrior from a neighboring clan abducts the boy. The Walksalong villagers fear the child and attempt to kill him, but Rumbler is ultimately saved by orphan child Little Wren, who leads the boy away from the Walksalong people. *Booklist* reviewer Diana Tixier Herald cited *People of the Masks* as "prehistoric epic at its finest," commending the "gripping plot, lots of action, [and] well-developed characters." A *Publishers Weekly* commentator also enjoyed the novel, describing it as "fast-paced, fluid, rich with smoothly integrated background detail and softened by a touch of romanticism that deflects the violence and brutality" of the times

People of the Owl features fifteen-year-old Mud Puppy, a visionary juvenile warrior who is given the responsible for his entire clan after being christened Salamander at his initiation ceremony. With three disloyal wives and a reputation for being the village idiot, Salamander must weather assaults from hidden enemies within his tribe while also battling the warring spirits of good and evil. A *Publishers Weekly* reviewer noted that *People of the Owl* is "propelled by the Gears' spry storytelling," while Brad Hooper commented in *Booklist* that the Gears "provide fascinating information on the customs of past times."

The Gears' series continues in the novels *People of the Raven, People of the Moon, People of the Nightland, People of the Weeping Eye, People of the Thunder,* and *People of the Longhouse,* all of which feature their compelling mix of history, archaeology, and adventure. Praised by *Booklist* critic Hooper as "one of the best novels" in the "First North Americans" series, *People of the Moon* is set in the region around what is now northern New Mexico, the home of the Chaco Anasazi. A hunter named Ripple is a member of a clan formed of Made People, the lesser of the two Anasazi castes. When the young man experiences a vision from a goddess urging him to destroy the power of the ruling First People, Ripple gathers a band of young hunters and

starts out on his quest, thereby setting in motion a tale of competing powers, ancient injustices, and revenge. In *People of the Nightland* the cave-dwelling People of the Nightland and the lodge-building People of the Sun are united by the visions of a young orphan in order to survive the melting of the glaciers and the flooding of the lake region now separating the east-central area of North America. In *Booklist* Margaret Flanagan praised *People of the Nightland* for its "authentically detailed evocation of a world and a people on the verge of an epic transformation," while a *Publishers Weekly* critic dubbed the Gears' novel "a timely saga of environmental catastrophe and misguided hubris."

In *People of the Weeping Eye* and *People of the Thunder* the Gears follow a small band of ancient natives on their travel across what is now Alabama and Mississippi. Praised by Flanagan as "historical fiction at its best," *People of the Weeping Eye* captures the beginning of an epic journey. After years of wandering, the ancient Old White knows that it is time to return home. On his way, he meets up with the mystical Two Petals, a woman who experiences life backward, as well as another wanderer named Trader, who has a dark secret in his past. In *People of the Thunder* the wise and powerful Old White joins shaman Two Petals and the secretive Trader on their journey to Moundville's Split Sky City, where the Sky Hand people are ruled by the misguided Flying Hawk and his war-hungry nephew Smoke Shield. While noting the violence that marks the Gears' compelling tale, a *Publishers Weekly* contributor praised *People of the Thunder* for its "court intrigues, colorful characters and sharp plot twists." The novel treats readers to the Gears' "superbly researched and rendered" fiction, added Flanagan, the *Booklist* critic suggesting that this installment in the Gears' "First North Americans" series "is as good a place as any . . . to jump in and begin enjoying the authors' talents."

The region that now comprises New York State is the setting for *People of the Longhouse,* a novel that portrays Iroquois society several centuries before the arrival of the European colonists. It is a time of scarcity, and tribes are forced to raid the longhouses of their neighbors in order to survive. When a Yellowtail village is left destroyed in the wake of a war party led by the Mountain People, tribal war chief Koracoo is determined to search for the Iroquois attackers, who have enslaved her two children to replenish their tribe's waning population. As their parents search for them, young Odion and Tutelo suffer under the captivity of the evil magician Gannajero, and bravely attempt to inspire their fellow captives to escape. In *Library Journal* Elsbernd praised *People of the Longhouse* as "a saga brimming with intrigue and adventure," while a *Kirkus Reviews* contributor recommended the Gears' entire "First North Americans" series to fans of Jean Auel's prehistoric novel *Clan of the Cave Bear.*

The Visitant, a novel in the Gears' "Anasazi Mystery" series, alternates between the past and present in telling the story of archeologist Dusty Stewart and anthropologist Maureen Cole. Looking for clues as to why the Chaco Anasazi Indians disappeared from northwestern New Mexico centuries before, the two discover several mass graves of young women whose skulls have been smashed. Meanwhile, after Anasazi war chief Browser's wife winds up dead and several other deaths of young women in the tribe follow, Browser's uncle Stone Ghost is called upon to deal with the situation. As the two situations converge, Stewart and Cole bring in the office of the Native American Graves Protection and Repatriation Act and a holy woman named Hail arrives to sort out the mystery. "Readers will enjoy the wide range of characters and thick suspense," predicted Susan A. Zappia in *Library Journal*. Praising the "breathtaking descriptions [that] evoke the harsh beauty of the desert in both winter and summer," a *Publishers Weekly* reviewer commended the Gears' "lucid, erudite historical perspectives," and Herald wrote that "the vividly depicted characters and settings are satisfying."

The Summoning God, the second book in the "Anasazi Mystery" series, centers upon the Katsinas people in the 1200s and explains the mystery of the Anasazi extinction. An afterword cautions that the fate of this people may befall human civilization as well. A *Publishers Weekly* contributor called *The Summoning God* a "memorable novel" and stated that, while it is a book "not for the squeamish," "the Gears offer unusual insight into Anasazi culture and history."

The Gears focus on conquest in their novel *Coming of the Storm.* The first novel in their "Contact: The Battle for America" series, it introduces the Chicaza (Chicksaw) trader and mystic Black Shell, who lives on lands that now comprise southern Florida. When Spanish conqueror Hernando de Soto invades the area in 1539, Black Shell is captured and enslaved. Freed by his beloved Pearl Hand, the man gathers a rag-tag army of native wanderers and vows to stop de Soto's quest for gold and efforts to force the Native Americans to accept Catholicism. The Gears interweave their characteristic adventure-filled story with "rich historical details and keen characterizations," according to a *Publishers Weekly* critic, making *Coming of the Storm* a "smooth, brisk-paced narrative." Flanagan noted in *Booklist* that the novel showcases the Gears' "usual narrative finesse" by mixing "history, archaeology, and anthropology" in "an irresistibly intriguing story." The "riveting plot" of *Coming of the Storm* "leaves the reader intensely engaged," noted *Library Journal* critic Mary Ellen Elsbernd, the reviewer predicting that the Gears' novel will leave fans "thirsting for [*Fire in the Sky,*] the next book" in their "Contact" series.

The Gears address themselves to a younger audience in their novel *Children of the Dawnland,* which introduces a preteen living in northeastern North America at the end of the Ice Age. Haunted by vivid dreams, Twig knows that she is destined to be a Dreamer for the Clo-

vis tribe. Her mother attempts to discourage the girl, worried that her daughter's skill at foretelling the future will only bring danger. When Twig's dreams begin to align with the predations of a warring tribe, she decides to seek out the illusive Cobia and learn to decipher her visions so that she can help her own people. Although Ragan O'Malley noted in *School Library Journal* that the first part of the novel is burdened with anthropological details and a "heavy emphasis . . . given to dreams and visions," readers "won't be able to read fast enough" when Twig and friend Greyhawk set off on their dangerous quest. Praising Twig as "bright and strong," Kara Dean added in her *Booklist* review of *Children of the Dawnland* that the couple's "character-driven fantasy will appeal to fans of epic series."

In addition to their series fiction set in North America's past, the Gears have also penned contemporary novels, as well as revisioning the live of Jesus in *The Betrayal: The Lost Life of Jesus.* With its focus on Yeshua ben Miriam, a version of Jesus that is far more outspoken and confrontational than the man depicted in the New Testament, the novel draws on up-to-date historical and archeological findings. In their notes to the novel, the coauthors also reference the many gospels about early Christianity that were discarded by the Roman Church during the Council of Nicea in the second century, *The Betrayal* "is guaranteed both to ignite controversy and attract a large readership," according to *Booklist* critic Flanagan.

Moving from distant past to present, the Gears' novel *Dark Inheritance* centers on the efforts of British pharmaceutical manufacturer Smyth-Archer Chemicals (SAC) to create a "smart" chimpanzee. To do so, the company has placed apes with scientists and their families, among them single father Jim Dutton and his daughter, Brett. Umber, a bonobo ape—a variety of chimpanzee—has been raised alongside Brett, and the pair is as close as human sisters. Umber communicates with Brett and Jim via sign language and a hand-held computer, and Jim soon discovers that the chimp is capable of solving simple math problems as well. When Umber asks about the existence of a higher being, Jim grows suspicious about her true origins. Meanwhile, questions are raised regarding SAC's experiments and the fact that certain chimps that do not achieve some level of intellectual advancement may become violent. *Booklist* critic William Beatty called *Dark Inheritance* a "lively, thought-provoking, and convincing story."

In addition to collaborations with her husband, Kathleen O'Neal Gear has published several novels for adult readers, among them her "Powers of Light" and "Black Falcon" trilogies and various standalone novels. Set in seventeenth-century Quebec, *This Widowed Land* finds Jesuit ministers clashing with the Huron tribe until one of the Europeans falls in love with a Huron woman named Andiora. A contributor to *Publishers Weekly* called Gear's characters "static and two-dimensional" but noted that "her use of period detail breathes life into daily events at the Huron village."

Thin Moon and Cold Mist is set during the U.S. Civil War and features Robin Walkingstick Heatherton, a female spy who masquerades as a black male soldier in order to infiltrate the Union army and spy for the Confederacy. When Robin finds herself on the run from a Union major who blames her for his brother's death, she flees to Colorado with her five-year-old son, Jeremy, and there falls in love with another Union soldier. A *Publishers Weekly* critic noted that Gear imbues *Thin Moon and Cold Mist* "with historical detail and intriguing plot twists, delivered in lively prose."

It Sleeps in Me, part of Gear's "Black Falcon" trilogy, finds the leadership of Black Falcon high chieftess Sora threatened by duplicitous allies and haunted by the shadow soul of her dead husband as she attempts to lead her people and sustain her life. In *It Wakes in Me* Sora is suspected of murder, but she is unsure of her innocence because of lapses in her own memories. Eventually confined and placed in the custody of a priest of the Loon tribe, the priestess is aided in recovering her past and gaining the tools required to reestablish leadership over her people. *Booklist* contributor Lynne Welch dubbed *It Sleeps in Me* "a riveting story of murder and madness" as well as "a tantalizing expose of Machiavellian intrigue," while *It Wakes in Me* was described as a "vivid" story "full of interesting cultural facts" and "intrigue" by a *Kirkus Reviews* writer. The concluding novel of the "Black Falcon" trilogy, *It Dreams in Me,* finds the still-banished Sora searching to regain her healing powers through dreams and rituals. "Fans of the series . . . will welcome the final chapter chronicling the steamy exploits of Sora," predicted Flanagan in her *Booklist* review of *It Dreams in Me.*

Biographical and Critical Sources

PERIODICALS

Booklist, January 1, 1996, Kathleen Hughes, review of *People of the Lightning,* p. 786; January 1, 1997, Margaret Flanagan, review of *People of the Silence,* p. 818; February 1, 1998, Eric Robbins, review of *People of the Mist,* p. 898; October 15, 1998, Diana Tixier Herald, review of *People of the Masks,* p. 401; January 1, 1999, review of *People of the Mist,* p. 781; July, 1999, Diana Tixier Herald, review of *The Visitant,* p. 1893; December 1, 2000, William Beatty, review of *Dark Inheritance,* p. 675; May 15, 2003, Brad Hooper, review of *People of the Owl,* p. 1619; April 15, 2005, Lynne Welch, review of *It Sleeps in Me,* p. 1431; August, 2005, Brad Hooper, review of *People of the Moon,* p. 1952; May 15, 2006, Lynne Welch, review of *It Wakes in Me,* p. 23; July 1, 2007, Margaret Flanagan, review of *It Dreams in Me,* p. 28; March 1, 2008, Margaret Flanagan, review of *People of the Weeping Eye,* p. 29; April 15, 2008, Margaret Flanagan, review of *The Betrayal: The Lost Life of Jesus,* p. 6; November 15, 2008, Margaret Flanagan, review of *People of the Thunder,* p. 5; July 1, 2009, Kara Dean, review of *Children of the Dawnland,* p. 60; November 15, 2009, Margaret Flanagan, review of *Coming of the Storm: Contact: The Battle for America,* p. 3; April 15, 2010, Margaret Flanagan, review of *People of the Longhouse,* p. 4.

Gazette (Colorado Springs, CO), April 22, 2001, Linda DuVal, "Defining Humanity," p. B6.

Kirkus Reviews, June 1, 2002, review of *Raising Abel,* p. 756; August 1, 2005, review of *People of the Moon,* p. 821; August 1, 2005, review of *People of the Moon,* p. 821; April 15, 2006, review of *It Wakes in Me,* p. 368; June 1, 2009, review of *Children of the Dawnland.*

Library Journal, February 1, 1998, Mary Ellen Elsbernd, review of *People of the Mist,* p. 110; November 1, 1998, Mary Ellen Eisbernd, review of *People of the Masks,* p. 125; August, 1999, Susan A. Zappia, review of *The Visitant,* p. 139; May 15, 2003, Mary Ellen Elsbernd, review of *People of the Owl,* p. 123; April 15, 2005, Mary Ellen Elsbernd, review of *It Sleeps in Me,* p. 72; February 15, 2010, Mary Ellen Elsbernd, review of *Coming of the Storm,* p. 87; June 18, 2010, Mary Ellen Elsbernd, review of *People of the Longhouse.*

Post & Courier (Charleston, SC), January 14, 2001, Michael A. Green, review of *The Summoning God,* p. 3.

Publishers Weekly, June 1, 1992, review of *People of the River,* p. 51; January 18, 1993, Sybil S. Steinberg, review of *This Widowed Land,* p. 448; September 13, 1993, review of *People of the Sea,* p. 89; June 12, 1995, Sybil S. Steinberg, review of *Thin Moon and Cold Mist,* p. 47; October 30, 1995, review of *People of the Lightning,* p. 46; June 3, 1996, review of *The Morning River,* p. 61; December 2, 1996, review of *People of the Silence,* p. 42; November 24, 1997, review of *People of the Mist,* p. 52; November 2, 1998, review of *People of the Masks,* p. 71; July 5, 1999, review of *The Visitant,* p. 62; June 26, 2000, review of *The Summoning God,* p. 53; February 5, 2001, review of *Dark Inheritance,* p. 65; July 1, 2002, review of *Raising Abel,* p. 55; May 26, 2003, review of *People of the Owl,* p. 49; November 17, 2008, review of *People of the Thunder,* p. 42; December 14, 2009, review of *Coming of the Storm,* p. 41; May 10, 2010, review of *People of the Longhouse,* p. 28.

St. Louis Post-Dispatch, March 23, 1997, Dick Richmond, "Rise and Fall of Ancient Civilization," p. T9.

School Library Journal, December, 2009, Ragan O'Malley, review of *Children of the Dawnland,* p. 118.

ONLINE

Kathleen O'Neal and W. Michael Gear Home Page, http://www.gear-gear.com (December 20, 2010).

Kathleen O'Neal and W. Michael Gear Web log, http://www.gear-gear.com/blog (December 20, 2010).*

GEAR, W. Michael 1955-

Personal

Born May 20, 1955, in Colorado Springs, CO; son of William Gear (a television anchor) and Katherine Perry Cook (an artist); married Kathleen O'Neal (an historian and writer), October 1, 1982. *Education:* Colorado State University, B.A., 1976, M.A. (physical anthropology), 1979. *Politics:* "Libertarian/Republican." *Religion:* "Native American." *Hobbies and other interests:* Hunting, shooting, reloading, motorcycle touring, bison, travel.

Addresses

Home—P.O. Box 1329, Thermopolis, WY 82443. *Office*—415 Park St., Thermopolis, WY 82443. *Agent*—Owen Laster, William Morris Literary Agency, 1325 Avenue of the Americas, New York, NY 10019.

Career

Novelist, archeologist, and rancher. Western Wyoming College, Rock Springs, archaeologist, 1979-81; Metcalf-Zier Archaeologists, Inc., Eagle, CO, archaeologist, 1981; Pronghorn Anthropological Association, Casper, WY, owner and principal investigator, 1982-84; Wind River Archaeological Consultants, founder, with wife Katherine Gear, and principal investigator, 1988-2000.

Member

American Anthropological Association, American Association of Physical Anthropology, Society for American Archaeology, Paleopathology Association, National Bison Association, Western Writers of America, Wyoming Writers.

Awards, Honors

Pulitzer Prize nomination, and National Book Award nomination, both 1998, both for *Morning River;* Golden Spur Award for best novel of the West (with Kathleen O'Neal Gear), Western Writers of America, 2005, for *People of the Raven;* Golden Spur Award finalist, 2006, for *People of the Moon;* Literary Contribution Award (with W. Michael Gear), Mountain Plains Library Association, 2007.

Writings

NOVELS

Long Ride Home, Tor Books (New York, NY), 1988.
Big Horn Legacy, Pinnacle (New York, NY), 1988.
The Artifact, DAW (New York, NY), 1990.
Starstrike, DAW (New York, NY), 1990.
The Morning River, Forge (New York, NY), 1996.
Coyote Summer, Forge (New York, NY), 1997.

(With wife Kathleen O'Neal Gear) *Dark Inheritance* (thriller), Warner Books (New York, NY), 2001.
(With Kathleen O'Neal Gear) *Raising Abel* (thriller), Warner Books (New York, NY), 2002.
The Athena Factor, Forge (New York, NY), 2005.
(With Kathleen O'Neal Gear) *The Betrayal: The Lost Life of Jesus,* Forge (New York, NY), 2008.
(With Kathleen O'Neal Gear) *Children of the Dawnland* (for children), Forge (New York, NY), 2009.

"SPIDER" NOVEL TRILOGY

The Warriors of Spider, DAW (New York, NY), 1988.
The Way of Spider, DAW (New York, NY), 1989.
The Web of Spider, DAW (New York, NY), 1989.

"FORBIDDEN BORDERS" NOVEL TRILOGY

Requiem for the Conqueror, DAW (New York, NY), 1991.
Relic of Empire, DAW (New York, NY), 1992.
Countermeasures, DAW (New York, NY), 1993.

"FIRST NORTH AMERICANS" NOVEL SERIES; WITH KATHLEEN O'NEAL GEAR

People of the Wolf, Tor Books (New York, NY), 1990.
People of the Light, DAW Books (New York, NY), 1991.
People of the Fire, Tor Books (New York, NY), 1991.
People of the Earth, Tor Books (New York, NY), 1992.
People of the River, Tor Books (New York, NY), 1992.
People of the Sea, Tor Books (New York, NY), 1993.
People of the Lakes, Tor Books (New York, NY), 1994.
People of the Lightning, Tor Books (New York, NY), 1995.
People of the Silence, Tor Books (New York, NY), 1996.
People of the Mist, Tor Books (New York, NY), 1997.
People of the Masks, Tor Books (New York, NY), 1998.
People of the Owl, Tor Books (New York, NY), 2003.
People of the Raven, Tor Books (New York, NY), 2004.
People of the Moon, Tor Books (New York, NY), 2005.
People of the Nightland, Forge (New York, NY), 2007.
People of the Weeping Eye, Forge (New York, NY), 2008.
People of the Thunder, Forge (New York, NY), 2009.
People of the Longhouse, Forge (New York, NY), 2010.
The Dawn Country, Forge (New York, NY), 2011.

"ANASAZI MYSTERY" NOVEL SERIES; WITH KATHLEEN O'NEAL GEAR

The Visitant, Forge (New York, NY), 1999.
The Summoning God, Forge (New York, NY), 2000.
Bone Walker, Forge (New York, NY), 2001.

"CONTACT: THE BATTLE FOR AMERICA" NOVEL SERIES; WITH KATHLEEN O'NEAL GEAR

Coming of the Storm, Gallery Books (New York, NY), 2010.
Fire in the Sky, Gallery Books (New York, NY), 2011.

Adaptations

Several of the Gears' novels have been adapted as audiobooks, including *People of the Owl,* Books on Tape, 2003.

Sidelights

Frequently collaborating with his wife, fellow author and historian Kathleen O'Neal Gear, W. Michael Gear began his writing career penning Western novels such as *The Morning River,* but has gone on to produce modern thrillers like *The Athena Factor* as well as books that meld the historical Western with elements of science fiction. Calling Gear "a vigorous writer," a *Publishers Weekly* contributor added in a review of *The Morning River* that the author "writes a superbly rolling prose with flair, confidence, wit, an ear for sounds and an eye for details."

The Gears are both trained archeologists—in fact, they met during an annual meeting of the Wyoming Association of Professional Archeologists—and the novels they write together center on the native peoples of prehistoric North America. Their "First North Americans" series, which includes *People of the Wolf, People of the Mist, People of the Moon,* and *People of the Longhouse,* blends whodunit suspense, historical romance, compelling characters, and a wealth of anthropological details in stories focusing on primitive native tribes.

A fourth-generation Coloradoan, Gear earned an advanced anthropology degree. In 1979 he became a field archaeologist and within a few years had started working independently as an archaeological consultant. The seasonal nature of the profession left him with free time during the long winter months, and he began writing western novels, although no publisher showed interest. In 1982 Gear married O'Neal and four years later the couple decided to devote their energies to writing on a full-time basis. They moved to a remote mountain cabin near Empire, Colorado, that was built by Gear's great-uncle and lived there for three years, with no running water and only a pair of stoves to provide heat. The focus that this setting allowed proved worthwhile, however: Gear's first book, the western novel *Long Ride Home,* was accepted by Tor Books in early 1987.

After a second western, *Big Horn Legacy,* Gear wrote *The Warriors of Spider,* the first novel in his "Spider" trilogy. Here he blends science fiction and Native American beliefs in a story that finds a lost colony of Native American and Hispanic descendants "discovered" by an advanced civilization. After continuing the story though two subsequent books, *The Way of Spider* and *The Web of Spider,* Gear devised the premise for a new series. He imagined an educated Bostonian lost in the wilderness of the American west during the 1820s, and this idea became *The Morning River,* published in 1996.

The Morning River centers on Richard Hamilton, a pretentious Harvard University philosophy student whose father decides to send him west on business as a way to

teach the young man a bit about the world. Hamilton lands in trouble soon after arriving at his destination: he is assaulted and robbed of his money, then sold as an indentured servant on a trade boat heading into Indian Territory. Help comes in the form of a boat passenger named Travis Hartman, a mountain man who knows several Native-American languages and teaches the Bostonian to appreciate Native customs. A young Shoshone woman, Heals like the Willow, is also being held as a slave, and her life and Hamilton's soon intersect. Hamilton's saga continues in *Coyote Summer,* as he and Heals like the Willow fall in love, battle various enemies, and begin a family. A writer for *Publishers Weekly* described the novel as "a well-plotted page-turner that distinguishes itself from other westerns in the depth and quality of its historical reconstruction."

The Gears began their collaborative "First North Americans" series with 1990's *People of the Wolf.* The saga presents an ancient people who purportedly traveled from Asia across an ice bridge to North America during the Ice Age. The plot centers upon the power struggle between two brothers, Wolf Dreamer and Raven Hunter. In the fourth novel of the series, *People of the River,* the Gears imagine events among the earth-mound-builder culture that lived in southern Illinois between 700 A.D. and 1500 A.D., while *People of the Sea* is set among a coastal California Native American community circa 10,000 B.C.E., as an Ice Age is ending and rising water levels are wreaking havoc for the area's ecosystem. "Fast-paced and engrossing, the novel has the ring of authenticity as well," stated a contributor to *Publishers Weekly* in reviewing *People of the Sea,* and a *Publishers Weekly* reviewer praised the Gears for "integrating a tremendous amount of natural and anthropological research into a satisfactory narrative." The reviewer went on to call *People of the Sea* "a vivid and fascinating portrait."

People of the Lightning is set within the Windover community of prehistoric Florida, where the Standing Hollow Horn clan is led by a tyrant named Cottonmouth. During a kidnapping raid on a rival clan, Cottonmouth captures Musselwhite, a warrior woman who had killed Cottonmouth's son in a previous skirmish. "A wealth of rich historical detail once again bolsters a pulsing narrative set in a turbulent time," noted a reviewer for *Publishers Weekly.* *People of the Silence* is set among the Anasazi culture in New Mexico around 1000 B.C.E, while *People of the Mist* takes place inside a matrilineal society in the Chesapeake Bay region. *People of the Mist* involves an arranged marriage between two neighboring clans, but this political alliance goes awry when the bride is slain on her wedding day and more than one potential culprit surfaces. "Suffused with suspense, their imaginative story offers a fascinating portrait of an ancient matrilineal culture," noted *Library Journal* reviewer Mary Ellen Eisbernd of the Gears' work, while a *Publishers Weekly* critic termed *People of the Mist* a "fluid, suspenseful mix of anthropological research and character-driven mystery" with "a solid, satisfying resolution."

People of the Masks, set in long-ago New York State, finds a dwarf born to a member of the Earth Thunderer clan and fated to be both revered and feared, while *People of the Owl* takes readers to the area that would one day be the state of Louisiana where a fifteen year old named Salamander inherits leadership of the clan as well as three wives following the death of his older brother. In *Booklist,* Diana Tixier Herald termed *People of the Masks* "prehistoric epic at its finest," and commended the Gears for their "gripping plot, lots of action, [and] well-developed characters."

The Gears' "First North Americans" series continues in the novels *People of the Raven, People of the Moon, People of the Nightland, People of the Weeping Eye, People of the Thunder,* and *People of the Longhouse,* all of which feature their compelling mix of history, archaeology, and adventure. Praised by *Booklist* critic Brad Hooper as "one of the best novels" in the saga, *People of the Moon* is set in the region around what is now northern New Mexico, the home of the Chaco Anasazi. A hunter named Ripple is a member of a clan formed of Made People, the lesser of the two Anasazi castes. When the young man experiences a vision from a goddess urging him to destroy the power of the ruling First People, he gathers a band of young hunters and sets out on his quest, setting in motion a tale of competing powers, ancient injustices, and revenge. In *People of the Nightland* the cave-dwelling People of the Nightland and the lodge-building People of the Sun are united by the visions of a young orphan in order to survive the melting of the glaciers and the flooding of the lake region now separating the east-central area of North America. In *Booklist* Margaret Flanagan praised *People of the Nightland* for its "authentically detailed evocation of a world and a people on the verge of an epic transformation," while a *Publishers Weekly* critic dubbed the Gears' novel "a timely saga of environmental catastrophe and misguided hubris."

In both *People of the Weeping Eye* and *People of the Thunder* the Gears follow a small band of ancient natives on their travel across what is now Alabama and Mississippi. Praised by Flanagan as "historical fiction at its best," *People of the Weeping Eye* captures the beginning of an epic journey. After years of wandering, the ancient Old White knows it is time to return home. On his way, he meets up with the mystical Two Petals, a woman who experiences life backward, and another wanderer named Trader, who has a dark secret in his past. In *People of the Thunder* the wise and powerful Old White joins shaman Two Petals and the secretive Trader on their journey to Moundville's Split Sky City, where the Sky Hand people are ruled by the misguided Flying Hawk and his war-hungry nephew Smoke Shield. While noting the violence that marks the Gears' compelling tale, a *Publishers Weekly* contributor praised *People of the Thunder* for its "court intrigues, colorful characters and sharp plot twists." The novel treats readers to the Gears' "superbly researched and rendered" fiction, added Flanagan, the *Booklist* critic suggesting

that this installment in the "First North Americans" series "is as good a place as any . . . to jump in and begin enjoying the authors' talents."

As in *People of the Mask,* the region that now comprises New York State is the setting for *People of the Longhouse,* a novel that brings to life Iroquois society several centuries before the arrival of the European colonists. It is a time of scarcity, and tribes are forced to raid the longhouses of their neighbors in order to survive. When a Yellowtail village is left destroyed in the wake of a war party led by the Mountain People, tribal war chief Koracoo is determined to search for the Iroquois attackers, who have enslaved her two children to replenish their tribe's waning population. As their parents track their path, young Odion and Tutelo suffer under the captivity of the evil magician Gannajero and bravely attempt to inspire their fellow captives to escape from the Mountain People tribe. In *Library Journal* Elsbernd praised *People of the Longhouse* as "a saga brimming with intrigue and adventure," while a *Kirkus Reviews* contributor recommended the Gears' entire "First North Americans" series to fans of Jean Auel's prehistoric novel *Clan of the Cave Bear.*

The first volume in the Gears' "Anasazi" series, *The Visitant,* focuses on archeologist Dusty Stewart and anthropologist Maureen Cole. The two pair up to determine why the Chaco Anasazi Indians once disappeared in northwestern New Mexico, but soon they find themselves embroiled in murder when mass graves are discovered. The series continues in *The Summoning God* and *Bone Walker,* the latter which finds Dusty a suspect in the ritualized murder of his uncle, a murder that has links to the history of the Chaco Canyon excavation site. "Readers will enjoy the wide range of characters and thick suspense," predicted Susan A. Zappia in her *Library Journal* review of *The Summoning God.* Herald, writing for *Booklist,* praised "the vividly depicted characters and settings are satisfying and leave the reader hoping for more titles in this promising series."

The Gears focus on conquest in their novels *Coming of the Storm* and *Fire in the Sky.* The first novel in their "Contact: The Battle for America" series, *Coming of the Storm* introduces the Chicaza (Chicksaw) trader and mystic Black Shell, who lives in the lands that now comprise southern Florida. When Spanish conqueror Hernando de Soto invades the area in 1539, Black Shell is captured and enslaved. Freed by his beloved Pearl Hand, the man gathers a rag-tag army of native wanderers and vows to stop de Soto's quest for gold and efforts to force the Native Americans to accept Catholicism. The Gears' characteristic adventure-filled story includes "rich historical details and keen characterizations," according to a *Publishers Weekly* critic, making *Coming of the Storm* a "smooth, brisk-paced narrative." In *Booklist* Flanagan also praised the book, writing that the novel "display[s] their usual narrative finesse" by mixing "history, archaeology, and anthropology" in the "irresistibly intriguing story" that begins their "Contact" series.

The Gears turn their attention to younger readers in *Children of the Dawnland*, a novel that introduces a preteen living in northeastern North America at the end of the Ice Age. Haunted by vivid dreams, Twig knows that she is destined to be a Dreamer for the Clovis tribe. Her mother attempts to discourage the girl, worried that her daughter's skill at foretelling the future can only bring danger. When Twig's dreams begin to align with the aggressive actions of a warring tribe, she decides to seek out the illusive Cobia and learn to use her visions for the good of her own people. Although Ragan O'Malley noted in *School Library Journal* that the first part of the novel is burdened with anthropological details and a "heavy emphasis . . . given to dreams and visions," readers "won't be able to read fast enough" when Twig and friend Greyhawk set off on their dangerous quest. Praising Twig as "bright and strong," Kara Dean added in *Booklist* review of *Children of the Dawnland* that the Gears' "character-driven fantasy will appeal to fans of epic series."

While the stories of native cultures remains the Gears' main focus, they have also veered into other subjects. For example, they address modern technology in *Dark Inheritance*, which centers upon a British pharmaceutical maker and its attempt to create a "smart" chimpanzee through biological engineering. Problems come when the treated animals are then placed in the care of staff-members and their families. In *Booklist* William Beatty called *Dark Inheritance* a "lively, thought-provoking, and convincing story."

Research into the ancient past is also the inspiration for their nonfiction book *The Betrayal: The Lost Life of Jesus*, which is based on actual documents and details the life of Yeshua ben Miriam, a Jesus character who is far more outspoken and confrontational than the Jesus of the New Testament. In their notes to the book, the Gears explain the way the Christian gospels were evaluated and either accepted or outlawed at the Council of Nicea in 325 C.E. Drawing on up-to-date historical and archeological findings, *The Betrayal* "is guaranteed both to ignite controversy and attract a large readership," according to *Booklist* contributor Flanagan.

As Gear told Dale L. Walker in an interview for the *Rocky Mountain News*, he always strives to depict history from a balanced perspective in his books. "We've created a great many myths about our history," he explained of his collaborative work with his wife. "I appreciate the myths, but I think people like to read about the way it really was. Kathy and I both struggle to write that kind of book."

Biographical and Critical Sources

PERIODICALS

Booklist, January 1, 1996, Kathleen Hughes, review of *People of the Lightning*, p. 786; January 1, 1997, Margaret Flanagan, review of *People of the Silence*, p. 818; February 1, 1998, Eric Robbins, review of *People of the Mist*, p. 898; October 15, 1998, Diana Tixier Herald, review of *People of the Masks*, p. 401; January 1, 1999, review of *People of the Mist*, p. 781; July, 1999, Diana Tixier Herald, review of *The Visitant*, p. 1893; December 1, 2000, William Beatty, review of *Dark Inheritance*, p. 675; May 15, 2003, Brad Hooper, review of *People of the Owl*, p. 1619; August, 2005, Brad Hooper, review of *People of the Moon*, p. 1952; March 1, 2008, Margaret Flanagan, review of *People of the Weeping Eye*, p. 29; April 15, 2008, Margaret Flanagan, review of *The Betrayal: The Lost Life of Jesus*, p. 6; November 15, 2008, Margaret Flanagan, review of *People of the Thunder*, p. 5; July 1, 2009, Kara Dean, review of *Children of the Dawnland*, p. 60; November 15, 2009, Margaret Flanagan, review of *Coming of the Storm: Contact: The Battle for America*, p. 3; April 15, 2010, Margaret Flanagan, review of *People of the Longhouse*, p. 4.

Gazette (Colorado Springs, CO), April 22, 2001, Linda DuVal, "Defining Humanity," p. B6.

Kirkus Reviews, November 15, 2001, review of *Bone Walker*, p. 1582; June 1, 2002, review of *Raising Abel*, p. 756; May 15, 2005, review of *The Athena Factor*, p. 557; August 1, 2005, review of *People of the Moon*, p. 821; June 1, 2009, review of *Children of the Dawnland*.

Library Journal, February 1, 1998, Mary Ellen Elsbernd, review of *People of the Mist*, p. 110; November 1, 1998, Mary Ellen Elsbernd, review of *People of the Masks*, p. 125; August, 1999, Susan A. Zappia, review of *The Visitant*, p. 139; May 15, 2003, Mary Ellen Elsbernd, review of *People of the Owl*, p. 123; February 15, 2010, Mary Ellen Elsbernd, review of *Coming of the Storm*, p. 87; June 18, 2010, Mary Ellen Elsbernd, review of *People of the Longhouse*.

Post & Courier (Charleston, SC), January 14, 2001, Michael A. Green, review of *The Summoning God*, p. 3.

Publishers Weekly, June 1, 1992, review of *People of the River*, p. 51; September 13, 1993, review of *People of the Sea*, p. 89; October 30, 1995, review of *People of the Lightning*, p. 46; June 3, 1996, review of *The Morning River*, p. 61; December 2, 1996, review of *People of the Silence*, p. 42; July 14, 1997, review of *Coyote Summer*, p. 66; November 24, 1997, review of *People of the Mist*, p. 52; November 2, 1998, review of *People of the Masks*, p. 71; July 5, 1999, review of *The Visitant*, p. 62; June 26, 2000, review of *The Summoning God*, p. 53; February 5, 2001, review of *Dark Inheritance*, p. 65; July 1, 2002, review of *Raising Abel*, p. 55; May 26, 2003, review of *People of the Owl*, p. 49; November 17, 2008, review of *People of the Thunder*, p. 42; December 14, 2009, review of *Coming of the Storm*, p. 41; May 10, 2010, review of *People of the Longhouse*, p. 28.

Rocky Mountain News, June 16, 1996, Dale L. Walker, "Young Man Comes of Age in the Wild West," p. D30.

St. Louis Post-Dispatch, March 23, 1997, Dick Richmond, "Rise and Fall of Ancient Civilization," p. T9.

School Library Journal, December, 2009, Ragan O'Malley, review of *Children of the Dawnland,* p. 118.

ONLINE

Kathleen O'Neal and W. Michael Gear Home Page, http://www.gear-gear.com (December 20, 2010).
Kathleen O'Neal and W. Michael Gear Web log, http://www.gear-gear.com/blog (December 20, 2010).*

*   *   *

GIFFORD, Carrie

Personal

Married Hal Mertz. *Education:* Attended art school.

Addresses

Home—Seattle, WA. *Agent*—Steve Malk, Writer's House, 7660 Fay Ave., No. 338H, La Jolla, CA 92037. *E-mail*—info@redcapcards.com.

Career

Illustrator and graphic designer. Former teacher and director of children's theatre; Redcap Cards, Beverly Hills, CA, founder with husband Hal Mertz; Black Coffee (coffee roaster), Seattle, WA, cofounder with Mertz.

Carrie Gifford (Photograph by Amber Gress. Reproduced by permission.)

Illustrator

Gitty Daneshvari, *School of Fear,* Little, Brown (New York, NY), 2009.
Gitty Daneshvari, *Class Is Not Dismissed!,* Little, Brown (New York, NY), 2010.
Leslie Muir, *Barry B. Wary,* Hyperion (New York, NY), 2011.

Biographical and Critical Sources

PERIODICALS

Booklist, September 1, 2009, Abby Nolan, review of *School of Fear,* p. 91.
Kirkus Reviews, September 1, 2009, review of *School of Fear.*

ONLINE

Carrie Gifford Home Page, http://carriegifford.com (December 7, 2010).

*   *   *

GRAHAM, Christine 1952-

Personal

Born 1952, in Syracuse, NY; father a college professor; married; children: three. *Education:* College degree.

Addresses

Home—Salt Lake City, UT. *E-mail*—christine@christinegrahambooks.com.

Career

Author and educator. LDS Business College, Salt Lake City, UT, teacher of writing.

Writings

When Pioneer Wagons Rumbled West, illustrated by Sherry Meidell, Deseret Book Co. (Salt Lake City, UT), 1997.
Three Little Robbers, illustrated by Susan Boase, Henry Holt (New York, NY), 2007.
Peter Peter Picks a Pumpkin House, illustrated by Susan Boase, Henry Holt (New York, NY), 2009.

Sidelights

Christine Graham was inspired to write her history-themed picture book *When Pioneer Wagons Rumbled West* by her experience as a reenactor during the 150-year-anniversary celebration of the Mormon pioneer crossing of 1847. During that year, Mormon leader Brigham Young and the 149 members of his Vanguard Company traveled the 1,300 miles from Naauvoo, Illinois, to their new home in Salt Lake City, Utah. Featuring colorful water-color illustrations by Sherry Meidell, *When Pioneer Wagons Rumbled West* was recommended by *Booklist* contributor Kay Weisman as a "useful" historical story for "classes that combine religion and secular studies."

Although Graham was born in Upper New York State, she was raised in Provo, Utah, where the story of the Mormon migration is a well-known part of local history. Her father, a professor of geography at Brigham Young University, took his family on many excursions around the world, allowing his daughter the chance to experience cultures in Europe, Africa, and the Middle East in addition to benefitting from life in a college town.

Other books by Graham include *Three Little Robbers,* a story about Flo, Mo, and Jo, young thieves whose attempt to rob an elderly woman nearby winds up building a close friendship and a lesson in generosity. Illustrated with what a *Kirkus Reviews* writer described as "detailed and expressive" drawings by Susan Boase, the story features the "predictable but entertaining plot" and "short sentences" that will make it popular with beginning readers. Another collaboration with Boase, *Peter Peter Picks a Pumpkin House* finds a family's vegetable patch yielding an unusual crop of pumpkins: one pumpkin is so large, in fact, that it becomes the perfect replacement for the family's falling-down house. Noting the story's basis in popular nursery rhymes, a *Kirkus Reviews* writer asserted that Graham's "spare text favors repetition, and [the book's] short chapters and ample drawings suit newly independent readers."

Biographical and Critical Sources

PERIODICALS

Booklist, September 15, 1998, Kaye Weisman, review of *When Pioneer Wagons Rumbled West,* p. 236.

Kirkus Reviews, August 1, 2007, review of *Three Little Robbers;* June 15, 2009, review of *Peter Peter Picks a Pumpkin House.*

ONLINE

Christine Graham Home Page, http://christinegraham books.com (December 7, 2010).*

*   *   *

GRANSTRÖM, Brita 1969-

Personal

Born July 23, 1969, in Eskilstuna, Sweden; immigrated to England; married Mick Manning (a writer and illustrator); children: Max, Björn, Frej, Charlie. *Education:* Attended Örebro Konstskola; Konstfack (national college of art, craft, and design), Stockholm, Sweden, M.F.A.

Addresses

Home—North England. *E-mail*—brita@mickandbrita. com.

Career

Artist and illustrator of children's books. Has worked as a medical illustrator for African Medical and Research Foundation. *Exhibitions:* Paintings exhibited at University Gallery, Newcastle, England; for Society of American Illustrators, New York, NY; and elsewhere.

Member

Society of Authors.

Awards, Honors

Smarties Silver Award, 1996, for *The World's Full of Babies!; Times Educational Supplement* Award, 1997, for *What's under the Bed?;* shortlisted for Rhone Pou-

Christine Graham tells a rural-themed story in her picture book Peter Peter Picks a Pumpkin House, *featuring artwork by Susan Boase.*
(Illustration copyright © 2009 by Susan Boase. Reproduced by permission of Henry Holt & Company, LLC.)

lenc science prize, 1998, for *Yum-Yum!*, and *How Did I Begin?*, and 1999, for *Science School;* Key Stage 1 Nonfiction Award, English Association, 2000, for *Wash, Scrub, Brush!*, 2005, for *Voices of the Rainforest*, and 2008; Key Stage 2 Award shortlist, English Association, 2005, for *Roman Fort;* Oppenheim Toy Portfolio Gold Award, and Book of the Year citation, *Parenting* magazine, both for *Eyes, Nose, Fingers, Toes;* Oppenheim Toy Portfolio Platinum Award, for *Does a Cow Say Boo?;* Blue Peter Book Award shortlist, 2005, for *What's My Family Tree?*, 2009, for *Tail-End Charlie;* Highland Book Award shortlist (Scotland), 2006, for *Yuck!*

Writings

SELF-ILLUSTRATED

Ten in the Bed, Candlewick Press (Cambridge, MA), 1996.

Many Hands Counting Book, edited by Gale Pryor, Candlewick Press (Cambridge, MA), 1999.

My First Words and Pictures, Walker (London, England), 2004.

Other books include *Wof Här Kommer Jag!* and *Fina och Telefonen*, published by Raben & Sjögren.

ILLUSTRATOR

Mick Manning, *The World Is Full of Babies!*, Delacorte (New York, NY), 1996.

Mick Manning, *Art School*, Kingfisher (New York, NY), 1996.

Christine Morley and Carole Orbell, *Me and My Pet Dog*, World Book/Two-Can (Chicago, IL), 1996.

Christine Morley and Carole Orbell, *Me and My Pet Cat*, World Book/Two-Can (Chicago, IL), 1996.

Christine Morley and Carole Orbell, *Me and My Pet Rabbit*, World Book/Two-Can (Chicago, IL), 1997.

Mick Manning, *What's Up?*, Franklin Watts (London, England), 1997.

Christine Morley and Carole Orbell, *Me and My Pet Fish*, World Book/Two-Can (Chicago, IL), 1997.

Pippa Goodhart, *Bed Time*, Franklin Watts (London, England), 1997, published as *My Bed Time*, 2002.

Pippa Goodhart, *Morning Time*, Franklin Watts (London, England), 1997, published as *My Morning Time*, 2002.

Pippa Goodhart, *Play Time*, Franklin Watts (London, England), 1997.

Pippa Goodhart, *Shopping Time*, Franklin Watts (London, England), 1997.

Mick Manning, *How Did I Begin?*, Franklin Watts (London, England), 1997.

Mick Manning, *Rainy Day*, Franklin Watts (London, England), 1997.

Mick Manning, *Snowy Day*, Franklin Watts (London, England), 1997.

Mick Manning, *Sunny Day*, Franklin Watts (London, England), 1997.

Mick Manning, *Windy Day*, Franklin Watts (London, England), 1997.

Mick Manning, *Science School*, Kingfisher (New York, NY), 1998.

Mick Manning, *Collect-o-Mania*, Franklin Watts (London, England), 1998, published as *Make Your Own Museum*, 2003.

Judy Hindley, *Eyes, Nose, Fingers, and Toes: A First Book about You*, Candlewick Press (Cambridge, MA), 1999.

Sam McBratney, *Bert's Wonderful News*, Walker & Co. (London, England), 1999.

Mick Manning, *Drama School*, Kingfisher (New York, NY), 1999.

Mick Manning, *Let's Build a House!*, Franklin Watts (London, England), 1999.

Mick Manning, *Let's Party!: Celebrate with Children All around the World*, Big Fish (London, England), 2000.

Mick Manning, *Wheels Keep Turning*, Franklin Watts (London, England), 2000.

Maddie Stewart, *Clever Daddy*, Early Learning Centre (Swindon, England), 2000.

Pippa Goodhart, *Molly and the Beanstalk*, Walker & Co. (London, England), 2001.

Kathy Henderson, *Baby Knows Best*, Little, Brown (Boston, MA), 2001.

Mick Manning, *What's My Family Tree?*, Franklin Watts (London, England), 2001, Franklin Watts (New York, NY), 2004.

Mick Manning, *How Should I Behave?*, Franklin Watts (London, England), 2002.

Mick Manning, *The Power Cut*, Franklin Watts (London, England), 2002.

Mick Manning, *Watch Out! Builders About!*, Franklin Watts (London, England), 2002.

Judy Hindley, *Does a Cow Say Boo?*, Candlewick Press (Cambridge, MA), 2002.

Joyce Dunbar, *A Chick Called Saturday*, Eerdmans (Grand Rapids, MI), 2003.

Kathy Henderson, *Dog Story*, Bloomsbury (London, England), 2004.

Paeony Lewis, *No More Cookies!*, Chicken House (New York, NY), 2005.

Judy Hindley, *Baby Talk: A Book of First Words and Phrases*, Candlewick Press (Cambridge, MA), 2006.

Lynn Brittney, *Christine Kringle*, BookSurge, 2007.

Mick Manning, *Woolly Mammoth*, Frances Lincoln (London, England), 2007, Frances Lincoln (New York, NY), 2011.

Mick Manning, *Under Your Skin: Your Amazing Body*, Albert Whitman (Morton Grove, IL), 2007.

Judy Hindley, *Does a Cow Say Boo?*, Candlewick Press (Cambridge, MA), 2008.

Paeony Lewis, *No More Yawning!*, Chicken House/Scholastic (New York, NY), 2008.

Illustrator of *Ben's Bring Your Bear Party*, by Martin Waddell, Walker & Co.; and *Kisses Are Little, Smiles Are Wide*, Candlewick Press.

ILLUSTRATOR WITH PARTNER, MICK MANNING

Mick Manning, *Nature Watch*, Kingfisher (New York, NY), 1997.

Mick Manning, *Honk! Honk! A Story of Migration*, Kingfisher (New York, NY), 1997.

Mick Manning, *Yum-Yum!*, Franklin Watts (London, England), 1997.

Mick Manning, *My Body, Your Body*, Franklin Watts (London, England), 1997.

Mick Manning, *Splish, Splash, Splosh!*, Franklin Watts (London, England), 1997.

Mick Manning, *What's under the Bed?*, Franklin Watts (London, England), 1997.

Mick Manning, *Nature School*, Kingfisher (New York, NY), 1997.

Mick Manning, *Out There Somewhere*, Franklin Watts (London, England), 1998.

Mick Manning, *What If? A Book about Recycling*, Franklin Watts (London, England), 1998.

Mick Manning, *Wild and Free*, Franklin Watts (London, England), 1998.

Mick Manning, *Super School*, Kingfisher (New York, NY), 1999.

Mick Manning, *Super Mum*, Franklin Watts (London, England), 1999, published as *Supermom*, Albert Whitman (Morton Grove, IL), 2001.

Mick Manning, *Wash, Scrub, Brush!*, Franklin Watts (London, England), 1999, Albert Whitman (Morton Grove, IL), 2001.

Mick Manning, *Stone Age, Bone Age*, Franklin Watts (London, England), 2000.

Mick Manning, *What a Viking!*, Raben & Sjögren (New York, NY), 2000.

Mick Manning, *Dinomania: Things to Do with Dinosaurs*, Franklin Watts (London, England), 2001, Holiday House (New York, NY), 2002.

Mick Manning, *The Story of a Storm*, Franklin Watts (London, England), 2001.

Mick Manning, *High Tide, Low Tide*, Franklin Watts (London, England), 2001.

Mick Manning, *Seasons Turning*, Franklin Watts (London, England), 2001.

Mick Manning, *When the Sun Goes Down*, Franklin Watts (London, England), 2001.

Mick Manning, *How Will I Grow?*, Franklin Watts (London, England), 2002.

Mick Manning, *Voices of the Rainforest*, Franklin Watts (London, England), 2004.

Mick Manning, *Seaside Scientist*, Franklin Watts (London, England), 2004.

Mick Manning, *Roman Fort* ("Fly on the Wall" series), Frances Lincoln (London, England), 2004.

Mick Manning, *Yuck!*, Frances Lincoln (London, England), 2005.

Mick Manning, *Pharaoh's Egypt* ("Fly on the Wall" series), Frances Lincoln (London, England), 2005.

Mick Manning, *Viking Longship* ("Fly on the Wall" series), Frances Lincoln (London, England), 2006.

Mick Manning, *Snap!*, Frances Lincoln (London, England), 2006.

Mick Manning, *Cock-a-doodle-hooooooo!*, Good Books (Intercourse, PA), 2007.

Mick Manning, *Dino-dinners!*, Holiday House (New York, NY), 2007.

Mick Manning, *Greek Hero* ("Fly on the Wall" series), Frances Lincoln (London, England), 2007.

Mick Manning, *Tail-End Charlie*, Frances Lincoln (London, England), 2008.

Mick Manning, *Planet Patrol*, Frances Lincoln (London, England), 2009.

Mick Manning, *Our Baby Inside!*, Frances Lincoln (London, England), 2009.

What Mr Darwin Saw, Frances Lincoln (London, England), 2009.

Taff in the WAAF, Frances Lincoln (London, England), 2010.

My Uncle's Dunkirk, Franklin Watts (London, England), 2010.

Collaborator, with Manning, on "Max and Kate" series for *Ladybug* magazine, beginning 1999.

Books have been translated into Welsh, Japanese, Korean, German, Serbo-Croat, Chinese, Dutch, Portugese, Swedish, Spanish, and Brazilian.

Sidelights

Swedish-born artist Brita Granström is well known for her work as an illustrator, much of which is done in collaboration with her husband, writer and illustrator Mick Manning. A prolific team, Manning and Granström have produced picture books for young readers as well as nonfiction titles. Because both studied art and design, they work together on both the writing and illustration stages of their books, although Granström explains that her input in the writing process is "collaborative" and credits her husband as author. "We try to stay flexible," the couple explained in an interview with Pam Kelt that was posted on their home page. In their illustrations, Granström typically focuses on human characters while Manning draws the animals. "In some books, one of us might draw and the other might colour the same artwork," the author/illustrators explained to Kelt. "Then we enjoy it when people say they can't see the join!" Along with their many books, Manning and Granström have also written and illustrated a five-page feature for *Ladybug* magazine called "Max and Kate," which features the amusing adventures of two preschool neighbors.

Manning and Granström's *Wash, Scrub, Brush!*, a book of instruction about personal hygiene, is one of several collaborations that has won an award. The title teaches basic behaviors in washing and grooming through a story of children preparing for a party. "The authors skillfully cover basic grooming and hygiene within a story framework," complimented Marilyn Ackerman in *School Library Journal*. *Booklist* contributor Connie Fletcher praised the pair's use of art, commenting that "the illustrations, crowded with happy kids sprucing up, are bright and lively."

Other titles by the pair focus on the science of daily life or on science topics that appeal to young readers. Their book *Supermom* shows the similarities between human

A curious little chick is determined to fly the coop and see the world in Joyce Dunbar's engaging picture book A Chick Called Saturday, *featuring illustrations by Brita Granström.* (Eerdmans Books for Young Readers, 2003. Illustration copyright © 2003 by Brita Granström. Reproduced by permission.)

mothers and their animal counterparts as they care for their young ones, while *Woolly Mammoth* combines cartoon watercolor-and-pencil art with a rhyming text that takes readers back to prehistoric times when these giant, long-tusked creatures roamed much of the earth. "The watercolor, graphite, and crayon artwork reflects the light approach to scientific facts," wrote Carolyn Janssen in a *School Library Journal* review of *Supermom,* while *Booklist* critic Carolyn Phelan noted that the "wonderfully scruffy" line drawings in *Woolly Mammoth* "depict mammoths foraging, warding off wolves, defending their . . . calves, as well as being hunted by Ice Age humans."

Featuring a subject that lived even further back in time, *Dinomania: Things to Do with Dinosaurs* focuses on modern paleontology and provides hands-on activities for young people who want to learn more about dinosaurs, while its companion volume *Dino-Dinners* looks at the favorite foodstuffs consumed by ten different dinosaurs. Augusta R. Malvagno, writing for *School Library Journal,* cited *Dinomania* for its "kid-friendly text, expressive and colorful illustrations, and creative activities and crafts," and Ellen Mandel commented in *Booklist* that the crafts included are "fun activities for hands-on learning." *Dino-Dinners* combines what *Booklist* critic Randall Enos described as a "playful, first-person narrative" with "large, eye-catching, dramatic" watercolor-and-pencil illustrations that make the book "a feast for the eyes."

In the picture books *Yuck!* and *Snap!* Manning and Grandström focus on the food chain. Described by a *Kirkus Reviews* contributor as "an enjoyable gross-out game to share with very young listeners," *Yuck!* shows

slimy, gross, and disgusting meals eaten by various animal babies. *Snap!* follows along the food chain as a frog is eaten by a duckling, which is eaten by a large fish, which is eaten by a fisherman. However, something lurks in the pictures that prompts readers to realize that the fisherman is not the end of the food chain after all. In reviewing the cumulative story in *Snap!,* a *Kirkus Reviews* writer noted that Grandström's "lighthearted, humorous illustrations will draw children in to this accessible" tale, while a *Publishers Weekly* critic wrote that Granström's "generous sense of scale, along with bold colors and a thick, exuberant ink line give the pictures a spontaneous quality and energy."

The husband-and-wife team turns to history in several picture books, among them *What Mr. Darwin Saw, Tail-End Charlie,* and the volumes in their "Fly on the Wall" series: *Pharaoh's Egypt, Roman Fort,* and *Greek Hero,* among others. Mixing a straight-forward story with journal entries and text boxes, *What Mr. Darwin Saw* recounts the journey of nineteenth-century scientist Charles Darwin's voyage aboard the *Beagle* as he developed his groundbreaking and still-controversial theory of evolution. The book's "cartoon illustrations in pencil and watercolor aim for the gross and startling aspects" of Darwin's journey, wrote *School Library Journal* critic Ellen Heath, while in *Booklist* Phelan observed that the use of "thought and speech balloons add informal appeal to the illustrations while giving voice to even minor characters." Published to coincide with the 200-year anniversary of Darwin's birth, *What Mr. Darwin Saw* "will provide younger readers with an accurate, if sketchy, introduction to Darwin's big ideas," according to a *Kirkus Reviews* writer.

Manning's family history serves as the inspiration for two of the couple's picture-book projects. In *Tail-End*

Charlie they capture the experiences of Manning's father during his service as a tail-gunner in the Royal Air Force during World War II, while his mother's experiences as a wireless operator in the Women's Auxiliary Air Force are captured in *Taff in the WAAF.* The books feature comic-book-style illustrations in Grandström's characteristic watercolor-and-ink art that are supplemented by photographs and images of wartime ephemera. According to *School Library Journal* contributor Linda Ludke, "reluctant readers will be drawn to the graphic format" of *Tail-End Charlie* "and quickly engaged by the authentic voice" of Manning's first-person narrative text. Although Phelan noted that their "picture book is an unusual format for tales of combat,. . .Manning and Granstrom use it very effectively here," combining cartoons with speech balloons and collage elements to present their "highly illustrated account."

Along with her collaborations with Manning, Granström has also illustrated a range of children's books by authors that include Pippa Goodhart, Sam McBratney, Joyce Dunbar, Paeony Lewis, and Judy Hindley. A *Kirkus Reviews* contributor labeled her work for Hindley's *Does a Cow Say Boo?* as "delightful pencil, watercolor, and crayon illustrations." A *Publishers Weekly* critic commented on the "vibrantly colored farm scenes" in the same title, while *Booklist* reviewer Diane Foote considered them "bright, energetic illustrations." Grandström's watercolor images for Lewis's *No More Cookies!* earned praise from *Booklist* critic Ilene Cooper,

who maintained that she "shows considerable talent in capturing the moods (and occasional frenzy) that fairly shriek 'preschooler.'"

Discussing Grandström's work for Dunbar's *A Chick Called Saturday,* a *Kirkus Reviews* contributor commented that the artist's "loose watercolor-and-pencil pictures and a touch of appropriately 'scratchy' calligraphy put readers in the right farm—uh, frame—of mind." A *Publishers Weekly* critic called the same book "sunnyhued," while Cooper noted in *Booklist* that the mix of small spot art and large illustrations makes "a dynamic combination that will keep kids' interest." Granström was honored when the Society of American Illustrators invited her to exhibit an image from *A Chick Called Saturday* at their annual show.

Granström once told *SATA:* "I love my job. It's a dream come true. When I'm not illustrating children's books, I go out painting. I fill the baby's pram with acrylic paints and go painting on the spot." Granström lives in northern England with her husband and children.

Biographical and Critical Sources

PERIODICALS

Booklist, January 1, 2000, review of *Eyes, Nose, Fingers, and Toes: A First Book about You,* p. 824; March 15, 2001, Ellen Mandel, review of *Supermom,* p. 1404;

Grandström and her husband, Mick Manning, team up to create the picture book **Tail-end Charlie.** (Frances Lincoln Children's Books, 2008. Illustration copyright © 2008 by Mick Manning and Brita Granström. Reproduced by permission.)

May 1, 2001, Connie Fletcher, review of *Wash, Scrub, Brush!,* p. 1686; June 1, 2002, Ellen Mandel, review of *Dinomania,* p. 1717, and Diane Foote, review of *Does a Cow Say Boo?,* p. 1738; August, 2003, Ilene Cooper, review of *A Chick Called Saturday,* p. 1988; May 1, 2005, Ilene Cooper, review of *No More Cookies!,* p. 1591; February 15, 2006, Ilene Cooper, review of *Baby Talk: A Book of First Words and Phrases,* p. 102; September 1, 2007, Randall Enos, review of *Dino-Dinners,* p. 121; September 15, 2007, Carolyn Phelan, review of *Under Your Skin: Your Amazing Body,* p. 71; November 15, 2007, Shelle Rosenfeld, review of *Viking Longship,* p. 42; January 1, 2008, Krista Hutley, review of *No More Yawning!,* p. 95; March 15, 2009, Carolyn Phelan, review of *What Mr. Darwin Saw,* p. 59; September 1, 2009, Carolyn Phelan, review of *Tail-End Charlie,* p. 88; November 15, 2009, Carolyn Phelan, review of *Woolly Mammoth,* p. 41.

Bulletin of the Center for Children's Books, March, 2010, Deborah Stevenson, review of *Woolly Mammoth,* p. 294.

Horn Book, May-June, 2006, Bridget T. McCaffrey, review of *Baby Talk,* p. 297.

Kirkus Reviews, May 1, 2002, review of *Does a Cow Say Boo?* p. 656; July 1, 2003, review of *A Chick Called Saturday,* p. 909; March 1, 2005, review of *Dog Story,* p. 287 and *No More Cookies!,* p. 290; June 15, 2005, review of *Yuck!,* p. 686; January 15, 2006, review of *Pharaoh's Egypt,* p. 87; October 15, 2006, review of *Snap!,* p. 1074; January 1, 2008, review of *No More Yawning!*

Publishers Weekly, June 21, 1999, review of *Eyes, Nose, Fingers, and Toes,* p. 66; May 13, 2002, review of *Does a Cow Say Boo?,* p. 69; June 2, 2003, review of *A Chick Called Saturday,* p. 50; October 30, 2006, review of *Snap!,* p. 60.

School Librarian, winter, 2004, Don Brothwell, review of *Roman Fort,* p. 209.

School Library Journal, July, 1999, Olga R. Barnes, review of *Eyes, Nose, Fingers, and Toes,* p. 73; September, 1999, Cris Riedel, review of *Drama School,* p. 214; April, 2001, Marilyn Ackerman, review of *Wash, Scrub, Brush!,* and Carolyn Janssen, review of *Supermom,* p. 133; April, 2002, Jean Pollock, review of *Let's Party!: Celebrate with Children All around the World,* and Augusta R. Malvagno, review of *Dinomania,* p. 137; August, 2003, Bina Williams, review of *A Chick Called Saturday,* p. 126; May, 2005, Shawn Brommer, review of *No More Cookies!,* p. 88; July, 2005, Lynda S. Poling, review of *Roman Fort,* p. 91; March, 2006, Gay Lynn Van Vleck, review of *Baby Talk,* p. 192; April, 2006, Coop Renner, review of *Pharaoh's Egypt,* p. 130; May, 2007, Maura Bresnahan, review of *Cock-a-Doodle-Hooooooo!,* p. 104; October, 2007, Susan E. Murray, review of *Dino-Dinners,* p. 137; April, 2008, Catherine Threadgill, review of *No More Yawning!,* p. 115; June, 2008, Lynda Ritterman, review of *Under Your Skin,* p. 128; August, 2008, Angela J. Reynolds, review of *Greek Hero,* p. 98; March, 2009, Ellen Heath, review of *What Mr. Darwin Saw,* p. 166; August, 2009, Linda Ludke, review of *Tail-End Charlie,* p. 91; January, 2010, Janet S. Thompson, review of *Woolly Mammoth,* p. 88.

ONLINE

Brita Granström and Mick Manning Home Page, http://www.mickandbrita.com (December 27, 2010).*

H

HADDIX, Margaret Peterson 1964-

Personal
Born April 9, 1964, in Washington Court House, OH; daughter of John Albert (a farmer) and Marilee Grace (a nurse) Peterson; married Doug Haddix (a newspaper editor), October 3, 1987; children: Meredith, Connor. *Education:* Miami University, B.A. (English/journalism; summa cum laude), 1986. *Religion:* Presbyterian. *Hobbies and other interests:* Travel.

Addresses
Home—Columbus, OH. *Agent*—Tracey Adams, McIntoch & Otis, 353 Lexington Ave., New York, NY 10016.

Career
Author and educator. Fort Wayne Journal-Gazette, Fort Wayne, IN, copy editor, 1986-87; *Indianapolis News,* Indianapolis, IN, reporter, 1987-91; Danville Area Community College, Danville, IL, member of adjunct faculty, 1991-93; freelance writer, beginning 1991.

Member
Society of Children's Book Writers and Illustrators, Phi Beta Kappa.

Awards, Honors
Honorable mention, *Seventeen* magazine fiction contest, 1983; fiction contest award, National Society of Arts and Letters, 1988; American Bestseller Pick-of-the-Lists selection, Edgar Allan Poe Award nomination, Mystery Writers of America, Quick Pick for Reluctant Young-Adult Readers and Best Book for Young Adults designations, Young-Adult Library Services Association (YALSA), Notable Children's Trade Books in the Field of Social Studies selection, National Council for Social Studies/Children's Book Council, Sequoyah Young-Adult Book Award, and Black-eyed Susan Award, all 1996-97, Arizona Young Readers Award, 1998, and

Margaret Peterson Haddix (Reproduced by permission.)

American Library Association (ALA) Best Book for Young Adults designation, all for *Running out of Time;* Children's Book Award (older reader category), International Reading Association (IRA), and YALSA Quick Pick for Reluctant Young-Adult Readers and Best Book for Young Adults designations, all 1997, Black-eyed Susan Award, 1998-99, and Nebraska Golden Sower Award, 2000, all for *Don't You Dare Read This, Mrs. Dunphrey;* YALSA Best Books for Young Adults designation, and American Bookseller Pick-of-the-Lists selection, both 1997, both for *Leaving Fishers;* YALSA Top Ten Best Books for Young Adults selection, and

Quick Picks Top-Ten designation, both 2000, and California Young Readers Medal, Maud Hart Lovelace Award, and Nevada Young Readers Award, all 2001, all for *Among the Hidden;* American Bookseller Pick-of-the-Lists selection, 2000, for *Turnabout,* and 2001, for both *The Girl with 500 Middle Names* and *Among the Imposters;* American Bookseller Pick-of-the-Lists selection, ALA Best Book for Young Adults designation, YALSA Quick Pick for Reluctant Young-Adult Readers designation, and IRA Young Adults' Choices selection, 2001, all for *Just Ella;* Eleanor Cameron Award for Middle Grades, 2003, for *Escape from Memory;* IRA Children's Choice selection, Book for the Teen Age selection, New York Public Library, and YALSA Quick Pick for Reluctant Young-Adult Readers selection, all 2003, and Lamplighter Award, 2004, all for *Among the Betrayed;* Book for the Teen Age selection, New York Public Library, 2007, for *Among the Free;* Book for the Teen Age selection, Ohioana Book Award for Juvenile Literature, and International IMPAC Dublin Literary Award nomination, all 2007, all for *Uprising;* numerous other awards and honors.

Writings

YOUNG-ADULT NOVELS

Running out of Time, Simon & Schuster (New York, NY), 1995.
Don't You Dare Read This, Mrs. Dunphrey, Simon & Schuster (New York, NY), 1996.
Leaving Fishers, Simon & Schuster (New York, NY), 1997.
Just Ella, Simon & Schuster (New York, NY), 1999.
Turnabout, Simon & Schuster (New York, NY), 2000.
Takeoffs and Landings, Simon & Schuster (New York, NY), 2001.
Escape from Memory, Simon & Schuster (New York, NY), 2003.
The House on the Gulf, Simon & Schuster (New York, NY), 2004.
Double Identity, Simon & Schuster (New York, NY), 2005.
Uprising, Simon & Schuster (New York, NY), 2007.
Palace of Mirrors, Simon & Schuster (New York, NY), 2008.
Claim to Fame, Simon & Schuster Books for Young Readers (New York, NY), 2009.
Into the Gauntlet ("39 Clues" series), Scholastic (New York, NY), 2010.

Contributor of short stories to anthologies, including *Indiannual and The Luxury of Tears,* National Society of Arts and Letters, 1989; *On the Edge,* Simon & Schuster (New York, NY), 2000; *I Believe in Water,* HarperCollins (New York, NY), 2000; and *Make Me Over: 11 Original Stories about Transforming Ourselves,* Dutton (New York, NY), 2005.

Author's works have been translated into Italian.

JUVENILE NOVELS

The Girl with 500 Middle Names, illustrated by Janet Hamlin, Simon & Schuster (New York, NY), 2001.
Because of Anya, Simon & Schuster (New York, NY), 2002.
Say What?, illustrated by James Bernardin, Simon & Schuster (New York, NY), 2004.
Dexter the Tough, illustrated by Mark Elliott, Simon & Schuster (New York, NY), 2007.

"SHADOW CHILDREN" NOVEL SERIES

Among the Hidden (also see below), Simon & Schuster (New York, NY), 1998.
Among the Imposters (also see below), Simon & Schuster (New York, NY), 2001.
Among the Betrayed, Simon & Schuster (New York, NY), 2002.
Among the Barons, Simon & Schuster (New York, NY), 2003.
Among the Brave, Simon & Schuster (New York, NY), 2003.
Among the Enemy, Simon & Schuster (New York, NY), 2005.
Among the Free, Simon & Schuster (New York, NY), 2006.
Among the Hidden/Among the Impostors, Simon & Schuster Books for Young Readers (New York, NY), 2009.
Shadow Children Bind-up (omnibus), Simon & Schuster Books for Young Readers (New York, NY), 2009.

"MISSING" NOVEL SERIES

Found, Simon & Schuster (New York, NY), 2008.
Sent, Simon & Schuster Books for Young Readers (New York, NY), 2009.
Sabotaged, Simon & Schuster Books for Young Readers (New York, NY), 2010.
Torn, Simon & Schuster Books for Young Readers (New York, NY), 2011.

Adaptations

Many of Haddix's books, including *Just Ella, Leaving Fishers, Don't You Dare Read This, Mrs. Dunphrey,* and her "Shadow Children" novels, have been adapted as audiobooks.

Sidelights

Award-winning author Margaret Peterson Haddix writes novels for young adults and juvenile readers that deal with topics ranging from religious cults to modern-day science fiction and reality-based situations. Haddix's debut novel, *Running out of Time,* a time-slip story with a twist, has become something of a classic of the form, and was adopted for use in middle-school classrooms around the United States. Haddix has written several other mainstream novels for middle-grade and younger readers, such as *Don't You Dare Read This, Mrs. Dunphrey, The Girl with 500 Middle Names,* and *Dexter the Tough,* while the novels *Leaving Fishers, Turnabout, Takeoffs and Landings,* and *Turnabout* engage teens through more complex themes. Other popular works include her "Missing" time-slip novels and her long-running dystopian "Shadow Children" saga. While Haddix's novels for young adults share little in terms of plot, setting, or theme, critics have cited her characteristic ability to involve even reluctant readers in the lives of her realistic characters.

Haddix was born in Washington Court House, Ohio, in 1964, the daughter of a farming father and a mother who worked as a nurse. "I grew up on lots of stories," she once commented, "both from books and in my family. My father in particular was always telling tales to my brothers and sister and me—about one of our ancestors who was kidnaped, about some friends who survived lying on a railroad bridge while a train went over the top of them, about the kid who brought possum meat to the school cafeteria when my father was a boy. So I always thought that becoming a storyteller would be the grandest thing in the world. But I didn't want to just tell stories. I wanted to write them down."

Through adolescence and on into high school, Haddix maintained her love of both reading and writing. "For a long time, I tried to write two different kinds of stories: real and imaginary," she once recalled. As a student at Miami University, she "majored in both journalism and creative writing (and history, just because I liked it). After college, I got jobs at newspapers, first as a copy editor in Fort Wayne, then as a reporter in Indianapolis. It was a lot of fun, especially getting to meet and talk to people from all walks of life, from homeless women to congressmen."

Meanwhile, during her free time on weekends and in the evenings, Haddix continued to write short fiction. "This was frustrating," the author once observed, "because there was never enough time. So, in 1991, when my husband got a new job in Danville, Illinois, I took a radical step: I quit newspapers. I took a series of temporary and part-time jobs, such as teaching at a community college, and used the extra time to write."

The first large-story idea to percolate in Haddix's imagination was the seed of *Running out of Time.* "I'd gotten the idea when I was doing a newspaper story about a restored historical village," she recalled. "I kept wondering what it would be like if there was a historical village where all the tourists were hidden and the kids, at least, didn't know what year it really was." When completed, her manuscript was quickly accepted by an editor at Simon & Schuster, and Haddix was on her way as a juvenile author.

In *Running out of Time* thirteen-year-old Jessie Keyser lives with her family in a frontier village in 1840. When the town's children are stricken with diphtheria, Jessie's

Cover of Haddix's debut teen mystery **Running out of Time,** *featuring artwork by Cliff Nielsen.* (Aladdin Books, 1997. Cover illustration copyright © 1999 by Cliff Nielsen. Reproduced by permission of the illustrator.)

mother reveals that it is actually the 1990s and their village is actually a tourist exhibit and scientific experiment gone awry. Because she is strong, Jessie is sent to the outside world to get help; her mother is fearful that the one-time idealistic planners of this "ideal" village may have become perverted in the twelve years since it began. In fact, Jessie's mother is right: the idealism of community founder Mr. Clifton has been subverted by researchers who have deliberately introduced diphtheria into the closed community to see how patients will fare without modern medical care. Out in the real world of the 1990s, Jessie must learn to deal with telephones, traffic, flush toilets, and the seductions of fast food.

Writing in *School Library Journal,* Lisa Dennis dubbed *Running out of Time* "absorbing" and "gripping," further noting that the "action moves swiftly, with plenty of suspense." While *Voice of Youth Advocates* critic Ann Welton found Jessie's adjustment to the drastic shift in time to be "far too smooth, resulting in a lack of narrative tension," she nonetheless pointed out that *Running out of Time* has "potential as a model for writing assignments and provides an interesting perspective on American history." In his review of Haddix's novel for the *Bulletin of the Center for Children's Books,* Roger Sutton also commented that Jessie's "disorientation upon discovering the modern world would surely have been more pronounced than it seems," but concluded that readers "will be gripped by the concept, and the book, readable throughout, [is] exciting in spots." Dennis predicted in *School Library Journal* that young fans of *Running out of Time* "will look forward to more stories from this intriguing new author."

Haddix wrote *Don't You Dare Read This, Mrs. Dunphrey* when she was pregnant with her first child. "The story should have been very difficult to write," she later recalled, "because I had a happy childhood and wonderful parents, and should have had nothing in common with the main character—tough-talking, big-haired Tish, whose parents abandoned her. But I'd once worked on a newspaper series where I talked to more than a dozen abused and neglected kids, and their stories haunted me for years. So writing the book was almost like an exorcism—I did feel possessed by Tish's spirit. Actually, in a way, everything I've written has felt like that, like being possessed. When I'm writing, I feel like I must write."

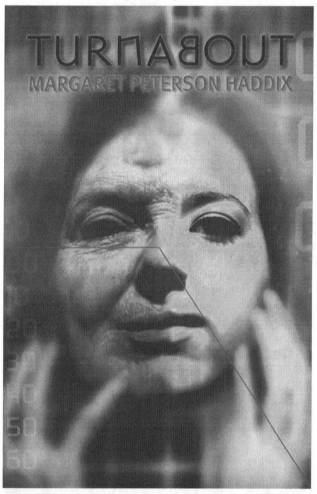

When Time begins to work in reverse, it threatens the teen heroine of Haddix's novel **Turnabout,** *featuring artwork by Cliff Nielsen.* (Simon & Schuster Books for Young Readers, 2000. Illustration copyright © 2000 by Cliff Nielsen. Reproduced by permission of the illustrator.)

In *Don't You Dare Read This, Mrs. Dunphrey* high schooler Tish is taking an English class where she is required to keep a journal. Since the teen has no one to confide in as she deals with an absent father, a depressed mother unable to care for her or her younger brother, and a part-time job where the manager subjects her to sexual harassment, this journal—and hence the reader—becomes her confidante. Tish feels safe in journaling because her teacher has promised to only read finished work inspired by students' journal entries, and not the individual entries themselves. Tish's predicament goes from bad to worse when she has to shoplift from a local store to feed herself and her brother Matthew, and faces eviction from her home as well. Finally Tish turns over the entire journal to her teacher, and the woman aids the teen in finding the assistance she needs.

"Tish's journal entries have an authentic ring in phrasing and tone and will keep readers involved," Carol Schene concluded in her *School Library Journal* review of *Don't You Dare Read This, Mrs. Dunphrey.* The result, according to Schene is a "brief, serious look at a young person who is isolated and faced with some seemingly overwhelming problems." Jean Franklin, writing in *Booklist,* called Haddix's novel "a brief, gritty documentary" and "a natural for reluctant readers." Jamie S. Hansen, writing in the *Voice of Youth Advocates,* echoed this sentiment: "The breezy style, short diary-entry format, and melodramatic subject matter will ensure popularity for this title, particularly with reluctant readers," concluded the critic.

In *Leaving Fishers* Haddix introduces Dorry, a teen whose life has been uprooted both geographically and economically. Suffering from diminished circumstances, Dorry has also found it difficult to make friends at her new school. When Angela, one of several attractive and friendly kids who congregate together, asks her to join her group at lunch, Dorry is eager to blend in. Her enthusiasm is not much diminished when she learns that these students are all part of a religious group called the Fishers of Men. She is introduced to their parties and retreats, and when pizza nights give way to prayer groups and retreats, Dorry becomes a member of the Fishers. Increasingly, the girl finds all her time taken up with the cult's activities. Totally immersed in the group, she fears she will go to hell if she does not do everything she is told to do by Angela and her fellow adherents. Neglecting family and school, Dorry soon finds herself in the grips of the Fishers. Only when she discovers herself terrifying young baby-sitting charges with threats of hell if they do not convert is she able to shake off the bonds of the cult.

"Haddix gives a fine portrayal of a teenager's descent into a cult," wrote *Booklist* critic Ilene Cooper, the reviewer adding that *Leaving Fishers* is a "good read and an informative one for young people who are constantly bombarded with challenges to their beliefs." In her *Voice of Youth Advocates* appraisal, Beverly Youree dubbed the novel "a definite page-turner, full of excitement and pathos" and concluded that "Dorry and readers learn that the world is neither black nor white, good nor bad, but shades of gray." A *Kirkus Reviews* critic called *Leaving Fishers* "a chilling portrait of an insecure teenager gradually relinquishing her autonomy to a religious cult," and went on to note that Haddix's novel, "tightly written, with well-drawn characters," is "in no way anti-religious." "Haddix's even-handed portrayal of the rewards of Christian fellowship and the dangers of a legalistic or black-and-white approach to religion" are, according to a reviewer for *Publishers Weekly,* the book's "greatest strength."

Including some of Haddix's most popular novels, the "Shadow Children" series take place in a future dystopia à la *1984* and *Brave New World,* wherein a totalitarian regime strictly observes a two-children-only policy. In series opener *Among the Hidden* twelve-year-old Luke Garner is the third child of a farming family and is thus illegal. When the government starts to log the woods around the family home in order to make way for new housing, Luke must hide from view, looking at the world outside through a small air vent in the attic. From this vantage point, he catches a glimpse of a shadowy figure in a nearby house and begins to suspect that this might be another hidden person like himself. One day he breaks into the seemingly empty house and discovers Jen. A hidden child with a tough exterior, Jen tells Luke about an entire subculture of hidden children who communicate via chat rooms on the Internet. He also learns about the repressive policies of the government. When Jen organizes a rally of other hidden children that ends in bloodshed and her death, Luke must finally make a decision as to how far he will go to defy the government and have a future worth living.

Critics responded positively to Haddix's futuristic focus, a *Publishers Weekly* contributor writing that "the unsettling, thought-provoking premise" in *Among the Hidden* "should suffice to keep readers hooked." Describing the novel as "exciting and compelling," Susan L. Rogers remarked in *School Library Journal* that readers "will be captivated by Luke's predicament and his reactions to it," and Debbie Earl noted in *Voice of Youth Advocates* that Haddix presents a "chilling vision of a possibly not-too-distant future" in her "bleak allegorical tale."

Haddix's "Shadow Children" saga continues in the novels *Among the Impostors, Among the Betrayed, Among the Barons, Among the Brave, Among the Enemy,* and *Among the Free. Among the Imposters* rejoins Luke as he adopts the alias Lee Grant and is sent to Hendricks School for Boys. The boarding school is a place of violence and fear, as terrified students quietly follow orders and newbies like Luke suffer nightly hazing at the hands of older boys. When he learns that some of his schoolmates, along with girls from a neighboring girls' school, are meeting secretly in the woods to plot their

escape, Luke decides to join the plotters in their dangerous plan. Brenda Moses-Allen, writing in *Voice of Youth Advocates,* wrote that *Among the Impostors* is filled with "tension and excitement."

In *Among the Betrayed* readers revisit thirteen-year-old Nina Ida, a character introduced in *Among the Impostors,* as she is arrested by the government's Population Police and charged with treason. An illegal third child, Nina faces death unless she agrees to help identify a group of third-born children who range in age from six to ten. The focus returns to Luke in *Among the Barons* as he meets the wealthy family of the dead boy whose name he has taken and feels a strange connection with Smits, the younger brother of the real Lee Grant. Noting that the relationship between the two boys "is compelling," a *Publishers Weekly* contributor concluded of *Among the Barons* that Haddix includes "enough cliff-hangers and plot twists to keep readers hooked."

The fifth installment in Haddix's "Shadow Children" series, *Among the Brave,* finds executions of third children increasingly more frequent now that the leader of the Population Police heads the government. Hoping to rescue Luke from a bad situation, Trey teams up with Luke's brother, Mark, but when Mark is captured he must turn to the adult-led resistance for help. "Once again, Haddix makes real how hard ordinary and not-so-ordinary actions would be" for her hidden heroes, Tina Zubak asserted in a *School Library Journal* review of *Among the Brave.* In *Booklist* Carolyn Phelan described Trey as "an interesting, sympathetic protagonist."

Like Luke, third child Matthias bravely infiltrates the ranks of the Population Police, hoping to learn enough about their system to save his friends in *Among the Enemy.* Now posing as a member of the Population Police, Luke realizes that his cover will be blown unless he follows murderous orders in *Among the Free,* and with that realization he initiates his planned rebellion against the deadly government forces. Writing that "Haddix's storytelling hums along quickly," *School Library Journal* reviewer Catherine Threadgill described *Among the Free* as "a light, easy read that delivers what it promises." The novel's "brisk, efficient pacing," fueled by "abrupt plot turns," has successfully "cemented Haddix's strong following among both avid and reluctant readers," according to *Booklist* contributor Jennifer Mattson.

Like her "Shadow Children" series, many of Haddix's books for teen readers are futuristic novels. *Turnabout* is set in 2085, in a world where pavement is made of foam rubber and society favors singles. At the heart of the novel is the question: "What if people could turn back the aging clock?" Haddix explores this question through characters Melly and Anny Beth, aged 100 and 103 respectively. When readers meet them, the year is 2001 and Melly and Anny Beth reside in a nursing home. As participants in an experiment to "un-age," the two women are given PT-1, a drug in the Project Turnabout program that will reverse the aging process, allowing the participant to grow younger every year until they reach a self-determined perfect age. At that point, they will receive another injection which will stop the process. The only problem is that this second shot proves fatal, and now the members of Project Turnabout are doomed to continue "un-aging" until they reach age zero. The novel switches between the present and 2085 when Melly and Anny Beth have reached their teens. While they are desperate to find someone to parent them as they grow increasingly younger, a reporter has gotten wind of the project and is trying to contact Melly. Publicity would destroy any chance of privacy these refugees from age have, and now their challenge is to flee from unwanted exposure.

A contributor to *Publishers Weekly* described *Turnabout* as a "thought-provoking science fiction adventure," adding that Haddix "keeps the pacing smooth and builds up to a surprising face-off." Debbie Carton, reviewing the novel in *Booklist,* wrote that the need for love and protection "is poignantly conveyed, as is the isolation of the elderly in society." Carton also suggested that Haddix's book "will provoke lively discussion in middle-school book clubs." In *School Library Journal* Beth Wright commented that, although the novel's futuristic setting "is scarily believable," the themes addressed in *Turnabout* will spark "thoughtful discussion about human life and human potential."

Time travel of a different sort is the focus of Haddix's "Missing" series, which follows the adventures of two boys who are misplaced in time in *Found, Sent, Sabotaged,* and *Torn.* In *Found* thirteen-year-old friends Jonah and Chip are adopted. When both boys receive the same strange letter, warning them of an impending threat, they join together to solve the mystery. In the process, they also discover that their pasts are linked with those of thirty-six other teens who, as babies, were pulled from early deaths in other historical epoch s. Given a new life as passengers on a mysterious aircraft, they were ultimately discovered abandoned in this aircraft, with no adults on board, in the late twentieth century. Reviewing the novel in *Booklist,* Lisa Von Drasek wrote that in *Found* "Haddix once again demonstrates her talent for penning page-turners kids will like," while *School Library Journal* contributor Heather M. Campbell noted that the book's fast-paced story "is driven by an exciting plot" that leads to a "cliff-hanger ending" guaranteed to "leave readers . . . begging for more."

Chip and Jonah return in *Sent,* as Chip uses a time-travel device called the Elucidator to travel back to his rightful place in time—the mid-1400s—along with another boy named Alex. Providentially, Jonah and friend Katherine travel back in time as well, as the group discovers that Chip and Alex are in fact the ill-fated English princes Edward and Richard. Trapped in the Tower of London, the boys are destined to be murdered by their uncle, Richard of Gloucester, the man who will eventual become England's King Richard III. As the boy's ill-fated destiny unfolds, James must find a way to return them to the future without disturbing the historical record. *Sabotaged* continues the adventures of the two friends, as they attempt to aid a fellow time traveler named Andrea after they learn that she is actually Virginia Dare, the first child born to the English colonists on Roanoke Island and destined to disappear without a trace along with the rest of the Roanoke Colony less than three years after her birth in 1587. When the Elucidator goes missing, James and Chip learn that Andrea sabotaged their journey, encouraged by a mysterious stranger who promised that he could help her modern-day parents avoid a fatal car crash. Praising the mix of adventure and history in *Sent,* Necia Blundy wrote in *School Library Journal* that "Haddix ratchets up the tension here, letting it mount in moment-by-moment near misses and escapes," while also positing some "interesting 'what if'" questions about the still-unsolved real-life mystery of the princes in the tower.

Memories of an alien past haunt fifteen-year-old Kira in *Escape from Memory,* a standalone novel that, like the "Missing" series, features time-travel elements. When a successful attempt at hypnosis during a sleep-over party unlocks visions of an exotic world and a mother very different from the woman raising her, the Ohio teen is determined to discover the truth behind these visions. Her quest takes her to Crythe, a small, Eastern European enclave of Roman descendants. Efforts to learn about her past soon draw Kira and her family into danger in a story that *Booklist* contributor John Green described as "tightly plotted and *Matrix*-esque in its thought-provoking complexity." "A startling and intricate thriller," in the opinion of a *Kirkus Reviews* writer, *Escape from Memory* treats readers to an "exciting adventure, climaxing in a tense armed standoff."

Haddix's mysteries *Double Identity* and *The House on the Gulf* are set squarely in the contemporary world. Praised by a *Publishers Weekly* contributor as "another suspenseful pageturner" by Haddix, *Double Identity* finds thirteen-year-old Bethany Cole worried. Her mom is constantly crying and her dad is acting unusually overprotective. Then, out of the blue, Dad drives her out to Illinois and leaves her at the home of Aunt Myrlie, with no explanation. Living with a relative she never knew, the teen is full of questions. As she attempts to understand the strange behavior of the adults around her, a looming danger unearths family secrets which force Bethany to reinterpret her own life. "Haddix conveys Bethany's dismay and fear through believable dialogue and thoughts," the *Publishers Weekly* reviewer noted, while in *Booklist* Kay Weisman cited the author's "carefully crafted, gripping prose" and her ability to smoothly introduce "secondary themes concerning cloning ethics and personal identity." "Bethany's courage and intelligence will win over readers," concluded Claire Rosser in a *Kliatt* review of *Double Identity.*

Although twelve-year-old Britt is excited when older brother Bran finds a house-sitting job that will let the family exchange their small apartment for a beach house during the summer, this proves not to be the case as the events of *The House on the Gulf* play out. Suddenly, Bran becomes rude and secretive, and Britt is determined to discover the reason for his change in behavior. First she learns that her brother has only been hired to mow the lawn for the vacationing homeowners, but Britt finds that this is only a partial explanation as Haddix's story takes numerous twists and turns. While noting that the complex plot in *The House on the Gulf* "stretches credibility" at times, Britt's first-person narration "makes riveting reading," according to *Booklist* critic Carolyn Phelan.

The versatile Haddix has crossed other genre boundaries on occasion, turning to fantasy in both *Just Ella* and *Palace of Mirrors* and historical fiction in *Uprising. Just Ella* presents the aftermath of the Cinderella story, as the charmed young teen finds life in the royal palace stifling and hardly worth the lifelong love of Prince Charming. Another royal family figures in *Palace of Mirrors,* as fourteen-year-old Cecilia battles imposters and danger in her attempt to gain her rightful position as princess of the kingdom of Suala. Calling *Palace of Mirrors* "a lively companion to *Just Ella,*" Caitlin Augusta added in her *School Library Journal* review that Haddix weaves humor and likeable characters into a story in which "the suspense builds to a well-paced climax." A *Kirkus Reviews* writer dubbed the same novel "plenty of fun."

Sharing unfortunate circumstances, immigrants Bella and Yetta, along with friend Jane, watch their livelihood go up in flames during the deadly Triangle Shirtwaist Factory fire that is the focus of *Uprising.* Set amid the events leading up to the 1911 fire as well as featuring 1927 flashbacks in which only one of the three will survive to recall the tragedy, *Uprising* was praised by Rosser as "a dramatic story, filled with all the elements we like: friendship, romance, bravery, and suspense." Writing that Haddix's "deftly crafted historical novel unfolds dramatically," Renee Steinberg added in her *School Library Journal* review that the tale is made the more riveting due to "well-drawn characters who readily evoke empathy and compassion."

Haddix dabbles in supernatural mystery in *Claim to Fame,* where sixteen-year-old Lindsay Scott suffers from a problem that has already destroyed her promising career as a child actor. No matter how far away from the speaker, Lindsay can hear every word uttered about her, and the constant chatter in her mind has prevented her from continuing a career that would keep her in the news. Home has been her only refuge for five years, but when her father dies a pair of local ruffians forces her out in the world again. As the reclusive Lindsay braves the outside world once more, she learns the reason for her ability as a "hearer," and also uncovers some important secrets about her family's past. Writing that the teen's "powers have fascinating, sometimes heartbreaking results" in Haddix's "compelling" story, a *Publishers Weekly* reviewer called *Claim to Fame* a "thought-provoking story," while in *School Library Journal* Tracy Weiskind predicted that teen readers "will relate to [Lindsay's] . . . feelings of isolation and the need for others' help" in coping with her own future. Praising Haddix's ability to create identifiable characters, a *Kirkus Reviews* writer also enjoyed *Claim to Fame,* calling it "an intriguing and often exciting" coming-of-age story that resolves into "a parable about finding the strength to confront fears."

A prolific writer, Haddix continues to entertain young readers and teens with entertaining and thought-provoking novels that can be difficult to put down. Her background in journalism helps fuel her meticulous, well-researched plots, allowing her to challenge older readers while also entertaining them. In fact, creating fiction that is able to engage children on its own merits is her primary goal as a writer. "Like the library programs where you read so many minutes and win a prize at the end of the summer," Haddix commented in an interview for the *Akron Beacon Journal,* "I like seeing the emphasis on reading, but I'm almost afraid the more we push it, the more [young readers] will think of it like broccoli or spinach, that it doesn't taste good or isn't fun. I'd like to see them pick up a book and read it and not think 'I've read for fifteen minutes.' The more they read and begin to enjoy it, the more likely they are to continue."

Biographical and Critical Sources

PERIODICALS

Akron Beacon Journal, November 2, 2000, interview with Haddix, p. E10.

Booklist, October 1, 1995, Mary Harris Veeder, review of *Running out of Time,* p. 314; October 15, 1996, Jean Franklin, review of *Don't You Dare Read This, Mrs. Dunphrey,* p. 413; December 15, 1997, Ilene Cooper, review of *Leaving Fishers,* p. 691; September 1, 1999, Shelle Rosenfeld, review of *Just Ella,* p. 123; October 15, 2000, Debbie Carton, review of *Turnabout,* p. 431; April 15, 2001, Sally Estes, review of *Among the Imposters,* p. 1557; November 15, 2001, Gillian Engberg, review of *Takeoffs and Landings,* p. 565; May, 15, 2003, Ed Sullivan, review of *Among the Barons,* p. 1661; September 1, 2003, John Green, review of *Escape from Memory,* p. 114; February 15, 2004, Lauren Peterson, review of *Say What?,* p. 1059; May 15, 2004, Carolyn Phelan, review of *Among the Brave,* p.

1619; September 1, 2004, Carolyn Phelan, review of *The House on the Gulf,* p. 124; June 1, 2005, Jennifer Mattson, review of *Among the Enemy,* p. 1809; October 1, 2005, Kay Weisman, review of *Double Identity,* p. 58; June 1, 2006, John Peters, review of *Among the Free,* p. 70; September 15, 2007, Lynn Rutan, review of *Uprising,* p. 66; May 1, 2008, Lisa Von Drasek, review of *Found,* p. 47; July 1, 2008, Jennifer Hubert, review of *Palace of Mirrors,* p. 55; August 1, 2009, Cindy Welch, review of *Sent,* p. 60.

Bulletin of the Center for Children's Books, November, 1995, Roger Sutton, review of *Running out of Time,* p. 91; January, 1997, review of *Don't You Dare Read This, Mrs. Dunphrey,* p. 172; November, 1999, review of *Just Ella,* pp. 93-94; July, 2000, review of *Turnabout,* p. 402; September, 2001, review of *Among the Impostors,* p. 17; October, 2002, review of *Among the Betrayed,* p. 58; November, 2003, Elizabeth Bush, review of *Escape from Memory,* p. 105; April, 2004, Karen Coats, review of *Say What?,* p. 329; October, 2004, Timnah Card, review of *The House on the Gulf,* p. 75; November, 2005, Deborah Stevenson, review of *Double Identity,* p. 138; April, 2007, Hope Morrison, review of *Dexter the Tough,* p. 330.

Kirkus Reviews, October 1, 1997, review of *Leaving Fishers,* p. 1532; July 1, 2001, review of *Takeoffs and Landings,* p. 938; May 15, 2002, review of *Among the Betrayed,* p. 733; August 15, 2003, review of *Escape from Memory,* p. 1073; January 1, 2004, review of *Say What?,* p. 37; August 1, 2004, review of *The House on the Gulf,* p. 741; September 15, 2005, review of *Double Identity,* p. 1027; November 15, 2006, review of *Dexter the Tough,* p. 1174; September 1, 2007, review of *Uprising,* p. 196; April 1, 2008, review of *Found;* August 1, 2008, review of *Palace of Mirrors;* July 1, 2009, review of *Sent;* October 1, 2009, review of *Claim to Fame.*

Kliatt, September, 2003, Claire Rosser, review of *Escape from Memory,* p. 8; September, 2005, Claire Rosser, review of *Double Identity,* p. 8; September, 2007, Claire Rosser, review of *Uprising,* p. 13.

Publishers Weekly, June 11, 2001, review of *Among the Imposters,* p. 86; June 10, 2002, review of *Among the Betrayed,* p. 61; April 28, 2003, review of *Among the Barons,* p. 71; October 13, 2003, review of *Escape from Memory,* p. 80; January 26, 2004, review of *Say What?,* p. 254; December 19, 2005, review of *Double Identity,* p. 66; January 1, 2007, review of *Dexter the Tough,* p. 50; September 24, 2007, review of *Uprising,* p. 73; March 17, 2008, review of *Found,* p. 71; November 23, 2009, review of *Claim to Fame,* p. 57.

School Library Journal, August, 2001, B. Allison Gray, review of *Takeoffs and Landings,* p. 182; February, 2004, Susan Patron, review of *Say What?,* p. 113; March, 2004, Farida S. Dowler, review of *Escape from Memory,* p. 212; June, 2004, review of *Among the Brave,* p. 143; October, 2004, Saleena L. Davidson, review of *The House on the Gulf,* p. 165; November, 2005, Michele Capozzella, review of *Double Identity,* p. 136; August, 2006, Catherine Threadgill, review of *Among the Free,* p. 120; January, 2007, Catherine

Callegari, review of *Dexter the Tough,* p. 97; September, 2007, Renee Steinberg, review of *Uprising,* p. 196; May, 2008, Heather M. Campbell, review of *Found,* p. 124; November, 2008, Caitlin Augusta, review of *Palace of Mirrors,* p. 122; October, 2009, Necia Blundy, review of *Sent,* p. 126; December, 2009, Tracy Weiskind, review of *Claim to Fame,* p. 118; July, 2010, Cheri Dobbs, review of *Sabotaged,* p. 88.

Voice of Youth Advocates, December, 1995, Ann Welton, review of *Running out of Time,* p. 302; Jamie S. Hansen, review of *Don't You Dare Read This, Mrs. Dunphrey,* p. 270; February, 1998, Beverly Youree, review of *Leaving Fishers,* p. 386; October, 1998, Debbie Earl, review of *Among the Hidden,* p. 283; December, 1999, Cynthia Grady, review of *Just Ella,* p. 346; August, 2001, Brenda Moses-Allen, review of *Among the Imposters,* p. 213; June, 2002, review of *Among the Betrayed,* p. 126; August, 2003, review of *Among the Barons,* p. 236; October, 2003, review of *Escape from Memory,* p. 324; August, 2004, review of *Among the Brave,* p. 230; October, 2005, review of *Double Identity,* p. 323; February, 2006, review of *Among the Free,* p. 487.

ONLINE

Cincinnati Library Web site, http://www.cincinnatilibrary. org/ (March 15, 2008), "Margaret Peterson Haddix."

Fantastic Fiction Web site, http://www.fantasticviction.co. uk/ (March 15, 2008), "Margaret Peterson Haddix."

Margaret Haddix Peterson Home Page, http://www.haddix books.com (December 27, 2010).*

*   *   *

HANSEN, Thore 1942-

Personal

Born January 10, 1942, in Fredrikstad, Norway. *Education:* Attended Kunstakademiet (Copenhagen, Denmark).

Addresses

Home—Frederikstad, Norway.

Career

Author and comics artist. Comics author, beginning 1960; illustrator of role-playing game Itras By.

Awards, Honors

Kultur-og kirkedepartementets pris, 1988, for *Skogland;* Nordisk Skolebibliotekarforenings Børnebogspris, 2002, for "Skogland" series; Bokkunstprisen for illustration, 2004; Kong Frederiks Hederspris, 2007; Hans Christian Andersen Award nomination for illustration (Norway), 2010.

Writings

SELF-ILLUSTRATED; FOR CHILDREN

Grimaster (short stories), 1975.

De flygende hvaler land, Gyldendal (Oslo, Norway), 1976.

Leonard R. Wompers vidunderlige hemmelighet, Gyldendal (Oslo, Norway), 1978.

Drømmen om de blomstrende kaninene, Gyldendal (Oslo, Norway), 1979.

Bobadillas cirkus eller: Den dagen toget gikk fem minutter før tiden, Gyldendal (Oslo, Norway), 1980.

Huset på den skarlagensrøde sletten, Gyldendal (Oslo, Norway), 1982.

Lyset fra heksas hus, Gyldendal (Oslo, Norway), 1984.

Skumringer: tre fortellinger, Tiden (Oslo, Norway), 1984.

Tor og Midgardsormen: gammel forteller, Gyldendal (Oslo, Norway), 1984.

Han som lengtet til stjernene, Gyldendal (Oslo, Norway), 1985.

Kunsten å leve lat en tilfred i en verden som vår, Tiden (Oslo, Norway), 1990.

Der elven gjør en sving, Gyldendal (Oslo, Norway), 1991.

En vind fylt av tusen sommere, Gyldendal (Oslo, Norway), 1994.

Vår verden, Victoria, Gyldendal (Oslo, Norway), 1995.

Høstfabel, Gyldendal (Oslo, Norway), 1996.

Sindbad sjøfareren, Gyldendal (Oslo, Norway), 2000.

Ali Baba og de 40 røverne, Gyldendal (Oslo, Norway), 2001.

Sjør verdronningen, Gyldendal (Oslo, Norway), 2002.

Bobadilla Brun og den udødelige makrellen, Gyldendal (Oslo, Norway), 2003.

Enhjørninger gresser i skumring, Gyldendal (Oslo, Norway), 2004.

Madagaskar, Gyldendal (Oslo, Norway), 2005.

Hombabo og jeg mater fuglene, Gyldendal (Oslo, Norway), 2008.

Hombabo og jeg møter indianere, Gyldendal (Oslo, Norway), 2009.

Creator of comics, including "Papegøye Olsen" for *Vi Menn,* 1963; "Satyren," for *Alle Menn,* beginning 1967; (with Jon Bing) "Fare, Fare Krigsmann," 1972; (with Bing) "Stasjon Nexus"; "Old," for *Magne,* c. 1980s; and "Fabelsvansen," for *Norsk Barneblad.*

"SKOGLAND" SERIES: SELF-ILLUSTRATED; FOR CHILDREN

Skogland: Gutten i dragereiret, Gyldendal (Oslo, Norway), 1988.

Reisen til den glemte byen, Gyldendal (Oslo, Norway), 1989.

Dragebyen, Gyldendal (Oslo, Norway), 1990.

Demonene ved elvens munning, Gyldendal (Oslo, Norway), 1992.

Der skogstiene møtes, Gyldendal (Oslo, Norway), 1993.

Frost og varme, Gyldendal (Oslo, Norway), 1997.

Den vidunderlige leken, Gyldendal (Oslo, Norway), 1998.

Alvens lengsel, Gyldendal (Oslo, Norway), 1999.

Skogene kommer, Gyldendal (Oslo, Norway), 2001.

OTHER

Satyren, Gyldendal (Oslo, Norway), 1976.

Karivold, Gyldendal (Oslo, Norway), 1978.

Båsen, Gyldendal (Oslo, Norway), 1983.

Skumringer, Gyldendal (Oslo, Norway), 1984.

Smilende streker (humor), Gyldendal (Oslo, Norway), 1986.

Båsen & Co., Gyldendal (Oslo, Norway), 1988.

Død manns blues, Gyldendal (Oslo, Norway), 1989.

Kunsten å leve lat & tilfreds i en verden som vår (humor), Gyldendal (Oslo, Norway), 1990.

Kunsten å unngå erotiske tilnærmelser (humor), Gyldendal (Oslo, Norway), 1991.

Kunsten å tilberede den perfekte makrellsuppe (humor), Gyldendal (Oslo, Norway), 1991.

Blues for en aldrende morder (adult novel), Gyldendal (Oslo, Norway), 2004.

Død manns Zarzuela (adult novel), Gyldendal (Oslo, Norway), 2006.

ILLUSTRATOR

Tor Åge Bringsværd, *Det Blaå Folket og karamellfabrikken,* Gyldendal (Oslo, Norway), 1974.

Tor Åge Bringsværd, *En gang til!,* Gyldendal (Oslo, Norway), 1985.

Fartein Horgar, *Ridder Remi: gutten som ble skylt ut med badevennaet,* Eide (Bergen Norway), 1992.

Anne Østgaard, *Historien om Oscar,* Gyldendal (Oslo, Norway), 1996.

Gustav Lorentzen, *Hest i huset: snille og ville vers,* Gyldendal (Oslo, Norway), 1999.

Bjarte Bjørkum, *Skatten på Snørøverøya,* Gyldendal (Oslo, Norway), 2000.

Knut Fredrik Samset, *Elmers klode,* Fritt (Norway), 2010.

Illustrator of numerous other books published in Norway.

ILLUSTRATOR; "RUFFEN" SERIES

Tor Åge Bringsværd, *Ruffen, den sjøormen som ikke kunne svømme,* Bokklubben (Oslo, Norway), 1972, translated as *Ruffen: The Sea Serpent Who Couldn't Swim,* MacKenzie Smiles (Smyrna, TN), 2008.

Tor Åge Bringsværd, *Ruffen på nye eventyr,* Bokklubben (Oslo, Norway), 1975, translated by James Anderson as *Ruffen Escapes to Loch Ness,* MacKenzie Smiles (Smyrna, TN), 2009.

Tor Åge Bringsværd, *Ruffen og den flyvende hollender,* Bokklubben (Oslo, Norway), 1982.

Tor Åge Bringsværd, *Den store boken om Ruffen,* Bokklubben (Oslo, Norway), 1998.

Tor Åge Bringsværd, *Ruffen og det mystiske hullet,* Bokklubben (Oslo, Norway), 2005.

Tor Åge Bringsværd, *Ruffen og drageslottet,* Gyldendal (Oslo, Norway), 2006.

Tor Åge Bringsværd, *Ruffen og det hemmelige havfolket,* Bokklubben (Oslo, Norway), 2007.

Tor Åge Bringsværd, *Den store Ruffenboken,* Bokklubben (Oslo, Norway), 2008.

Biographical and Critical Sources

PERIODICALS

Bookbird, April, 2010, "Thore Hansen: Norway Illustrator."

Children's Bookwatch, September, 2008, review of *Ruffen: The Sea Serpent Who Couldn't Swim.*

Kirkus Reviews, September 15, 2008, review of *Ruffen.*

School Library Journal, May, 2009, Marianne Saccardi, review of *Ruffen Escapes to Loch Ness,* p. 71.

ONLINE

Gyldendal Norsk Forlag Web site, http://www.gyldendal.no/ (December 27, 2010), "Thore Hansen."*

*   *   *

HARTMAN, Bob 1955-

Personal

Born 1955; married; children: two. *Religion:* Baptist.

Addresses

Home—Pittsburgh, PA.

Career

Storyteller, author, and pastor. Baptist minister; youth pastor in Pittsburgh, PA. Recordings include *First Love,* 1999. Presenter at schools, libraries, festivals, and museums.

Writings

Lobster for Lunch, illustrated by JoEllen McAllister Stammen, Down East Books (Camden, ME), 1992.

Johnny Thumbs, illustrated by Richard Max Kolding, Standard Publishing (Cincinnati, OH), 1993.

The Birthday of a King, illustrated by Michael McGuire, Victor Books (Wheaton, IL), 1993.

The Edge of the River, illustrated by Michael McGuire, Victor Books (Wheaton, IL), 1993.

The Middle of the Night, illustrated by Michael McGuire, Victor Books (Wheaton, IL), 1993.

The Morning of the World, illustrated by Michael McGuire, Victor Books (Wheaton, IL), 1993.

The One and Only Delgado Cheese: A Tale of Talent, Fame, and Friendship, illustrated by Donna Kae Nelson, Lion Publishing (Batavia, IL), 1993.

Aunt Mabel's Table, illustrated by Richard Max Kolding, Standard Publishing (Cincinnati, OH), 1994.

Who Brought the Bread?: A Bible Mystery, Standard Publishing (Cincinnati, OH), 1994.

Who Wrecked the Roof?: A Bible Mystery, illustrated by Terri Steiger, Standard Publishing (Cincinnati, OH), 1994.

A Night the Stars Danced for Joy, illustrated by Tim Jonke, Lion Publishing (Colorado Springs, CO), 1996.

Cheer Up Chicken!, illustrated by Mike Spoor, Lion Publishing (Colorado Springs, CO), 1998.

Early Saints of God, foreword by Walter Wangerin, Jr, illustrated by Doug Oudekerk, Augsburg (Minneapolis, MN), 1998.

The Lion Storyteller Bedtime Book, illustrated by Susie Poole, Lion Publishing (Colorado Springs, CO), 1998, new edition, illustrated by Krisztina Kállai Nagy, 2009.

Brother Gabriel and the Secret of Christmas: A Family Read-aloud Book, illustrated by Matthew Archambault, Augsburg (Minneapolis, MN), 1999.

Silly Stories: Three Fun-to-read-aloud Stories with a Message, illustrated by Nancy Ellen Hird, Standard Publishing (Cincinnati, OH), 1999.

The Easter Angels, illustrated by Tim Jonke, Lion Publishing (Colorado Springs, CO), 1999, illustrated by Sophy Williams, Lion Children's (Oxford, England), 2009.

Time to Go, Hippo!, illustrated by Kate Siimpson, Lion Children's Books (Colorado Springs, CO), 1999.

Bible Bad Guys, illustrated by Ron Tiner, Augsburg (Minneapolis, MN), 2000.

Granny Mae's Christmas Play, illustrated by Lynne Cravath, Augsburg (Minneapolis, MN), 2001.

More Bible Bad Guys—and Gals, illustrated by Jeff Anderson, Augsburg Fortress (Minneapolis, MN), 2001.

Parables to Learn By: Based on Stories Told by Jesus, illustrated by Terry Julien, Pauline Books & Media (Boston, MA), 2001.

Anyone Can Tell a Story: Bob Hartman's Guide to Storytelling, Lion (Oxford, England), 2002.

The Wolf Who Cried Boy, illustrated by Tim Raglin, Putnam's Sons (New York, NY), 2002.

Grumblebunny, illustrated by David Clark, G.P. Putnam's Sons (New York, NY), 2003.

Polly and the Frog and Other Folk Tales, Brett Hudson, Lion Children's (Oxford, England), 2004.

The Noisy Stable, illustrated by Brett Hudson, Lion Children's (Oxford, England), 2004.

The Littlest Camel, and Other Christmas Stories, illustrated by Brett Hudson, Lion Children's (Oxford, England), 2004.

Noah's Big Boat, illustrated by Janet Samuel, Lion Children's (Oxford, England), 2006.

Telling the Bible: One Hundred Stories to Read out Loud, Lion Children's (Oxford, England), 2006.

Dinner in the Lions' Den, illustrated by Tim Raglin, Lion's Children (Oxford, England), 2006, G.P. Putnam's Sons (New York, NY), 2007.

The Three Billy Goats' Stuff, illustrated by Jacqueline East, Lion's Children (Oxford, England), 2007, Lion (New York, NY), 2009.

The Lion Storyteller Easter Book, illustrated by Nadine Wickenden, Lion Children's (Oxford, England), 2007.

The Lion Storyteller Bible, illustrated by Krisztina Kállai Nagy, Lion Children's (Oxford, England), 2008.

Stories from the Stable, Lion Children's (Oxford, England), 2008.

Carol: A New Christmas Story, Lion (Oxford, England), 2009.

The Lion Storyteller Christmas Book, illustrated by Krisztina Kállai Nagy, Lion Children's (Oxford, England), 2010.

Telling the Gospel: Seventy Stories about Jesus to Read out Loud, Lion Children's (Oxford, England), 2010.

The Lion Storyteller Book of Animal Tales, illustrated by Krisztina Kállai Nagy, Lion Children's (Oxford, England), 2011.

Author's work has been translated into Welsh.

Sidelights

Bob Hartman is a pastor and storyteller whose performances for children include retelling tales from the Bible as well as traditional folk stories from many countries which feature both humor and a child-friendly twist. In addition to working with audiences and teaching storytelling, Hartman has also created several book-length collections of stories, among them *Stories from the Stable, The Lion Storyteller Christmas Book, The Lion Storyteller Book of Animals,* and *Telling the Bible: One Hundred Stories to Read Aloud.* He also shares his years of performance experience in *Anyone Can Tell a Story: Bob Hartman's Guide to Storytelling.* Noting the diverse sources drawn on by Hartman in *The Lion Storyteller Book of Animal Stories, School Library Journal* critic Jane Barrer recommended the book to teachers as a good choice for "relaxing and listening [to] at the end of the day."

While the majority of Hartman's books collect tales with a shared theme, some, such as *Grumblebunny, A Night the Stars Danced for Joy, The Noisy Stable,* and *Dinner in the Lion's Den,* feature solo stories that are paired with engaging illustrations. In *Dinner in the Lion's Den* Hartman retells the story of King Darius and Daniel, replacing the bloodcurdling themes of the original with a "lighthearted tone" and Tim Raglin's "cartoon artwork," according to *School Library Journal* reviewer Shelley B. Sutherland. Featuring colorful illustrations by David Clark, *Grumblebunny* plays on the tendency for all picture-book bunnies to be loving and cuddly. Unlike his cousins, the appropriately named Cuddlemop, Pretty, and Sweetsnuffle, Grumblebunny is a curmudgeonly creature who never enjoys a sunny day.

His discontented nature serves him well, however, when all four bunnies are captured by a hungry wolf with ideas about cooking up some rabbit stew for dinner. In *Publishers Weekly* a critic noted of *Grumblebunny* that "Hartman's ironic sense" creates a "delectably twisted" parody of standard picture books and Clark adds even more humor in his "deep-toned watercolors" featuring the buck-toothed characters.

In *The Wolf Who Cried Boy* and *The Three Billy Goats' Stuff* Hartman gives a whimsical spin to a pair of well-known stories by factoring human children into the action. In *The Wolf Who Cried Boy,* for example, Little Wolf is tired of the lamb, deer, and muskrat that are served up for dinner each night, so he demands that boy-burgers be served instead. Fortunately, when a real boy appears at the door of the family wolf den—in the form of a boy scout who has become separated from his troop during a forest hike—Little Wolf shows that his dinner-table demands have all been made in fun. Calling *The Wolf Who Cried Boy* "a fun twist on a traditional tale," Donna L. Scanlon added in *School Library Journal* that the "spare storytelling style" of the text is paired with pen-and-ink illustrations by Raglin that "are packed with nifty details." Hartman's artful humor combines with "the time-honored message that truthfulness pays, make this a wonderful addition to any fairy-tale collection," concluded a *Kirkus Reviews* writer, while in *Horn Book* Peter D. Sieruta praised *The Wolf Who Cried Boy* for its "upside-down version of the familiar fable" and the slapstick comedy in its "cartoonish pen-and-ink illustrations."

Hartman's version of "The Three Billy Goats' Gruff" gains a new setting and supporting cast in *The Three Billy Goats' Stuff,* a picture book illustrated by Jacqueline East. Instead of lurking under a bridge, the troll in this version hides under the climbing ladder on a school playground. Although the students—goats and other assorted creatures—tire of being bullied by the troll, who constantly demands that they relinquish various possessions in order to complete their climb, it is up to a brave little billy goat to report the problem to school authorities. In *School Library Journal* Michele Sealander wrote that Hartman's intent is to make his "unique retelling . . . a cautionary tale about bullying," and a *Kirkus Reviews* critic acknowledged the author's success by noting that "the fun's in the text" of his "fractured-fairy-tale read-aloud."

In addition to including several of his favorite stories in *Anyone Can Tell a Story,* Hartman discusses his belief in the ability of stories to share basic values and traditions. The book also includes tale-telling techniques and sources to mine for stories, Sharing his own storytelling inspiration in an online interview for the Lion Hudson Web site, Hartman explained: "I remember things that happened to me when I was a child. Or I retell stories other people have told—local legends, or tales from long ago. I love to retell stories from the

Bible; I find that crawling into a text, asking questions and then coming out the other side is the best way to discover what it's all about—to be surprised, challenged, moved, and won over."

Biographical and Critical Sources

PERIODICALS

Booklist, July, 2002, Ilene Cooper, review of *The Wolf Who Cried Boy,* p. 1860.

Horn Book, May-June, 2002, Peter D. Sieruta, review of *The Wolf Who Cried Boy,* p. 314.

Kirkus Reviews, April 1, 2002, review of *The Wolf Who Cried Boy,* p. 491; June 15, 2009, review of *The Three Billy Goats' Stuff.*

Publishers Weekly, July 20, 1992, review of *Lobsters for Lunch,* p. 248; September 30, 1996, review of *A Night the Stars Danced for Joy,* p. 92; September 27, 1999, review of *Brother Gabriel and the Secret of Christmas: A Family Read-aloud Book,* p. 62; September 24, 2001, review of *Granny Mae's Christmas Play,* p. 50; April, 2002, review of *The Wolf Who Cried Boy,* p. 491; May 5, 2003, review of *Grumblebunny,* p. 220; August, 2004, Jane Barrer, review *The Lion Storyteller Book of Animal Tales,* p. 108; January 29, 2007, review of *Dinner in the Lions' Den,* 75.

School Library Journal, June, 2002, Donna L. Scanlon, review of *The Wolf Who Cried Boy,* p. 97; July, 2003, Kathy Piehl, review of *Grumblebunny,* 98; April, 2007, Shelley B. Sutherland, review of *Dinner in the Lions' Den,* p. 122; August, 2009, Michele Sealander, review of *The Three Billy Goats' Stuff,* p. 76.

ONLINE

Lion Hudson Web site, http://www.lionhudson.com/ (December 15, 2010), "Bob Hartman."*

*   *   *

HAVEL, Jennifer
See HAVILL, Juanita

*   *   *

HAVILL, Juanita 1949-
(Jennifer Havel)

Personal

Born May 11, 1949, in Evansville, IN; daughter of Frank Walden (an oil producer) and Ruth Denise (a homemaker) Havill; married Pierre Masure (a technical writer), 1976; children: Laurence Aimee, Pierre Gustav.

Education: Attended Université de Rouen, 1969-70; University of Illinois at Urbana-Champaign, B.A. (English and French), 1971, M.A. (English and French), 1973. *Hobbies and other interests:* Movies, music, swimming.

Addresses

Home and office—28232 N. 58th St., Cave Creek, AZ 85331.

Career

Author and educator. Freelance writer, beginning 1981. Translator for companies in France and United States; adjunct writing instructor at École Bi-Lingue de Fontainebleau, Wabash Valley College, The Loft, Writer's Voice Project, Phoenix College, Ottawa University, Phoenix, and Pima Community College; WestEd, consultant, 2007-08. Worked in personnel department, Organisation for Economic Cooperation and Development, Paris, France.

Member

Authors Guild, Authors League, Society of Children's Book Writers and Illustrators, Children's Reading Roundtable, Phi Beta Kappa.

Awards, Honors

Child Study Children's Book Award, Bank Street College, Children's Choices designation, Children's Trade Books, and Children's Book of the Year selection, Library of Congress, all 1986, and Ezra Jack Keats New Writer Award, 1987, all for *Jamaica's Find;* Child Study Children's Book Award, Bank Street College, 1989, and Mrs. Bush's Story Hour selection, 1992-93, both for *Jamaica Tag-Along;* Minnesota Book Award nomination, 1991, for *Leona and Ike.*

Writings

PICTURE BOOKS

Leroy and the Clock, illustrated by Janet Wentworth, Houghton (Boston, MA), 1988.

The Magic Fort, illustrated by Linda Shute, Houghton (Boston, MA), 1991.

Treasure Nap, illustrated by Elivia Savadier, Houghton (Boston, MA), 1992.

Sato and the Elephants, illustrated by Jean and Mou-Sien Tseng, Lothrop (New York, NY), 1993.

Kentucky Troll (folktale), illustrated by Bert Dodson, Lothrop (New York, NY), 1993.

Jennifer, Too, illustrated by J.J. Smith-Moore, Hyperion (New York, NY), 1994.

Saving Owen's Toad, Hyperion (New York, NY), 1994.

Embarcadero Upset, Lothrop (New York, NY), 1999.

Juanita Havill's series chapter book **Jamaica and the Substitute Teacher** *features realistic artwork by Anne Sibley O'Brien.* (Illustration copyright © 1999 by Anne Sibley O'Brien. Reproduced by permission of Houghton Mifflin Harcourt Publishing Company.)

The Blue Racer, illustrated by Judy Love, Zaner-Bloser (Columbus, OH), 2004.

Zox, illustrated by Reggie Holladay, Zaner-Bloser (Columbus, OH), 2004.

The Lincoln Penny, illustrated by Larry Reinhart, Zaner-Bloser (Columbus, OH), 2004.

I Heard It from Alice Zucchini, and Other Poems about the Garden, illustrated by Christine Davenier, Chronicle Books (San Francisco, CA), 2005.

Just like a Baby, illustrated by Christine Davenier, Chronicle Books (San Francisco, CA), 2009.

"JAMAICA" PICTURE-BOOK SERIES

Jamaica's Find, illustrated by Anne Sibley O'Brien, Houghton (Boston, MA), 1986.

Jamaica Tag-Along, illustrated by Anne Sibley O'Brien, Houghton (Boston, MA), 1989.

Jamaica and Brianna, illustrated by Anne Sibley O'Brien, Houghton (Boston, MA), 1993.

Jamaica's Blue Marker, illustrated by Anne Sibley O'Brien, Houghton (Boston, MA), 1995.

Jamaica and the Substitute Teacher, illustrated by Anne Sibley O'Brien, Houghton (Boston, MA), 1999.

Brianna, Jamaica, and the Dance of Spring, illustrated by Anne Sibley O'Brien, Houghton (Boston, MA), 2002.

Jamaica Is Thankful, illustrated by Anne Sibley O'Brien, Houghton (Boston, MA), 2009.

NOVELS

It Always Happens to Leona, Crown (New York, NY), 1989.

Leona and Ike, Crown (New York, NY), 1990.
Eyes like Willy's, HarperCollins (New York, NY), 2004.
Grow (verse novel), illustrated by Stanislawa Kodman, Peachtree (Atlanta, GA), 2008.
Call the Horse Lucky, Gryphon Press (Minneapolis, MN), 2010.

OTHER

(Under pseudonym Jennifer Havel) *The Wacky Rulebook,* Parker Brothers, 1984.
I Love You More, Western Publishing, 1990.
(Editor) *Booklove: Creating Good Books for Children in an Age That Values Neither,* Phoenix College Press (Phoenix, AZ), 2000.

Contributor to periodicals, including *Cricket, Jack and Jill, U.S. Kids,* and *Children's Magic Window.*

Sidelights

Juanita Havill began her children's book career with *Jamaica's Find,* and her engaging young African-American heroine has continued to appear in other books in the years since. Apart from her "Jamaica" books, Havill has also written many other picture books and has also produced elementary-grade novels such as *Eyes like Willy's.* She turns to poetry in her verse novel *Grow,* while *I Heard It from Alice Zucchini, and Other Poems about the Garden* features short rhymes designed for the story-hour set. Illustrated by Christine Davenier, *I Heard It from Alice Zucchini* serves up "a bountiful harvest of

Grow, a novel in verse, pairs Havill's creative rhymes with artwork by Stanislawa Kodman. (Illustration © copyright 2008 by Stanislawa Kodman. All rights reserved. Reproduced courtesy of Peachtree Publishers.)

lyrical poems that expresses delight in the world of nature," according to *School Library Journal* contributor Teresa Pfeifer, and in *Booklist* Gillian Engberg noted that the range of its poems—from "factual" to "instructional"—"offer excellent opportunities for studying sound, imagery, and poetry's range."

"In a sense, even before I could print, I began to write," Havill once told *SATA.* "I dictated stories to my mother and she wrote them down for me. . . . When I went to school, I learned to print, then to write in cursive, and I experienced all the frustration of not being able to get the words down as fast as I thought them. I began to write down stories and ideas and poems."

In high school Havill wrote for her school newspaper, contributing editorials, articles, and even poetry. "I learned how to be straightforward and factual and how to argue in print, and I loved it." Following college, she found a job as a typist and then worked as a teacher and a translator. "I traveled and married, and when my children were born, I settled down to write. When I took a course in Minneapolis taught by Emilie Buchwald, I discovered my audience: young people. I have been writing for them ever since."

Readers first meet Jamaica in *Jamaica's Find,* which also introduces the girl's sometime-friend Brianna, her brother Ossie, and assorted teachers and classmates. After Brianna makes fun of Jamaica for wearing a pair of Ozzie's worn-out boots to school in *Jamaica and Brianna,* the clever young girl finds a way to make peace with her sometimes jealous friend, while in *Jamaica's Blue Marker* she realizes that the annoying scribbling of a classmate are actually caused by the lonely child's need for attention. In *Brianna, Jamaica, and the Dance of Spring* the fierce competition for plum parts in an upcoming ballet school recital ends when Brianna and sister Nikki both wind up with strep throat, while a pet kitten hidden by Jamaica causes the allergic Ozzie to suffer a sneezing fit in *Jamaica Is Thankful.*

Throughout her "Jamaica" series Havill "displays a clear grasp of what matters to children," noted a *Publishers Weekly* contributor in reviewing *Jamaica and Brianna,* adding that Havill's likeable young characters are convincingly brought to life in Anne Sibley O'Brien's detailed water-color illustrations. In a review for *Horn Book,* Maeve Visser Knoth commended the inclusion of multicultural elements—Brianna and her family are Asian American—and noted that both "text and illustrations work together to create a portrait of a warm family, ethnically diverse school, and close friendship between the two girls." Havill and O'Brien "work . . . well together in portraying realistic children in an ethnically diverse setting," asserted *School Library Journal* contributor Dorian Chong in a review of *Brianna, Jamaica, and the Dance of Spring,* while a *Kirkus Reviews* writer deemed the same book valuable in its focus on disappointment, "an issue that is hard for kids (and parents) to face," according to the critic.

Havill's entertaining childhood saga **Just like a Baby** *comes to life in Christina Davenier's lighthearted art.* (Illustration copyright © 2009 by Christine Davenier. Used with permission of Chronicle Books, LLC, San Francisco. Visit ChronicleBooks.com.)

In addition to the "Jamaica" books, Havill has also authored a number of stand-alone picture books. In *Jennifer, Too* she introduces a tag-along seven-year-old sister determined to prove herself as brave and adventurous as the older boys who play with her big brother. The realization of a young ivory carver—that in order for him to practice the craft of his ancestors elephants must be killed—is the focus of *Sato and the Elephants,* a picture book that *Booklist* contributor Deborah Abbott cited as an effective story to begin a discussion of the African ivory trade. Featuring artwork by Davenier, *Just like a Baby* finds a newly born baby given the advice of a host of loving relatives, each of whom encourages the infant to dedicate herself to his or her favorite career. From fisherman to truck driver to professional athlete, the conflicting aspirations of these family members ultimately prompt a loud yelp from the future adult in question. With its simple, large-scaled text and "bright, expressive" illustrations, *Just like a Baby* features a "message of doing whatever your heart desires [that] will appeal to all children," according to *School Library Journal* contributor Rachel Kamin.

In her middle-grade novel *Eyes like Willy's* Havill focuses on the meaning of friendship through her story of two young friends—one Austrian and one American—who grow up and find themselves on the opposite sides of the battlefield during World War I. Praising the history-themed tale in a *Booklist* review, Carolyn Phelan noted that *Eyes like Willy's* succeeds as a "spare, thoughtful story [that] does a superb job of personalizing the pain of this brutal, futile war."

Illustrated by Stanislawa Kodman, *Grow* is geared for slightly younger readers and captures the thoughts of a twelve year old as she watches her urban Minnesota

neighborhood come together to create a city garden. Near the building where Kate and her family live is a vacant lot that is littered with trash, but when boisterous ex-teacher Beneetha decides that it would be the perfect place for a garden, the woman has the determination and bossiness to make her vision a reality. Soon the lot is abustle with activity as neighbors young and old help dig, weed, plant, and water their fledgling garden, from troubled young people to local business owners to a fireman who works in the area and defends the neighbors' right to reclaim the unused land. Readers "will hear the freshness in Kate's voice as she delivers a message of hope and resilience," wrote a *Publishers Weekly* critic in a review of *Grow,* and *School Library Journal* contributor Anne Knickerbocker noted of the book that "Havill creates characters with depth" and her "verse . . . filled with meaningful phrases . . . is a joy to read." In her *Booklist* review of *Grow* Rochman recommended Davinier's "quiet, scribbly drawings" for the book, writing that they enhance Havill's story embracing "the power of working as a community."

Discussing her motivations as an author for children, Havill once explained: "I write to find out what I think, to give form to thought. That is why I have stacks of journals on my office floor. The act of writing helps me to get what is hidden out in the open so that I may examine it, study it, describe it, remember it, perhaps understand it."

Biographical and Critical Sources

PERIODICALS

Booklist, October 15, 1993, Hazel Rochman, review of *Jamaica and Brianna,* and Deborah Abbott, review of

Sato and the Elephants, both p. 452; June 1, 1994, Julie Corsaro, review of *Jennifer, Too,* p. 1820; July, 1995, Hazel Rochman, review of *Jamaica's Blue Marker,* p. 1883; February 15, 1999, Hazel Rochman, review of *Jamaica and the Substitute Teacher,* p. 1975; March 15, 2002, Hazel Rochman, review of *Briana, Jamaica, and the Dance of Spring,* p. 1262; March 1, 2004, Carolyn Phelan, review of *Eyes like Willy's,* p. 1189; April 1, 2006, Gillian Engberg, review of *I Heard It from Alice Zucchini: Poems about the Garden,* p. 45; June 1, 2008, Hazel Rochman, review of *Grow,* p. 74.

Horn Book, November-December, 1993, Maeve Visser Knoth, review of *Jamaica and Brianna,* p. 732; May, 1999, Terri Schmitz, review of *Jamaica and the Substitute Teacher,* p. 314.

Kirkus Reviews, February 15, 2002, review of *Brianna, Jamaica, and the Dance of Spring,* p. 257; May 15, 2004, review of *Eyes like Willy's,* p. 492; March 15, 2006, review of *I Heard It from Alice Zucchini,* p. 291; March 15, 2008, review of *Grow;* September 1, 2009, review of *Jamaica Is Thankful.*

Publishers Weekly, March 8, 1993, review of *Kentucky Troll,* p. 78; July 26, 1993, review of *Jamaica and Brianna,* p. 71; March 24, 2008, review of *Grow,* p. 70; March 9, 2009, review of *Just like a Baby,* p. 46.

School Library Journal, April, 2002, Dorian Chong, review of *Brianna, Jamaica, and the Dance of Spring,* p. 110; July, 2004, Kristen Oravec, review of *Eyes like Willy's,* p. 106; April, 2006, Teresa Pfeifer, review of *I Heard It from Alice Zucchini,* p. 126; May, 2008, Anne Knickerbocker, review of *Grow,* p. 126; June, 2009, Rachel Kamin, review of *Just like a Baby,* p. 90; October, 2009, Alyson Low, review of *Jamaica Is Thankful,* p. 94.

ONLINE

ChildrensLit.com, http://www.childrenslit.com/ (January 27, 2009), Anna Olswanger, "Juanita Havill."

Underdown.org, http://www.underdown.org/ (1998), Anna Olswanger, interview with Havill.

*   *   *

HEUVEL, Eric 1960-

Personal

Born May 25, 1960, in Amsterdam, Netherlands. *Education:* Attended college.

Addresses

Home—Zaandam, Netherlands.

Career

Comics artist and author and commercial illustrator. Formerly worked as a customs officer and history teacher. Creator of comic strips, including "Een avont-

uur van January Jones," "Bud Broadway," "Geheim van de tijd," "De zaak Sven," "Bureau Warmoestraat," and "Alleen Rond de wereld." *Military service:* Served in the Dutch military, 1980-82.

Awards, Honors

Three awards from Dutch Comics Association, including for *De ontdekking* and *De zoektocht.*

Writings

De avontuuren van meneer van Looij: kan ik effe vangen? (comic book), E/S Productions (Amsterdam, Netherlands), 1993.

De ontdekking (graphic novel), Big Balloon (Haarlem, Netherlands), 2003, translated by Lorraine T. Miller as *A Family Secret,* Farrar, Straus & Giroux (New York, NY), 2009.

De zaak Sven (collected comic strips), De Inktvis (Dordrecht, Netherlands), 2004.

De Schuilhoek, Markt 12 Museum (Aalten, Netherlands), 2005.

(With Ruud van der Rol and Lies Schippers) *De zoektocht* (graphic novel), Reproduct (Amsterdam, Netherlands), 2007, translated by Lorraine T. Miller as *The Search,* Farrar, Straus & Giroux Books for Young Readers (New York, NY), 2009.

Author and illustrator of comic strip "Bureau Warmoestraat," beginning 2007; illustrator of comic strip "Alleen Rond de wereld," by Rob van Bavel, beginning 2009. Contributor to periodicals, including *Algemeen Dagblad, Eppo, Het Parool, Krest, Rebel Comics, Sjosji,* and *Yèch.*

Author's work has been translated into Danish, French, German, Hungarian, Italian, Japanese, Polish, and Spanish.

"EEN AVONTUUR VAN JANUARY JONES" COMICS SERIES

Een avontuur van January Jones (collected comic strips; originally published in *Sjosji*), illustrated by Martin Lodewijk, Oberon (Haarlem, Netherlands), 1988.

Story arcs published in comic-book form as *Dodenrit naar Monte Carlo,* Oberon (Haarlem, Netherlands), 1988; *De schedel van sultan Mkwawa,* Big Balloon (Heemstede, Netherlands), 1990; *De schatten van koning Salomo,* Big Balloon, 1992; and *Het Pinkerton-draaiboek,* Big Balloon, 1995. Author of new story arc, beginning 2009.

"BUD BROADWAY" COMICS SERIES

Bud Broadway (collected comic strips; originally published in *Algemeen Dagblad*), Boumaar (Zutphen, Netherlands), 2002.

Story arcs published in comic-book form as *De weg naar Java,* Boumar (Zutphen, Netherlands), 2002; *Het geheim van Raffles,* Boumaar, 2002; *Banzaï op Borneo,* Boumaar, 2004; *Het einde van Indie,* Boumaar, 2005; *Show in de Sahara,* Boumaar, 2006; *De toorts van Caesar,* Boumaar, 2007; and *De dubbele duce,* Boumaar, 2010.

"GEHEIM VAN DE TIJD" COMICS SERIES

Geheim van de tijd (title means "The secret of time"; collected comic strips; originally published in *Algemeen Dagblad*), illustrated by Frits Jonker, Luytingh (Amsterdam, Netherlands), 2004.

Story arcs published in comic-book form as *Het gat in de cirkel,* Meulenhoff (Amsterdam, Netherlands), 2004; *Eerste tekens,* Luytingh (Amsterdam, Netherlands), 2005; *De Tijdwachters,* Luytingh, 2005; and *Een nieuw begin,* Luytingh, 2007.

Sidelights

Dutch illustrator and writer Eric Heuvel has been creating comic strips both on his own and in collaboration with other writers, since the mid-1970s. His stories focus on the early twentieth century and, particularly, on the World War II era. Outside his native Netherlands, Heuvel is best known for his history-themed graphic novels *De ontdekking* and *De zoektocht,* both of which won awards from the Dutch Comics Association.

Born and raised in Amsterdam, Heuvel worked in customs and then taught history before beginning his career in comics. As an artist, he adopted the clear line style first made popular in the "Tintin" comics created in the 1940s by Belgian artist Hergé, and his early comic strips appeared in several independent magazines. Heuvel's script for "Een avontuur van January Jones," a strip that ran for a decade following its start in 1986, was illustrated by another award-winning Dutch comics artist, Martin Lodewijk. "Een avontuur van January Jones" attracted critical notice for its 1930s-era story about a globe-trotting woman pilot and included the episodes *Dodenrit naar Monte Carlo,*, *De schedel van sultan Mkwawa De schatten van koning Salomo,* and *Het Pinkerton-draaiboek.* Another popular comics series, Heuvel's "Bud Broadway" strip ran in the newspaper *Algemeen Dagblad* for five years, while his collaboration with artist Frits Jonker, "Het geheim van de tijd," replaced "Bud Broadway" beginning in 2003.

Released in early 2003 and subsequently translated into English as *A Family Secret, De ontdekking* marked Heuvel's move to the graphic-novel format, a successful medium through which to tell his dramatic story of the Nazi occupation of the Netherlands during World War II. In the story, a teen named Jeroen is cleaning out his grandmother Helena's attic in preparation for a family yard sale when he comes upon an album of old photographs. For Helena, seeing these pictures rekindles long-suppressed memories about her life in occupied Holland, particularly as they regard her best friend Esther, who as a teenaged Jew was ultimately sent to a Nazi concentration camp. As Jeroen listens to his grandmother's recollections of that time, he realizes that he holds a secret that she does not know, one that might change her feelings of guilt at being the daughter of a Nazi collaborator. Acclaimed by critics and educators, *De ontdekking* was produced with the support of both the Anna Frank Haus and the Resistance Museum of Friesland, and the work has been distributed to over 200,000 Dutch ang German schoolchildren as part of their history curriculum.

Again with the support of the Anna Frank Haus and joined by several coauthors, Heuvel continues Helena's story in *De zoektocht,* a graphic novel that focuses on the memories of Helena's friend Esther. Now living in the United States and still close to Helena, she relates to Jeroen and her own grandson, Daniel, her own memories of the Nazi occupation. While she was able to escape, Ellie's parents died in the German camps, and she is still haunted by unanswered questions regarding their fate. Daniel encourages his grandmother to seek out the truth, and with his help she locates a resident of Israel who was with Esther's parents during their last days at Auschwitz.

According to *New York Times Book Review* contributor Michael Kimmelman, the publication of both *De ontdekking* and *De zoektoch* marked a shift in the way the Holocaust is viewed and taught. "Without excusing anyone or spreading blame," according to Kimmelman, Heuvel's story avoids both the political context within which Germany supported Adolph Hitler and the calculated violence with which Nazi leaders planned and set into motion their "Final Solution" of eradicating the Jews. Instead, Heuvel's graphic novels capture "instances where ordinary individuals—farmers, shopkeepers, soldiers, prison guards, even camp inmates—faced dilemmas, acted selfishly or ambiguously: showed themselves to be human." The "intimacy and immediacy" of the comic-book format, with its colorful pastel-toned pages and likeable characters, "help boil down a vast subject to a few lives that young readers, and old ones too, can grasp," the critic added. Praising the "gripping story" and "highly detailed" art in *A Family Secret,* Hazel Rochman compared Heuvel's work to Art Spiegelman's "Maus" books, adding in her *Booklist* review that both works share "the unsentimental truth of the complex humanity: victims are far from saints, survivors are haunted by guilt." While *School Library Journal* contributor Douglas P. Davey predicted that U.S. readers "may find the cartoon style" of both Heuvel's graphic novels "somewhat at odds with the often tragic nature of the narratives," a *Kirkus Reviews* author praised *The Search* as "evocatively written and deftly illustrated." "Heuvel holds little back," added the critic, calling both volumes a "gripping and visceral" introduction to Holocaust history.

Biographical and Critical Sources

PERIODICALS

Booklist, September 15, 2009, Hazel Rochman, review of *A Family Secret,* p. 58.
Bulletin of the Center for Children's Books, January, 2010, Elizabeth Bush, review of *A Family Secret,* p. 200.
Kirkus Reviews, September 15, 2009, review of *The Search.*
New York Times Book Review, February 27, 2008, Michael Kimmelman, "No Laughs, No Thrills, and Villians All Too Real."
School Library Journal, May, 2010, Douglas P. Davey, review of *A Family Secret,* p. 140.
Voice of Youth Advocates, December, 2009, Geri Diorio, review of *A Family Secret,* p. 406.

ONLINE

Eric Heuvel Home Page, http://www.eric-heuvel.nl (December 27, 2010).*

* * *

HOPGOOD, Tim 1961-

Personal

Born 1961, in England; married; children: Ava, Bill. *Education:* Kingston University, degree. *Hobbies and other interests:* Jazz music, painting, cooking.

Addresses

Home—York, North Yorkshire, England. *Agent*—Celia Catchpole, 56 Gilpin Ave., East Sheen, London SW14 8QY, England. *E-mail*—tim@timhopgood.com.

Career

Author and illustrator of children's book. Worked in art department of *i-D* and *Vogue* magazines; freelance graphic designer and art director in retail fashion industry for twenty years. Presenter at festivals and conferences.

Awards, Honors

Cambridgeshire Read It Again Picture-Book Award, and Kate Greenaway Medal nomination, both 2007, both for *Our Big Blue Sofa;* British Book Design Award shortlist, 2007, Red House Children's Book Award shortlist, and Best Emerging Illustrator award, Book-

Tom Hopgood (Reproduced by permission.)

trust Early Years Award, both 2008, and Hampshire Picture-Book Award shortlist, 2009, all for *Here Comes Frankie!;* Booktrust Early Years Award shortlist in preschool category, 2009, for *Wow! Said the Owl;* Kate Greenaway Medal nomination, 2011, for *Tip Tap Went the Crab.*

Writings

Our Big Blue Sofa, Macmillan Children's (London, England), 2006.
A Dog Called Rod, Macmillan Children's (London, England), 2007.
Here Comes Frankie!, Macmillan Children's (London, England), 2008.
Wow! Said the Owl, Farrar, Straus & Giroux (New York, NY), 2009.
Tip Tap Went the Crab, Macmillan Children's (London, England), 2010.
It Was a Cold, Dark Night, Collins Educational (London, England), 2010.
Playing, Collins Educational (London, England), 2010.
Unpoppable, Macmillan Children's (London, England), 2011.
Thank You for Looking after Our Pets, Simon & Schuster (London, England), 2011.

Sidelights

Tim Hopgood was inspired to write his first book for children by contemplating his family's couch. Passed from relative to relative over many years, the lumpy, old-fashioned sofa was now a playground for Hopgood's young children, and like a cat it gains yet another life as the star of the picture book *Our Big Blue Sofa.* Hopgood has continued to pair his whimsical stories with original art in other highly praised picture books, among them *A Dog Called Rod, Here Comes Frankie!, Wow! Said the Owl,* and *Tip Tap Went the Crab.*

Born and raised in England, Hopgood studied art at Kingston University and then established a career as a graphic designer. His first job was in the art department at *i-D* magazine, and from there he moved to *Vogue* and then to work as a freelance art director and commercial illustrator in the retail fashion industry. After almost twenty years in this field, Hopgood grew tired of working hard to create images that were used only briefly, with the changing fashion seasons. Turning to children's books, he found that he had a knack for writing and illustrating real-life stories that combine lighthearted humor with the tupical ups and downs of childhood.

In *Here Comes Frankie!*, for example, a young musician learns about the different ways people can perceive colors when his parents "hear" his music as a panorama of different colors. Colors also feature in the award-winning picture book *Wow! Said the Owl*, in which an owlet stays awake during the sunlit hours and is amazed by the many colors of nature. Praising the text in *Wow! Said the Owl* as "straightforward and flowing," *School Library Journal* critic Julie Roach recommended Hopgood's picture book as "a satisfying introduction to the colors of the day."

Since his college days, Hopgood has worked to develop a distinct illustration style. He begins with a black-and-white ink or marker drawing and then adds color and texture through paint and computer manipulation. His illustrations sometimes feature distinctive elements, such as sparkly glitter or glossy spot varnish. According to a *Kirkus Reviews* writer, the artist's "graphic-design background is evident in his illustrations," which are "a mixture of color and texture," according to the critic. In *Horn Book*, Susan Dove Lempke praised Hopgood's mixture of "vivid colors" and "delicate lines and textures," the critic adding that the author/illustrator adds "just enough embellishment to flesh out each sentence" of *Wow! Said the Owl* "without distracting from the story's simplicity."

Biographical and Critical Sources

PERIODICALS

Horn Book, September-October, 2009, Susan Dove Lempke, review of *Wow! Said the Owl,* p. 542.
Kirkus Reviews, August 15, 2009, review of *Wow! Said the Owl.*
School Library Journal, September, 2009, Julie Roach, review of *Wow! Said the Owl,* p. 125.

ONLINE

Book Trust Web site, http://www.booktrust.org.uk/ (December 15, 2010), Madelyn Travis, interview with Hopgood.

Tim Hopgood Home Page, http://www.timhopgood.com (December 7, 2010).*

*   *   *

HOWE, James 1946-

Personal
Born August 2, 1946, in Oneida, NY; son of Lee Arthur (a clergyman) and Lonnelle (a teacher) Howe; married Deborah Smith (a writer and actress), September 28, 1969 (died June 3, 1978); married Betsy Imershein (a photographer), April 5, 1981 (divorced); partner of Mark Davis (an attorney), beginning January, 2001; children: (second marriage) Zoey. *Education:* Boston University, B.F.A., 1968; Hunter College of the City University of New York, M.A., 1977. *Hobbies and other interests:* Bicycling, hiking, skiing, movies, theater, traveling, reading.

Addresses
Home—NY. *Agent*—Amy Berkower, Writers House Inc., 21 W. 26th St., New York, NY 10010.

Career
Author. Freelance actor and director, 1971-75; Lucy Kroll Agency, New York, NY, literary agent, 1976-81; children's writer, 1981—. *Military service:* Civilian public service, 1968-70.

Member
Society of Children's Book Writers and Illustrators, Writers Guild of America East.

Awards, Honors
Notable Book citation, American Library Association (ALA), 1979, Pacific Northwest Young Readers' Choice Award, 1982, and *Booklist* Fifty All-Time Favorite Children's Books inclusion, all for *Bunnicula: A Rabbit-Tale of Mystery; Boston Globe/Horn Book* Honor Book in Nonfiction selection, ALA Notable Book citation, and Children's Book of the Year citation, Library of Congress, all 1981, and nonfiction nomination, American Book Award in Children's Books (now National Book Award), 1982, all for *The Hospital Book;* CRABbery Honor Book selection, 1984, for *The Celery Stalks at Midnight;* Volunteer State award, 1984, for *Howliday Inn;* Washington Irving Younger Fiction Award, and Colorado Children's Book Award runner-up, both 1988, both for *There's a Monster under My Bed;* Garden State Children's Book Award for Younger Fiction, 1990, for *Nighty-Nightmare;* North Dakota Children's Choice Picture Book selection, 1992, for *Harold and Chester in Scared Silly;* ALA Notable Children's Book selection, and E.B. White Read Aloud Award, Association of

James Howe (Photograph by Betsy Imershein. Reproduced by permission.)

Booksellers for Children, 2007, for *Houndsley and Catina;* Children's Choices selection, International Reading Association/Children's Book Council, for *Bunnicula Meets Edgar Allan Crow;* Whitney and Scott Cardozo Award for Children's Literature, Library of Virginia, 2009, for *Houndsley and Catina: Plink and Plunk;* recognition from American Booksellers Association, Child Study Children's Book Committee, and National Science Teachers Association; recipient of numerous children's choice awards.

Writings

FOR CHILDREN

(With wife, Deborah Howe) *Teddy Bear's Scrapbook,* illustrated by David S. Rose, Atheneum (New York, NY), 1980.

The Hospital Book (nonfiction), photographs by Mal Warshaw, Crown (New York, NY), 1981, Morrow (New York, NY), 1994.

Annie Joins the Circus (spin-off from movie *Annie*), illustrated by Leonard Shortall, Random House (New York NY), 1982.

The Case of the Missing Mother, illustrated by William Cleaver, Random House (New York NY), 1983.

A Night without Stars, Atheneum (New York, NY), 1983.

The Muppet Guide to Magnificent Manners; Featuring Jim Henson's Muppets, illustrated by Peter Elwell, Random House (New York NY), 1984.

How the Ewoks Saved the Trees: An Old Ewok Legend (spin-off from movie *Return of the Jedi*), illustrated by Walter Velez, Random House (New York NY), 1984.

Morgan's Zoo, illustrated by Leslie Morrill, Atheneum (New York, NY), 1984.

The Day the Teacher Went Bananas (picture book), illustrated by Lillian Hoban, Dutton (New York, NY), 1984.

Mister Tinker in Oz ("Brand-New Oz" adventure series), illustrated by D. Rose, Random House (New York NY), 1985.

When You Go to Kindergarten, photographs by Betsy Imershein, Knopf (New York, NY), 1986, revised second edition, Morrow (New York, NY), 1995.

There's a Monster under My Bed (picture book), illustrated by D. Rose, Atheneum (New York, NY), 1986.

A Love Note for Baby Piggy, Marvel (New York, NY), 1986.

(Reteller) *Babes in Toyland* (adaptation of 1903 operetta by Victor Herbert and Glen MacDonough), illustrated by Allen Atkinson, Gulliver Books, 1986.

(Reteller) *The Secret Garden* (adaptation of novel by Frances Hodgson Burnett), illustrated by Thomas B. Allen, Random House (New York NY), 1987, illustrated by Nancy Sippel Carpenter, 2004.

I Wish I Were a Butterfly (picture book), illustrated by Ed Young, Gulliver Books, 1987.

Carol Burnett: The Sound of Laughter ("Women of Our Time" series), illustrated by Robert Masheris, Viking (New York, NY), 1987.

(Adaptor) *Dances with Wolves: A Story for Children* (adapted from the screenplay by Michael Blake), Newmarket Press, 1991.

Playing with Words, photographs by Michael Craine, R.C. Owen, 1994.

There's a Dragon in My Sleeping Bag, illustrated by D. Rose, Macmillan (New York, NY), 1994.

The New Nick Kramer; or, My Life as a Baby-Sitter, Hyperion (New York, NY), 1995.

The Watcher, Atheneum (New York, NY), 1997.

Horace and Morris but Mostly Dolores, illustrated by Amy Walrod, Atheneum (New York, NY), 1999.

The Misfits (novel), Atheneum (New York, NY), 2001.

(Editor) *The Color of Absence: Twelve Stories about Loss and Hope,* Atheneum (New York, NY), 2001.

Horace and Morris Join the Chorus (but What about Dolores?), illustrated by Amy Walrod, Atheneum (New York, NY), 2002.

(Editor) *13: Thirteen Stories That Capture the Agony and Ecstasy of Being Thirteen,* Atheneum (New York, NY), 2003.

Kaddish for Grandpa in Jesus' Name Amen, illustrated by Catherine Stock, Atheneum (New York, NY), 2004.

Totally Joe (novel), Atheneum (New York, NY), 2005.

Horace and Morris Say Cheese (Which Makes Dolores Sneeze!), illustrated by Amy Walrod, Atheneum (New York, NY), 2009.

Brontorina, illustrated by Randy Cecil, Candlewick Press (Somerville, MA), 2010.

Addie on the Inside (novel), Atheneum (New York, NY), 2011.

"BUNNICULA" SERIES

(With Deborah Howe) *Bunnicula: A Rabbit-Tale of Mystery,* illustrated by Alan Daniel, Atheneum (New York, NY), 1979, reprinted, Aladdin Paperbacks (New York, NY), 2006.

Howliday Inn, illustrated by Lynn Munsinger, Atheneum (New York, NY), 1982, reprinted, Aladdin Paperbacks (New York, NY), 2006.

The Celery Stalks at Midnight, illustrated by Leslie Morrill, Atheneum (New York, NY), 1983, reprinted, Aladdin Paperbacks (New York, NY), 2006.

Nighty-Nightmare, illustrated by Leslie Morrill, Atheneum (New York, NY), 1987.

The Fright before Christmas, illustrated by Leslie Morrill, Morrow (New York, NY), 1988.

Scared Silly: A Halloween Treat, illustrated by Leslie Morrill, Morrow (New York, NY), 1989.

Hot Fudge, illustrated by Leslie Morrill, Morrow (New York, NY), 1990.

Creepy-Crawly Birthday, illustrated by Leslie Morrill, Morrow (New York, NY), 1991.

Return to Howliday Inn, illustrated by Alan Daniel, Atheneum (New York, NY), 1992, reprinted, Aladdin Paperbacks (New York, NY), 2007.

The Bunnicula Fun Book, illustrated by Alan Daniel, Morrow (New York, NY), 1993.

Rabbit-Cadabra!, illustrated by Alan Daniel, Morrow (New York, NY), 1993.

Bunnicula Escapes!: A Pop-up Adventure, illustrated by Alan and Lea Daniel, paper engineering by Vicki Teague-Cooper, Tupelo Books, 1994.

Bunnicula's Wickedly Wacky Word Games, illustrated by Alan Daniel, Little Simon (New York, NY), 1998.

Bunnicula's Pleasantly Perplexing Puzzlers, illustrated by Alan Daniel, Little Simon (New York, NY), 1998.

(With Louis Phillips) *Bunnicula's Long-lasting Laugh-Alouds,* illustrated by Alan Daniel, Little Simon (New York, NY), 1999.

Bunnicula's Frightfully Fabulous Factoids, illustrated by Alan Daniel, Little Simon (New York, NY), 1999.

Bunnicula Strikes Again!, illustrated by Alan Daniel, Atheneum (New York, NY), 1999.

The Bunnicula Collection: Three Hare-raising Tales in One Volume, Atheneum (New York, NY), 2003.

Bunnicula Meets Edgar Allan Crow, illustrated by Eric Fortune, Atheneum (New York, NY), 2006.

"TALES FROM THE HOUSE OF BUNNICULA" SERIES; ILLUSTRATED BY BRETT HELQUIST

It Came from beneath the Bed, Atheneum (New York, NY), 2002.

Invasion of the Mind Swappers from Asteroid 6!, Atheneum (New York, NY), 2002.

Howie Monroe and the Doghouse of Doom, Atheneum (New York, NY), 2002.

Screaming Mummies of the Pharaoh's Tomb II, Atheneum (New York, NY), 2003.

Bud Barkin, Private Eye, Atheneum (New York, NY), 2003.

The Amazing Odorous Adventures of Stinky Dog, Atheneum (New York, NY), 2003.

"SEBASTIAN BARTH" MYSTERY SERIES

What Eric Knew, Atheneum (New York, NY), 1985.
Stage Fright, Atheneum (New York, NY), 1986.
Eat Your Poison, Dear, Atheneum (New York, NY), 1986.
Dew Drop Dead, Atheneum (New York, NY), 1990.

"PINKY AND REX" SERIES; ILLUSTRATED BY MELISSA SWEET

Pinky and Rex, Atheneum (New York, NY), 1990.

Pinky and Rex Get Married, Atheneum (New York, NY), 1990.

Pinky and Rex and the Spelling Bee, Atheneum (New York, NY), 1991.

Pinky and Rex and the Mean Old Witch, Atheneum (New York, NY), 1991.

Pinky and Rex Go to Camp, Atheneum (New York, NY), 1992.

Pinky and Rex and the New Baby, Macmillan (New York, NY), 1993.

Pinky and Rex and the Double-Dad Weekend, Atheneum (New York, NY), 1995.

Pinky and Rex and the Bully, Atheneum (New York, NY), 1996.

Pinky and Rex and the New Neighbors, Atheneum (New York, NY), 1997.

Pinky and Rex and the Perfect Pumpkin, Atheneum (New York, NY), 1998.

Pinky and Rex and the School Play, Atheneum (New York, NY), 1998.

Pinky and Rex and the Just-Right Pet, Atheneum (New York, NY), 2001.

"HOUNDSLEY AND CANTINA" SERIES; ILLUSTRATED BY MARY-LOUISE GAY

Houndsley and Catina, Candlewick Press (Cambridge, MA), 2006.

Houndsley and Catina and the Birthday Surprise, Candlewick Press (Cambridge, MA), 2006.

Houndsley and Catina and the Quiet Time, Candlewick Press (Cambridge, MA), 2008.

Houndsley and Catina: Plink and Plunk, Candlewick Press (Somerville, MA), 2009.

OTHER

My Life as a Babysitter (television play), The Disney Channel, 1990.

Also compiler of *365 New Words-a-Year Shoelace Calendar for Kids*, Workman Publishing, 1983-85. Contributor to *Horn Book* and *School Library Journal*.

Author's work has been translated into Danish, Dutch, French, German, Italian, Japanese, Spanish, and Swedish.

Adaptations

Bunnicula was adapted as an animated television movie produced by Ruby-Spears Productions, ABC, 1982, a sound recording narrated by Lou Jacobi, Caedmon Records, 1982, and a videocassette produced by World Vision Home Video. *Howliday Inn* was adapted as a sound recording narrated by Jacobi, Caedmon Records, 1984. *The Celery Stalks at Midnight* was adapted as a sound recording, 1987. *Nighty-Nightmare* was adapted as a sound recording narrated by George S. Irving, Caedmon, 1988. Listening Library recordings narrated by Victor Garber and produced in 2000 include *Bunicula, Howliday Inn, The Celery Stalks at Midnight, Nighty Nightmare, Return to Howliday Inn,* and *Bunnicula Strikes Again. The Misfits* was adapted as an audiobook produced by Full Cast, 2003. *It Came from beneath the Bed!, Invasion of the Mind-Swappers from Asterlid 6!, Howie Monroe and the Doghouse of Doom,* and *Screaming Mummies of the Pharaoh's Tomb II* were adapted as sound recordings narrated by Joe Grifasi, Listening Library, 2003. Recorded Books adapted the "Pinky and Rex" books as audiobooks. The "Bunnicula" stories were adapted by Heather Henson as the "Bunnicula and Friends" easy readers, illustrated by Jeff Mack, Atheneum, 2004-07.

Sidelights

Best known for creating the laugh-out-loud tales of vampire bunnies and talking pets that comprise his "Bunnicula" books, James Howe is also the author of sometimes painfully funny coming-of-age stories for middle graders. He also serves up stories of close friendship in his "Pinky and Rex" and "Houndsley and Catina" chapter books and spins a mystery with an often-humorous twist in each of his "Sebastian Barth" tales. "Humor is the most precious gift I can give to my reader," Howe once noted in *Horn Book*.

Although he is best known for his humor, Howe moved into more serious territory with his novel *The Watcher,* which focuses on child abuse, and he has also courted controversy by dealing with teen homosexuality in his novels *The Misfits* and *Totally Joe*. In addition, he has collected writings by a number of popular authors into anthologies such as *The Color of Absence: Twelve Stories about Loss and Hope* and *13: Thirteen Stories That Capture the Agony and Ecstasy of Being Thirteen,* which directly address the realities of adolescence. "It is the writer's privilege and responsibility to give children a world they can enter, recognize, at times be

frightened of, but which ultimately, they can master and control," Howe observed in *Horn Book*. "We must not leave them feeling stranded in an unfamiliar world where the questions, let alone the answers, are beyond their grasp."

Born in Oneida, New York, in 1946, Howe grew up in a family that loved language. As a child he began what has become his trademark—wordplay—in an effort to win the attention of his three older brothers. At Boston University he earned a degree in fine arts, then worked as an actor and director for several years before returning to graduate school where a seminar in playwriting rekindled his childhood love of words. For several years, Howe also worked as a literary agent in New York City, and by the time he and his first wife, the late Deborah Howe, thought of collaborating on a children's book, he was familiar with the world of publishing.

The Howes' first collaborative effort led to the publication of *Bunnicula: A Rabbit-Tale of Mystery,* winner of a Dorothy Canfield Fisher award and an instant success with young readers. The perennially popular story, which has been republished in several anniversary editions, revolves around Chester, an arrogant cat who relishes horror stories, and Harold, a lumbering, shaggy dog who narrates the tale under the discrete pseudonym Harold X. (to protect the innocent). The sleuths team up when their owners, the Monroes, innocently adopt a bunny abandoned at a movie theater and name it Bunnicula, after the chilling film *Dracula* that had been playing at the time. Convinced that Bunnicula is really a vampire rabbit—the bunny *does* have oddly shaped teeth resembling fangs *and* the vegetables in the house seemed to be mysteriously drained of their color soon after Bunnicula's arrival—the cat-and-dog twosome attempts to warn the unsuspecting Monroes of the evil they have invited into their lives. *Bunnicula*'s "stylish, exuberant make-believe," observed a reviewer in *Publishers Weekly,* arises from the Howes' "unreined imagination and . . . glinting sense of humor." Zena Sutherland, reviewing the book for the *Bulletin of the Center for Children's Books,* summed up its appeal by noting that "the plot is less important in the story than the style." Sutherland went on to characterize that style as "blithe, sophisticated, and distinguished for the wit and humor of the dialogue."

"Bunnicula" soon evolved into a series, as well as several related spin-offs, with the completion of such light-hearted and comic tales as *Howliday Inn, The Celery Stalks at Midnight,* and *Bunnicula Strikes Again!* Chateau Bow-Wow provides the locale for *Howliday Inn* (so named because Chester is convinced that it shelters werewolves). In the story, Chester and Harold are lodged at a boarding house from which cats and dogs strangely disappear almost daily. Frantic when Louise, the French poodle, vanishes, the distressed pair fears that a villainous murderer may be afoot. "Wonderfully witty dialogue and irresistible characters" fill the story, wrote a *Publishers Weekly* reviewer.

The Celery Stalks at Midnight follows the duo's efforts to track Bunnicula, who has disappeared from his cage in the Monroe house. Along with Howie, a tiny pup who insists that Chester is his "pop," the three also join forces to destroy (i.e. puncture with toothpicks) the vegetables Chester is sure have been transformed into killer zombies by the vampire rabbit. Many reviewers called special attention to the slapstick humor and abundant puns that fill *The Celery Stalks at Midnight.*

In *Bunnicula Meets Edgar Allan Crow* Harold and Chester go on the alert when an eccentric mystery writer and his unusual pet visit the Monroe household and exhibit an eerie fascination with the rabbit, who then mysteriously vanishes. "The writing style is a mixture of chills and chuckles," Elaine E. Knight commented in her *School Library Journal* review of *Bunnicula Meets Edgar Allan Crow*, and *Booklist* reviewer Carolyn Phelan praised Howe's ability to craft "dramatic and comical situations."

Howie Monroe, the dachshund puppy introduced in the "Bunnicula" books, comes into his own in several picture books that follow his efforts to become a famous writer like his uncle Harold. In *It Came from beneath the Bed* Howie spins a story about a stuffed koala bear that grows out of control after it soaks up some stray concoction from Pete Monroe's science project. In *Howie Monroe and the Doghouse of Doom* Howe parodies the popular "Harry Potter" books, throwing in a bungled version of Hamlet's soliloquy for good measure. *Invasion of the Mind Swappers from Asteroid 6!* describes the efforts of a group of fiendish aliens to control earthlings, specifically, turning Howie's friend Delia into a squirrel. A play on hardboiled detective fiction is served up by the ambitious dachshund in *Bud Barkin, Private Eye,* as Howie pens a whodunit that features a detective, a dame in distress, and a suspicious ex-convict.

Alongside the text of each of Howie's fictional masterpieces are his hand-written notes about the writing process, alternating the tail-wagging scribbler's glowing references to his many talents as a writer with sage advice from mentor Harold. Praising the series, *Booklist* reviewer Anne O'Malley noted in her review of *Invasion of the Mindswappers from Asteroid 6!* that the series format allows Howe to present beginning writers "with an ingenious lesson" in creative writing "seamlessly blended with two first-rate tales starring a whimsical protagonist." In a similar vein, John Sigwald noted in *School Library Journal* that the "Tales from the House of Bunnicula" books "could easily become the standard textbook for creative writing classes."

In *Rabbit-Cadabra!,* another of the many picture-book spin-offs to the antics of Harold and Chester, the Amazing Karlovsky is coming to town and the Monroes are

excited. Chester and Harold, however, are having second thoughts about the show: the rabbit displayed in publicity posters looks awfully like Bunnicula, the faux or maybe all-too-real vampire bunny. In an attempt to ward off an invasion of vampire bunnies spilling from the magician's hat, dog and cat wield garlic pizza and steal the show, revealing the magician to be none other than the Monroes' cousin Charlie. A *Kirkus Reviews* contributor concluded that Howe's book is "predictable, but fans will love it," while Kay Weisman writing in *Booklist* called *Rabbit-Cadabra!* an "appealing story."

The "Sebastian Barth" mystery series is a bit more plot-oriented, relating four sleuthing tales about a middle-school-aged fledgling detective whose exploits lead him into both dangerous and humorous situations. A flu epidemic at school is actually a case of food poisoning, as Sebastian discovers in *Eat Your Poison.* Sebastian suspects, among others, the cafeteria manager. In the fourth book of the series, *Dew Drop Dead,* Howe inserts serious elements in a tale of a discovered body, looking at the issue of homelessness in the process of telling an

Howe teams up with artist Marie-Louise Gay to create the entertaining animal team that stars in **Houndsley and Catina.** *(Illustration copyright © 2006 by Marie-Louise Gay. Reproduced by permission of the publisher Candlewick Press, Somerville, MA.)*

old-fashioned, fast-paced yarn. In *Stage Fright,* Howe draws on his love of the theater when he writes about Sebastian's desire to work with a famous actress.

Another popular series from Howe is "Pinky and Rex," written for younger readers just advancing to chapter books. The series features two young best friends whose relationship is lovingly detailed in a series of small yet piquant and telling mini-adventures. In *Pinky and Rex* the two children test their new friendship when both covet a pink dinosaur. Pinky has twenty-seven stuffed animals and Rex has twenty-seven dinosaurs. So when they see a one-of-a-kind pink dinosaur in the museum gift shop that would enhance each of their collections, they need a little help from Pinky's annoying little sister, Amanda, to decide what to do.

In *Pinky and Rex and the Spelling Bee,* the desire to win at a spelling bee is mixed with the embarrassment of a peeing accident, while fears about summer camp are broached in *Pinky and Rex Go to Camp.* Kindly Mrs. Morgan moves away in *Pinky and Rex and the New Neighbors,* and the two friends fear that their new neighbor will not be nearly so nice. A pumpkin hunt forms the backdrop for familial rivalries and a clash between Rex and Pinky in *Pinky and Rex and the Perfect Pumpkin,* while in *Pinky and Rex and the Just-Right Pet* Pinky's disappointment over the family's new pet turns to love when the new kitten shows that it likes Pinky best.

The "Pinky and Rex" books have been well received by critics. Reviewing *Pinky and Rex and the New Baby,* a contributor to *Kirkus Reviews* called Howe's book "another strong entry" in the ongoing series and one that is noteworthy for its "lively, believable dialogue and realistic situation that gently tests the likable pair's mettle." Valerie F. Patterson noted in *School Library Journal* that those ready for chapter books "will appreciate this gentle story of two friends who really care about each other." Praising the series illustrations by Melissa Sweet, *School Library Journal* contributor Olga R. Kuharets wrote that in *Pinky and Rex and the Just-Right Pet* Howe presents young readers with "a realistic story with just the right amount of suspense and drama."

Howe's "Houndsley and Cantina" series of easy readers concerns the warm and supportive relationship between a thoughtful canine and his feline companion. In the debut title, *Houndsley and Catina,* Howe offers three humorous tales about ambition and honesty. In one story, Houndsley tries to avoid upsetting the literary-minded Catina after she asks for his opinion about her poorly written memoir. The work will "hit home with kids just learning about their own particular talents and passions," Gillian Engberg commented in *Booklist.* In *Houndsley and Catina and the Birthday Surprise,* the pair finds ways to cheer one another after they realize that they do not know the dates of their own birthdays. According to Phelan, Howe's book "will appeal to children's compassion as well as their sense of humor," and a contributor in *Kirkus Reviews* observed that the author "crafts a knowing paean . . . to the care and feeding of friendship."

In *Houndsley and Catina and the Quiet Time* the talented duo plans a musical concert for friends, but when a snowstorm hits and forces them to cancel their performance, Houndsley devises a way to comfort his crestfallen pal. "These endearing characters shine in this gentle and reflective read," a *Kirkus Reviews* critic remarked. The two friends learn the importance of communication when their canoe and bicycle trips fall flat in *Houndsley and Catina: Plink and Plunk.* Rebecca Dash, writing in *School Library Journal* stated that "the language is playful and precise," while Phelan described the work as "an encouraging book on overcoming fears."

Howe's stand-alone books for children include a retelling of Frances Hodgson Burnett's *The Secret Garden,* a classic novel about a young orphaned girl who joins her invalid cousin in uncovering the secrets of a locked garden in her new home in rural England. In the more fanciful *Brontorina,* a picture book illustrated by Randy Cecil, a young dinosaur pursues her dreams of becoming a ballerina despite a host of obstacles. Although initially denied entry into Madame Lucille's Dance Academy for Boys and Girls, Brontorina eventually convinces the instructor to give her a chance, and she is soon leaping about the studio. Because of her enormous size, however, the new student causes extensive damage to the ceiling until Madame Lucille devises a clever solution to the problem. A *Publishers Weekly* critic described *Brontorina* as "a humorous and inspiring tale," and Sara Lissa Paulson, writing in *School Library Journal,* dubbed Howe's tale a "quiet fusion of pathos, comedy, and passion."

Kaddish for Grandpa in Jesus' Name Amen is geared for children who are raised in more than one religious tradition; the story focuses on how five-year-old Emily incorporates the memories of her Christian grandfather with the Jewish faith of her immediate family after her grandfather passes away. While sermons about angels and Christian prayers are new to her when she attends the man's church funeral, when Emily and her family return home her father, who converted to Judaism as an adult, decides to mourn his father in the Jewish tradition, by sitting shivah. Noting that few books for children address interfaith families, *Booklist* reviewer Stephanie Zvirin dubbed *Kaddish for Grandpa in Jesus' Name Amen* exceptional, while Jane Marin wrote in *School Library Journal* that Howe's unusual book serves as "a good vehicle to explain the rituals of death to children."

Howe is also well recognized as a novelist for middle-grade readers as well as young adults. His breezy dialogue comes into play with *The New Nick Kramer; or,*

Randy Cecil contributes the artwork to Howe's humorous picture book Brontorina. (Illustration copyright © 2010 by Randy Cecil. Reproduced by permission of Candlewick Press, Somerville, MA.)

My Life as a Baby-Sitter, a spin-off of an original script Howe wrote for the Disney Channel. Nick desperately wants to beat popular Mitch at something; he finally settles on getting a date with Jennifer, betting Mitch that she will ask him to a girl-ask-guy dance. To convince shallow Jennifer that he is not just another macho guy, Nick takes a babysitting class. The subsequent babysitting job he takes, and the girl he meets as a result, make all bets moot. Carrie A. Guarria noted in *School Library Journal* that "Nick's first-person narrative adds believability" to the story, as do the "ploys he erroneously uses to gain Jennifer's trust and companionship." Writing in the *New York Times Book Review,* Robin Tzannes commented that Howe "tells Nick Kramer's story with remarkably natural dialogue and a hilarity that owes a great deal to television sitcoms, making this book hard for kids to put down."

Howe takes a different approach with his novels for older readers, such as *The Watcher* and *The Misfits.* A "somber, ambitious novel (about child abuse)," according to Stephanie Zvirin in *Booklist, The Watcher* employs three different narrative viewpoints as Howe tells the story of a solitary teen whose best friend at an island beach resort seems to be her notebook. Called "the Watcher" by others at the beach due to her habit of staring intently at nearby families and appearing to record her impressions in a notebook, the young girl, Margaret latches on to one family in particular and weaves herself fancifully into their lives. Other narrative viewpoints come from Evan, who is afraid his parents are divorcing, and the lifeguard Chris, a teen who is trying to find his place with his family and the world.

Leigh Ann Jones, reviewing *The Watcher* in *School Library Journal,* had high praise, writing that the book is "so powerful that even after the last page is read, and Margaret is mercifully saved, her story may be reflected upon again and again." Nancy Thackaberry noted in *Voice of Youth Advocates* that "fans of Howe's middle-level books will not be shocked or disappointed by his realistic fiction. He handles these more mature topics in a way that bridges the younger reader to YA literature."

Twelve-year-old Bobby Goodspeed is the focus of *The Misfits,* which finds the part-time tie salesman joining three other friends—"Faggot" Joe, "Know-it-All" Addie, and "ree-tard" Skeezie—to turn the tables on the school bullies now that they have reached the seventh grade. Overweight Bobby has been assailed by taunts like "Lardo" and "Fatso" for years; now, when he finds the courage to speak out about name-calling during his run for student council, he transcends labels and gains the respect of his peers. While noting that Howe's characters seem "wiser than their years . . . and remarkably well-adjusted," a *Publishers Weekly* reviewer praised *The Misfits* as "an upbeat, reassuring novel that encourages preteens and teens to celebrate their individuality." *Booklist* reviewer Hazel Rochman described the dialogue between characters as "right-on and funny," while a *Kirkus Reviews* critic wrote that Bobby's "winsome and funny" viewpoint prompts readers to "discover how the names we call each other shape our vision of ourselves."

Howe reprises a character from *The Misfits* in *Totally Joe,* a novel "about tolerance, self-knowledge and the vacuity of teenage popularity," a critic wrote in *Publishers Weekly.* The work unfolds as a series of entries in Joe Bunch's "alphabiography," a writing assignment from the seventh grader's English teacher in which he records his thoughts about his classmates and his observations about life, including his growing awareness of his homosexuality. "Throughout, Joe demonstrates that he truly is a one-of-a-kind kid," Maria B. Salvadore commented in *School Library Journal,* and a *Kirkus Reviews* contributor noted that "the story is nothing but realistic."

The Misfits and *Totally Joe* are intensely personal works for Howe, who came out as a gay man at the age of fifty-one. In those works, as he remarked to a Tolerance.org interviewer, "an underlying theme that kept surfacing had to do with my own feelings of being different as a boy and then a man. My own shame about being gay, my own discomfort, my own wish that I could be open and accepting and be accepted. These feelings kept bubbling up in my work, which often celebrated difference and feeling good about who you are." Howe further noted, "In coming out, I set my stories—and myself—free. My hope is that my stories can now help others set their stories free."

Whether penning continuing chapters in the ongoing saga of "Bunnicula," writing bracingly humorous picture books, or creating hard-hitting YA literature, Howe continues to directly address and entertain his young readers. His "books are clever, often spoofs, and filled with contemporary references that entertain," commented Jane Anne Hannigan in an essay for the *St. James Guide to Children's Writers.* More than entertainment, however, Howe recognizes that his work serves a deeper purpose. "In the end," the author once commented in *Horn Book,* "my primary responsibility as a writer is to the hidden child in the reader and in myself, and to the belief that—though we are years apart—when I open my mouth to speak, the child will understand. Because in that hidden part of ourselves, we are one."

Cover of Howe's teen novel The Misfits, *featuring cover art by Bagram Ibatoulline.* (Atheneum Books for Young Readers, 2001. Illustration copyright © 2001 by Bagram Ibatoulline. Reproduced by permission of the illustrator.)

Biographical and Critical Sources

BOOKS

Children's Literature Review, Volume 9, Gale (Detroit, MI), 1985.
St. James Guide to Children's Writers, edited by Sara Pendergast and Tom Pendergast, St. James Press (Detroit, MI), 1999.

PERIODICALS

Booklist, April 15, 1993, Kay Weisman, review of *Rabbit-Cadabra!,* p. 1523; April 15, 1995, Lauren Peterson, review of *Pinky and Rex and the Double-Dad Week-*

end, p. 1500; April 1, 1996, Carolyn Phelan, review of *Pinky and Rex and the Bully,* p. 1364; June 1-15, 1997, Stephanie Zvirin, review of *The Watcher* p. 1685; March 1, 1998, Janice Del Negro, review of *Pinky and Rex and the New Baby,* p. 1230; September 1, 1998, Carolyn Phelan, review of *Pinky and Rex and the Perfect Pumpkin,* p. 119; October 15, 2000, Patricia Austin, review of *The Celery Stalks at Midnight,* p. 472; January 1, 2001, Jean Hatfield, review of *Howliday Inn,* p. 987; March 1, 2001, Stephanie Zvirin, review of *Pinky and Rex and the Just-Right Pet,* p. 1278; November 15, 2001, Hazel Rochman, review of *The Misfits,* p. 572; August, 2002, Anne O'Malley, review of *Invasion of the Mind Swappers from Asteroid 6!,* p. 1961; October 1, 2002, Kathleen Odean, review of *Howie Monroe and the Doghouse of Doom,* p. 326; November, 15, 2002, Ilene Cooper, review of *Horace and Morris Join the Chorus (but What about Dolores?),* p. 610; May 1, 2004, Shelle Rosenfeld, review of *Bud Barkin, Private Eye,* p. 1528; January 1, 2004, Gillian Engberg, review of *13: Thirteen Stories That Capture the Agony and Ecstasy of Being Thirteen,* p. 843; May 15, 2004, Stephanie Zvirin, review of *Kaddish for Grandpa in Jesus' Name Amen,* p. 1621; February 15, 2006, Gillian Engberg, review of *Houndsley and Catina,* p. 102; October 1, 2006, Carolyn Phelan, review of *Houndsley and Catina and the Birthday Surprise,* p. 58; January 1, 2007, Carolyn Phelan, review of *Bunnicula Meets Edgar Allan Crow,* p. 81; May 1, 2009, Carolyn Phelan, review of *Houndsley and Catina: Pink and Plunk,* p. 78; August 1, 2009, Ilene Cooper, review of *Horace and Morris Say Cheese (Which Makes Dolores Sneeze!),* p. 78; May 15, 2010, Carolyn Phelan, review of *Brontorina,* p. 40.

Bulletin of the Center for Children's Books, July-August, 1979, Zena Sutherland, review of *Bunnicula: A Rabbit-Tale of Mystery,* p. 192.

Horn Book, March-April, 1985, James Howe, "Writing for the Hidden Child," pp. 156-161; September, 2001, Bridget McCaffrey, review of *The Color of Absence,* p. 586; November-December, 2001, Peter D. Sieruta, review of *The Misfits,* p. 750; January-February, 2003, Susan P. Bloom, review of *Horace and Morris Join the Chorus (but What about Dolores?),* p. 56; September-October, 2009, Jennifer M. Brabander, review of *Horace and Morris Say Cheese (Which Makes Dolores Sneeze!),* p. 542.

Kirkus Reviews, March 15, 1993, review of *Pinky and Rex and the New Baby,* p. 372; May 1, 1995, review of *Rabbit-Cadabra!,* p. 599; September 1, 2001, review of *The Misfits,* p. 1291; October 1, 2002, review of *Horace and Morris Join the Chorus (but What about Dolores?),* p. 1471; November 15, 2002, review of *Screaming Mummies from the Pharaoh's Tomb II,* p. 1695; September 15, 2003, review of *13,* p. 1176; January 15, 2004, review of *Bunnicula and Friends,* p. 84; April 15, 2004, review for *Kaddish for Grandpa in Jesus' Name Amen,* p. 394; October 1, 2005, review of *Totally Joe,* p. 1080; October 1, 2006, review of *Houndsley and Catina and the Birthday Surprise,*

p. 1016; August 1, 2008, review of *Houndsley and Catina and the Quiet Time;* June 1, 2009, review of *Horace and Morris Say Cheese (Which Makes Dolores Sneeze!).*

Kliatt, May, 2003, Francisca Goldsmith, review of *The Color of Absence,* p. 28; July, 2003, Paula Rohrlick, review of *The Misfits,* p. 23.

New York Times Book Review, November 12, 1995, Robin Tzannes, review of *The New Nick Kramer; or, My Life as a Baby-Sitter,* p. 49.

Publishers Weekly, March 19, 1979, review of *Bunnicula,* p. 94; March 19, 1982, review of *Howliday Inn,* p. 71; October 29, 2001, review of *The Misfits,* p. 64; October 14, 2002, review of *Horace and Morris Join the Chorus (but What about Dolores?),* p. 83; November 17, 2003, review of *13,* p. 65; April 26, 2004, review of *Kaddish for Grandpa in Jesus' Name Amen,* p. 62; October 3, 2005, review of *Totally Joe,* p. 71; March 20, 2006, review of *Houndsley and Catina,* p. 55; July 5, 2010, review of *Brontorina,* p. 41.

School Library Journal, June, 1993, Valerie F. Patterson, review of *Pinky and Rex and the New Baby,* p. 76; January, 1996, Carrie A. Guarria, review of *The New Nick Kramer; or, My Life as a Baby-Sitter,* p. 108; April, 1996, Marilyn Taniguchi, review of *Pinky and Rex and the Bully,* p. 110; May, 1997, Leigh Ann Jones, review of *The Watcher,* p. 134; October, 2000, Ann Elders, review of *Bunnicula Strikes Again!,* p. 92; May, 2001, Olga R. Kuharets, review of *Pinky and Rex and the Just-Right Pet,* p. 124; September, 2001, Susan Riley, review of *The Color of Absence,* p. 225; November, 2001, Louie Lahana, review of *The Misfits,* p. 158; November, 2002, Shelley B. Sutherland, review of *Horace and Morris Join the Chorus (but What about Dolores?),* p. 126, and John Sigwald, review of *It Came from beneath the Bed,* JoAnn Jonas, review of *Howie Monroe and the Doghouse of Doom,* and Wendy S. Carroll, review of *Invasion of the Mid Swappers from Asteroid 6!,* all p. 169; August, 2003, Elaine E. Knight, review of *Bud Barkin, Private Eye,* p. 129; October, 2003, Janet Hilbun, review of *13,* p. 167; July, 2004, Jane Marino, review of *Kaddish for Grandpa in Jesus' Name, Amen,* p. 78; May, 2005, Jennifer Ralston, review of *Pinky and Rex and the Bully,* p. 50; November, 2005, Maria B. Salvadore, review of *Totally Joe,* p. 137; February, 2007, Elaine E. Knight, review of *Bunnicula Meets Edgar Allan Crow,* p. 118; September, 2008, Mary Elam, review of *Houndsley and Catina and the Quiet Time,* p. 150; May, 2009, Rebecca Dash, review of *Houndsley and Catina: Plink and Plunk,* p. 80; July, 2009, Lauralyn Persson, review of *Horace and Morris Say Cheese (Which Makes Dolores Sneeze!),* p. 64; July, 2010, Sara Lissa Paulson, review of *Brontorina,* p. 61.

Voice of Youth Advocates, August, 1997, Nancy Thackaberry, review of *The Watcher,* p. 185.

PERIODICALS

Candlewick Web site, http://www.candlewick.com/(January 15, 2011), interview with Howe.

Scholastic Web site, http://www2.scholastic.com/ (January 15, 2011), "James Howe."

Tolerance.org, http://www.tolerance.org/ (spring, 2006), interview with Howe.*

* * *

HYDE, Catherine Ryan 1955-

Personal

Born Catherine Feinberg, 1955, in Buffalo, NY; father a part-time musician father, mother a writer. *Hobbies and other interests:* Hiking, kayaking, photography.

Addresses

Home—Cambria, CA. *Agent*—Laura Rennert, Andrea Brown Literary Agency, 2225 E. Bayshore Rd., Ste. 200, Palo Alto, CA 94303. *E-mail*—ryanhyde@ cryanhyde.com.

Career

Novelist and short-story writer. Formerly worked as a dog trainer, pastry chef, auto mechanic, shopkeeper, and tour guide at Hearst Castle, San Simeon, CA; Cuesta College Writers' Conference, teacher of fiction workshops. Member of administrative staff, Santa Barbara Writers' Conference; member of editorial board, *Santa Barbara Review;* member of fiction fellowship panel, Arizona Commission on the Arts, 1998. Pay It Forward Foundation, founder and president, 2000-09.

Awards, Honors

Raymond Carver Short Story Contest honors, 1994, for "Love Is Always Running Away," and 1996, for "Dante"; second-place award, *Bellingham Review* Tobias Wolff Award, 1997, for "Breakage"; numerous Pushcart Prize nominations for short stories; citation in *Best American Short Stories 1999,* for "Castration Humor," and 2002, for both "Bloodlines" and "The Man Who Found You in the Woods"; Best Books for Young Adults designation, American Library Association (ALA), 2001, for *Pay It Forward;* British Book Award shortlist, c. 2006, for *Love in the Present Tense;* ALA Rainbow Project selection, c. 2006, for *Becoming Chloe;* Best Fiction for Young Adults selection, and Rainbow Project selection, both ALA, both 2010, both for *Jumpstart the World.*

Writings

Pay It Forward, Simon & Schuster (New York, NY), 2000.
Becoming Chloe, Knopf (New York, NY), 2006.
The Year of My Miraculous Reappearance, Knopf (New York, NY), 2007.

The Day I Killed James, Knopf (New York, NY), 2008.
Diary of a Witness, Knopf (New York, NY), 2009.
Jumpstart the World, Knopf (New York, NY), 2010.
Second Hand Heart, Transworld UK (London, England), 2010.

FOR ADULTS

Funerals for Horses, Russian Hill Press (San Francisco, CA), 1997.
Earthquake Weather (short stories), Russian Hill Press (San Francisco, CA), 1998.
Electric God, Simon & Schuster (New York, NY), 2000.
Walter's Purple Heart, Simon & Schuster (New York, NY), 2002.
Love in the Present Tense, Doubleday (New York, NY), 2006.
Chasing Windmills, Doubleday/Flying Dolphin Press (New York, NY), 2008.
When I Found You, Black Swan (London, England), 2009.

Contributor to literary journals, including *Antioch Review, Amherst Review, Sun, Manoa, Puerto del Sol, Virginia Quarterly Review, Ploughshares, New Letters,* and *Michigan Quarterly Review.* Contributor to anthologies, including *Santa Barbara Stories,* John Daniel & Company, 1998, *California Shorts,* Heyday Books, 1999, and *Dog Is My Co-Pilot.*

Adaptations

Pay It Forward was adapted as a film starring Kevin Spacey and Helen Hunt, released by Warner Brothers, and as an audiobook, Simon & Schuster Audio, both 2000.

Sidelights

An award-winning short-story writer and novelist, Catherine Ryan Hyde is best known for her phenomenally successful work *Pay It Forward,* which follows the exploits of an optimistic and kind-hearted youngster and was adapted as a major motion picture. In addition to her numerous short stories, which have appeared in such publications as the *Virginia Quarterly Review* and *Ploughshares,* Hyde has more than a dozen other books to her credit, including the critically acclaimed young-adult novels *The Day I Killed James,* and *Jumpstart the World.*

Written for adults, *Pay It Forward* was Hyde's first novel to gain popularity with teen readers. Given an extra-credit assignment by his social studies teacher to think of a plan that would change society, twelve-year-old Trevor McKinney conceives of a "good will chain." He will do something good for three people, but rather than have them in his debt, he asks them to "pay it forward" by doing good turns for three other people. One of Trevor's good acts is to try to bring his hard-working single mom, Arlene, together with his social studies teacher, Reuben St. Clair. The two do not seem to have much in common to start. Arlene is white, pretty, and works two jobs while trying to recover from alcohol addiction; Reuben is black, well-educated, and missing half his face from an explosion in Vietnam. Although the outlook on this romance seems tenuous at first, like Trevor's other good works the relationship picks up steam before long. Trevor's extra-credit project soon escalates into a major movement through the work of journalist Chris Chandler, whose articles interweave throughout Hyde's fictional narrative.

Pay It Forward received a great deal of critical attention. Although *Time* contributor R.Z. Sheppard dubbed Trevor's project "an idealistic Ponzi scheme" and found the romantic aspects of the plotline "plodding," *Booklist* reviewer Carolyn Kubisz called *Pay It Forward* a "beautifully written, heartwarming story of one boy's belief in the goodness of humanity." *Chicago Tribune* contributor Scott Eyman praised Hyde's "powerful narrative" as well as her ability to tell the story

Cover of Catherine Ryan Hyde's young-adult novel Diary of a Witness, *which focuses on a teen forced to address the bullying in his life.* (Illustration copyright © 2009 by Melissa Nelson. Jacket photograph copyright © 2009 by Rubberball/Jupiter Images. Reproduced by permission of Alfred A. Knopf, an imprint of Random House Children's Books, a division of Random House, Inc.)

"with an easy, beneficent wisdom about the ways of the world." A *Publishers Weekly* contributor maintained of *Pay It Forward* that "Trevor's ultimate martyrdom, and the extraordinary worldwide success of his project, catapult the drama into the realm of myth, but Hyde's simple prose rarely turns preachy." Ultimately, commented *San Francisco Chronicle* reviewer David Field Sunday, Hyde's "fable speaks to the hunger so many of us feel for something to believe in that can give us hope for a future that looks increasingly bleak."

Hyde's *Becoming Chloe* centers on the unlikely friendship between a pair of homeless teens. Jordan, a gay seventeen year old who was tossed from his home after surviving a beating from his father, now lives in a cellar in New York City and resorts to prostitution to survive. After he rescues Chloe, a traumatized young woman, from a rapist, the two form an intense bond and embark on a cross-country odyssey, searching for signs of hope and beauty in the world. The novel's "powerful questions about responsibility and forgiveness will affect readers," Gillian Engberg predicted in her *Booklist* review of *Becoming Chloe*, while a *Kirkus Reviews* critic dubbed the novel "vibrant and heartbreaking."

A thirteen year old battles addiction in *The Year of My Miraculous Reappearance,* a tale of "risk and redemption with a hopeful ending," observed *Booklist* contributor Heather Booth. Cynnie is crushed when her grandparents institutionalize her beloved younger brother, Bill, who suffers from Down syndrome. Heartbroken, the young woman begins drinking heavily, following in the footsteps of her alcoholic mother. A reckless decision to kidnap Bill has devastating consequences for the girl, but with the help of a patient and caring sponsor in Alcoholics Anonymous she begins to reconstruct her life. According to *Journal of Adolescent and Adult Literacy* critic Helen Wanamaker, "*The Year of My Miraculous Reappearance* tells the ugly truth about alcoholism and the ravaging effects it has on a family." "Always heartfelt, often suspenseful, the work stays appropriate for its target audience," a contributor in *Kirkus Reviews* noted.

In Hyde's *The Day I Killed James* a teenage girl's callous act leads to disaster. Attempting to make her on-again, off-again boyfriend jealous, Theresa invites James, who harbors a crush on her, to accompany her to a friend's party. Theresa's ploy works, but when James realizes that he has been used he hops on his motorcycle and drives off a cliff. Knowing that she is responsible for his death, Theresa runs away, moves into a trailer park, and forges a new identity. When she encounters an abused youngster she finds a path to redemption. "Theresa's voice is both raw and witty, capturing the emotion and ambiguity of a young woman in pain," wrote Janis Flint-Ferguson in *Kliatt,* and a *Kirkus Reviews* critic described *The Day I Killed James* as an "original, gripping story."

Bullying is the focus of *Diary of a Witness*. Here Hyde centers on Ernie, a graceless, overweight teen who survives routine humiliation at the hands of the school jocks with the help of a supportive family and friend Will Manson, a classmate who is also bullied. When Will's younger brother drowns in a boating accident, a guilt-ridden Will attempts suicide. Although he survives, the harassment at school only worsens. When Ernie learns that Will has brought a gun to school he must make a fateful decision. "The moment of crisis is chillingly believable and will have readers on the edge of their seats," a *Publishers Weekly* reviewer maintained. "Overall, the story is engrossing, and it compassionately depicts the ever-increasing fury of Will," a critic in *Kirkus Reviews* observed.

Hyde explores another sensitive topic—transgender issues—in *Jumpstart the World*, Dumped into her own apartment at the request of her mother's new boyfriend, fifteen-year-old Elle finds solace in her kindly and wise next-door neighbor, Frank. Although Frank is much older than Elle, she falls for him anyway, then discovers than her neighbor is transgender, transitioning from female to male. At first angry and confused, Elle is able to discard her prejudices and reexamine her relationship with Frank. A *Publishers Weekly* reviewer applauded "Elle's thoughtful and honest narration, which genuinely reads like someone sorting through a complex situation," and Gina Bowling, writing in *School Library Journal*, called Hyde's heroine "a likable, well-developed character with whom teens will identify." According to *Booklist* contributor Michael Cart, *Jumpstart the World* "deserves a wide readership."

Discussing her fictional characters with *Publishers Weekly* interviewer Roxane Farmanfarmaian, Hyde stated: "The world I live in is not all white people, not all straight people, and it's not all people who have their acts together either. Any point I'm trying to make in my writing is that if you go deep enough inside any human being, through all the layers that are different from you, you're going to find the place that's not different. If we could get better at seeing that in each other, we could get over our racism, our classism, our sexism, the here's us and that's them, and I don't know about them."

Biographical and Critical Sources

PERIODICALS

Booklist, December 15, 1999, Carolyn Kubisz, review of *Pay It Forward,* p. 757; November 15, 2000, Carolyn Kubisz, review of *Electric God,* p. 609; March 15, 2002, Carolyn Kubisz, review of *Waiter's Purple Heart,* p. 1212; January 1, 2006, Gillian Engberg, review of *Becoming Chloe,* p. 84; April 1, 2006, Carolyn Kubisz, review of *Love in the Present Tense,* p. 19; March 1, 2007, Heather Booth, review of *The Year of My Miraculous Reappearance,* p. 74; November 15, 2010, Michael Cart, review of *Jumpstart the World,* p. 43.

Chicago Tribune, March 3, 2000, Scott Eyman, "Capraesque Fable Fosters Inspirational Feeling."

Denver Post, April 7, 2002, Kelly Milner-Halls, review of *Walter's Purple Heart.*

Journal of Adolescent and Adult Literacy, March, 2008, Helen Wanamaker, review of *The Year of My Miraculous Reappearance,* p. 521.

Kirkus Reviews, February 15, 2002, review of *Walter's Purple Heart,* p. 210; January 15, 2006, review of *Becoming Chloe,* p. 86; March 15, 2006, review of *Love in the Present Tense,* p. 254; March 1, 2007, review of *The Year of My Miraculous Reappearance,* p. 223; January 1, 2008, review of *Chasing Windmills;* April 1, 2008, review of *The Day I Killed James;* July 1, 2009, review of *Diary of a Witness.*

Kliatt, March, 2006, Myrna Marler, review of *Becoming Chloe,* p. 12; March, 2007, Myrna Marler, review of *The Year of My Miraculous Reappearance,* p. 18; May, 2008, Janis Flint-Ferguson, review of *The Day I Killed James,* p. 10.

Library Journal, August, 1997, David A. Berona, review of *Funerals for Horses,* p. 130; April 15, 1998, Charlotte L. Glover, review of *Earthquake Weather,* pp. 117-118; November 1, 2000, Michele Leber, review of *Electric God,* p. 134; April 1, 2002, Michele Leber, review of *Walter's Purple Heart,* p. 138; February 1, 2008, Bette-Lee Fox, review of *Chasing Windmills,* p. 62.

New Times, April 30, 1998, Joan McCray Tucker, review of *Earthquake Weather.*

Publishers Weekly, April 28, 1997, review of *Funerals for Horses,* p. 52; February 9, 1998, review of *Earthquake Weather,* p. 75; February 22, 1999, John F. Baker, "On the Map," p. 13; November 1, 1999, review of *Pay It Forward,* p. 72; October 16, 2000, review of *Electric God,* p. 47; December 4, 2000, Roxane Farmanfarmaian, interview with Hyde, p. 48; February 18, 2002, review of *Walter's Purple Heart,* p. 74; March 6, 2006, review of *Love in the Present Tense,* p. 46; January 14, 2008, review of *Chasing Windmills,* p. 39; August 17, 2009, review of *Diary of a Witness,* p. 63; October 18, 2010, review of *Jumpstart the World,* p. 51.

San Francisco Chronicle, February 6, 2000, David Field Sunday, "One Boy's Attempt to Change the World."

San Jose Mercury News, May 31, 1998, Jill Wolfson, review of *Earthquake Weather.*

San Luis Obispo Telegram-Tribune, April 3, 1998, Michael Ray, review of *Earthquake Weather.*

School Library Journal, July, 2000, Claudia Moore, review of *Pay It Forward,* p. 127; September, 2002, Julie Dasso, review of *Walter's Purple Heart,* p. 256; October, 2006, Kim Dare, review of *Love in the Present Tense,* p. 187; April, 2007, Stephanie L.

Petruso, review of *The Year of My Miraculous Reappearance,* p. 138; February, 2008, Sondra Vander-Ploegg, review of *Chasing Windmills,* p. 141; June, 2008, Geri Diorio, review of *The Day I Killed James,* p. 144; September, 2009, Diane P. Tuccillo, review of *Diary of a Witness,* p. 162; November, 2010, Gina Bowling, review of *Jumpstart the World,* p. 116.

Time, February 14, 2000, R.Z. Sheppard, review of *Pay It Forward,* p. 86.

ONLINE

BookPage.com, http://www.bookpage.com/ (September 15, 2001), "Meet the Author: Catherine Ryan Hyde."

Catherine Ryan Hyde Web Site, http://www.catherine ryanhyde.com (January 1, 2011).

Pay It Forward Foundation Web Site, http://www.payit forwardfoundation.org/ (January 1, 2011).

K-L

KEHOE, Tim 1970-

Personal
Born 1970, in St. Paul, MN; married, 1995; wife's name Sherri; children: five. *Education:* University of Minnesota, degree.

Addresses
Home—St. Paul, MN. *Office*—Kehoe Companies, 1043 Grand Ave., Ste. 259, Saint Paul, MN 55105-3002. *E-mail*—tim@kehoecompanies.com.

Career
Inventor, toy designer, and writer. Freelance toy designer; Lund & Company, Chicago, IL, toy designer, for one year; Kick Design (toy company), MN, founder; freelance Web site designer; Adaytum (software company), Minneapolis, MN, designer, until 2003; Ascadia, Inc. (toy company), St, Paul, MN, founder, 2004—.

Awards, Honors
Best of What's New Grand Award for Innovation, *Popular Science,* 2005, for Zubbles.

Writings

The Unusual Mind of Vincent Shadow, illustrated by Guy Francis and Mike Wohnoutka, Little, Brown (New York, NY), 2009.
The Unusual Mind of Vincent Shadow: The Whizzer Wishbook, illustrated by Guy Francis, Little, Brown (New York, NY), 2010.

Sidelights
An award-winning inventor and toy designer, Tim Kehoe has also found success in the world of children's literature with the release of *The Unusual Mind of Vin-*

cent Shadow, a fantastical tale about a boy genius and his wondrous creations. In the wider world, Kehoe is best known as the inventor of Zubbles, the world's first brightly colored soap bubbles. "If you said to me, 'You're going to spend a quarter of your life playing with bubbles,' I'd have said you were crazy," Kehoe admitted of his creation *Wired.com* interviewer John Booth.

A native of St. Paul, Minnesota, Kehoe first became interested in toy design while spending Christmas with the family of his girlfriend (now wife) Sherri. After a rousing game of Pictionary, Kehoe decided to "solve the problem of how to have fun," as he remarked to Mike Haney inr *Popular Science.* By 1989 he had completed work on his first board game, Save the Earth. Although the game's stodgy recycling theme failed to impress toy companies, Kehoe made an important contact in Frank Young, who offered the aspiring inventor his first job in the industry. "Young's confidence (and the casual, come-and-go schedule) fueled Kehoe's creativity," Haney noted, "and the ideas poured out: a toy truck with tires that children could pump to monster-truck size; colored sand that hardens in an Easy-Bake toy oven; colored soap bubbles."

Although Kehoe quickly became obsessed with developing the colored bubbles, they proved more difficult to create than he imagined. At first, nothing he used to color the soap mixture—Jell-O, hair dye, fruit juice—would adhere to the bubble's viscous surface. Kehoe even tried nitric acid, which gives off red fumes under certain conditions. "I got it making a really cool bubble, but it could've killed somebody," he recalled to Haney. "It ate through clothes." As the years passed, Kehoe began working out of his kitchen, and though he finally discovered a dye that bonded to the soap, the result was disastrous. "The problem was that if the bubbles touched you, they stained your skin for weeks," he remembered. "It ruined everything. Everybody said the same thing: Call me when you get it right. So I went back to work."

Tim Kehoe's chapter book **The Unusual Mind of Vincent Shadow** *features artwork by Guy Francis.* (Copyright © 2009 by Vincent Shadow, Inc. Reproduced by permission of Little, Brown Company.)

Kehoe's breakthrough came in 2004. With financial backing from the software company where he then worked, he developed a colored bubble that incorporated a washable, pigment-based dye. Still, the product needed tweaking. "You can't go to market with something that leaves that much color, even if it is washable," he told Haney. "It freaks people out." Enlisting the aid of Ram Sabnis, a chemist, Kehoe finally came up with a winning design: vivid orbs colored with an easy-to-clean dye that disappears by simply dabbing it with water or rubbing it gently. "They kind of look like Christmas balls in the air," Kehoe told Leslie Brooks Suzukamo in the *St. Paul Pioneer Press.* Zubbles, as Kehoe dubbed the toy, received 2005's Best of What's New Grand Award for Innovation from *Popular Science,* but it took another four years until the product was ready for large-scale production; Zubbles hit toy-store shelves in 2009.

Kehoe has also parlayed his zeal for invention into his books *The Unusual Mind of Vincent Shadow* and *The Unusual Mind of Vincent Shadow: The Whizzer Wishbook.* The first introduces an eleven-year-old inventor who experiences blinding flashes of inspiration much like those of his idol, famed scientist Nikola Tesla. These moments result in astonishing toys that Vincent builds in his secret attic lab. When Vincent's father remarries and his cranky stepmother forces him to sleep in the basement, the youngster begins to lose his creative drive until he learns of a contest sponsored by an eccentric toy designer. *The Unusual Mind of Vincent Shadow* is "gee-whiz fun for young tinkerers," according to *Booklist* reviewer Ian Chipman, and in *School Library Journal* Jeffrey Hastings called Kehoe's book "a solid, whimsically illustrated writing debut from a real-life toy inventor."

Biographical and Critical Sources

PERIODICALS

Booklist, October 15, 2009, Ian Chipman, review of *The Unusual Mind of Vincent Shadow,* p. 65.

Bulletin of the Center for Children's Books, January, 2010, Karen Coats, review of *The Unusual Mind of Vincent Shadow,* p. 202.

Current Science, April 20, 2007, Chris Jozefowicz, "Mr. Bubble: Tim Kehoe Got His Science Education While Inventing the World's First Colored Bubbles," p. 10.

Kirkus Reviews, October 1, 2009, review of *The Unusual Mind of Vincent Shadow.*

Popular Science, December 1, 2005, Mike Haney, "Building a Better Bubble," p. 98.

Publishers Weekly, November 2, 2009, review of *The Unusual Mind of Vincent Shadow,* p. 52.

St. Paul Pioneer Press, November 7, 2005, Leslie Brooks Suzukamo, "Inventor Unveils Colored but Temporary Soap Bubbles."

School Library Journal, December, 2009, Jeffrey Hastings, review of *The Unusual Mind of Vincent Shadow,* p. 122.

Science World, March 27, 2006, Cody Crane, "Bubble Blower," p. 6.

Star Tribune (Minneapolis, MN), April 12, 2006, Curt Brown, "Inventor's Disappearing Act Is Getting Noticed," p. 1B.

ONLINE

Tim Kehoe Home Page, http://www.timkehoe.com (January 1, 2011).

Unusual Mind of Vincent Shadow Web site, http://www.vincentshadow.com (January 1, 2011).

Wired.com, http://www.wired.com/ (July 26, 2009), John Booth, "Bubbles, Zubbles, Toys and Troubles."*

*   *   *

KRASNESKY, Thad 1969(?)-

Personal

Born c. 1969; married; wife's name Robin; children: Rachael, Isabelle. *Hobbies and other interests:* Marathon running.

Addresses

Home—West Point, NY.

Career

Military officer, educator, and author. U.S. Army, soldier, recruiting officer in Brooklyn, NY, then major, Office of Military Intelligence; U.S. Military Academy at West Point, West Point, NY, instructor.

Writings

I Always, Always Get My Way, illustrated by David Parkins, Flashlight Press (Brooklyn, NY), 2009.

That Cat Can't Stay, illustrated by David Parkins, Flashlight Press (Brooklyn, NY), 2010.

Sidelights

Thad Krasnesky was inspired to write his first children's book by his daughters Rachael and Isabelle, to whom he told rhyming stories beginning when they were very young. Eventually, Krasnesky began to write them down and submitted several to a publisher. Featuring illustrations by artist David Parkins, his first two tales were published as the humorous children's books *I Always, Always Get My Way* and *That Cat Can't Stay.* In his non-writing life, Krasnesky is known as Major Krasnesky; a career officer in the U.S. Army, he served three deployments in Iraq before becoming an instructor at the U.S. Military Academy at West Point.

Emily, the young heroine of *I Always, Always Get My Way,* is three years old and a quick study of the rules of the game of life. Emily is not punished for spilling

Thad Krasnesky tells an humorous story brought to life in David Parkins' art in **The Cat Can't Stay.** (Flashlight Press, 2010. Illustration copyright © 2010 by David Parkins. Reproduced by permission.)

juice on her father's work trousers, and she gets a pass when she makes a mess of her big sister's things. The girl concludes that being young and cute will allow her to get away with almost anything. Emily's assumption is not quite true, however, as readers find out in what a *Publishers Weekly* contributor described as "a fast-moving crowd-pleaser made for reading aloud." "Krasnesky tells the story with flowing rhyme that accommodates the humor of the plot and heightens Parkins's comical cartoon illustrations," asserted Adrienne Wilson in *School Library Journal*, while a *Kirkus Reviews* contributor likened the "subversiveness" in *I Always, Always Get My Way* to the work of noted children's author Shel Silverstein.

In his characteristic rhyming text, Krasnesky introduces another close-knit family in *That Cat Can't Stay*. Mom loves cats and when a stray arrives at her door, she lets it in. When Dad puts up an objection, promises are made by Mom: the cat will only stay for a day or two . . . or three. Then the next cat arrives, and the next, until Dad realizes that he is outnumbered by felines five to one, and any objections to a home overrun by cats will elicit empassioned pleas from his cat-loving children. *That Cat Can't Stay* "expertly combines a comic, rhyming text with hilarious cartoon illustrations to create a completely enjoyable romp," according to Teri Markson in *School Library Journal*, the critic going on to praise the continuing collaboration between Krasnesky and Parkins. Also recommending Parkins' "high-spirited cartoons," a *Publishers Weekly* critic added that the book's "energetic rhymed couplets" propel its comedic view of "family dynamics."

On the Flashlight Press Web site Krasnesky discussed the reaction he gets when people find out that he is a soldier who also writes children's books . . . or, conversely, a children's book author who is also a soldier. "Some people find it odd to reconcile the image of a children's writer with the image that they have of a soldier," he explained. "Some people wonder if writing is my escape from being a soldier. No more so than soldiering is my escape from being a writer. They are both who I am. . . . Most of us, most soldiers, are that way. We are more than simply one-dimensional images. We are fathers and mothers, sons and daughters, husbands and wives. We are founding families and immigrants. We are conservative and liberal, religious and agnostic, scholars and clowns. We are Midwest farmers, west coast activists, southern belles, and urban rappers. Everything that you can possibly imagine, anyone that you have ever known, that is us. We are you."

Biographical and Critical Sources

PERIODICALS

Kirkus Reviews, July 1, 2009, review of *I Always, Always Get My Way*.

Publishers Weekly, September 28, 2009, review of *I Always, Always Get My Way*, p. 63; March 15, 2010, review of *That Cat Can't Stay*, p. 51.

School Library Journal, December, 2009, Adrienne Wilson, review of *I Always, Always Get My Way*, p. 86; May, 2010, Teri Markston, review of *That Cat Can't Stay*, p. 86.

ONLINE

Flash Light Press Web site, http://www.flashlightpress. com/ (November 11, 2010), Thad Krasnesky, "Veterans' Day: A Soldier and Children's Author Celebrates"; (December 27, 2010) "Thad Krasnesky."*

* * *

LEHMAN-WILZIG, Tami 1950-

Personal

Born 1950; immigrated to Israel; married Samuel Wilzig (a university professor); children: two sons. *Education:* Suffolk University, B.A. (English literature); Boston University, M.A. (communications). *Religion:* Jewish. *Hobbies and other interests:* Cooking.

Addresses

Home—Petach Tikva, Israel. *E-mail*—Tamisam@ writestuff.co.il.

Career

Author of children's books. WNET-TV, New York, NY, former on-air copywriter; Teleprompter Cable TV, New York, NY, production assistant, then associate director of programming; TRC Productions (film company), marketing film producer; The Write Stuff (advertising copywriter), Israel, founder, 1980, and chief executive officer.

Awards, Honors

International Reading Association Teacher's Choice Award, 2005, for *Keeping the Promise*.

Writings

FOR CHILDREN

Khlik Lak, Yediot Ahranot (Israel), 1997.
Tasty Bible Stories: A Menu of Tales and Matching Recipes, illustrated by Katherine Janus Kahn, Kar-Ben (Minneapolis, MN), 2003.
Keeping the Promise: A Torah's Journey, illustrated by Craig Orback, Kar-Ben (Minneapolis, MN), 2004.
Lotty's Lace Tablecloth, illustrated by Ksenia Topaz, Gefen Publishing House 2007.

Mayer Aaron Levi and His Lemon Tree, illustrated by Ksenia Topaz, Gefen Publishing House 2007.

Passover around the World, illustrated by Elizabeth Wolf, Kar-Ben (Minneapolis, MN), 2007.

Hanukkah around the World, illustrated by Vicki Wharman, Kar-Ben (Minneapolis, MN), 2009.

Zvuvi's Israel, illustrated by Ksenia Topaz, Kar-Ben (Minneapolis, MN), 2009.

Greener Pastures: Ecological Stories from the Bible, illustrated by Durga Bernhard, Kar-Ben (Minneapolis, MN), 2011.

Nathan Blows Out the Hanukkah Candles, illustrated by Jeremy Tugeau, Kar-Ben (Minneapolis, MN), 2011.

Author's work has been translated into Hebrew.

OTHER

The Melting Pot (cookbook; in Hebrew), Palphot (Israel), 1993.

A Taste of Egypt (cookbook), Palphot (Israel), 1995.

Contributor of articles to magazines.

Sidelights

Tami Lehman-Wilzig draws on her Jewish heritage in many of her books for children. An American-born writer now living in Israel, Lehman-Wilzig writes in English, providing an engaging and international focus in books that include *Passover around the World, Hanukkah around the World,* and *Zvuvi's Israel.* "I believe that being involved in a book makes reading extra fun," Lehman-Wilzig told readers on her home page. "That's why I create original stories around themes that let YOU get involved. I want you to be a part of each and every one of my books . . . and I want you to start writing and dreaming up your own stories."

Lehman-Wilzig grew up in New York State and earned both a bachelor's and a master's degree before moving to Israel with her husband in the late 1970s. With her command of English and her talent for writing, she started a copywriting firm called The Write Stuff and has gained a reputation for producing effective English-language advertising copy as well as translations. On her own initiative, Lehman-Wilzig wrote magazine articles as well as a cookbook before creating her first children's book, a story about a reluctant silkworm that was written in Hebrew and titled *Khlik Lak.* Her next book, *Tasty Bible Stories: A Menu of Tales and Matching Recipes,* was illustrated by Katherine Janus Kahn. *Tasty Bible Stories* earned her a U.S. publisher and started her picture-book career.

Both *Passover around the World* and *Hanukkah around the World* follow the history of two of the most prominent Jewish holidays. Threaded with fictional stories about families living in North America, Europe, Australia, Africa, and the Middle East, *Hanukkah around the World* presents the historic origins of the Festival of

Lights and the diverse ways it is represented by various Jewish communities, while *Passover around the World* introduces the Seder traditions of families living in India, Gibraltar, North America, and Israel. In both *Hanukkah around the World* and *Passover around the World* Lehman-Wilzig includes recipes, songs, and other rituals associated with the celebration. Together with "soft impressionistic" illustrations by Elizabeth Wolf, *Passover around the World* is a "vibrant picture book" that "invites readers to travel the globe," according to a *Publishers Weekly* critic. Lehman-Wilzig's "engaging text and attractive illustrations will make this a good choice for families wishing to explore diverse ways of celebrating," concluded *Booklist* critic Kay Weisman in her review of *Hanukkah around the World,* and Teri Markson noted in *School Library Journal* that the book's "densely colored illustrations" and maps by Kahn are "generally appealing."

Another faith-based book by Lehman-Wilzig, *Keeping the Promise: A Torah's Journey,* is set during the Holocaust of World War II. Rabbi Simon Dasberg lived in the Netherlands when the Nazis began to round up Dutch Jews, and he was eventually sent to Bergen-Belsen, a concentration camp in northwestern Germany. In captivity Rabbi Dasberg retained possession of a miniature Torah scroll, and after performing a Bar Mitzvah for a young fellow captive he passed his Torah to the boy with the request that he tell the truth of the camps if he survived. The poignant story ends in 2003, as the same Torah was taken aboard the Columbia space shuttle by Israeli astronaut Ilan Ramon. Recommended for "Hebrew day schools and synagogue libraries" by

Tami-Lehman-Wilzig teams up with artist Ksenia Topaz to create the picture book Zvuvi's Israel. (Illustration copyright © 2009 by Ksenia Topaz. Reproduced by permission of Kar-Ben, a division of Lerner Publishing Group. No part of this excerpt may be used or reproduced in any manner whatsoever without the prior written permission of Lerner Publishing Group, Inc.)

School Library Journal contributor Sandra Kitain, *Keeping the Promise* was also praised as a profile of "a true hero's journey as well as a lesson in history and humanity."

Other books by Lehman-Witzig include *Zvuvi's Israel,* which takes reader on a tour of Israel using an unusual perspective: the viewpoint of fly cousins named Zahava and Zvuvi. With their literal "fly on the wall" perspective on life, the flies travel from historic sites to beaches and zoos, their "whirlwind . . . tour" captured in "detailed pictures" by Ksenia Topaz, according to *School Library Journal* critic Heidi Estrin. A *Kirkus Reviews* writer described horsefly tour guides Zvuvi and Zahava as "likable" and added that "the overall design and wealth of information" in *Zvuvi's Israel* makes Lehman-Witzig's picture book "a friendly introduction to the country."

Biographical and Critical Sources

PERIODICALS

Booklist, May 15, 2007, Hazel Rochman, review of *Passover around the World,* p. 43; December 1, 2009, Kay Weisman, review of *Hanukkah around the World,* p. 40.
Kirkus Reviews, August 1, 2009, review of *Zvuvi's Israel*; September 15, 2009, review of *Hanukkah around the World.*
Publishers Weekly, December 18, 2006, review of *Passover around the World,* p. 66; October 19, 2009, review of *Hanukkah around the World,* p. 52.
School Library Journal, February, 2004, Sandra Kitain, review of *Tasty Bible Stories: A Menu of Tales and Matching Recipes,* p. 134; August, 2004, Sandra Kitain, review of *Keeping the Promise: A Torah's Journey,* p. 111; April, 2007, Lisa Silver, review of *Passover around the World,* p. 123; October, 2009, Teri Markson, review of *Hanukkah around the World,* p. 81; November, 2009, Heidi Estrin, review of *Zvuvi's Israel,* p. 83.

ONLINE

Tami Lehman-Wilzig Home Page, http://www.tlwkids books.com (December 27, 2010).*

*   *   *

LIDDIMENT, Carol

Personal

Born in Widnes, Cheshire, England; children. *Education:* Goldsmiths College London, degree (textile design), 1985; Anglia Ruskin, M.F.A. (children's book illustration), 2005.

Addresses

Home—Suffolk, England. *Agent*—The Organisation, 69 Caledonian Rd., Kings Cross, London N1 9BT, England.

Career

Illustrator and designer. Ericson Beamon London, London, England, former jewelry designer; founder of retail jewelry company in London; freelance illustrator; teacher.

Awards, Honors

Coventry Inspirational Book Award, 2008, for *Happy I'm a Hippo* by Richard Edwards; Sharjah World Book Fair Children's Book Award, 2010, for *How Many Donkeys?* by Margaret Read MacDonald.

Illustrator

Richard Edwards, *Happy I'm a Hippo,* Alison Green (London, England), 2007.
Richard Edwards, *Happy Birthday, Bear,* Alison Green (London, England), 2008.
Margaret Read MacDonald and Nadia Jameel Taibah, retellers, *How Many Donkeys?: An Arabic Counting Tale,* Albert Whitman (Morton Grove, IL), 2009

Biographical and Critical Sources

PERIODICALS

Booklist, September 15, 2009, Diane Foote, review of *How Many Donkeys?: An Arabic Counting Tale,* p. 61.
Kirkus Reviews, September 1, 2009, review of *How Many Donkeys?*
School Library Journal, October, 2009, Mary Jean Smith, review of *How Many Donkeys?,* p. 112.

ONLINE

Carol Liddiment Home Page, http://www.organisart.co.uk (December 7, 2010).*

*   *   *

LIEB, Josh 1972-

Personal

Born June 4, 1972, in SC; married; wife's name Beata; children: two. *Education:* Harvard University, degree.

Addresses

Home—New York, NY.

Career

Television producer and author. Writer of animated films and television scripts; television series work includes (executive story editor, supervising producer, co-executive producer, then co-producer) *NewsRadio,* 1995-99, (consulting producer) *Nikki,* 2000, (consulting producer) *The Simpsons,* 2002, (consulting producer, then executive consultant) *Drawn Together,* 2005-08, and (co-executive producer) *The Daily Show,* 2007-11.

Member

Writer's Guild of America.

Awards, Honors

(With others) Emmy Award nomination for Outstanding Animated Program, 2002, for *The Simpsons;* Emmy Award for Outstanding Writing for a Variety, Music, or Comedy Series, nomination, 2007, 2008, 2010, and award, 2009, Emmy Award for Outstanding Variety, Music, or Comedy Series, 2007, 2008, 2009, and Writer's Guild of America Award for Best Comedy/Variety, nomination, 2009, and award, 2010, all for *The Daily Show with Jon Stewart.*

Writings

I Am a Genius of Unspeakable Evil and I Want to Be Your Class President, Razorbill (New York, NY), 2009.

Author of filmscripts, including *Big Stan,* 2007; (with Billiam Coronel) *Immigrants* (animation), 2008. Author of scripts for television episodes of *The Daily Show with Jon Stewart, Twisted Puppet Theatre, NewsRadio,* and *The Simpsons.* Contributor to *Harvard Lampoon.*

Adaptations

I Am a Genius of Unspeakable Evil and I Want to Be Your Class President was optioned for film by Wonderland Productions, 2009.

Sidelights

Josh Lieb is a television producer and writer whose professional credits include a four-year stint as executive producer of the popular *Daily Show with Jon Stewart,* which airs on the Comedy Central cable network. In 2007, Lieb's first year with the show, his trade union went on a prolonged strike. With free time on his hands and no idea how long the Writer's Guild strike would last, he planned the outline and first four chapters of what would become his first teen novel, *I Am a Genius of Unspeakable Evil and I Want to Be Your Class President.*

Oliver Watson is the ambitious and maniacal middle-schooler who stars in *I Am a Genius of Unspeakable Evil and I Want to Be Your Class President.* Pudgy, ma-

levolent, and brilliant to a fault, Oliver lives in Omaha, Nebraska, where his parents lead their uneventful lives oblivious to the fact that their son has spent his childhood years building a globe-spanning empire of wealth and power. With a penchant for cruelty—but also with a hidden need for parental approval—Oliver decides to outdo his father's own adolescent triumph and win the upcoming student-body election at Gale Sayers Middle School. In true megalomaniac fashion, he uses bribery, threats, and boated campaign promises to orchestrate his election victory, pulling all the strings from his secret hideout and using 007-style technology. In a simple text mixed with humorous photographs, "Lieb perfectly captures the wise-guy sarcasm and trash mouth of a seventh-grade evil genius," wrote Connie Tyrrell Burns in *School Library Journal,* while a *Publishers Weekly* critic predicted that the "ample scatalogical humor" in *I Am a Genius of Unspeakable Evil and I Want to Be Your Class President* will appeal to Leib's intended readership. Comparing *I Am a Genius of Unspeakable Evil and I Want to Be Your Class President* to Eoin Colfer's novels about evil genius Artemis Fowl, a *Kirkus Reviews* writer added that "Lieb's creative and twisted first novel gets a positive vote."

Biographical and Critical Sources

PERIODICALS

Kirkus Reviews, September 1, 2009, review of *I Am a Genius of Unspeakable Evil and I Want to Be Your Class President.*

Publishers Weekly, October 12, 2009, review of *I Am a Genius of Unspeakable Evil and I Want to Be Your Class President,* p. 50.

School Library Journal, October, 2009, Connie Tyrrell Burns, review of *I Am a Genius of Unspeakable Evil and I Want to Be Your Class President,* p. 130.

USA Today, October 22, 2009, Bob Minzesheimer, "*Daily Show* Writer Channels Teen 'Genius'," p. D6.

Voice of Youth Advocates, December, 2009, Jenny Ingram, review of *I Am a Genius of Unspeakable Evil and I Want to Be Your Class President,* p. 410.

ONLINE

MediaBistro.com, http://www.mediabistro.com/ (October 21, 2009), Amanda Ernst, interview with Lieb.*

M

MADIGAN, Lisa Kay
See MADIGAN, L.K.

*   *   *

MADIGAN, L.K. (?)-2011
(Lisa Kay Madigan)

Personal
Died of cancer, February 23, 2011, in OR; married; children: Nathan. *Hobbies and other interests:* Travel, bike riding, photography.

Career
Novelist and financial analyst. Presenter at schools and conferences.

Awards, Honors
William C. Morris Young-Adult Debut Award, and Best Books for Young Adults selection, both American Library Association, and Rhode Island Teen Book Award nomination, all 2010, all for *Flash Burnout.*

Writings

Flash Burnout, Houghton Mifflin (Boston, MA), 2009.
The Mermaid's Mirror, Houghton Mifflin Harcourt (Boston, MA), 2010.

Adaptations
Flash Burnout was adapted for audiobook, narrated by Macleod Andrews, Aududible, Inc., 2010.

Sidelights
A year before she died of cancer, L.K. Madigan won the William C. Morris Y-A Debut Award for her novel *Flash Burnout,* about a teen whose love of photography opens his eyes to the complications of true friendships and the demands of love. A children's writing class given by her local community college inspired Madigan to consider writing for children, and the tragedy of September 11, 2001 convinced her to pursue her long-held dream of authorship while she had the opportunity. During the seven years until *Flash Burnout* found a publisher, she moved from picture books to young-adult fiction, sought out the advice and support of other writers, and completed three novel-length manuscripts. Although Madigan's writing moved from a hobby to something more serious, it remained her second job; she planned the plots of her teen fiction while working the numbers at a money manager in her home state of Oregon.

When readers meet Blake in *Flash Burnout,* the teen seems to be lucky in love: Shannon, one of the most beautiful girls in school is his girlfriend. He also has a really good friend who shares his interest in photography, and that is where his problems arise. That really good friend is a girl, Marissa, and as Blake is drawn into Marissa's troubled home life (her mother is a meth addict) their relationship becomes increasingly intimate. While Blake navigates the fall out from his shifting emotions, he also deals with his own parents and his younger brother in a family where responsibility for personal choices is consistently modeled. Madigan's "rich romance explores the complexities of friendship and love, and the all-too-human limitations of both," wrote *Booklist* contributor Frances Bradburn, while in *Kirkus Reviews* a contributor praised the author's skill in creating dialogue that "feels genuinely alive." Remarking on Blake's "quick witted" and humorous dialogue, Sue Lloyd added in *School Library Journal* that *Flash Burnout* features a "beautifully developed" coming-of-age story that "is thought-provoking on many levels."

Although *Flash Burnout* was the first of Madigan's manuscripts to find a publisher, it was actually the third novel she completed; her second was published in 2010 as *The Mermaid's Mirror.* Although her single father

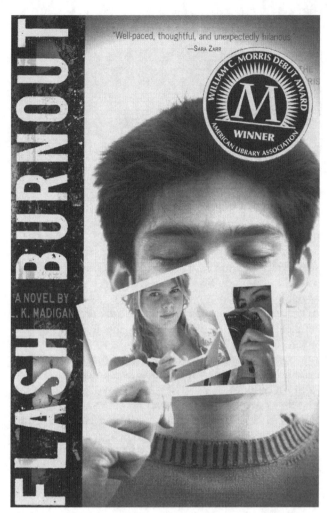

Cover of L.K. Madigan's young-adult novel Flash Burnout, *which focuses on the emotional world of a teen photographer.* (Cover photographs 2009 by Photoalto and Rian Hughes. Reproduced by permission of Houghton Mifflin Harcourt Publishing Company.)

has raised her to keep away from the ocean because of a terrible surfing accident, almost-sixteen-year-old Lena feels strangely drawn to the sea in this supernatural story. While gaining her skill as a surfer, Lena begins to catch glimpses of a mermaid swimming nearby. Her determination to follow this vision draws her out into dangerous waters of Magic Crescent Cove, off the northern California coast. Although she almost drowns, the teen is saved by the mermaid and given a small golden key. Soon Lena finds herself in an underwater world where many of her questions are answered, including who—or what—her mother really is. Described by *Booklist* contributor Francisca Goldsmith as "a rewarding and credible story that uses fantasy elements to bare truths about family ties," *The Mermaid's Mirror* is strengthened by Madigan's skill in creating "highly imagistic descriptions and savvy dialogue," according to the critic. The book's combination of "exquisite writing . . . and a compelling plot set in vivid scenery" create a tale with realistic teen appeal, wrote *School Library Journal* contributor Tara Kehoe, the critic recommending *The Mermaid's Mirror* as "one fantasy worth reading."

Biographical and Critical Sources

PERIODICALS

Booklist, September 15, 2009, Frances Bradburn, review of *Flash Burnout,* p. 68; September 15, 2010, Francisca Goldsmith, review of *The Mermaid's Mirror,* p. 63.

Bulletin of the Center for Children's Books, January, 2010, Jeff Chang, review of *Flash Burnout,* p. 207.

Kirkus Reviews, September 15, 2009, review of *Flash Burnout.*

Publishers Weekly, December 21, 2009, "Flying Starts," p. 18; October 4, 2010, review of *The Mermaid's Mirror,* p. 49.

School Library Journal, November, 2009, Sue Lloyd, review of *Flash Burnout,* p. 114; December, 2010, Tara Kehoe, review of *The Mermaid's Mirror,* p. 120.

ONLINE

L.K. Madigan Home Page, http://www.flashburnout.com (December 7, 2010).

L.K. Madigan Web log, http://lkmadigan.livejournal.com (December 27, 2010).*

*   *   *

MEISEL, Paul

Personal

Married Cheryl Clark; children: Peter, Andrew, Alex. *Education:* Wesleyan University, B.A.; Yale University, M.F.A. *Hobbies and other interests:* Tennis.

Addresses

Home and office—Newtown, CT.

Career

Illustrator and graphic artist. Has also worked in editorial and advertising illustration.

Awards, Honors

Best Children's Book of the Year selection, Bank Street College of Education, Parent's Guide to Children's Media Award, and Children's Literature Choices, all 2000, all for *The Cool Crazy Crickets Club* by David Elliott; Parent's Guide to Children's Media Award, 2001, for *The Cool Crazy Crickets to the Rescue; Oppenheim Toy Portfolio Gold Award, 2005, for *Dear Baby* by Sarah Sullivan; Oppenheim Toy Portfolio Gold Award, and Best of the Best listee, Chicago Public Library, both 2009, both for *Harriet's Had Enough!* by Elissa Haddon Guest.

Writings

SELF-ILLUSTRATED

Zara's Hats, Dutton Children's Books (New York, NY), 2003.

See Me Run, Holiday House (New York, NY), 2011.

ILLUSTRATOR

Patricia McKissack, *Monkey-Monkey's Trick: Based on an African Folktale,* Random House (New York, NY), 1988.

Jill A. Davidson, *And That's What Happened to Little Lucy,* Random House (New York, NY), 1989.

Billy Goodman, *A Kid's Guide to How to Save the Planet,* Avon Books (New York, NY), 1990.

William H. Hooks, *Mr. Monster,* Bantam Books (New York, NY), 1990.

Billy Goodman, *A Kid's Guide to How to Save the Animals,* Avon Books (New York, NY), 1991.

Ira Wolfman, *My World and Globe: From the Seven Continents to the Seven Seas, from Katmandu to Kalamazoo: An Interactive First Book of Geography,* Workman Publishing (New York, NY), 1991.

Joanna Cole, *Your Insides,* Putnam (New York, NY), 1992.

Christel Kleitsch, *Cousin Markie and Other Disasters,* Dutton Children's Books (New York, NY), 1992.

Alvin Schwartz, *Busy Buzzing Bumblebees, and Other Tongue Twisters,* HarperCollins (New York, NY), 1992.

Sarah Albee, *Halloween ABC,* Western Publishing Company (Racine, WI), 1993.

Carol Diggory Shields, *I Am Really a Princess,* Dutton Children's Books (New York, NY), 1993.

Andrea Zimmerman, *The Cow Buzzed,* HarperCollins (New York, NY), 1993.

William H. Hooks, *Mr. Dinosaur,* Bantam Books (New York, NY), 1994.

Barbara Ann Kipfer, *1,400 Things for Kids to Be Happy about: The Happy Book,* Workman Publishing (New York, NY), 1994.

Janice Lee Smith, *Wizard and Wart,* HarperCollins (New York, NY), 1994.

Games and Giggles Just for Girls!, Pleasant Company (Middleton, WI), 1995.

Carol Diggory Shields, *Lunch Money, and Other Poems about School,* Dutton Children's Books (New York, NY), 1995.

Janice Lee Smith, *Wizard and Wart at Sea,* HarperCollins (New York, NY), 1995.

Stephanie Calmenson, *Engine, Engine, Number Nine,* Hyperion Books for Children (New York, NY), 1996.

Janet Frank, *Daddies: All about the Work They Do,* Western Publishing Company (Racine, WI), 1996.

Kirby Puckett and Andrew Gutelle, *Kirby Puckett's Baseball Games,* Workman Publishing (New York, NY), 1996.

William H. Hooks, *Mr. Dinosaur,* Gareth Stevens Publishing (Milwaukee, WI), 1997.

Margo Lundell, *Mommies: All about the Work They Do,* Golden Books (Racine, WI), 1997.

Joan L. Nodset, *Go Away, Dog,* HarperCollins (New York, NY), 1997.

Carol Diggory Shields, *I Wish My Brother Was a Dog,* Dutton Children's Books (New York, NY), 1997.

B.G. Hennessy, *Mr. Bubble Gum,* Gareth Stevens Publishing (Milwaukee, WI), 1997.

William H. Hooks, *Mr. Baseball,* Gareth Stevens Publishing (Milwaukee, WI), 1998.

Kathleen Weidner Zoehfeld, *What Is the World Made of?: All about Solids, Liquids, and, Gases,* HarperCollins (New York, NY), 1998.

Karen Magnuson Beil, *A Cake All for Me!,* Holiday House (New York, NY), 1998.

William H. Hooks, *Mr. Monster,* Gareth Stevens Publishing (Milwaukee, WI), 1998.

Cobi Jones and Andrew Gutelle, *Cobi Jones' Soccer Games,* Workman Publishing (New York, NY), 1998.

Anne Mazer, *The Fixits,* Hyperion Books for Children (New York, NY), 1998.

Betty Miles, *The Three Little Pigs,* Simon & Schuster Books for Young Readers (New York, NY), 1998.

Betty Miles, *The Tortoise and the Hare,* Simon & Schuster Books for Young Readers (New York, NY), 1998.

Janice Lee Smith, *Wizard and Wart in Trouble,* HarperCollins (New York, NY), 1998.

Jeanette Ryan Wall, *More Games and Giggles: Wild about Animals!,* Pleasant Company (Middleton, WI), 1998.

William C. Harvey. *Spanish for Gringos: Shortcuts, Tips, and Secrets to Successful Learning,* Barron's (Hauppauge, NY), 1999, 3rd edition, 2008.

On beyond a Million: An Amazing Math Journey, Random House (New York, NY), 1999.

Melvin Berger, *Why I Sneeze, Shiver, Hiccup, and Yawn,* HarperCollins (New York, NY), 2000.

David Elliott, *The Cool Crazy Crickets,* Candlewick Press (Cambridge, MA), 2000, published as *The Cool Crazy Crickets Club,* 2010.

Jean Craighead George, *How to Talk to Your Cat,* HarperCollins (New York, NY), 2000.

Kathleen Karr, *It Happened in the White House: Extraordinary Tales from America's Most Famous Home,* Hyperion Books for Children (New York, NY), 2000.

J. Philip Miller and Sheppard M. Greene, *We All Sing with the Same Voice,* HarperCollins (New York, NY), 2001.

Anne Rockwell, *Morgan Plays Soccer,* HarperCollins (New York, NY), 2001.

David Elliott, *The Cool Crazy Crickets to the Rescue!,* Candlewick Press (Cambridge, MA), 2001.

Michelle Edwards and Phyllis Root, *What's That Noise?,* Candlewick Press (Cambridge, MA), 2002.

Joan Holub, *Hooray for St. Patrick's Day!,* Puffin Books (New York, NY), 2002.

Bill Martin, Jr., and Michael Sampson, *Trick or Treat?,* Simon & Schuster Books for Young Readers (New York, NY), 2002.

Kimberly Brubaker Bradley, *Energy Makes Things Happen,* HarperCollins (New York, NY), 2003.

Anne Rockwell, *Katie Catz Makes a Splash,* HarperCollins (New York, NY), 2003.

Carol Diggory Shields, *Almost Late to School, and More School Poems,* Dutton Children's Books (New York, NY), 2003.

Judy Sierra, *Coco and Cavendish: Circus Dogs,* Random House (New York, NY), 2003.

Karen Magnuson Beil, *Mooove Oover!: A Book about Counting by Twos,* Holiday House (New York, NY), 2004.

Lynn Brunelle, *Pop Bottle Science,* Workman Publishing (New York, NY), 2004.

Judy Cox, *Go to Sleep, Groundhog,* Holiday House (New York, NY), 2004.

Anne Rockwell, *Chip and the Karate Kick,* HarperCollins (New York, NY), 2004.

Michael Elsohn, *What's the Matter in Mr. Whisker's Room?,* Candlewick Press (Cambridge, MA), 2004.

Judy Sierra, *Coco and Cavendish: Fire Dogs,* Random House (New York, NY), 2004.

Kimberly Brubaker Bradley, *Forces Make Things Move,* HarperCollins (New York, NY), 2005.

Kathy Duval, *The Three Bears' Christmas,* Holiday House (New York, NY), 2005.

Sheila Keenan, *Looking for Leprechauns,* Scholastic (New York, NY), 2005.

Anne Rockwell, *Brendan and Belinda and the Slam Dunk,* HarperCollins (New York, NY), 2005.

Sarah Sullivan, *Dear Baby: Letters from Your Big Brother,* Candlewick Press (Cambridge, MA), 2005.

B.G. Hennesey, *Mr. Ouchy's First Day,* Putnam's (New York, NY), 2006.

Anne Rockwell, *Why Are the Ice Caps Melting?: The Dangers of Global Warming,* Collins (New York, NY), 2006.

Shelley Moore Thomas, *Take Care, Good Knight,* Dutton Children's Books (New York, NY), 2006.

Kathy Duval, *The Three Bears' Halloween,* Holiday House (New York, NY), 2007.

Linda Ashman, *Stella, Unleashed: Notes from the Doghouse,* Sterling Publishing (New York, NY), 2008.

Dian Curtis Regan, *Barnyard Slam,* Holiday House (New York, NY), 2009.

Elissa Haden Guest, *Harriet's Had Enough!,* Candlewick Press (Somerville, MA), 2009.

Anne Rockwell, *What's So Bad about Gasoline?: Fossil Fuels and What They Do,* Collins (New York, NY), 2009.

Kelly Bennett, *Dad and Pop: An Ode to Fathers and Stepfathers,* Candlewick Press (Somerville, MA), 2010.

Alyssa Satin Capucilli, *Scat, Cat!,* HarperCollins (New York, NY), 2010.

Leslie Kimmelman, *The Little Red Hen and the Passover Matzah,* Holiday House (New York, NY), 2010.

Carol Diggory Shields, *Someone Used My Toothbrush! and Other Bathroom Poems,* Dutton Children's Books (New York, NY), 2010.

Sidelights

An award-winning illustrator, Paul Meisel has created artwork for more than seventy children's books, including Dian Curtis Regan's *Barnyard Slam* and Elissa Haden Guest's *Harriet's Had Enough!* Using a variety of techniques, including acrylics, gouache, water color,

and mixed media, Meisel "adds child appeal" to the often humorous narratives, according to *Booklist* critic Ilene Cooper. In addition, with the 2003 picture book *Zara's Hats,* Meisel turned author as well, drawing inspiration from a family photograph. *Zara's Hats* tells a story about Selig the hat maker and his daughter Zara. When Selig runs out of the special feathers he uses to design his hats, he is forced to travel far from home to obtain more. While her father is away, Zara begins crafting hats of her own, using materials found within her family's house. Before long, word spreads about the girl's unique hats and they become the newest fashion trend in town. As *School Library Journal* reviewer Martha Topol commented of Meisel's original picture book, *Zara's Hats* treats readers to "a fully fleshed out and engaging story" that comes to life in the author/illustrator's colorful artwork.

In illustrating author Anne Rockwell's environmental-themed picture book *Why Are the Ice Caps Melting?: The Dangers of Global Warming,* Meisel also contributes to the "Let's Read and Find Out Science" series. In the book, Rockwell offers a straightforward text while Meisel provides colorful and detailed illustrations that speak to the book's young audience. As Cooper commented in her review of *Why Are the Ice Caps Melting?* for *Booklist,* the illustrator's "ink-and-watercolor art,

Paul Meisel's illustration work includes creating the amusing art for Priscilla Paton's Howard and the Sitter Surprise. (Illustration copyright © 1996 by Paul Meisel. All rights reserved. Reproduced by permission of Houghton Mifflin Harcourt Publishing Company.)

brimming with action, has a lightness the subject belies." In a companion volume, *What's So Bad about Gasoline?: Fossil Fuels and What They Do,* Rockwell examines the history of petroleum-based energy sources and looks at renewable energy resources. A *Kirkus Reviews* critic noted that "Meisel's ink-and-watercolor illustrations nicely illustrate/summarize the key concepts in the text."

Other books featuring Meisel's art include one of his favorite projects: Judy Cox's humorous picture book *Go to Sleep, Groundhog!* The book finds a restless groundhog awaking sporadically in time to sample a winter's worth of other holidays. When he learns what he has been missing by hibernating, the animal is tempted to emerge from his hole earlier than the appointed Groundhog Day. Reviewing *Go to Sleep, Groundhog!* for *School Library Journal,* Kathleen Kelly MacMillan wrote that Meisel's "vibrant acrylic-and-gouache illustrations will help make this a favorite in storytimes." In *School Library Journal,* Grace Oliff and Ann Blanche Smith also praised Meisel's work for B.G. Hennessey's *Mr. Ouchy's First Day.* In addition to noting that the illustrator's "watercolor, gouache, and pen-and-ink" images inspire Hennessey's story with a "cozy feel," Oliff and Smith asserted that Meisel's images both "amplify humorous situations" in the text and "create them when the text does not." Discussing his illustrations for Sarah Sullivan's scrapbook-style picture book *Dear Baby: Letters from Your Big Brother,* a *Kirkus Reviews* writer concluded that "Meisel's mixed-media pictures are cheerful and engaging."

In his role as illustrator, Meisel has collaborated with author Kathy Duval on a pair of holiday stories. In *The Three Bears' Christmas,* a tale inspired by "Goldilocks," Papa Bear, Mama Bear, and Baby Bear discover that their home has been visited by a jolly old elf bearing gifts. Meisel's illustrations "provide an atmosphere of comfort and warmth" to the story, a critic in *Horn Book* stated. The bruin family gets a wonderful surprise while trick-or-treating at a witch's house in *The Three Bears' Halloween.* "Observant readers will giggle over the hidden details in Meisel's acrylics," noted a *Kirkus Reviews* contributor.

A trio of dragons agrees to babysit a wizard's cats—with predictably disastrous results—in *Take Care, Good Knight,* a work by Shelley Moore Thomas. According to *Booklist* reviewer Carolyn Phelan, "Meisel's ink-and-watercolor illustrations, full of lively details, are as entertaining as the story." Linda Ashman's *Stella, Unleashed: Notes from the Doghouse,* a collection of twenty-nine poems, offers a canine's ground-eye perspective of life with its new family. Here "Meisel's illustrations bring Stella and her family to life with a bright palette of cheerful colors," wrote a critic in *Kirkus Reviews.* Animals also take center stage in Regan's *Barnyard Slam,* which details a lively poetry competition headed by Yo Mama Goose. Meisel's pictures "convey the story's humor and energy," a reviewer commented in *Publishers Weekly.*

Meisel's illustrations for **Morgan Plays Soccer** *capture the summertime fun of Anne Rockwell's tale.* (Illustration copyright © 2001 by Paul Meisel. Used by permission of HarperCollins Children's Books, a division of HarperCollins Publishers.)

A familiar childhood scenario is the focus of *Harriet's Had Enough!,* a picture book by Guest. After a disagreement with her mother, a raccoon named Harriet decides to run away from home, until her wise grandparents intervene. Meg Smith, writing in *School Library Journal,* applauded Meisel's contributions to the work, stating that "Harriet's shifting emotions are conveyed through her varied expressions." Another family-oriented tale, Kelly Bennett's *Dad and Pop: An Ode to Fathers and Stepfathers,* offers a young girl's thoughts on her two loving but very different caretakers. "Expressive faces and gentle humor add charm to the pictures," Heidi Estrin noted in *School Library Journal,* and *USA Today* contributor Bob Minzesheimer also complimented Meisel's brightly colored illustrations, stating that they "add a festive flavor."

Meisel's cartoon-like artwork is also featured in *The Little Red Hen and the Passover Matzah,* a tale by Leslie Kimmelman. With the Jewish holiday approaching, Little Red Hen turns to her companions for help in preparing the matzah for her Seder dinner, to no avail. Frustrated and prepared to dine alone, Little Red Hen recalls a lesson about forgiveness when her lazy friends arrive for a meal. Meisel's pictures "add exactly the right touch of humor to this holiday version of a classic folktale," maintained a contributor in *Kirkus Reviews,*

Meisel's art captures the antics of the raccoon characters that star in Harriet's Had Enough!, *a story by Elissa Haden Guest.* (Illustration copyright © 2009 by Paul Meisel. Reproduced by permission of Candlewick Press, Somerville, MA.)

and Ilene Cooper wrote in *Booklist* that "the ink-and-watercolor art amusingly captures both the Little Red Hen's aggravation and the animals' turnaround." According to *School Library Journal* critic Lauralyn Persson, Meisel's "colorful cartoons add just the right tone" to *Someone Used My Toothbrush! and Other Bathroom Poems,* a collection by Carol Diggory Shields.

Biographical and Critical Sources

PERIODICALS

Audubon, May-June, 1997, review of *Why Are the Ice Caps Melting?: The Dangers of Global Warming,* p. 94.

Booklist, December 15, 1999, Ilene Cooper, review of *How to Talk to Your Cat,* p. 787; September 15, 2000, John Peters, review of *The Cool Crazy Crickets,* p. 240; September 1, 2001, Ellen Mandel, review of *The Cool Crazy Crickets to the Rescue,* p. 104; September 15, 2002, Stephanie Zvirin, review of *Trick or Treat?,* p. 246; February 1, 2003, review of *Energy Makes Things Happen,* p. 996; February 15, 2003, Gillian Engberg, review of *Zara's Hats,* p. 1075; August, 2003, review of *Almost Late to School!,* p. 1994; November 15, 2003, review of *Go to Sleep, Groundhog!,* p. 599; May 1, 2004, Jennifer Mattson, review of *Chip and the Karate Kick,* p. 1564; September 1, 2005, Il-

ene Cooper, review of *The Three Bears' Christmas,* p. 124; September 15, 2005, Carolyn Phelan, review of *Forces Make Things Move,* p. 67; August 1, 2006, Hazel Rochman, reviews of *Letters from Your Big Brother,* p. 75, and *Mr. Ouchy's First Day,* p. 95; September 15, 2006, Carolyn Phelan, review of *Take Care, Good Knight,* p. 68; December 15, 2006, Ilene Cooper, review of *Why Are the Ice Caps Melting?,* p. 50; July 1, 2007, Randall Enos, review of *Brendan and Belinda and the Slam Dunk!,* p. 64; August, 2007, Ilene Cooper, review of *The Three Bears' Halloween,* p. 86; May 1, 2008, Stephanie Zvirin, review of *Stella, Unleashed: Notes from the Doghouse,* p. 94; February 15, 2009, Carolyn Phelan, review of *What's So Bad about Gasoline?: Fossil Fuels and What They Do,* p. 93; April 1, 2009, Randall Enos, review of *Harriet's Had Enough,* p. 43; February 1, 2010, Ilene Cooper, review of *The Little Red Hen and the Passover Matzah,* p. 46; February 15, 2010, Randall Enos, review of *Dad and Pop: An Ode to Fathers and Stepfathers,* p. 80; April 1, 2010, Hazel Rochman, review of *Someone Used My Toothbrush! and Other Bathroom Poems,* p. 44.

Bulletin of the Center for Children's Books, January, 2004, Janice Del Negro, review of *Go to Sleep, Groundhog!,* p. 186; December, 2006, Elizabeth Bush, review of *Why Are the Ice Caps Melting?,* p. 187; February, 2007, Elizabeth Bush, review of *Take Care, Good Knight,* p. 270.

Horn Book, November-December, 2005, review of *The Three Bears' Christmas,* p. 692; May-June, 2010, Elissha Gershowitz, review of *The Little Red Hen and the Passover Matzah,* p. 69.

Kirkus Reviews, July 1, 2002, review of *What's That Noise?,* p. 953; September 15, 2002, review of *Trick or Treat?,* p. 1395; February 1, 2003, review of *Zara's Hats,* p. 236; June 1, 2003, review of *Almost Late to School!,* p. 811; December 15, 2003, review of *Go to Sleep, Groundhog!,* p. 1449; May 1, 2004, review of *Chip and the Karate Kick,* p. 447; August 15, 2004, review of *What's the Matter in Mr. Whisker's Room?,* p. 812; September 15, 2004, review of *Mooove Oover!: A Book about Counting by Twos,* p. 910; July 1, 2005, review of *Forces Make Things Move,* p. 731; August 1, 2005, review of *Letters from Your Big Brother,* p. 859; November 1, 2005, review of *The Three Bears' Christmas,* p. 1192; June 1, 2006, review of *Mr. Ouchy's First Day,* p. 573; August 1, 2006, review of *Take Care, Good Knight,* p. 796; October 15, 2006, review of *Why Are the Ice Caps Melting?,* p. 1079; September 1, 2007, review of *The Three Bears' Halloween;* March 1, 2008, review of *What's So Bad about Gasoline?;* April 15, 2009, review of *Harriet's Had Enough!;* June 15, 2009, review of *Barnyard Slam;* January 15, 2010, review of *The Little Red Hen and the Passover Matzah.*

Publishers Weekly, January 15, 2001, review of *We All Sing with the Same Voice,* p. 74; July 16, 2001, review of *Morgan Plays Soccer,* p. 179; September 23, 2002, review of *Trick or Treat?,* p. 23; December 16, 2002, review of *Zara's Hats,* p. 66; January 13, 2003, review of *How to Talk to Your Dog; How to Talk to Your Cat,* p. 63; May 5, 2003, review of *Katie Catz*

Makes a Splash, p. 220; August 11, 2003, review of *Poetry for Teacher's Pets,* p. 282; January 12, 2004, review of *Go to Sleep, Groundhog!,* p. 53; September 13, 2004, review of *Fun, by Nature,* p. 81; January 10, 2005, review of *We All Sing with the Same Voice,* p. 58; September 24, 2007, review of *The Three Bears,* p. 75; June 12, 2006, review of *Mr. Ouchy's First Day,* p. 52; August 17, 2009, review of *Barnyard Slam,* p. 61; January 18, 2010, review of *The Little Red Hen and the Passover Matzah,* p. 47.

School Library Journal, August, 2000, Kate McLean, review of *The Cool Crazy Crickets,* p. 154; February, 2001, Genevieve Ceraldi, review of *We All Sing with the Same Voice,* p. 113; August, 2001, Blair Christolon, review of *Morgan Plays Soccer,* p. 158; December, 2002, Susan Marie Pitard, review of *What's That Noise?,* p. 94; Martha Topol, February, 2003, review of *Zara's Hats,* p. 116; August, 2003, Helen Foster James, review of *Almost Late to School!,* p. 152; February, 2004, Kathleen Kelly MacMillan, review of *Go to Sleep, Groundhog!,* p. 104; June, 2004, Gay Lynn Van Vleck, review of *Chip and the Karate Kick,* p. 118; October, 2004, Laurie Edwards, review of *Mooove Oover!,* p. 109, and Sandra Weizenback, review of *What's the Matter in Mr. Whisker's Room?,* p. 148; September, 2005, Kara Schaff Dean, review of *Letters from Your Big Brother,* p. 187; July, 2006, Grac Oliff and Ann Blanche Smith, review of *Mr. Ouchy's First Day,* p. 79; August, 2007, Susan Moorhead, review of *The Three Bears' Halloween,* p. 80; April, 2008, Gay Lynn Van Vleck, review of *Stella, Unleashed,* p. 102; February, 2009, Sandra Welzenbach, review of *What's So Bad about Gasoline?,* p. 94; April, 2009, Meg Smith, review of *Harriet's Had Enough!,* p. 106; August, 2009, Laura Butler, review of *Barnyard Slam,* p. 83; March, 2010, Heidi Estrin, review of *Dad and Pop,* p. 114; May, 2010, Lauralyn Persson, review of *Someone Used My Toothbrush! and Other Bathroom Poems,* p. 101.

USA Today, June 17, 2010, Bob Minzesheimer, review of *Dad and Pop,* p. D6.

ONLINE

Paul Meisel Home Page, http://www.paulmeisel.com (January 11, 2011).

Walker Books Web site, http://www.walker.co.uk/ (January 11, 2011), "Paul Meisel."*

*   *   *

MESSNER, Kate

Personal

Born in Medina, NY; married; children: two. *Education:* Syracuse University, B.A (broadcast journalism); State University of New York Plattsburgh, teaching degree; National Board Certification in early adolescent English language arts, 2006. *Hobbies and other interests:* Hiking, kayaking, cross-country skiing, downhill skiing, traveling, reading, blogging.

Addresses

Home—Plattsburgh, NY. *E-mail*—kmessner@katemessner.com.

Career

Educator and author. Television news producer and reporter in Syracuse, NY, and Burlington, VT, for seven years; Stafford Middle School, Plattsburgh, NY, English teacher.

Member

Society of Children's Book Writers and Illustrators.

Awards, Honors

Adirondack Literary Award, 2007, for *Spitfire;* E.B. White Read Aloud Award for Older Readers, Association of Booksellers for Children, 2010, for *The Brilliant Fall of Gianna Z.*

Writings

FOR CHILDREN

Spitfire, North Country Books (Utica, NY), 2007.

Champlain and the Silent One, illustrated by Martha Gulley, North Country Books (Utica, NY), 2008.

The Brilliant Fall of Gianna Z., Walker Books for Young Readers (New York, NY), 2009.

Sugar and Ice, Walker Books for Young Readers (New York, NY), 2010.

Marty McGuire, illustrated by Brian Floca, Scholastic Press (New York, NY), 2011.

Seamonster's First Day, illustrated by Andy Rash, Chronicle Books (San Francisco, CA), 2011.

Over and Under the Snow, Chronicle Books (San Francisco, CA), 2011.

Marty McGuire Digs Worms, illustrated by Brian Floca, Scholastic Press (New York, NY), 2012.

OTHER

Real Revision: Authors; Strategies to Share with Student Writers, Stenhouse Publishing (Portland, ME), 2011.

Sidelights

In *The Brilliant Fall of Gianna Z.,* her award-winning novel for young adults, Kate Messner presents a humorous tale about a sensitive girl who faces a host of personal and academic challenges. Messner, a former television broadcaster who teaches middle school in northern New York State, has a number of other works to her credit, including picture books for young readers as well as works of historical fiction set in the Lake Champlain region. "I've loved writing since I was old enough to hold a pencil, but to be honest, it never occurred to me that I could be a real, live author some-day," Messner observed on her home page. "I grew up in a really small town, and we didn't have authors visit our schools, so I didn't know any authors. To me, they were far away people—not just ordinary people like me who loved to write."

The Brilliant Fall of Gianna Z. focuses on Gianna Zales, a seventh grader facing a chaotic week both at school and at home. Informed that she must improve her grade in science to be eligible for an important cross-country meet, Gianna has just days to complete a labor-intensive leaf-collecting project for that course; failing that, her spot on the team will go to Bianca, her haughty and beautiful rival. The youngster must turn to her loyal friend, Zig, for help after her parents focus their attention on Gianna's Nonna, whose health is failing. "Messner's engaging debut features a well-drawn protagonist and diverse secondary characters," observed *Booklist* critic Shelle Rosenfeld. A contributor in *Kirkus Reviews* expressed similar sentiments, noting that the author "succeeds in creating an engaging saga," and Kim Dare, writing in *School Library Journal,* predicted that "Messner's warm and humorous tone will capture even reluctant readers."

"When my first nationally published book, *The Brilliant Fall of Gianna Z.* won the 2010 E.B. White Read Aloud Medal, I was beyond thrilled because reading has always been such a big part of my life," Messner told *SATA.* "Growing up the youngest of four kids in a busy house, I was always on the lookout for someone who might want to read to me. When my parents, brothers, and sister grew weary, I'd wait in the kitchen for unsuspecting visitors. As soon as the doorbell rang, I'd run for the bookshelf. My parents still have photos of a pre-school me, bringing piles of books to the table at their dinner parties, hoping to find a reader.

"When I became a parent, reading aloud became a huge part of my life again. It doesn't matter that everyone in our house is an independent reader now; read-aloud time is a treasured part of every day. Curled up by the fireplace in winter. On the deck by the lake in summer. And just before bed at night. I have read the end of [E.B. White's] *Charlotte's Web* aloud more times than I can count, and never without tears. I have read every word of all seven "Harry Potter" books out loud—twice—since my kids are five years apart and were ready for them at different times.

"Sometimes people ask why I choose to write for kids. It's because the books I read when I was young are the books that have meant the most to me. I think the stories we read as children shape the kind of people we become and stay with us long after the reading is through.

"My second nationally published book, *Sugar and Ice,* is about a figure skater from a small-town maple farm who earns a scholarship to train with the elite in Lake Placid. The book grew out of my daughter's love of figure skating. *Sugar and Ice* was a particularly fun book to research because I got to spend lots of time at high-level figure skating competitions, paying attention to how the skaters performed, what they did both on and off the ice, what they wore, and what they shared with me about their experiences.

"My first book for younger readers, *Marty McGuire,* was also inspired by my own family's experiences. There's a pond not far from Lake Placid, New York, where we like to go exploring and catching frogs, and Marty McGuire is a girl who loves nature, too. She's a third grader who would rather be a scientist than a fancy pink ballerina, so when she's forced to play the part of the princess in the school play, the results are hilarious. Marty finds a way to make the part her own and discovers that even a princess in muddy sneakers can live happily ever after. *Marty McGuire* is the first in a series of books for Scholastic Press. The second book, *Marty McGuire Digs Worms,* is about an environmental contest at Marty's school that leads her to set up a worm farm in the elementary school cafeteria.

"Because I love reading all kinds of books, it's probably no surprise that I write picture books for even younger readers, too. My first picture book, *Sea Monster's First Day,* was inspired by my fascination with Champ, the legendary sea monster of Lake Champlain. I live on the lake in Northern New York, and one afternoon when my kids were very small we saw a slithery something swimming along the shoreline. It looked like it was more than twenty feet long, and it swam like some kind of serpent. Was it Champ? We have no idea and haven't seen it since that day many years ago, but I love the idea that there might be a mystery in our lake. Thinking about Champ led me to wonder what it must be like for a creature so different from everything else in the water, and that's where I got the idea for *Sea Monster's First Day,* about a nervous sea monster's first day in a new school . . . of fish!

"I wrote the first draft of my second picture book, *Over and Under the Snow,* on the back of an attendance paper on the bus home from an animal tracking field trip my seventh-grade students took to the Adirondacks. We spent the day snowshoeing through the woods, looking for signs of deer, coyotes, and other forest creatures. One of our guides pointed out a tunnel that led under the snow, to the subnivean zone, where small animals like mice and voles stay warm and safe from predators. I'm an avid cross-country skier, and I loved the idea of a whole secret world existing under the snow while I was skiing over it. *Over and Under the Snow* is about a girl who goes cross-country skiing with her father and discovers that secret kingdom under the snow.

"Most of my ideas start out as scribbles in the little writing notebook that I carry with me almost everywhere I go, but when it's time to sit down and write, I usually do that in a special writing room in the back of our house, overlooking the lake. I usually start a new book by making some kind of outline, and what kind depends on what the book seems to need. I love graphic organizers, chapter outlines, and timelines because they help me to keep my ideas organized. After I write a first draft, I spent a lot of time revising, making sure my characters feel like real people, my writing has descriptive details to make readers feel like they're really there, and my ideas are clear. Because I'm also an English teacher, I share writing and revision strategies with my students and with my colleagues online. I think it really help students to see how published authors revise, so after doing a lot of writing about my own revision process and interviewing other authors, I wrote a book for teachers about how to help students revise. It's called *Real Revision: Authors' Strategies to Share with Student Writers,* and it's published by Stenhouse. Mostly, I wrote that book because I love talking about writing and learning how other writers' processes are similar to or different from mine.

"Writing is something I've always loved, and I find with each book I write, it's more and more fun. My research trips have sent me to a high-tech weather research center in Oklahoma, the Smithsonian Museum of American History in Washington, DC, and the rain forest of Costa Rica. I really can't imagine a better job."

Biographical and Critical Sources

PERIODICALS

Booklist, August 1, 2009, Shelle Rosenfeld, review of *The Brilliant Fall of Gianna Z.,* p. 65.
Kirkus Reviews, August 15, 2009, review of *The Brilliant Fall of Gianna Z.*
School Library Journal, December, 2009, Kim Dare, review of *The Brilliant Fall of Gianna Z.,* p. 128.

ONLINE

All Points North Web site, http://www.apnmag.com/ (winter, 2010), Gabrielle Bilik, "A Brilliant Fall for Kate Messner."
Kate Messner Home Page, http://www.katemessner.com (January 1, 2011).
Kate Messner Web log, http://kmessner.livejournal.com (January 1, 2011).

*   *   *

MONTGOMERY, Lewis B.
See ROCKLIFF, Mara

*   *   *

MOORE, Margie

Personal

Born in Belmar, NJ; daughter of William and Lillian Kelly; married Kenny Moore; children: three daughters.

Margie Moore (Photograph by Theresa Artigas. Reproduced by permission.)

Hobbies and other interests: Sewing, baking, her pets, collecting antique sterling silver.

Addresses

Home and office—NJ. *Agent*—Herman Agency, 350 Central Park W., New York, NY 10025. *E-mail*—margiemooreillustration@gmail.com.

Career

Freelance illustrator. *Exhibitions:* Work exhibited at Meridian International Center, 2006.

Awards, Honors

Cooperative Children's Book Center Choice Best-of-the-Year designation, and Best Children's Books of the Year selection, Bank Street College of Education, both 2006, both for *Ruby Paints a Picture.*

Illustrator

PICTURE BOOKS

Jonathan London, *Count the Ways, Little Brown Bear,* Dutton Children's Books (New York, NY), 2002.
Frank Finale, *A Gull's Story: A Tale of Learning about Life, the Shore, and the ABCs,* Jersey Shore (Bay Head, NJ), 2002.
Nursery Rhymes, Publications International (Lincolnwood, IL), 2003.

Susan Hill, *Ruby Bakes a Cake,* HarperCollins (New York, NY), 2004.

Stephanie S. Tolan, *Bartholomew's Blessing,* HarperCollins (New York, NY), 2004.

Susan Hill, *Ruby Paints a Picture,* HarperCollins (New York, NY), 2005.

Jonathan London, *Do Your ABC's, Little Brown Bear,* Dutton Children's Books (New York, NY), 2005.

Frank Finale, *A Gull's Story, Part 2: Counting at the Shore,* Jersey Shore Publications (Bay Head, NJ), 2006.

Susan Hill, *Ruby's Perfect Day,* HarperCollins (New York, NY), 2006.

Joanne Ryder, *Bear of My Heart,* Simon & Schuster Books for Young Readers (New York, NY), 2006.

Hope Vestergaard, *Hillside Lullaby,* Dutton Children's Books (New York, NY), 2006.

Frank Finale, *A Gull's Story, Part 3: Colors at the Shore,* Jersey Shore Publications (Bay Head, NJ), 2007.

Susan Lubner, *A Horse's Tale: A Colonial Williamsburg Adventure,* Abrams Books for Young Readers (New York, NY), 2008.

Dori Chaconas, *Looking for Easter,* Albert Whitman (Morton Grove, IL), 2008.

Nancy White Carlstrom, *It's Your First Day of School, Annie Claire,* Abrams Books for Young Readers (New York, NY), 2009.

Sidelights

An award winning, self-taught children's book illustrator, Margie Moore developed a deep interest in both art and nature while growing up near the New Jersey shore. Using her signature pen-and-ink and watercolor style, Moore creates images that often incorporate childhood memories and reflect the influences of favorite illustrators such as Beatrix Potter and Nancy Tafuri. Her work has appeared in books such as Jonathan London's *Count the Ways, Little Brown Bear,* Hope Vestergaard's *Hillside Lullaby,* Joanne Ryder's *Bear of My Heart,* Nancy White Carlstrom's *It's Your First Day of School, Annie Claire,* and Susan Hill's easy-reader series about young Ruby the Raccoon.

Moore's first illustration project, *Count the Ways, Little Brown Bear,* brings to life London's engaging story about the everyday activities of Mama Brown Bear and her cub, activities that take young readers from numbers one to ten. In *School Library Journal* Gay Lynn Van Vleck had special praise for the book's "splendid" artwork, writing that Moore's "cozy scenes" of brown-bear domesticity "steal the show," while a *Publishers Weekly* contributor cited the artist for showing "real aesthetic strength and emotional depth in her close-up work." In *Kirkus Reviews* a critic also expressed enthusiasm for the visual aspects of *Count the Ways, Little Brown Bear,* noting that the first-time illustrator's "playful pictures depicting the duo savoring each other's company underscore [London's] . . . tender message." A second collaboration between London and Moore, *Do Your ABC's, Little Brown Bear,* earned similar praise, Jennifer Locke remarking in *Booklist* that the "delight-

ful book" comes to life in "bright, cheery illustrations [that] have a charmingly old-fashioned air about them." Reviewing Moore's contribution to yet another bear-centered story, Ryder's *Bear of My Heart,* a *Publishers Weekly* critic maintained that the "velvety textures and soft hues" featured in Moore's watercolors "convey an idyllic life."

In her illustrations for Vestergard's *Hillside Lullaby,* Moore creates "luminous" images in which sleepy animals and the coming of night "evoke both the cozy comforts of bedtime and the dreamy mystery of the nighttime world," according to *Booklist* reviewer Gillian Engberg. In *School Library Journal* Angela J. Reynolds wrote that "the delightful animals, painted with soft edges, are the main feature here, and youngsters will enjoy nodding off with these gentle, twilight-hued images in their heads." A *Kirkus Reviews* critic also praised Moore's work, calling *Hillside Lullaby* "a must for every child with a window to the great outdoors and a heart that will listen to nature's song."

Susan Hill's engaging racoon heroine in **Ruby Bakes a Cake** *comes to life in Moore's watercolor-and-ink art.* (Illustration copyright © 2004 by Margie Moore. Used by permission of HarperCollins Children's Books, a division of HarperCollins Publishers.)

Ruby the Raccoon makes her introduction to beginning readers in *Ruby Bakes a Cake,* along with her animal friends: a duck, a fox, and a rabbit. In Hill's story, the optimistic Ruby hopes to create the perfect cake, but the ingredients that are suggested by her helpful friends do not come together in an appetizing way. Ruby is also open to suggestions in *Ruby Paints a Picture,* as each friend wants to be included in her painting of a tree, as well as in *Ruby's Perfect Day.* According to a *Kirkus Reviews* writer, the "softly shaded watercolor-and-ink illustrations" that bring to life *Ruby Bakes a Cake* "add personality to each animal character and charming details to Ruby's cozy kitchen." In *Booklist* Hazel Rochman noted that Hill's story for *Ruby's Perfect Day* is enriched by "exuberant line-and-watercolor pictures [that] show the small raccoon as part of a cheerful community," while *School Library Journal* critic Corrina Austin cited the "endearing illustrations" Moore contributes to series installment *Ruby Paints a Picture* as "fresh, stimulating, and full of charm."

Moore casts a frisky puppy in her illustrations for Carlstrom's picture book *It's Your First Day of School, Annie Claire,* a story in which "preschool jitters are gently explored," according to *School Library Journal* contributor Anne Beier. As Annie asks question after question about how to handle an imaginatively improbable series of "What If . . . ?" worries, Moore's "soothing watercolors . . . emphasize the fun, excitement and positive aspects" of a child's first day at school, Beier explained. Carlstrom's "reassuring" story balances well with the artist's "delicate ink-and-watercolor paintings," according to a *Kirkus Reviews* writer, while in *Booklist* Diane Foote concluded of *It's Your First Day of School, Annie Claire* that, "if reassurance is what's needed, there's plenty to be found here."

Courtesy of Moore, views of America's colonial past await readers of Susan Lubner's picture book *A Horse's Tale: A Colonial Williamsburg Adventure.* When Lancer the horse trots away from its owner, Garrick the Gardener, with a sad look in its eye, everyone in town has a theory about why the horse seems so dispirited. As Lubner chronicles these theories in rhyming verse, Moore "lovingly re-creates scenes featuring the historical buildings and . . . costumed folk" of the historical Williamsburg visitor site in her ink and water-color wash art, according to *Booklist* reviewer Carolyn Phelan. Moore's depiction of the colonial townspeople as "cheerful cuddly animals" dressed in period costume inspired Lucinda Snyder Whitehurst to recommend *A Horse's Tale* as "a nice introduction to Williamsburg for very young visitors" in her *School Library Journal* review.

Biographical and Critical Sources

PERIODICALS

Booklist, April 15, 2005, Jennifer Locke, review of *Do Your ABC's, Little Brown Bear,* p. 1460; May 15,

Moore's illustration projects include It's Your First Day of School, Annie Claire, *a picture book by Nancy White Carlstrom.* (Abrams Books for Young Readers, 2009. Illustration copyright © 2009 by Margie Moore. Reproduced by permission.)

2005, Hazel Rochman, review of *Ruby Paints a Picture,* p. 1665; February 15, 2006, Gillian Engberg, review of *Hillside Lullaby,* p. 105; December 1, 2006, Hazel Rochman, review of *Ruby's Perfect Day,* p. 52; May 1, 2008, Carolyn Phelan, review of *A Horse's Tale: A Colonial Williamsburg Adventure,* p. 92; September 1, 2009, Diane Foote, review of *It's Your First Day of School, Annie Claire,* p. 98.

Bulletin of the Center for Children's Books, April, 2005, Karen Coats, review of *Do Your ABC's Little Brown Bear,* p. 346; April, 2006, Deborah Stevenson, review of *Hillside Lullaby,* p. 375.

Horn Book, March-April, 2005, Susan Dove Lempke, review of *Do Your ABC's, Little Brown Bear,* p. 191.

Kirkus Reviews, November 15, 2001, review of *Count the Ways, Little Brown Bear,* p. 1613; April 15, 2004, review of *Ruby Bakes a Cake,* p. 394; November 1, 2004, Stephanie S. Tolan, review of *Bartholomew's Blessing,* p. 1054; May 15, 2005, review of *Ruby Paints a Picture,* p. 590; March 1, 2006, review of *Hillside Lullaby,* p. 241; June 15, 2009, review of *It's Your First Day of School, Annie Claire.*

Publishers Weekly, November 19, 2001, review of *Count the Ways, Little Brown Bear,* p. 66; September 27, 2004, review of *Bartholomew's Blessing,* p. 62; January 31, 2005, review of *Do Your ABC's, Little Brown Bear,* p. 69; December 4, 2006, review of *Bear of My Heart,* p. 57; July 13, 2009, review of *It's Your First Day of School, Annie Claire,* p. 58.

School Arts, January, 2007, Ken Marantz, review of *Ruby Paints a Picture,* p. 54.

School Library Journal, April, 2002, Gay Lynn Van Vleck, review of *Count the Ways, Little Brown Bear,* p. 116; June, 2004, Melinda Piehler, review of *Elvis the Rooster and the Magic Words,* p. 104; March, 2005, Linda L. Walkins, review of *Do Your ABC's, Little Brown Bear,* p. 175; July, 2005, Corrina Austin, review of *Ruby Paints a Picture,* p. 75; February, 2006,

Angela J. Reynolds, review of *Hillside Lullaby,* p. 111; October, 2006, Susan Lissim, review of *Ruby's Perfect Day,* p. 112; February, 2007, Kara Schaff Dean, review of *Bear of My Heart,* p. 96; June, 2008, Lucinda Snyder Whitehurst, review of *A Horse's Tale,* p. 108; August, 2009, Anne Beier, review of *It's Your First Day of School, Annie Claire,* p. 72.

ONLINE

Herman Agency Web site, http://www.hermanagencyinc.com/ (February 15, 2011), "Margie Moore."

Margie Moore Home Page, http://margiemooreillustration.com (December 20, 2010).

Margie Moore Web log, http://margiemooreillustration.blogspot.com (December 20, 2010).

*   *   *

MORRIS, Richard 1969-

Personal

Born 1969; married; children: two. *Education:* College degree.

Addresses

Home—Maplewood, NJ. *Office*—Janklow & Nesbit Associates, 445 Park Ave., New York, NY 10022.

Career

Literary agent and author. Janklow & Nesbit Associates, New York, NY, agent.

Writings

Bye-bye, Baby!, illustrated by Larry Day, Walker & Co. (New York, NY), 2009.

Biographical and Critical Sources

PERIODICALS

Booklist, September 15, 2009, Hazel Rochman, review of *Bye-bye, Baby!,* p. 62.

Kirkus Reviews, August 15, 2009, review of *Bye-bye, Baby!.*

School Library Journal, November, 2009, Anne Beier, review of *Bye-bye, Baby!,* p. 84.*

MURPHY, Jim 1947-
(Tim Murphy)

Personal

Born James John Murphy, September 25, 1947, in Newark, NJ; son of James K. (a certified public accountant) and Helen Irene (a bookkeeper and artist) Murphy; married Elaine A. Kelso (a company president), December 12, 1970 (marriage ended); married Allison Blank (a television producer, writer, and editor); children (second marriage): Michael, Benjamin. *Education:* Rutgers University, B.A., 1970 (English); graduate study at Radcliffe College, 1970. *Hobbies and other interests:* Cooking, reading, gardening, collecting old postcards of ships and trains.

Addresses

Home—Maplewood, NJ. *E-mail*—jimmurphybooks@gmail.com.

Career

Children's book author. Seabury Press, Inc. (now Clarion Books), New York, NY, 1970-77, began as assistant editorial secretary in juvenile department, became managing editor; freelance writer and editor, 1977—, for clients including Crowell, Crown, Farrar, Straus & Giroux, and Macmillan. Formerly worked in construction in New York and New Jersey.

Member

Asian Night Six Club (founding member).

Awards, Honors

Children's Choice designation, International Reading Association (IRA), 1979, for *Weird and Wacky Inventions;* Children's Choice designation, IRA, and Children's Book of the Year designation, Child Study Association, both 1980, both for *Harold Thinks Big;* Best Book for Young Adults designation, American Library Association (ALA), 1982, for *Death Run;* Outstanding Science Trade Book for Children designation, National Science Teachers Association (NSTA)/Children's Book Council (CBC), 1984, for *Tractors;* Children's Choice designation, IRA, 1988, for *The Last Dinosaur;* Recommended Book for Reluctant Readers, ALA, and International Best Book designation, Society of School Librarians, both 1990, both for *Custom Car;* Golden Kite Award for nonfiction, Society of Children's Book Writers and Illustrators (SCBWI), 1990, Dorothy Canfield Fisher Book Award nomination, 1991-92, William Allen White Children's Book Award nomination, 1992-93, and Children's Book of the Year designation, Bank Street College of Education, all for *The Boys' War;* Nevada Young Readers Award, and Outstanding Science Trade Book for Children, NSTA/CBC, both 1992, both for *The Call of the Wolves;* Pick of the Lists designation, *American Bookseller,* 1992, for *Backyard Bear;* Golden Kite Award for nonfiction, 1992, for *The Long Road to Gettysburg;* Orbis Pictus Award, National

Council of Teachers of English (NCTE), and *Jefferson Cup Award, Virginia Librarians*, both 1994, both for *Across America on an Emigrant Train*; *Boston Globe/Horn Book* Award for nonfiction, 1995, Orbis Pictus Award, Jefferson Cup, and Newbery Medal Honor Book designation, ALA, all 1996, all for *The Great Fire*; Robert F. Sibert Informational Book Award, Association of Library Services to Children, Jefferson Cup Award, and ALA Notable Book and Best Books for Young People designations, all 2000, all for *Blizzard!*; National Book Award finalist, Robert F. Sibert Informational Book Award, ALA Notable Children's Book designation, YALSA Best Book for Young Adults designation, Orbis Pictus Award, and Newbery Honor designation, all 2004, and Margaret A. Edwards Award, YALSA, 2010, all for *An American Plague*; ALA Best Book for Young Adults designation, 2004, for *Inside the Alamo*; NCSS/CBC Notable Social Studies Trade Book designation, and ALA Best Biography of the Year selection, both 2008, both for *The Real Benedict Arnold*; Orbis Pictus Recommended selection, and ALA Best Book for Young Adults and Notable Book selections, all 2009, and Notable Book for a Global Society selection, 2010, all for *Truce*; NCSS/CBC Notable Social Studies Trade Book selection, Bank Street College Best Books selection, and ALA Best Book selection, all 2010, all for *A Savage Thunder*; nominations for several regional awards.

Writings

NONFICTION; FOR CHILDREN AND YOUNG ADULTS

Weird and Wacky Inventions, Crown (New York, NY), 1978.
Two Hundred Years of Bicycles, Harper (New York, NY), 1983.
The Indy 500, Clarion (New York, NY), 1983.
Baseball's All-Time All-Stars, Clarion (New York, NY), 1984.
Tractors: From Yesterday's Steam Wagons to Today's Turbo-charged Giants, Lippincott (Philadelphia, PA), 1984.
The Custom Car Book, Clarion (New York, NY), 1985.
Guess Again: More Weird and Wacky Inventions (sequel to *Weird and Wacky Inventions*), Four Winds Press (New York, NY), 1985.
Napoleon Lajoie: Modern Baseball's First Superstar, Four Winds Press (New York, NY), 1985.
Custom Car: A Nuts-and-Bolts Guide to Creating One, Clarion (New York, NY), 1989.
The Boys' War: Confederate and Union Soldiers Talk about the Civil War, Clarion (New York, NY), 1990.
The Long Road to Gettysburg, Clarion (New York, NY), 1992.
Across America on an Emigrant Train, Clarion (New York, NY), 1993.
Into the Deep Forest with Henry David Thoreau, illustrated by Kate Kiesler, Clarion (New York, NY), 1995.

The Great Fire, Scholastic (New York, NY), 1995.
A Young Patriot: The American Revolution as Experienced by One Boy, Clarion (New York, NY), 1995.
Gone A-Whaling: The Lure of the Sea and the Hunt for the Great Whale, Clarion (New York, NY), 1998.
Pick-and-Shovel Poet: The Journeys of Pascal D'Angelo, Clarion (New York, NY), 2000.
Blizzard!: The Storm That Changed America, Scholastic (New York, NY), 2000.
An American Plague: The True and Terrifying Story of the Yellow Fever Epidemic of 1793, Clarion (New York, NY), 2003.
Inside the Alamo, Delacorte Press (New York, NY), 2003.
The Real Benedict Arnold, Clarion Books (New York, NY), 2007.
A Savage Thunder: Antietam and the Bloody Road to Freedom, Margaret K. McElderry Books (New York, NY), 2009.
Truce: The Day the Soldiers Stopped Fighting, Scholastic Press (New York, NY), 2009.
The Crossing: How George Washington Saved the American Revolution, Scholastic Press (New York, NY), 2010.

Contributor of articles to periodicals, including *Cricket* magazine, some under the name Tim Murphy.

PICTURE BOOKS

Rat's Christmas Party, illustrated by Dick Gackenbach, Prentice-Hall (Englewood Cliffs, NJ), 1979.
Harold Thinks Big, illustrated by Susanna Natti, Crown (New York, NY), 1980.
The Last Dinosaur, illustrated by Mark Alan Weatherby, Scholastic (New York, NY), 1988.
The Call of the Wolves, illustrated by Mark Alan Weatherby, Scholastic (New York, NY), 1989.
Backyard Bear, illustrated by Jeffrey Greene, Scholastic (New York, NY), 1992.
Dinosaur for a Day, illustrated by Mark Alan Weatherby, Scholastic (New York, NY), 1992.
Fergus and the Night-Demon: An Irish Ghost Story, illustrated by John Manders, Clarion Books (New York, NY), 2006.

FICTION; FOR YOUNG ADULTS

Death Run (novel), Clarion (New York, NY), 1982.
Night Terrors (short stories), Scholastic (New York, NY), 1993.
West to a Land of Plenty: The Diary of Teresa Angelino Viscardi, New York to Idaho Territory, 1883 (novel), Scholastic (New York, NY), 1998.
The Journal of James Edmond Pease: A Civil War Union Soldier, Virginia, 1863 (novel), Scholastic (New York, NY), 1998.
My Face to the Wind: The Diary of Sarah Jane Price, a Prairie Teacher (novel), Scholastic (New York, NY), 2001.
The Journal of Brian Doyle: A Greenhorn on an Alaskan Whaling Ship (novel), Scholastic (New York, NY), 2004.

Desperate Journey (novel), Scholastic Press (New York, NY), 2006.

Adaptations

The Great Fire and *The Boys' War* were released on audio cassette by Recorded Books in 1998 and 1999, respectively.

Sidelights

Called "one of the best writers of nonfiction for young people today" by a reviewer in *Voice of Youth Advocates,* award-winning author Jim Murphy writes on a variety of topics, among them sports, transportation, inventions, dinosaurs, animal life, mechanical devices, and historical figures. In addition, Murphy has created picture books such as *Fergus and the Night-Demon: An Irish Ghost Story,* that appeal to younger children, as well as historical fiction, contemporary realistic fiction, and a collection of horror stories for teen readers. A prolific writer, he is perhaps best known for his books on U.S. military history and natural disasters that include Chicago's Great Fire of 1871, the blizzard that paralyzed the northeastern United States in 1888, and the yellow fever epidemic of the late eighteenth century.

"One of the problems of history writing for children is the perception that the text is heavy with names, dates, and facts," Murphy noted in an interview with *School*

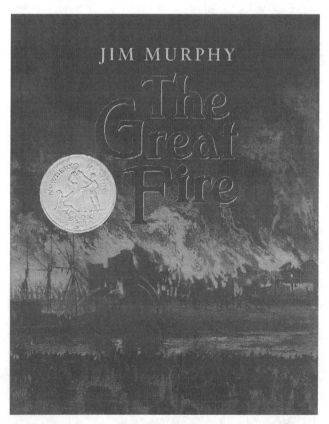

Cover of Murphy's **The Great Fire,** *which features a painting of the Chicago Fire of 1871 by John Thompson.* (Illustration © 1995 by John Thompson. Reproduced by permission of Scholastic, Inc.)

Library Journal contributor Anita Silvey. "So I always tell kids that I don't write history books; I write experience books. I want the reader to feel that they are viewing past events shoulder to shoulder with those who actually experienced them." He begins each book by investigating the diaries, memoirs, journals, and letters of characters central to his topic, and he embroiders his narrative with fictional details such as thoughts and emotions, descriptions of physical surroundings, and discussions of the social conditions and prejudices of the time. Combined through Murphy's insightful analysis and enhanced by a range of visual images, a book emerges that captures a particular moment in history wherein ordinary people were involved in dramatic events. By frequently including eyewitness accounts by young people, he makes his story relevant to young readers, showing that children have made valuable contributions to history. As a *St. James Guide to Children's Writers* essayist noted, in his book for young readers Murphy "has consistently made fact more interesting than any fiction."

Born in Newark, New Jersey, Murphy was raised in the nearby suburb of Kearny, where "my friends and I did all the normal things—played baseball and football endlessly, explored abandoned factories, walked the railroad tracks to the vast Jersey Meadowlands, and, in general, cooked up as much mischief as we could," as he recalled. Murphy and his friends also enjoyed exploring Newark and New York City, both of which were close by, and playing games of "let's pretend."

Murphy was an indifferent reader as a boy, partially because he had an eye condition that went undiagnosed until he was nine or ten. He once commented, "I hardly cracked open a book willingly until a high school teacher announced that we could 'absolutely, positively *not* read' Hemingway's *A Farewell to Arms.* I promptly read it, and every other book I could get ahold of that I felt would shock my teacher. I also began writing, mostly poetry, but with an occasional story or play tossed in there." Murphy became a voracious reader, moving from historical fiction and mysteries to poetry to books about medicine or history as his interests shifted during middle school.

In college, Murphy's interests centered on history, English, geology, art history, and track. After graduating from Rutgers, he briefly attended graduate school, then returned home and worked at a variety of construction jobs. At the same time, he looked for a job in publishing, especially in the area of children's books. After thirty or forty interviews, he was hired as a secretarial assistant at the Seabury Press (now Clarion Books), where he learned about all stages of book writing and production. After rising to the position of managing editor at Clarion, Murphy realized that he wanted to write his own books. In 1977, he left Clarion to become a freelance writer.

In Murphy's first published book, 1978's *Weird and Wacky Inventions,* he mined the files of the U.S. Patent

Office to present young readers with a selection of the often-bizarre gadgets and contraptions that have been registered since the 1700s. The inventions include such creations as a dimple-maker, a bird diaper, an automatic hat-tipper, a portable fire escape, a portable bathtub, jumping shoes, and the safety pin. Together with a reproduction of the picture that originally accompanied each invention, Murphy asks readers to guess its use; the answer and a further explanation are given on the following page. Final chapters discuss how one invention leads to another and detail the process of getting a patent. A reviewer in *Publishers Weekly* wrote that "the reaction of kids to an aptly named book will range from smiles to giggles to guffaws," and Barbara Elleman, writing in *Booklist,* called *Weird and Wacky Inventions* "a browser's delight." Continuing the theme, *Guess Again: More Weird and Wacky Inventions* uses a similar format to introduce readers to a coffin with an escape hatch, a trap for tapeworms, and training pants for dogs. A critic for *Publishers Weekly* dubbed *Guess Again* "just as wacky as its predecessor," and in *Appraisal* Arrolyn H. Vernon concluded that Murphy's book "should be fun for those who enjoy the cryptic, especially when imaginative visualization is exercised."

On of Murphy's first books geared for young children, *The Last Dinosaur,* is a fact-based fictional speculation on the passing of the age of dinosaurs. Set sixty-five million years in the past, the book features paintings by Mark Alan Weatherby. In the book, a female Triceratops finds herself alone after the males in her herd are killed in a fight with a T-Rex. After she abandons her nest to escape a forest fire, her eggs are eaten by some small shrewlike mammals. On the last page, the triceratops pads away, in search of food and perhaps another herd. Another collaboration with Weatherby, *Dinosaur for a Day,* follows a mother hypsilophodon and her eight children on their search for food. When the family encounters a deinonychus pack that charges their clearing, Mother Hypsilophodon must outrun the carnivores and divert them from her babies. Janet Hickman, writing in *Language Arts,* called *The Last Dinosaur* "surprisingly poignant," adding that "it's quite an accomplishment to make a sixty-five-million-year-old setting seem immediate." Hickman deemed Murphy's book "a welcome companion for . . . informational books that examine possible reasons for the dinosaurs' extinction," and *Bulletin of the Center for Children's Books* contributor Betsy Hearne concluded that "the scenario certainly renders the end of the Age of Dinosaurs more immediate than many nonfiction accounts." *Dinosaur for a Day* prompted Nicholas Hotton III to write in *Science Books & Films* that "this very attractive book is simple in concept, well executed, and gorgeously illustrated."

Weatherby also provided the illustrations for *The Call of the Wolves,* in which Murphy follows a young wolf that becomes separated from its pack while hunting for caribou in the Arctic. Trapped by illegal hunters who shoot at it from a plane, the wolf plunges over a cliff,

Like many of Murphy's books, **A Young Patriot** *features historic images of the period.* (Clarion Books, 1995.)

injuring its leg. A painful and dangerous journey through a snowstorm through another pack's territory follows as the injured creature makes its way home. Hearne noted of *The Call of the Wolves* that, "with an involving text and arresting art, this is a nature narrative that commands attention without ever becoming sentimental or anthropomorphic." A critic in *Kirkus Reviews* dubbed Murphy's book an "effective plea for respect for and conservation of an often misunderstood fellow creature."

Many of Murphy's books focus on U.S. history, and he captures the dramatic formation of this young country in *A Young Patriot: The American Revolution as Experienced by One Boy, The Real Benedict Arnold,* and *The Crossing: How George Washington Saved the American Revolution.* Reviled in most history texts for switching his allegiance from colony to crown during the American Revolution, Benedict Arnold had reasons for his decision, as Murphy shows in *The Real Benedict Arnold.* His case for reconsidering Arnold's reputation is based on Arnold's own writings, as well as those of his contemporaries, many of whom distorted the man's actions and opinions for their own purposes. From Arnold's childhood through his early efforts in business, readers see how the man's quick intelligence and strong opinions both helped and hurt him, earning him a reputation for being argumentative and belligerent. Amid the partisan cliques that flourished during the government's first years, Arnold's lack of political savvy earned him many enemies, "leaving him the bitter and disillusioned man who lost faith in his cause and defected to the British side," according to *School Library Journal* contributor Mary Mueller. Murphy's "fascinating, well-researched volume" will be a book to "buffs of the era," Mueller added, while a *Kirkus Reviews* writer praised the book's "clear and detailed" text and "numerous reproductions of paintings, engravings and drawings." Although noting the limited amount of primary sources that are available on Arnold—Mrs. Arnold destroyed her husband's correspondence after his death—Lynn Rutan noted in *Booklist* that Murphy avoids speculation while "carefully contrast[ing] . . . popular myth with historical fact" in his "splendid biography."

When yellow fever overran Philadelphia in 1793, the disease killed thousands and caused a mass exodus from that city. With little knowledge of the disease—which is in fact carried by mosquitoes—and fearing its spread, the governments of surrounding states ordered their militias to prevent frightened Philadelphians to enter their own borders. In *An American Plague: The True and Terrifying Story of the Yellow Fever Epidemic of 1793* Murphy places the Philadelphia crisis within the context of its age and discusses the sometimes humorous ways people attempted to guard against the disease as well as the way both citizens and governments responded to the catastrophic illness and resulting hysteria. Calling the book "a mesmerizing, macabre account that will make readers happy they live in the 21st century," a *Kirkus Reviews* writer added that Murphy also introduces many of the individuals who played an important part in dealing with the tragedy, and his assessment of the contemporary accounts upon which he draws present readers with "a valuable lesson in reading and writing history."

Moving forward in time to February of 1836, *Inside the Alamo* benefits from the "thorough research and solid narrative style" that *Booklist* reviewer Kay Weisman cited as characteristic of Murphy. Here readers are transported to the rustic mission at San Antonio de Bexar, where less than 200 Texans led by Lieutenant Colonel William Travis and including Jim Bowie and Davie Crockett held off a Mexican military force led by General Antonio Lopez de Santa Ana for thirteen days before being overrun. Murphy discusses the complex political changes that precipitated this stand-off, which took place on what was then Mexican soil as part of the Texas War for Independence. Noting the myths and legends that have grown up around this historic event, Weisman wrote that *Inside the Alamo* takes care to address such elements, "allowing readers to judge where the truth may lie and giving them insight into how historical research works." A *Publishers Weekly* contributor commended Murphy for "ably captur[ing] . . . the mood of suspense" that existed up to the Mexican Army's attack and providing "a compelling behind-the-scenes look at the defeat that, ironically, helped create the state of Texas." "This is history writing at its finest," proclaimed a *Kirkus Reviews* writer of *Inside the Alamo*, the critic citing the book's "lively prose, sidebars, profiles of key players," and "abundance" of photographs, paintings, and other visual images.

Nineteenth-century history and the U.S. Civil War have yielded a wealth of book ideas for Murphy. One of his most highly praised works, *The Boys' War: Confederate and Union Soldiers Talk about the Civil War,* incorporates eyewitness accounts by soldiers aged twelve to sixteen, a group that made up as much as twenty percent of the total number of enlisted men, to present a unique view of the War between the States. Inspiration for the book came from the journal of a fifteen-year-old Union soldier that Murphy found in a library. The book covers battles, living conditions, imprisonment, suffering and death, the mixed emotions brought on by returning home following war, and the psychological effects of war on these young people. Writing in *Voice of Youth Advocates,* Joanne Johnson stated that "the excerpts from the diaries and letters written home by this group of young men" make the Civil War "come alive in a way that the diaries and letters of adults may not." Margaret A. Bush, writing in *Horn Book,* noted that "it is startling to learn of the large numbers of very young soldiers whose lives were given to the war, and this well-researched and readable account provides fresh insight into the human cost of a pivotal event in United States history." A *St. James Guide to Children's Literature* essayist observed that, with *The Boys' War,* Murphy's mix of primary sources and a compelling, informative text has become characteristicand stands as an "important contribution to children's and young adult literature."

On September 17, 1862, the armies of Confederate General Robert E. Lee and Union General George McClellan clashed along the banks of a small creek near Sharpsburg, Maryland. In *A Savage Thunder: Antietam and the Bloody Road to Freedom,* Murphy chronicles the history of what has become known as the bloodiest battle in U.S. history, as well as the first large-scale confrontation on Union ground. Although Lee's forces numbered little more than half those of McClellan, the combined assaults of Union officers that included Major Generals Ambrose Burnside and Joseph Hooker were unable to defeat the Confederate troops, although Lee withdraw south of the Potomac River in the face of continued Union pursuit. In addition to his compelling description of this pivotal battle and its aftermath— 22,717 men lost their lives that day—Murphy includes first-person narratives and battlefield maps as well as photographs and other images that bring the ill-fated day to life. He also "makes a direct connection between the battle and the signing of the Emancipation Proclamation" that ended slavery, observed a *Kirkus Reviews* writer, while in *Horn Book* Betty Carter noted that his use of "personal quotes . . . reiterate the human toll" of Antietam. Praising Murphy's skill in "bring[ing] the battle's horrors and poignancy into sharper focus," Phelan cited *A Savage Thunder* as "a stirring, well-researched addition to Civil War shelves."

In *The Long Road to Gettysburg* Murphy includes excerpts from the journals of nineteen-year-old Confederate lieutenant John Dooley and seventeen-year-old Union corporal Thomas Galway, both of whom were involved in one of the most pivotal battles of the War between the States. Beginning and ending with the dedi-

Murphy focuses on a favorite topic in his nonfiction work A Savage Thunder: Antietam and the Bloody Road to Freedom. (Illustration courtesy of the Library of Congress.)

cation ceremony at Gettysburg, Pennsylvania, during which President Abraham Lincoln delivered his famous address, Murphy recounts the battle from the point of view of both young men. His text does not spare readers the grim details of the battle; in his epilogue the author outlines the postwar lives of Dooley and Galway. Writing in *Horn Book,* Silvey commented that *The Long Road to Gettysburg* draws on Murphy's "fine skills as an information writer—clarity of detail, conciseness, understanding of his age group, and ability to find the drama appealing to readers—to frame a well-crafted account of a single battle in the war." Carolyn Phelan maintained in her *Booklist* review that the inclusion of "firsthand accounts . . . give the narrative immediacy and personalize the horrors of battle," and described *The Long Road to Gettysburg* as "an important addition to the Civil War shelf." Writing in *School Library Journal,* Elizabeth M. Reardon concluded that, "by focusing on these two ordinary soldiers, readers get a new perspective on this decisive and bloody battle."

Murphy mines an interesting facet of nineteenth-century history in *Across America on an Emigrant Train,* an informational books directed to young adults. The 1879 journey of twenty-nine-year-old Scottish author Robert Louis Stevenson is the basis by which he explores the development of the transcontinental railroad and the growth of the westward movement in the 1800s. Stevenson traveled by boat and train from Edinburgh, Scotland, to Monterey, California, to visit his friend Fanny Osbourne, an American woman who had become gravely ill with brain fever. On his journey, the writer traveled with other newcomers to the United States, immigrants who faced cramped, unsanitary conditions on the train but were nonetheless filled with hope. While quoting Stevenson's point of view, Murphy adds historical context and discusses topics such as the roles of various ethnic groups in building the railroads, how the railroads helped to destroy the traditional Native-American way of life, and the true nature of the "Wild West." He ends the book with a joyful reunion between Stevenson and Osbourne, who recovered from her illness and eventually became his wife; an epilogue summarizes Stevenson's subsequent rise to fame and brief last years. Noting Murphy's "delightfully effective narrative device," a *Kirkus Reviews* critic called *Across America on an Emigrant Train* a "fascinating, imaginatively structured account that brings the experience vividly to life in all its details; history at its best." In *School Library Journal,* Diane S. Marton deemed the same book "a readable and valuable contribution to literature concerning expansion into the American West." *Booklist* contributor Hazel Rochman stated that the facts and feelings Murphy represents in *Across America on an Emigrant Train* "tell a compelling story of adventure and failure, courage and cruelty, enrichment and oppression" and "revitalizes the myths of the West."

In 1871, the city of Chicago was devastated by a conflagration that killed 300 people and destroyed 17,500 buildings. In *The Great Fire* Murphy explores the causes and effects of this disaster, one of the most extensive in American history. Combining details of the fire and its damage with personal anecdotes from newspaper accounts and quotes from historians and commentators, Murphy suggests that the fire could have been contained. He also argues that factors such as architectural and human errors, the dry weather, the high winds, and the city fire brigade's lack of organization contributed to the ultimate tragedy. The author also notes the discrimination that surfaced as a result of the blaze. Rich residents, many of whom lost their homes, were quick to blame the city's poor immigrant population for the fire; as a result, the poor were forced into slums or out of Chicago permanently. Writing in the *Bulletin of the Center for Children's Books,* Elizabeth Bush noted that Murphy's account "offers not only the luridly enticing details disaster junkies crave, but also a more complex analysis . . . than is usually offered in children's history books." Frances Bradburn also praised the work in *Booklist,* calling Murphy's text "dramatic" and "riveting" before concluding that *The Great Fire* "will automatically draw readers with its fiery cover and illustrations of disasters." Writing in *School Library Journal,* Susannah Price added that the book "reads like an adventure/survival novel and is just as hard to put down"; in fact, according to Price, *The Great Fire* is "history writing as its best."

With *Blizzard!: The Storm That Changed America* Murphy gives an account of the snowstorm that hit the northeastern United States in March of 1888. Drawing on newspaper articles, letters, journals, and histories of the period, he describes the freak blizzard from the perspectives of people of various ages and social positions, some of whom survived the storm and others who did

The travails of eighteenth-century transportation are captured in this image from Murphy's Across America on an Emigrant Train. (Denver Public Library. Reproduced by permission.)

not. He also discusses the political and social conditions of the time and outlines how life in the United States changed following the storm: for example, the effects of the blizzard led to the founding of the U.S. Weather Bureau and to the development of subways in New York City. Writing in *Booklist,* Jean Franklin called *Blizzard!* "an example of stellar nonfiction," and a *Children's Literature Review* critic wrote that Murphy's "clear and even-handed approach to describing the details makes this a page-turner." In his review of the book for *School Library Journal,* Andrew Medlar concluded by calling *Blizzard!* "a superb piece of writing and history."

World War I is Murphy's focus in *Truce: The Day the Soldiers Stopped Fighting,* which frames an almost mythical moment in wartime history within the earth-shattering sequence of events that began in July of 1914, with the assassination of Austrian Archduke Franz Ferdinand and culminated in a war that made much of Europe a battlefield. By December of 1914 the lines of battle had been clearly drawn, with Austria-Hungary and Germany on one side and France, Great Britain, and Russia on the other. Only six months into a war that would rage for five years, the men on the front did not comprehend the complex reasons for this fragmentation of Europe, but the birth of Jesus on December 25th was something that most all of them celebrated in common. All along the front lines, infantrymen from both sides joined together in an informal truce, setting aside their differences in a moment of human brotherhood that honored their Christian traditions of good will toward their fellow man. Murphy sets the stage for this dramatic event by showing what *School Library Journal* contributor Ann Welton described as the "incredible carnage, [and] the complete senselessness" of World War I. He also discusses the technological advances that made World War II so devastating to Europe's psyche. "Murphy's research is impeccable, and his use of primary sources is both seamless and effective," Welton added, while in *Publishers Weekly* a critic dubbed *Truce* "a poignant and sometimes graphic introduction" to a conflict that marked a new age in warfare while also being ironically labeled by contemporaries as the "war to end all wars."

Murphy's first novel for young adults, *Death Run,* was published in 1982. Featuring a contemporary setting and told from different points of view, *Death Run* outlines how sophomore Brian Halihan begins by hanging out in the park with three older schoolmates, but ultimately becomes involved in the death of star high-school basketball player Bill Jankowski. When Brian and his friends see Bill coming through the park with his basketball, they tease and taunt him; gang leader Roger then slams Bill's basketball against his face, knocking the athlete down. Bill has an epileptic seizure, then a burst aneurysm. Brian wants to report the incident, but he is talked out of doing so by Roger. Brian becomes obsessed with Bill's death and begins hanging around the dead boy's home. Meanwhile, a de-

tective suspects that Bill's death was not an accident. Writing in the *ALAN Review,* Tony Manna noted that "the psychology of detection and the anatomy of fear . . . makes Murphy's first novel such an enticing read. Despite his inclination to tell more than he shows, Murphy is a master at creating tension and sustaining the complex emotions of the hunter and the hunted." Stephanie Zvirin, reviewing *Death Run* for *Booklist,* concluded that "few stories of this genre are written specifically for a teenage audience, and Murphy handles his competently, keeping a firm hold on tough talk, including plenty of fast-action sequences, and providing just enough character motivation to fill out the plot."

In his historical fiction, Murphy often draws on the same themes that he deals with in his nonfiction writing. Set in the late 1840s, *Desperate Journey* focuses on a family who works a boat along the Erie Canal in upstate New York. Taking place later in the century, *West to a Land of Plenty: The Diary of Teresa Angelino Viscardi, New York to Idaho Territory, 1883* is one of several books Murphy has contributed to the "My Name Is America" series. *West to a Land of Plenty* describes how a family of Italian immigrants journeys to the northwest territory by train and covered wagon. Written in the form of diary entries by fourteen-year-old Teresa and her younger sister Netta, the novel outlines the family's experiences as they go west to settle in an Idaho town optimistically called Opportunity. Teresa describes how her family survives the arduous journey, which includes sickness, danger, and, for Netta, even death. Throughout her narrative, Teresa has her first romance and also shows courage and presence of mind when she saves her grandmother from thieves. In an epilogue dated 1952, Teresa speaks of her happiness with her life, addressing herself to her late sister. Janet Gillen, writing in *School Library Journal,* noted that, "reminiscent of a Willa Cather heroine," Murphy's protagonist "is resourceful, strong-minded, and intelligent." For Bush, reviewing *West to a Land of Plenty* for the *Bulletin of the Center for Children's Books,* "what could have been merely another overland trail story is considerably enriched by Murphy's attention to the rapid and profound Americanization of these fictional Italian immigrants."

Murphy continues his diary approach in *The Journal of James Edward Pease: A Civil War Union Soldier, Virginia, 1863.* Here a sixteen-year-old private serving in the New York Volunteers is viewed by his comrades as a "Jonah," or bad-luck charm. Assigned, nonetheless, to be the historian of his company, James describes infantry life, the horrors of battle and of the medical practices of the period, and his own thoughts and emotions as he loses several friends to death and desertion. When he is lost behind enemy lines, James is hidden from Confederate soldiers by a slave family whom he has befriended. Throughout the course of the novel, the young man matures, learns the meaning of friendship, and receives a promotion for doing a good job. Writing in *Catholic Library World,* Carol L. Kennedy called

The Journal of James Edmond Pease an "excellent piece of historical fiction." In *Booklist*, Roger Leslie concluded that, despite ambiguities, the diary-like text "is very well written, and Pease's unassuming personality keeps him a vivid, accessible narrator throughout." Other contributions Murphy has made to the "My Name Is America" series include *My Face to the Wind: The Diary of Sarah Jane Price, a Prairie Teacher* and *The Journal of Brian Doyle: A Greenhorn on an Alaskan Whaling Ship.*

In assessing his career as a writer, Murphy once explained: "The nonfiction projects let me research subjects that I'm really interested in; they provide an opportunity to tell kids some unusual bits of information. The fiction lets me get out some of the thoughts and opinions that rattle around in my head." "I view research as a kind of detective work where I try to discover all of the secrets about any subject," he commented on the Scholastic Web site. "I really enjoy taking topics that might seem commonplace . . . and finding new ways to tell the story of the event. I do it specifically for young readers because I hope that in some way my enthusiasm will get them to read more about the subject."

"Life is made up of many kinds of journeys," Murphy concluded, waxing philosophical in his online commentary. "Some are physical, like moving from one home to another, but most are interior journeys of the heart or soul. The important thing is to face each with a positive attitude. And to try and learn as much about yourself and other as you can along the way. Oh, yes—and to have fun while you are experiencing all of these things."

Biographical and Critical Sources

BOOKS

Beacham's Guide to Literature for Young Adults, Volume 10, Gale (Detroit, MI), 2000.
Children's Literature Review, Volume 53, Gale (Detroit, MI), 1999.
Roberts, Patricia, *Taking Humor Seriously in Children's Literature,* Scarecrow Press (Metuchen, NJ), 1997.
St. James Guide to Children's Writers, 5th edition, St. James Press (Detroit, MI), 1999.

PERIODICALS

ALAN Review, fall, 1982, Tony Manna, review of *Death Run,* p. 21.
Appraisal, winter, 1987, Arrolyn H. Vernon, review of *Guess Again: More Weird and Wacky Inventions,* pp. 48-49.
Booklist, September 1, 1978, Barbara Elleman, review of *Weird and Wacky Inventions,* p. 52; May 1, 1982, Stephanie Zvirin, review of *Death Run,* p. 1153; May 15, 1992, Carolyn Phelan, review of *The Long Road to Gettysburg,* p. 1677; Hazel Rochman, review of *Across America on an Emigrant Train;* June 1, 1995, Frances Bradburn, review of *The Great Fire,* p. 1757; November 15, 1998, Roger Leslie, review of *The Journal of James Edmond Pease: A Civil War Union Soldier,* p. 581; February 15, 2001, Jean Franklin, review of *Blizzard!: The Storm That Changed America,* p. 1135; March 14, 2003, Kay Weisman, review of *Inside the Alamo,* p. 1323; September 1, 2006, Abby Nolan, review of *Fergus and the Night-Demon: An Irish Ghost Story,* p. 138; October 15, 2006, Hazel Rochman, review of *Desperate Journey,* p. 41; October 1, 2007, Lynn Rutan, review of *The Real Benedict Arnold,* p. 57; August 1, 2009, Carolyn Phelan, review of *A Savage Thunder: Antietam and the Bloody Road to Freedom,* p. 68; October 15, 2009, Carolyn Phelan, review of *Truce: The Day the Soldiers Stopped Fighting,* p. 51.
Bulletin of the Center for Children's Books, June, 1988, Betsy Hearne, review of *The Last Dinosaur,* p. 213; September, 1989, Betsy Hearne, review of *The Call of the Wolves,* p. 13; May, 1995, Elizabeth Bush, review of *The Great Fire,* pp. 297-298; March, 1998, Elizabeth Bush, review of *West to a Land of Plenty: The Diary of Teresa Angelino Viscardi,* p. 253; December, 2000, review of *Pick-and-Shovel Poet: The Journeys of Pascal D'Angelo,* p. 156; January, 2001, review of *Blizzard!,* p. 190; September, 2003, Elizabeth Bush, review of *Inside the Alamo,* p. 25.
Catholic Library World, June, 1999, Carol L. Kennedy, review of *The Journal of James Edmond Pease,* p. 64.
Horn Book, January-February, 1991, Margaret A. Bush, review of *The Boys' War: Confederate and Union Soldiers Talk about the Civil War,* pp. 86-87; July-August, 1992, Anita Silvey, review of *The Long Road to Gettysburg,* pp. 469-470; November, 1998, Kristi Beavin, review of *The Great Fire,* p. 768; January, 2001, reviews of *Blizzard!,* p. 113, and *Pick-and-Shovel Poet,* p. 114; July-August, 2003, Betty Carter, review of *Inside the Alamo,* p. 484; January-February, 2008, Betty Carter, review of *The Real Benedict Arnold,* p. 116; September-October, 2009, Betty Carter, review of *A Savage Thunder,* p. 582; November-December, 2009, Roger Sutton, review of *Truce,* p. 647.
Kirkus Reviews, November 15, 1989, review of *The Call of the Wolves,* p. 1674; November 15, 1993, review of *Across America on an Emigrant Train,* p. 1465; October 15, 2001, review of *My Face to the Wind: The Diary of Sarah Jane Price, a Prairie Teacher,* p. 1489; March 1, 2003, review of *Inside the Alamo,* p. 393; April 1, 2003, review of *An American Plague: The True and Terrifying Story of the Yellow Fever Epidemic of 1793,* p. 538; September 1, 2006, reviews of *Fergus and the Night-Demon,* p. 909, and *Desperate Journey,* p. 910; September 1, 2007, review of *The Real Benedict Arnold;* June 15, 2009, review of *A Savage Thunder;* September 15, 2009, review of *Truce.*
Language Arts, September, 1988, Janet Hickman, review of *The Last Dinosaur,* p. 500.
Publishers Weekly, July 17, 1978, review of *Weird and Wacky Inventions,* p. 168; June 27, 1986, review of

Guess Again, p. 97; January 25, 1993, review of *Backyard Bear,* p. 87; March 13, 1995, review of *Into the Deep Forest with Henry David Thoreau,* p. 69; May 8, 1995, review of *The Great Fire,* p. 297; December 9, 1996, review of *My Dinosaur,* p. 67; March 10, 2003, review of *Inside the Alamo,* p. 73; October 9, 2006, review of *Fergus and the Night-Demon,* p. 56; November 5, 2007, review of *The Real Benedict Arnold,* p. 66; October 26, 2009, review of *Truce,* p. 59.

School Library Journal, November, 1978, Robert Unsworth, review of *Weird and Wacky Inventions,* p. 66; June, 1992, Elizabeth M. Reardon, review of *The Long Road to Gettysburg,* p. 146; December, 1993, Diane S. Marton, review of *Across America on an Emigrant Train,* pp. 129-130; July, 1995, Susannah Price, review of *The Great Fire,* pp. 89-90; Janet Gillen, review of *West to a Land of Plenty;* December, 2000, Andrew Medlar, review of *Blizzard!,* p. 164; December, 2001, Lana Miles, review of *My Face to the Wind,* p. 139; April, 2003, Diane S. Marton, review of *Pick-and-Shovel Poet,* p. 105; May, 2004, Shelley B. Sutherland, review of *The Journey of Brian Doyle: A Greenhorn on an Alaskan Whaling Ship,* p. 154; September, 2004, David Bilmes, review of *An American Plague,* p. 82; August, 2005, Blair Christolon, review of *Inside the Alamo,* p. 49; August, 2006, Kirsten Cutler, review of *Fergus and the Night-Demon,* p. 94;

November, 2006, Adrienne Furness, review of *Desperate Journey,* p. 142; December, 2007, Mary Mueller, review of *The Real Benedict Arnold,* p. 156; August, 2009, Brian Odom, review of *A Savage Thunder,* p. 125; November, 2009, Ann Welton, review of *Truce,* p. 134; June, 2010, Anita Silvey, interview with Murphy, p. 22.

Science Books & Films, August-September, 1993, Nicholas Hotton III, review of *Dinosaur for a Day,* p. 180.

Voice of Youth Advocates, April, 1991, Joanne Johnson, review of *The Boys' War,* p. 60; June, 1996, review of *The Great Fire,* p. 88.

ONLINE

Jim Murphy Home Page, http://www.jimmurphybooks. com (December 27, 2010).

Scholastic Web site, http://teacher.scholastic.com/ (April 20, 2001), interview with Murphy.*

*   *   *

MURPHY, Tim
See MURPHY, Jim

P

PAPINEAU, Lucie 1962-

Personal

Born April 26, 1962, in Longueuil, Québec, Canada. *Education:* Université du Québec (Montréal), B.A. (communications).

Addresses

Home—Québec, Canada.

Career

Journalist and editor and author of children's books. *Petit Devoir* (periodical supplement of *Le Devoir*), editor, 1987-99; freelance book reviewer and author, beginning 1990; Dominique et compagnie (publisher), Saint-Lambert, Québec, Canada, editor and writer of educational material, beginning late 1990s. Presenter at schools.

Writings

FOR CHILDREN

La dompteuse de perruche, illustrated by Pierre Berthiaume, Boréal (Montréal, Québec, Canada), 1990.
La dompteuse de rêves, illustrated by Pierre Berthiaume, Boréal (Montréal, Québec, Canada), 1991.
Des bleuets dans mes lunettes, illustrated by Daniel Dumont, Boréal (Montréal, Québec, Canada), 1992.
La dompteuse de ouaouarons, illustrated by Pierre Berthiaume, Boréal (Montréal, Québec, Canada), 1993.
Chaminouille, illustrated by Marisol Sarrazin, Boréal (Montréal, Québec, Canada), 1994.
Chaminet, Chaminouille, illustrated by Marisol Sarrazin, Boréal (Montréal, Québec, Canada), 1994.
Francis Reddy comédien et Marifolle, Héritage (Saint-Lambert, Québec, Canada), 1995.
Casse-Noisette, illustrated by Stéphane Jorisch, Héritage (Saint-Lambert, Québec, Canada), 1996.

Monsieur Soleil, illustrated by Marie-Louise Gay, Héritage (Saint-Lambert, Québec, Canada), 1997.
Pas de taches pour une girafe, illustrated by Marisol Sarrazin, Dominique et cie. (Saint-Lambert, Québec, Canada), 1997, translated by Sheila Fischman as *No Spots for This Giraffe,* 1999, adapted by Michael Dahl as *No Spots for Gilda the Giraffe!,* Picture Window Books (Minneapolis, MN), 2006.
Les boutons du pirate, illustrated by Dominique Jolin, Boréal (Montréal, Québec, Canada), 1997.
Pas de bananes pour une girafe, illustrated by Marisol Sarrazin, Dominique et cie. (Saint-Lambert, Québec, Canada), 1998, new edition, 2003, translated by Carolyn Perkes as *No Bananas for This Giraffe,* 1998.
(Adaptor) *Hansel et Gretel,* illustrated by Luc Melanson, Les 400 Coups (Laval, Québec, Canada), 1998.
Le secret du spaghetti mou, illustrated by Dominique Jolin, Boréal (Montréal, Québec, Canada), 1998.
Papaye le panda, illustrated by Marisol Sarrazin, Dominique et cie. (Saint-Lambert, Québec, Canada), 1999, new edition, 2002, translation illustrated by Charles Phillips as *Papaya the Panda,* 1999.
Gontrand et le croissant des cavernes, illustrated by Alain Reno, Dominique et cie. (Saint-Lambert, Québec, Canada), 1999, translated by David Homel as *Gontrand and the Crescent Moon,* 1999.
Bambou à l'école des singes, illustrated by Dominique Jolin, Dominique et cie. (Saint-Lambert, Québec, Canada), 1999, translated as *Bamboo at Jungle School,* 1999, Picture Window Books (Minneapolis, MN), 2005.
Gloups! Bébé-vampire, illustrated by Pascale Constantin, Dominique et cie. (Saint-Lambert, Québec, Canada), 1999, translated by Charles Phillips as *Glup! Baby Vampire,* 1999.
Pouah! Bébé-sorciére, illustrated by Steve Beshwaty, Dominique et cie. (Saint-Lambert, Québec, Canada), 1999, translated by Charles Phillips as *Yuck! Baby Witch,* 1999.
Pouf! Bébé-fantôme, illustrated by Céline Malépart, Dominique et cie. (Saint-Lambert, Québec, Canada), 1999, translated by Charles Phillips as *Poof! Baby Ghost,* 1999.

Ouiiin! Bébé loups-garous, illustrated by Alain Reno, Dominique et cie. (Saint-Lambert, Québec, Canada), 2000, translated by David Homel as *Waaa! Baby Werewolves,* 2000.

Bambou à la plage, illustrated by Dominique Jolin, Dominique et cie. (Saint-Lambert, Québec, Canada), 2000, translated by David Homel as *Bamboo at the Beach,* 2000, Picture Window Books (Minneapolis, MN), 2005.

Léonardo le lionceau, illustrated by Marisol Sarrazin, Dominique et cie. (Saint-Lambert, Québec, Canada), 2000, new edition, 2003, translated by Sheila Fischman as *Leonardo the Lion Cub,* 2000.

Petit Gilles, illustrated by Steve Beshwaty, Dominique et cie. (Saint-Lambert, Québec, Canada), 2001, translated as *Little Gil,* 2001.

Bambou au pays des Bambous, illustrated by Dominique Jolin, Dominique et cie. (Saint-Lambert, Québec, Canada), 2001, translated as *Bamboo in Bamboo Land,* 2001.

Oscar, le drôle de ouistiti, illustrated by Marisol Sarrazin, Dominique et cie. (Saint-Lambert, Québec, Canada), 2001.

Marvin the Strange Little Marmoset, translated by Sheila Fischman, illustrated by Marisol Sarrazin, Dominique et cie. (Saint-Lambert, Québec, Canada), 2001.

Pépin le pingouin, illustrated by Marisol Sarrazin, Dominique et cie. (Saint-Lambert, Québec, Canada), 2002.

Les amours de Lulu, illustrated by Catherine Lepage, Dominique et cie. (Saint-Lambert, Québec, Canada), 2002.

Lulu et la boîte à malice, illustrated by Catherine Lepage, Dominique et cie. (Saint-Lambert, Québec, Canada), 2003, translated as *Lulu and the Magic Box,* Picture Window Books (Minneapolis, MN), 2005.

Pataras la panthère, illustrated by Marisol Sarrazin, Dominique et cie. (Saint-Lambert, Québec, Canada), 2004.

(Adaptor) *Un chant de Noël* (based on *A Christmas Carol* by Charles Dickens), illustrated by Stéphane Poulin, Dominique et cie. (Saint-Lambert, Québec, Canada), 2004, translated by Brigitte Shapiro as *Christmas Eve Magic,* Kids Can Press (Toronto, Ontario, Canada), 2006.

Petite ourse, tu m'aimes pour toujours?, illustrated by Fanny, Dominique et cie. (Saint-Lambert, Québec, Canada), 2005.

Le trésor de Jacob, illustrated by Steve Adams, Dominique et cie. (Saint-Lambert, Québec, Canada), 2005.

Le cirque des ouistitis, illustrated by Marisol Sarrazin, Dominique et cie. (Saint-Lambert, Québec, Canada), 2006.

Mimosa la mouffette, illustrated by Marisol Sarrazin, Dominique et cie. (Saint-Lambert, Québec, Canada), 2006.

Les gusses, illustrated by Daniel Dumont, Dominique et cie. (Saint-Lambert, Québec, Canada), 2006.

Les mousses, illustrated by Julie Cossette, Dominique et cie. (Saint-Lambert, Québec, Canada), 2007.

Les amis de Gilda la girafe, illustrated by Marisol Sarrazin, Dominique et cie. (Saint-Lambert, Québec, Canada), 2007.

Une girafe dans la lune, illustrated by Marisol Sarrazin, Dominique et cie. (Saint-Lambert, Québec, Canada), 2007.

Patatras la panthère, illustrated by Marisol Sarrazin, Dominique et cie. (Saint-Lambert, Québec, Canada), 2008.

Petite ourse, une amie pas comme les autres, illustrated by Fanny, Dominique et cie. (Saint-Lambert, Québec, Canada), 2008.

Mon pyjama à moi, illustrated by Stéphane Jorisch, Dominique et cie. (Saint-Lambert, Québec, Canada), 2008, translated as *Lulu's Pajamas,* Kids Can Press (Toronto, Ontario, Canada), 2009.

Les pounes, illustrated by Julie Cossette, Dominique et cie. (Saint-Lambert, Québec, Canada), 2009.

J'apprends à lire avec Bambou, illustrated by Dominique Jolin, Dominique et cie. (Saint-Lambert, Québec, Canada), 2009.

J'apprends à lire avec Lulu, illustrated by Catherine Lepage, Dominique et cie. (Saint-Lambert, Québec, Canada), 2009.

Mon premier amour, illustrated by Verginie Egger, Dominique et cie. (Saint-Lambert, Québec, Canada), 2009.

Ma coccinella à moi, illustrated by Stéphane Jorisch, Dominique et cie. (Saint-Lambert, Québec, Canada), 2009.

Les nouveaux amis de Gilda la girafe, illustrated by Mirasol Sarrazin, Dominique et cie. (Saint-Lambert, Québec, Canada), 2009.

Fanny et les doudous, illustrated by Julie Cossette, Dominique et cie. (Saint-Lambert, Québec, Canada), 2009.

Méchant Coco: le journal secret de Jojo Sapino, illustrated by Philippe Béha, Dominique et cie. (Saint-Lambert, Québec, Canada), 2010.

Une famille pour Mimosa, illustrated by Mirasol Sarrazin, Dominique et cie. (Saint-Lambert, Québec, Canada), 2010.

Author's work has been translated into Spanish.

OTHER

(Reteller) *The Nutcracker* (with CD), illustrated by Stéphane Jorisch, translated by Marina Orsini, Pocketaudio (Carignan, Québec, Canada), 2000.

(Translator) Edward Lear, *Sire Hibou et dame chat,* illustrated by Stéphane Jorisch, Dominique et cie. (Saint-Lambert, Québec, Canada), 2008.

Adaptations

Papaye le panda, Léonardo le lionceau, and *Une famille pour Mimosa* were adapted for music by Pierre-Daniel Rheault, beginning 2004. Papineau's characters have been adapted by Michael Dahl in the picture books *Gilda the Giraffe and Leonardo the Lion, Gilda the Giraffe and Lucky the Leopard, Gilda the Giraffe and Marvin the Marmoset, Gilda the Giraffe and Papaya the Panda,* and *No More Melons for Gilda the Giraffe,* all Picture Window Books (Minneapolis, MN), 2006.

Sidelights

Writing in French, Lucie Papineau began her career in children's books while working as an editor of the young readers' supplement of a Canadian newspaper, and by 1990 she was writing her own picture-book texts in addition to working as a journalist and book reviewer. A move to the staff of Québec-based publisher Dominique et Compagnie gave Papineau the chance to become even more involved in the book-creation process, and since the late 1990s she has produced numerous picture books for young children. Several of Papineau's books have been translated into English, among them *Gontrand and the Crescent Moon, Lulu's Pajamas,* and her "Gilda the Giraffe" books, which are colorfully illustrated by Marisol Serrazin and include *Leonardo the Lion Cub, No Spots for This Giraffe,* and *Papaya the Panda.*

One of several stories by Papineau that focus on a little gray mouse, *Lulu's Pajamas* features artwork by award-winning Canadian illustrator Stéphane Jorisch and was originally published as *Mon pyjama à moi.* In Papineau's story, Lulu the mouseling loves to put on her red pajamas and snuggle down to sleep with her pet ladybug, Lili-poo. Because her pajamas are so comfortable in bed, she decides to wear them all day long, even at school. In addition to being teased by her classmates, the little mouse learns that bedtime clothes are not the best clothing for daytime, as a messy art project, a lunch of spaghetti, and playground activities all take their toll on the treasured red pajamas. The narrator of her own tale, Lulu returns in several other stories by Papineau, among them *Lulu et la boîte à malice* and *Ma coccinella à moi.* Reviewing *Lulu's Pajamas* in *Resource Links,* Rachelle Gooden described the story as "charmingly written from a child's point of view," and Linda Staskus wrote in *School Library Journal* that Jorisch's "watercolor illustrations add an interesting quirkiness" to Papineau's tale. Dubbing *Lulu's Pajamas* "a charmer," a *Kirkus Reviews* writer predicted that "young readers will be entranced with Lulu."

Papineau taps into children's love of the supernatural in her series of books that includes *Yuck! Baby Witch, Gulp! Baby Vampire,* and *Poof! Baby Ghost.* Each volume focuses on a creature couple as their expected offspring arrives, and both parents do their part in instilling the appropriate tendencies while squashing any humane instincts. In *Glup! Baby Vampire,* for example, the green-skinned and pointy-toothed infant is encouraged to hunt mice and rip up his toys, while *Yuck! Baby Witch* finds a witch couple dealing with problems when a human child is delivered into their care by mistake.

Illustrated in oil paintings by Stéphane Poulin that evoke the Victorian setting of Charles Dickens' classic *A Christmas Carol, Christmas Eve Magic* finds Barton the pig totally unimpressed by the coming of Christmas. Fortunately for Barton, who is too spoiled to care about giving, a tiny mouse arrives in the nick of time and takes the grouchy piglet on a time-travel tour from Christmas time past through to Yuletides yet to come.

First published in French as *Un chant de Noël,* Papineau's holiday story "offers new delights" due to its "all-animal cast," according to a *Publishers Weekly* contributor, and Mara Alpert wrote in *School Library Journal* that the author's text combines with Poulin's "lovingly detailed" illustrations to "simplif[y] . . . a classic tale for young readers."

Biographical and Critical Sources

PERIODICALS

Canadian Review of Materials, October 27, 2006, Alicia Jinkerson, review of *Christmas Eve Magic;* October 20, 2009, Gregory Bryan, review of *Lulu's Pajamas.*
Kirkus Reviews, November 1, 2006, review of *Christmas Eve Magic,* p. 1133; August 1, 2009, review of *Lulu's Pajamas.*
Publishers Weekly, September 25, 2006, review of *Christmas Eve Magic,* p. 70.
Quill & Quire, September, 2006, Gwyneth Evans, review of *Christmas Eve Magic.*
Resource Links, December, 2006, Victoria Pennell, review of *Christmas Eve Magic,* p. 5; December, 2009, Rachelle Gooden, review of *Lulu's Pajamas,* p. 7.
School Library Journal, January, 2000, Nina Lindsay, reviews of *Papaya the Panda* and *No Spots for This Giraffe!,* both p. 109; February, 2000, Elizabeth Maggio, review of *Gontrand and the Crescent Moon,* p. 96; March, 2000, Martha Topol, reviews of *Gulp! Baby Vampire* and *Yuck! Baby Witch,* both p. 210; October, 2006, Mara Alpert, review of *Christmas Eve Magic,* p. 100; November, 2009, Linda Staskus, review of *Lulu's Pajamas,* p. 86.*

* * *

PAUL, Chris 1985-

Personal

Born May 6, 1985, in Lewisville, NC; son of Charles Paul and Robin Jones. *Education:* Attended Wake Forest University for two years. *Hobbies and other interests:* Bowling, music, mountain biking.

Addresses

Home—New Orleans, LA.

Career

Professional athlete and author. U.S. National Basketball Team, member, 2006, 2008; New Orleans Hornets (basketball team), New Orleans, LA, point guard, beginning 2005. Spokesperson for U.S. Bowling Congress. Founder, CP3 All-stars (local youth organization), and CP3 YWCA Youth Camp; cofounder, CP3 foundation; volunteer for charitable organizations.

Awards, Honors

Named National Basketball Association (NBA) Rookie of the Year, and ESPY Award for Best Breakthrough Athlete, both 2006; selected to NBA All-Rookie First

Team, 2006; selected to NBA All-Star Team, 2008, 2009, 2010 (replaced); named to All-NBA team and All-Defensive team, 2008, 2009; (with U.S. National Basketball Team) Gold Medal, 2008, Beijing Olympics; set several NBA records.

Writings

Long Shot: Never Too Small to Dream Big, illustrated by Frank Morrison, Simon & Schuster Books for Young Readers (New York, NY), 2009.

Sidelights

Known to his many fans as CP3, Chris Paul is a star NBA athlete who serves as point guard for the New Or-

leans Hornets. In his time off the basketball court, Paul frequently works with young people in his local community, and he also connects with young sports fans in his picture book *Long Shot: Never Too Small to Dream Big,* featuring illustrations by Frank Morrison.

During his high-school years in North Carolina, Paul played on the varsity basketball team for two years, and his on-the-court talent earned him nationwide recognition. A scholarship to Wake Forest University allowed him to play for the school's Demon Deacons, and he declared for the draft as a sophomore. A first-round draft pick by the New Orleans Hornets, Paul moved to New Orleans the same year the city was devastated by Hurricane Katrina. During his career with

Noted athlete Chris Paul tells an inspiring story of determination in **Long Shot,** *a picture book featuring artwork by Frank Morrison.* (Illustration copyright © 2009 by Frank Morrison. Reproduced by permission of Simon & Schuster Books for Young Readers, an imprint of Simon & Schuster Macmillan.)

the Hornets, Paul has been named NBA Rookie of the Year and was named to several NBA All-Star games, including the 2008 game hosted by the city of New Orleans. He also won an Olympic Gold Medal as a member of the U.S. National Basketball Team and has demonstrated his skill as a bowler through his appearances in celebrity and youth bowling tournaments.

The key to Paul's success as an athlete can be found in *Long Shot.* In the picture book a boy named Chris is teased for his short stature, even by his older brother's friends. Fortunately, Chris is big in determination, and the boy practices enough to overcome his deficit of height. In *Booklist* Karen Cruze noted Paul's success in avoiding a text that is "too preachy," praising *Long Shot* for its "first-person narration and bright, active language." "When the action concentrates on basketball, the writing soars," wrote a *Publishers Weekly* critic, and Morrison's animated paintings "exude a raucous energy." Paul's "bantering energy and the ensuing hard practice punctuated by sound family advice create a tight narrative," declared Sara Paulson-Yarovoy, reviewing the athlete's inspirational story for *School Library Journal,* and a *Kirkus Reviews* writer maintained that *Long Shot* shares "valuable lessons . . . about the importance of persistence, perspective and family support" when "learning to set goals and risk failure to accomplish them."

Biographical and Critical Sources

PERIODICALS

Booklist, September 1, 2009, Karen Cruze, review of *Long Shot: Never Too Small to Dream Big,* p. 110.
Kirkus Reviews, August 15, 2009, review of *Long Shot.*
Publishers Weekly, September 21, 2009, review of *Long Shot,* p. 57.
School Library Journal, October, 2009, Sara Paulson-Yarovoy, review of *Long Shot,* p. 101.
Sports Illustrated Kids, November, 2008, Duane Munn, interview with Paul, p. 28.
Success, July, 2009, Don Yaeger, "Favorite Son," p. 78.

ONLINE

Chris Paul Home Page, http://www.chrispaul3.com (December 27, 2010).
National Basketball Association Web site, http://www.nba.com/ (December 27, 2009), "Christ Paul."*

*   *   *

PETERS, Stephanie True 1965-

Personal

Born 1965; married Dan Peters; children: Jackson, Chloe. *Education:* Bates College, B.A. (history), 1987.

Addresses

Home—Mansfield, MA.

Career

Author and editor of books for children. Little, Brown Children's Books, Boston, MA, editor, 1989-99; freelance writer, beginning 1999.

Writings

FOR CHILDREN

Gary Paulsen, Learning Works (Santa Barbara, CA), 1999.
(Author of text) Matt Christopher, *Heads Up!,* illustrated by Daniel Vasconcellos, Little, Brown (Boston, MA), 2000.
(Adaptor) *Raggedy Ann and the Birthday Surprise* ("My First Raggedy Anne" series; based on the stories by Johnny Gruelle), illustrated by Kathryn Mitter, Simon & Schuster Books for Young Readers (New York, NY), 2000.
(Author of text) Matt Christopher, *Master of Disaster,* illustrated by Daniel Vasconcellos, Little, Brown (Boston, MA), 2001.
(Adaptor) *Raggedy Ann and Andy and the Magic Potion* ("My First Raggedy Anne" series; based on the stories by Johnny Gruelle), illustrated by Reg Sandland, Simon & Schuster Books for Young Readers (New York, NY), 2001.
(Author of text) Matt Christopher, *All Keyed Up,* illustrated by Daniel Vasconcellos, Little, Brown (Boston, MA), 2002.
(Author of text) Matt Christopher, *You Lucky Dog,* illustrated by Daniel Vasconcellos, Little, Brown (Boston, MA), 2002.
(Author of text) Matt Christopher, *Kick It!,* illustrated by Daniel Vasconcellos, Little Brown (New York, NY), 2003.
(Author of text) Matt Christopher, *Switch Play!,* illustrated by Daniel Vasconcellos, Little, Brown (New York, NY), 2003.
Day of the Dragon, illustrated by Michael Koelsch, Little, Brown (New York, NY), 2004.
(Author of text) Matt Christopher, *Making the Save,* illustrated by Daniel Vasconcellos, Little, Brown (New York, NY), 2004.
On Thin Ice, illustrated by Michael Koelsch, Little, Brown (New York, NY), 2004.
One Smooth Move, illustrated by Michael Koelsch, Little, Brown (New York, NY), 2004.
Rock On, illustrated by Michael Koelsch, Little, Brown (New York, NY), 2004.
Roller Hockey Rumble, illustrated by Michael Koelsch, Little, Brown (New York, NY), 2004.
Head to Head, illustrated by Michael Koelsch, Little, Brown (New York, NY), 2005.
Into the Danger Zone, illustrated by Michael Koelsch, Little, Brown (New York, NY), 2005.

On the Edge, illustrated by Michael Koelsch, Little, Brown (New York, NY), 2005.

Wild Ride, illustrated by Michael Koelsch, Little, Brown (New York, NY), 2005.

A Princess Primer: A Fairy Godmother's Guide to Being a Princess, Dutton Children's Books (New York, NY), 2006.

BMX Racer, illustrated by Michael Koelsch, Little, Brown (New York, NY), 2006.

Can It, LB Kids (New York, NY), 2006.

Catching Waves, Little, Brown (New York, NY), 2006.

Cloning Around, Little, Brown (New York, NY), 2006.

Comeback of the Home Run Kid, Little, Brown (New York, NY), 2006.

Game Over, Little, Brown (New York, NY), 2006.

Lacrosse Face-off, Little, Brown (New York, NY), 2006.

(Author of text) Matt Christopher, *The Super Bowl,* Little, Brown (New York, NY), 2006.

Thunderstruck, Little, Brown (New York, NY), 2006.

Time Warped, Little, Brown (New York, NY), 2006.

(Adaptor) *My First Nutcracker* (based on the opera by E.T.A. Hoffman), illustrated by Linda Bronson, Dutton Children's Books (New York, NY), 2007.

Sweet Nothings, Little, Brown (New York, NY), 2007.

(Author of text) Matt Christopher, *The World Series: Great Championship Moments,* Little, Brown (New York, NY), 2007.

Football Double Threat, Little, Brown (New York, NY), 2008.

Lacrosse Firestorm, Little, Brown (New York, NY), 2008.

The First and Final Voyage: The Sinking of the Titanic, illustrated by Jon Proctor, Stone Arch Books (Minneapolis, MN), 2008.

The Olympics: Unforgettable Moments of the Games, Little, Brown (New York, NY), 2008.

Great Moments in Basketball History, Little, Brown (New York, NY), 2009.

Karate Kick, Little, Brown (New York, NY), 2009.

Rumble Tum, illustrated by Robert Papp, Dutton Children's Books (New York, NY), 2009.

Storm of the Century: A Hurricane Katrina Story, illustrated by Jesus Aburto, Stone Arch Books (Mankato, MN), 2009.

Hot Shot, Little, Brown Books for Young Readers (New York, NY), 2010.

(Author of text) Matt Christopher, *Lacrosse Face-off,* Norwood House Press (Chicago, IL), 2010.

The Home Run Kid Races On, Little, Brown Books for Young Readers (New York, NY), 2010.

(Author of text) Matt Christopher, *World Cup,* Little, Brown (New York, NY), 2010.

Track Team Titans, illustrated by Aburtov, Andres Esparza, and Fares Maese, Stone Arch Books (Mankato, MN), 2011.

"LIBRARY OF CONSTELLATIONS" SERIES

Andromeda, PowerKids Press (New York, NY), 2003.

Gemini, PowerKids Press (New York, NY), 2003.

Orion, PowerKids Press (New York, NY), 2003.

Pisces, PowerKids Press (New York, NY), 2003.

The Big Dipper, PowerKids Press (New York, NY), 2003.

The Little Dipper, PowerKids Press (New York, NY), 2003.

"EPIDEMIC!" SERIES

Cholera: Curse of the Nineteenth Century, Benchmark Books (New York, NY), 2005.

Smallpox in the New World, Benchmark Books (New York, NY), 2005.

The 1918 Influenza Pandemic, Benchmark Books (New York, NY), 2005.

The Battle against Polio, Benchmark Books (New York, NY), 2005.

The Black Death, Benchmark Books (New York, NY), 2005.

"GRAPHIC SPIN" GRAPHIC-NOVEL SERIES

Rapunzel, illustrated by Jeffrey Stewart Timmins, Stone Arch Books (Minneapolis, MN), 2009.

(Reteller) *John Henry, Hammerin' Hero,* illustrated by Nelson Evergreen, Stone Arch Books (Minneapolis, MN), 2010.

(Adaptor) Hans Christian Andersen, *The Emperor's New Clothes,* illustrated by Jeffrey Stewart Timmins, Stone Arch Books (Minneapolis, MN), 2010.

(Reteller) *The Princess and the Pea,* illustrated by M.A. Lamoreaux, Stone Arch Books (Minneapolis, MN), 2010.

OTHER

(With Janet Anastasio and Michelle Bevilacqua) *The Everything Wedding Book: Absolutely Everything You Need to Know to Survive Your Wedding Day and Actually Even Enjoy It!,* second edition, Adams Media Corp. (Holbrook, MA), 2000.

Sidelights

A former editor for trade publisher Little, Brown, Stephanie True Peters is a prolific author of books for young readers as well as a ghost writer for fellow author Matt Christopher. From fictional stories such as *Rumble Tum* and the graphic-novel fairy-tale retellings *Rapunzel* and *The Princess and the Pea* to true-to-life books like *Great Moments in Basketball History,* and *The Battle against Polio,* Peters has developed her writing career while raising her own children. "That I am able to spend my days at such work is, on the whole, wonderful," she noted on the Our White House Web log. "I lose myself for hours in imagined scenarios, made-up people, or buried in research into a fascinating topic. I'm here when my kids and husband need me and can take a day off when I need some 'me' time. Sometimes I miss the office life I had years ago, when I was an editor. . . . Then I compare my commute then (a long ride on public transportation) versus now (a short climb up a flight of stairs) and realize just how lucky I am."

Peters' "Epidemic!" series includes *Cholera: Curse of the Nineteenth Century, Smallpox in the New World, The 1918 Influenza Pandemic, The Battle against Polio,* and *The Black Death.* Mixing the medical and historical discussion of each disease with the treatment of victims down through the centuries, Peters' books have been cited for their informative texts and up-to-the minute research. Discussing *The Battle against Polio* in *Booklist,* Hazel Rochman noted that the author "makes both the science and the social history compelling," while *School Library Journal* critic Ann Welton called all five volumes "exemplary information sources" that benefit from period photographs and Peters' "exceptionally lucid, interesting, and graceful" text.

Peters introduces young readers to a well-known ballet in *My First Nutcracker,* an adaptation of Tchaikovsky's classic work featuring illustrations by Linda Bronson. Reviewing the volume in *Horn Book,* Lolly Robinson praised the author's "assured storyteller's voice" and Bronson's "bold and jazzy" art. A fictional tale, Peters' *Rumble Tum* finds a little girl searching for her new kitten during a scary thunderstorm, resulting in what *School Library Journal* contributor Rachel G. Payne described as a "simple, sentimental story." A *Kirkus Reviews* also enjoyed the tale's upbeat depiction of pet ownership, writing that Peters' "inviting and straightforward story . . . is playful and full of charm."

Biographical and Critical Sources

PERIODICALS

Booklist, December 15, 2004, Hazel Rochman, review of *The Battle against Polio,* p. 733; March 1, 2009, Ian Chipman, review of *Rapunzel,* p. 64.

Horn Book, November-December, 2007, Lolly Robinson, review of *My First Nutcracker,* p. 631.

Kirkus Reviews, August 15, 2009, review of *Rumble Tum.*

School Library Journal, July, 2003, John Peters, reviews of *The Little Dipper, Orion, Pisces,* and *The Big Dipper,* all p. 116; February, 2005, Ann Welton, reviews of *The 1918 Influenza Pandemic, Smallpox in the New World,* and *The Battle against Polio,* all p. 151; October, 2007, Virginia Walter, review of *My First Nutcracker,* p. 99; September, 2009, Rachel G. Payne, review of *Rumble Tum,* p. 131, and Carrie Rogers-Whitehead, review of *Rapunzel,* p. 190.

ONLINE

Our White House Web site, http://www.ourwhitehouse.org/ (December 27, 2010), "Stephanie True Peters."*

* * *

POBLOCKI, Dan 1981-

Personal

Born August 10, 1981, in Providence, RI.

Addresses

Home—Brooklyn, NY. *E-mail*—danpoblocki@yahoo.com.

Career

Author of middle-grade fiction.

Writings

The Stone Child, Random House (New York, NY), 2009.
The Nightmarys, Random House (New York, NY), 2010.

Sidelights

Dan Poblocki has always enjoyed a good mystery, and the rich vein of local stories surrounding the towns he visited during his East Coast childhood helped to inspire his eventual career as a writer. "Growing up in small towns shaped my imagination," Poblocki noted on his home page. "I was always curious what was out in the dark of the woods or just over the horizon. Often,

Cover of Dan Poblocki's middle-grade novel **The Stone Child,** *featuring cover artwork by Steve Stone.* (Illustration copyright © 2009 by Steve Stone. Reproduced by permission of Yearling Books, an imprint of Random House Children's Books, a division of Random House, Inc.)

if my friends and I didn't have an answer, we would make one up. The stories we invented were much more interesting than the truth, at least to us. And yet, the tales to which I now find myself drawn are a blend of fact and fiction. Strangely, I like it when I can't tell the difference." In his middle-grade novels *The Stone Child* and *The Nightmarys* Poblocki evokes the same spookiness he thrilled to as a child.

Eddie Fennicks, the twelve-year-old narrator of *The Stone Child,* shares Poblocki's fascination for mysteries, and when his family moves to Gatesweed, a small New England town, he is thrilled to learn that his favorite mystery writer once lived there. In addition to writing mysteries, Nathaniel Olmstead was a mystery as well; he disappeared from Gatesweed thirteen years before, leaving no trace. When Eddie's mom goes to a flea market and finds an Olmstead manuscript that is written in code, the boy teams up with fellow mystery afficionado Harris as well as friend Maggie to decipher the story. The preteens quickly find themselves enmeshed in Olmstead's creepy vision, however, when the horrid creatures from his story suddenly become real. In addition to discovering the key to banishing these creatures—including the threatening Woman in Black—the friends must also discover Olmstead's fate, and their adventures play out in what *School Library Journal* contributor Mara Alpert described as a "briskly paced" story in which "the creep factor is high but not graphic." In *Kirkus Reviews* a critic praised Poblocki's "intricate plotting," noting that his story "ranges from Gatesweed to Dracula's Romania and the Garden of Eden" and should appeal to fans of author John Bellairs.

Another middle grader is the focus of *The Nightmarys,* Poblocki's second page-turning spine tingler. Things change for Timothy after Abigail Tremens joins his seventh-grade class and becomes the brunt of several cruel jokes. Not only do strange dreams now haunt his sleep, but even his teacher begins to sense that something is not right. Their shared sense of doom eventually bring Timothy and Abigail together, and they soon find themselves enmeshed in the ghostly hauntings of two sisters known as the Nightmarys. A half-century-old murder, a family curse, a painting called "The Edge of Doom," and some creepy jars of science specimens in the classroom all come together in Poblocki's intricate tale. The author's "deft handling of the[se] multiple threads makes [*The Nightmarys*] . . . a devilish delight," wrote Daniel Kraus in *Booklist,* and Karen E. Brooks-Reese noted in *School Library Journal* that the novel's "strong characters and deliciously frightening action will keep fans . . . engaged to the end." For a *Publishers Weekly* contributor, *The Nightmarys* "offers plenty of grisly, cinematically creepy imagery" and treats readers to "a good scare."

Biographical and Critical Sources

PERIODICALS

Booklist, August 1, 2010, Daniel Kraus, review of *The Nightmarys,* p. 49.

Bulletin of the Center for Children's Books, October, 2009, Kate McDowell, review of *The Stone Child,* p. 79; September, 2010, Karen Coats, review of *The Nightmarys,* p. 37.
Kirkus Reviews, July 1, 2009, review of *The Stone Child.*
Publishers Weekly, July 26, 2010, review of *The Nightmarys,* p. 76.
School Library Journal, November, 2009, Mara Alpert, review of *The Stone Child,* p. 118; December, 2010, Karen E. Brooks-Reese, review of *The Nightmarys,* p. 123.
Voice of Youth Advocates, December, 2009, Hilary Crew, review of *The Stone Child,* p. 423.

ONLINE

Dan Poblocki Home Page, http://danpoblocki.com (December 27, 2010).
Dan Poblocki Web log, http://enigmaticmanuscript. blogspot.com. (December 27, 2010).*

*   *   *

PODWAL, Mark 1945-

Personal

Born June 8, 1945, in Brooklyn, NY; son of Milton (a restaurant and bar owner) and Dorothy (a homemaker) Podwal; married Ayalah Siev-Or (a jewelry designer), March, 1977; children: Michael, Ariel. *Education:* Queens College of the City University of New York, B.A., 1967; New York University, M.D., 1970. *Religion:* Jewish.

Addresses

Home—Harrison, NY. *Office*—55 E. 73rd St., New York, NY 10021. *Agent*—Forum Gallery, 730 5th Ave., 2nd Fl., New York, NY 10019. *E-mail*—infomarkpodwal@ gmail.com.

Career

Physician, author, and artist. New York University, New York, NY, clinical associate professor of dermatology, beginning 1974; Tisch University Hospital and Bellevue Hospital, associate attending physician, beginning 1974. Artist and illustrator, 1971—. Member, Committee on Collections and Acquisitions and Committee on Art in Public Spaces, U.S. Memorial Holocaust Museum. Collaborator on documentary film *House of Life: The Old Jewish Cemetery in Prague,* 2010. *Exhibitions:* Works exhibited in solo and group exhibitions across the United States and abroad; works represented in permanent collections, including at Israel Museum, Library of Congress, Skirball Museum, Los Angeles, CA, Jewish Museum, New York, NY, Fogg Art Museum, Metropolitan Museum of Art, and Victoria & Albert Museum, London, England. *Military service:* U.S. Army Reserve, 1970-76; became captain.

Mark Podwal (Photograph by Darryl Pitt. Reproduced by permission.)

Member

American Academy of Dermatology (fellow).

Awards, Honors

Award of Excellence, Society of Newspaper Design, 1989, for drawing in *New York Times;* named chevalier, 1993, and officer, 1996, French Order of Arts and Letters; Sidney Taylor Award Honor Book designation, Association of Jewish Libraries, 1996, for *Dybbuk,* and 1998, for *You Never Know;* Aesop Prize, American Folklore Society, and Silver Medal, Society of Illustrators, both 1999, both for *King Solomon and His Magic Ring;* National Jewish Book Award, 1998, and Washington Irving Children's Choice Award Honor Book designation, Westchester Library Association, 2000, both for *You Never Know* by Francine Prose; honorary D.H.L., Hebrew College, 2003; Alumni Award for Medicine in the Humanities, New York University, 2010.

Writings

FOR CHILDREN; SELF-ILLUSTRATED

The Book of Tens, Greenwillow (New York, NY), 1994.

(Reteller) *Golem: A Giant Made of Mud,* Greenwillow (New York, NY), 1995.
The Menorah Story, Greenwillow (New York, NY), 1998.
A Sweet Year: A Taste of the Jewish Holidays, Random House (New York, NY), 2003.
Jerusalem Sky: Stars, Crosses, and Crescents, Doubleday (New York, NY), 2005.
Built by Angels: The Story of the Old-New Synagogue, Houghton Mifflin Harcourt (New York, NY), 2009.

ILLUSTRATOR; FOR CHILDREN

Francine Prose, *Dybbuk: A Story Made in Heaven,* Greenwillow (New York, NY), 1996.
Francine Prose, reteller, *The Angel's Mistake: Stories of Chelm,* Greenwillow (New York, NY), 1997.
Francine Prose, *You Never Know: A Legend of the Lamed-Vavniks,* Greenwillow (New York, NY), 1998.
Ileene Smith Sobel, *Moses and the Angels,* Delacorte (New York, NY), 1999.
Elie Wiesel, *King Solomon and His Magic Ring,* Greenwillow (New York, NY) 1999.
Francine Prose, *The Demon's Mistake: A Story from Chelm,* Greenwillow (New York, NY), 2000.

FOR ADULTS; SELF-ILLUSTRATED

The Decline and Fall of the American Empire, Darien House (New York, NY), 1971.
The Book of Lamentations, National Council on Art in Jewish Life, 1974.
Freud's da Vinci, Images Graphiques, 1977.
A Book of Hebrew Letters, Jewish Publication Society, 1977, reprinted, Aronson (Northdale, NJ), 1992.
Leonardo di Freud, Sperling & Kupfer Editori (Milan, Italy), 1982.
A Jewish Bestiary: A Book of Fabulous Creatures Drawn from Hebraic Legend and Lore, Jewish Publication Society, 1984.
Doctored Drawings, Bellevue Literary Press (New York, NY), 2007.

Also contributor to periodicals.

ILLUSTRATOR; FOR ADULTS

Let My People Go: A Haggadah, Darien House (New York, NY), 1972.
Paul Simon, *New Songs,* Knopf (New York, NY), 1975.
Francine Klagsbrun, *Voices of Wisdom,* Pantheon (New York, NY), 1979.
Elie Wiesel, *The Golem,* Summit Books (New York, NY), 1983.
Howard Schwartz, *The Captive Soul of the Messiah,* Schocken (New York, NY), 1983.
The Elie Wiesel Collection, fourteen volumes, Bibliophile Library (Paris, France), 1985–1988.
Elie Wiesel, *Six Days of Destruction,* Paulist Press, 1988.
Elie Wiesel, commentator, *A Passover Haggadah,* Simon & Schuster (New York, NY), 1993.

Francine Klagsbrun, *Jewish Days: A Book of Jewish Life and Culture around the Year,* Farrar, Straus & Giroux (New York, NY), 1996.

Harold Bloom, *Fallen Angels,* Yale University Press (New Haven, CT), 2007.

Contributor of illustrations to periodicals, including the *New York Times.*

Books featuring Podwal's illustrations have been translated into Dutch, French, German, Italian, and Portuguese.

OTHER

(Illustrator and creative consultant) *A Passover Seder Presented by Elie Wiesel* (children's video), Time Warner (New York, NY), 1994.

Author's papers are archived in the Princeton University Library, Princeton, NJ, and at the University of Connecticut, Storrs.

Sidelights

In addition to his career as a dermatologist and educator, New York City native Mark Podwal is an accomplished author and artist whose works have been exhibited internationally and recognized internationally. Podwal's creative work includes designing a Congressional Gold Medal and a medal for the U.S. Holocaust Memorial Council, designing a tapestry for a major New York City synagogue and a logo for Japan's *The Future of Hope* conference, creating posters for events held at Lincoln Center and cover art for musical recordings, and even crafting ceramics for the Metropolitan Museum of Art. In addition to these varied accomplishments, Podwal has also written and/or illustrated an equally diverse range of books for both children and adults. Much of his focus here has been on the events, symbols, and stories that inform his own Jewish faith and history.

Podwal's first self-illustrated picture book for children, *The Book of Tens,* appeared in 1994. In this work, readers learn about the significance of the number ten in Jewish lore, tales, and rituals, many of which come directly from the Old Testament and Talmud. For example, King David's harp had ten strings, there are ten commandments, and God created the world by speaking ten words. Each number-ten statement is accompanied by a detailed explanation and a large watercolor illustration. Ellen Mandel, writing in *Booklist,* described *The Book of Tens* as "attractive in format" and a work that "welcomes readers to an innovative approach to the Bible and Jewish history." While noting that younger children may need additional explanations to understand some of Podwal's stories, *New York Times* contributor Edward Hirsch deemed the "handsomely designed, clearly written and beautifully illustrated" book to be a treasure for "children of all ages."

Podwal once explained to *SATA* how he came up with his idea to write and illustrate *The Book of Tens.* "When the rabbi of my synagogue was planning his vacation a few winters ago, he asked me to deliver the Friday-night sermon. When I asked what the weekly Torah reading was, he told me, 'The Ten Commandments.' When I asked how long he wanted me to speak, he responded, 'ten minutes.' That Friday evening I spoke for ten minutes about the significance of the number ten in Judaism. My young sons liked the talk so much that I decided to expand it into a children's book. So I called Susan Hirschman, who for ten years had been urging me to do a children's book. The result was *The Book of Tens.*"

In creating *Golem: A Giant Made of Mud* Podwal selected the much-written-about Jewish legend of the golem, a sixteenth-century creature formed out of clay to protect the Jews from their enemies. In *Booklist* Hazel Rochman noted that while his version of the story "lacks a clear focus," Podwal's "folk-art illustrations of the medieval city [Prague] express the magical transformation of the powerful giant." *New York Times* contributor

Podwal brings to life an ancient building in his self-illustrated picture book **Built by Angels: The Story of the Old-New Synagogue.** (Copyright © 2009 by Mark Podwal. Reproduced by permission of Houghton Mifflin Harcourt Publishing Company. This material may not be reproduced in any form or by any means without the prior written permission of the publisher.)

Rodger Kamenets cited the illustrations in *Golem,* noting that they convey "wonder and delight," and a *Publishers Weekly* reviewer remarked on the "shadowy, mythic power" of Podwal's text and the author's "ability to work creatively and respectfully within the folktale tradition."

In another self-illustrated work for children, *The Menorah Story,* Podwal discusses the menorah and the story of Hanukkah, while *A Sweet Year: A Taste of the Jewish Holidays* rounds the holidays of the Jewish year with a discussion of the traditional foods prepared and eaten at each. In the latter book Podwal uses combinations of images—a solar system of fruit, or food tucked into envelopes like holiday cards, for example—to present these special holiday foods. Susan Pine, writing in *School Library Journal,* praised the "artful and witty illustrations" for *A Sweet Year,* noting that each illustration "creates a colorful and fanciful tableau." According to a *Publishers Weekly* reviewer, Podwal's "writing matches the art in eloquence and in its deceptively straightforward concentration of different ideas," while *Booklist* critic Ellen Mandel noted that "each page of creative art" in *A Sweet Year* "faces thoughtful, yet economically phrased, text explaining each holiday."

In *Jerusalem Sky: Stars, Crosses, and Crescents* Podwal once again revisits his Jewish faith. In addition to retelling a story of how the rains held off over Jerusalem long enough for King Solomon to build his temple, he describes Muhammad's ride across the night sky on a flying horse on his way up into heaven. The three major faiths of modern Jerusalem—Judaism, Christianity, and Islam—are also explained, and here Podwal observes that the prayers of the followers of all three religions travel up to the same sky. Recommending the book's "stylish, energetically textured" illustrations, a *Publishers Weekly* contributor deemed *Jerusalem Sky* "thought-provoking, inspirational and informative," while Susan Scheps praised the artist's "skillfully composed" paintings for "show[ing] the beauty and sacredness of the ancient city." Noting the use of *Jerusalem Sky* in discussing religious tolerance, a contributor to *Kirkus Reviews* added special praise for the book's "unusual paintings and the brevity and simple power" of Podwal's writing.

Podwal moves to another faith-based city in his self-illustrated picture book *Built by Angels: The Story of the Old-New Synagogue.* Completed in 1270 in the city of Prague, the world's oldest still-standing synagogue was constructed by angels, according to local tradition, and a golem has been trapped in the building's stone walls for all eternity. In his book, the Czech edition which features an introduction by Holocaust survivor Elie Wiesel, Podwal follows the history of the Old-New Synagogue, which has weathered wars, plagues, and even Nazi occupation throughout its existence. In the author's "spare, free-verse prose," *Built by Angels* captures "the magic and mystery" of this inspiring place, according to *School Library Journal* contributor Rachel Kamin, and a *Kirkus Reviews* writer deemed Podwal's picture book "a beautiful, impressionistic introduction to . . . a European architectural marvel."

In addition to illustrating his own work for children, Podwal has also illustrated the works of several other authors. *Dybbuk: The Story Made in Heaven, The Angel's Mistake: Stories of Chelm, You Never Know: A Legend of the Lamed-Vavniks,* and *The Demon's Mistake: A Story from Chelm* feature stories by Francine Prose that *Booklist* contributor Hazel Rochman described as "Jewish legend[s] of wry humanity." *Dybbuk* draws upon two Jewish tales of matchmaking angels and spirits living in another's body and forms what Marcia W. Posner described in her *School Library Journal* review as "a silly noodlehead story, charmingly illustrated." A *Publishers Weekly* critic observed of the same tale that Podwal's artwork gives "a vibrant flavor to the story," unlike many folktales with a similar background.

In *The Angel's Mistake* Prose describes the Yiddish tale of how Chelm became a town filled with fools and features some of its unusual inhabitants. Praising the work in *Booklist,* Rochman observed that Podwal's illustrations are as "deadpan, wild, solemn, and absurd as the storytelling." A *Kirkus Reviews* writer similarly noted that the artist's "sly yet strikingly beautiful gouache and colored-pencil paintings" serve as a "a perfect foil for Prose's understated, humorous narrative." *You Never Know* relates a legend about a poor shoemaker who, considered foolish by the townsfolk, turns out to have

Prose's retelling of a humorous tale in **The Angel's Mistake** *is given a contemporary flavor in Podwal's colorful illustrations.* (Illustration © 1997 by Mark Podwal. Used by permission of HarperCollins Children's Books, a division of HarperCollins Publishers. In the British Commonwealth by Georges Borchardt, Inc. on behalf of the illustrator.)

Podwal teams up with author Francine Prose to share a Yiddish folktale in Dybbuk: A Story Made in Heaven. (Illustration copyright © 1996 by Mark Podwal. Used by permission of HarperCollins Children's Books, a division of HarperCollins Publishers. In the British Commonwealth by Georges Borchardt, Inc. on behalf of the illustrator.)

the ear of God. Podwal's "glowing gems of illustrations capture the reverence and mystery of this legend," according to *Horn Book* critic Hannah B. Zeiger. "Prose and Podwal bring an unusual agility to their work," noted a *Publishers Weekly* reviewer, the critic calling Podwal's watercolor art for *You Never Know* as "light and springlike."

Podwal teamed up with Ileene Smith Sobel to create the picture book *Moses and the Angels.* "Rarely has the story of Moses been presented with such grace and economy," praised a *Publishers Weekly* reviewer. The collaborative work focuses on the part that angels played in the story of Moses, from the angel who foretells the man's birth to the angel who announces Moses' death. Commenting on Podwal's paintings for *Moses and the Angels,* the *Publishers Weekly* critic wrote that "their light yet bold images in supple colors . . . give great lift to the storytelling."

Podwal has provided illustrations for other Biblical stories, including one told by Nobel laureate Elie Wiesel and titled *King Solomon and His Magic Ring.* Drawing on tales from the Jewish holy books the Talmud and the Midrash, Wiesel tells of King Solomon's mythical adventures. Podwal's "carefully modulated abstractions are as striking in their embrace of the twentieth century as is the text's pleasure in tradition," noted a *Publishers Weekly* reviewer in appraising *King Solomon and His Magic Ring.* Weisel and Podwal have also worked together on several books for adults, and Podwal's art is featured in the children's film *A Passover Seder Presented by Elie Wiesel.*

As Podwal once told *SATA,* several events in his life directly led to and influenced his dual careers as an author/artist and a physician. "Because of a minor illness, perhaps just 'a bad cold,' I missed the first few days of kindergarten. As a result my name was not on the class roster. When my teacher read out the class list, as she did each morning, my name was never called. It was not until my teacher noticed a drawing of a train I had made that she asked, 'Who are you?' And so it seemed to me, at the age of five, that my existence depended on my drawing.

"Although I had the ability for drawing, my parents encouraged me to become a physician. In the words of my mother, 'Since you are such a fine artist, you'll make a great plastic surgeon.' Instead, I chose dermatology, since it requires visual discriminations and with its few emergencies allows me time to draw.

"While attending New York University School of Medicine, I began drawing anti-war posters for the New York Moratorium Committee. Then four students lay dead on the campus of Kent State. The tumultuous events of the weeks that followed inspired me to create some fifty drawings that were published in 1971 as my first book, *The Decline and Fall of the American Empire.* These drawings were brought to the attention of an art director at the *New York Times.* In 1972 my first drawing appeared in that newspaper."

Reflecting upon his career, Podwal once noted: "Over the years I have been fortunate to see my drawings published in many books, animated for television, engraved on medals, exhibited in museums, and woven into a tapestry to hang in the largest synagogue in the world. Perhaps it all stems from missing those first days of kindergarten and needing my drawings to say that I am here."

Biographical and Critical Sources

PERIODICALS

Booklist, September 15, 1994, Ellen Mandel, review of *The Book of Tens,* p. 134; October 1, 1995, Hazel Rochman, review of *Golem: A Giant Made of Mud,* p. 324; March 1, 1997, Hazel Rochman, review of *The Angel's Mistake: Stories of Chelm,* p. 1168; June 1, 1998, Hazel Rochman, review of *You Never Know: A Legend of the Lamed-Vavniks,* p. 1774; October 1, 2003, Ellen Mandel, review of *A Sweet Year: A Taste of the Jewish Holidays,* p. 334; October 1, 2005, Ilene Cooper, review of *Jerusalem Sky: Stars, Crosses and Crescents,* p. 68; October 1, 2007, June Sawyers, review of *Fallen Angels,* p. 24.

Horn Book, July-August, 1998, Hannah B. Zeiger, review of *You Never Know,* p. 504.

Kirkus Reviews, April 15, 1997, review of *The Angel's Mistake;* August 1, 2005, review of *Jerusalem Sky,* p. 856; March 1, 2009, review of *Built by Angels: The Story of the Old-New Synagogue.*

Library Journal, December 1, 2007, review of *Fallen Angels,* p. 123.

New York Times Book Review, April 9, 1995, Edward Hirsch, review of *The Book of Tens,* p. 25; December 17, 1995, Rodger Kamenets, review of *Golem,* p. 28.

Publishers Weekly, October 30, 1995, review of *Golem,* p. 61; February 12, 1996, review of *Dybbuk: A Story Made in Heaven;* May 18, 1998, review of *You Never Know,* p. 79; January 25, 1999, review of *Moses and the Angels,* p. 86; July 26, 1999, review of *King Solomon and His Magic Ring,* p. 83; August 25, 2003, review of *A Sweet Year,* p. 61; June 27, 2005, review of *Jerusalem Sky,* p. 67.

School Library Journal, November, 1995, Susan Scheps, review of *Golem,* p. 115; April, 1996, Marcia W. Posner, review of *Dybbuk,* pp. 127-128; October, 2000, Teri Markson, review of *The Demons' Mistake,* p. 152; August, 2003, Susan Pine, review of *A Sweet Year,* p. 151; September, 2005, Susan Scheps, review of *Jerusalem Sky,* p. 195; June, 2009, Rachel Kamin, review of *Built by Angels,* p. 111.

ONLINE

Forum Gallery Web site, http://www.forumgallery.com/ (July 15, 2005), "Mark Podwal."

Jewish Press Online, http://www.jewishpress.com/ (July 4, 2007), Menachem Wecker, review of *Doctored Drawings.*

Mark Podwal Home Page, http://markpodwal.com (December 15, 2010).

R

REGAN, Dian Curtis 1950-

Personal
Born May 17, 1950, in Colorado Springs, CO; daughter of Donald (a Denver & Rio Grande Railroad agent) and Katherine (a homemaker) Curtis; married John Regan (an engineer), August 25, 1979 (died, 2010). *Education:* University of Colorado, Boulder, B.S. (education; with honors), 1980. *Politics:* "Independent." *Religion:* Roman Catholic. *Hobbies and other interests:* Traveling, study of alternative healing, reading.

Addresses
Home—Wichita, KS. *Agent*—Curtis Brown Ltd., 10 Astor Pl., New York, NY 10003. *E-mail*—dian@diancurtis regan.com.

Career
Writer. Hewlett Packard, Colorado Springs, CO, inspector, 1968-70; Colorado Interstate Gas Company, Colorado Springs, clerk, 1971-78; Adams County District 12, Denver, CO, elementary school teacher, 1980-82; full-time author and speaker, 1982—.

Member
Society of Children's Book Writers and Illustrators (regional advisor, 1984-92), Authors Guild, National Coalition against Censorship.

Awards, Honors
International Reading Association/Children's Book Council Children's Choice designation, 1987, for *I've Got Your Number;* Recommended Book for Reluctant Readers selection, American Library Association (ALA), 1990, for *Game of Survival;* Oklahoma Cherubim Award, 1990, for *Game of Survival,* 1991, for *Jilly's Ghost,* 1992, for *Liver Cookies;* named Member of the Year, Society of Children's Books Writers and Illus-

Dian Curtis Regan (Reproduced by permission.)

trators, 1993; 100 Titles for Reading and Sharing selection, New York Public Library, and Muse Medallion, Cat Writers' Association, both for *The Friendship of*

Milly and Tug; inducted into Oklahoma Professional Writers' Hall of Fame, 1996; Distinguished Medal of Service in Children's Literature, Oklahoma Center for Poets and Writers, 1997; library at Escuela de las Américas in Venezuela was renamed the Dian Curtis Regan Library, 2001; Notable Trade Book in the Social Studies citation, National Council for the Social Studies/ Children's Book Council, and Best Book for Young Adults citation, ALA, both 2003, both for *Shattered;* 100 Titles for Reading and Sharing selection, New York Public Library, 2004, for *Barnyard Slam;* numerous awards from state reading associations.

Writings

YOUNG-ADULT FICTION

I've Got Your Number, Avon (New York, NY), 1986.
The Perfect Age, Avon (New York, NY), 1987.
Game of Survival, Avon (New York, NY), 1989.
Jilly's Ghost, Avon (New York, NY), 1990.
The Initiation, Avon (New York, NY), 1993.
Princess Nevermore, Scholastic (New York, NY), 1995, updated and expanded edition, Darby Creek Publishing (Plain City, OH), 2007.
Cam's Quest: The Continuing Story of Princess Nevermore and the Wizard's Apprentice, Darby Creek Publishing (Plain City, OH), 2007.

Contributor to anthologies, including *New Year, New Love,* Avon (New York, NY), 1996, *Dirty Laundry,* Viking (New York, NY), 1998, *Shattered: Stories of Children and War,* Knopf (New York, NY), 2001, *Soul Searching: Thirteen Stories about Faith and Belief,* Simon & Schuster (New York, NY), 2002, *First Crossing: Stories about Teen Immigrants,* Candlewick Press (Cambridge, MA), 2004, and *What a Song Can Do: 12 Riffs on the Power of Music,* Knopf, 2004.

Author's books have been translated into German.

MIDDLE-GRADE FICTION

The Kissing Contest, Scholastic (New York, NY), 1990.
Liver Cookies, Scholastic (New York, NY), 1991.
My Zombie Valentine, Scholastic (New York, NY), 1993.
The Vampire Who Came for Christmas, Scholastic (New York, NY), 1993.
Home for the Howl-idays, Scholastic (New York, NY), 1994.
Monster of the Month Club, illustrated by Laura Cornell, Holt (New York, NY), 1994.
Monsters in the Attic, illustrated by Laura Cornell, Holt (New York, NY), 1995.
Fangs-giving, Scholastic (New York, NY), 1996.
Monsters in Cyberspace, illustrated by Melissa Sweet, Holt (New York, NY), 1997.

Monsters and My One True Love, illustrated by Melissa Sweet, Holt (New York, NY), 1998.

Contributor to anthologies, including *Period Pieces: Stories for Girls,* HarperCollins (New York, NY), 2003, *Mysterious 13,* Scholastic (New York, NY), and *This Family Is Driving Me Crazy: Ten Stories about Surviving Your Family,* G.P. Putnam's (New York, NY), 2009.

"GHOST TWINS" SERIES

The Mystery at Kickingbird Lake, Scholastic (New York, NY), 1994.
The Mystery of One Wish Pond, Scholastic (New York, NY), 1994.
The Mystery on Walrus Mountain, Scholastic (New York, NY), 1994.
The Missing Moose Mystery, Scholastic (New York, NY), 1994.
The Mystery of the Disappearing Dogs, Scholastic (New York, NY), 1995.
The Haunted Campground Mystery, Scholastic (New York, NY), 1995.
The Mystery at Hanover School, Scholastic (New York, NY), 1995.
The Mystery of the Haunted Castle, Scholastic (New York, NY), 1995.

The "Ghost Twins" series has been translated into Finnish.

CHAPTER BOOKS

The Class with the Summer Birthdays, illustrated by Susan Guevara, Holt (New York, NY), 1991.
The Curse of the Trouble Dolls, illustrated by Michael Chestworth, Holt (New York, NY), 1992.
The Peppermint Race, illustrated by Anna Dewdney, Holt (New York, NY), 1993.
The Friendship of Milly and Tug, illustrated by Jennifer Danza, Holt (New York, NY), 1993.
The World according to Kaley, Darby Creek Publishing (Plain City, OH), 2005.
Cyberpals according to Kaley, Darby Creek Publishing (Plain City, OH), 2006.
Rocky Cave Kids, Marshall Cavendish (Tarrytown, NY), 2011.

Author's books have been translated into French.

PICTURE BOOKS

The Thirteen Hours of Halloween, illustrated by Lieve Baeten, Albert Whitman (Morton Grove, IL), 1993.
Daddies, illustrated by Mary Morgan, Scholastic (New York, NY), 1995.
Mommies, illustrated by Mary Morgan, Scholastic (New York, NY), 1995.
Dear Dr. Sillybear, illustrated by Randy Cecil, Holt (New York, NY), 1997.

A Sparkly Christmas Eve (board book), illustrated by Dawn Apperley, Little Simon (New York, NY), 2002.

Eight Nights of Chanukah Lights (board book), illustrated by Dawn Apperley, Little Simon (New York, NY), 2002.

How Do You Know It's Halloween? (board book), illustrated by Fumi Kosaka, Little Simon (New York, NY), 2002.

Chance, illustrated by Dee Huxley, Philomel (New York, NY), 2003.

How Do You Know It's Easter?: A Springtime Lift-the-Flap Book, illustrated by Fumi Kosaka, Little Simon (New York, NY), 2004.

I Know God Is Near, illustrated by Susan Mitchell, Little Simon (New York, NY), 2006.

Peek-a-Boo Zoo, illustrated by Amanda Gulliver, Silver Castle (Edmonton, Alberta, Canada), 2007.

Barnyard Slam, illustrated by Paul Meisel, Holiday House (New York, NY), 2009.

Monster Baby, illustrated by Doug Cushman, Clarion Books (New York, NY), 2009.

The Snow Blew Inn, illustrated by Doug Cushman, Holiday House (New York, NY), 2011.

OTHER

Juvenile market columnist, *Byline* magazine, 1983-89; contributor to periodicals, including *Writer's Digest* and *Scholastic Scope.*

Adaptations

The "Monster of the Month Club" series was adapted for audiobook. *Dear Dr. Sillybear, The Peppermint Race,* and *Monster Baby* were adapted as e-books. Several books by Regan have been published in electronic form by ipicturebooks.com.

Sidelights

Dian Curtis Regan is the author of more than fifty books, including middle-grade novels, chapter books, and the award-winning picture book *Barnyard Slam.* "I've published in all genres," Regan once explained to *SATA.* "I was 'warned' not to do this, and advised to stick to one area and become good at it," she added. "But the idea of writing the same kind of book over and over didn't appeal to me." The versatile and talented Regan has found success in multiple genres in part because she finds inspiration "at all times of the day or night," as she stated on her home page. "I think ideas buzz about in the air like tiny mosquitoes. Many 'land' on you and get brushed aside. But it's the ones that take a 'bite' out of you, the ones that really get into your blood that make you the most passionate about writing."

Regan was born in Colorado Springs, Colorado, in 1950, and among her favorite books as a child were *Anne of Green Gables, Little Women,* and the "Bobbsey Twins" books. "When I was in elementary school, I loved hearing the teacher say, 'We're going to write a story.'" she recalled. "Everyone would groan except me. I'd already be writing. The reason, I suppose, was that I always surprised myself with the end result—something I *still* try to do. And when the teacher chose my story to read to the class, it reinforced my instinct that what I'd written was good, or, at least, different from what everyone else had written."

After high school Regan was still interested in writing, but she confined her efforts to part-time freelancing while working another job. However, attending a writer's conference in the mid-1970s inspired her to begin seriously studying writing and literature. She enrolled in college and earned a bachelor's degree in education from the University of Colorado in 1980. After teaching for two years at elementary schools in Denver, Regan decided to divert her attention to writing full-time, figuring that if she did not find success after a year she could return to the teaching profession. Her first books, *I've Got Your Number* and *The Perfect Age,* were written that year, published several years later by Avon, and also found their way to publishers in Germany.

Many of Regan's books are geared toward an elementary school-aged readership, such as her "Monster of the Month" quartet. In *Monster of the Month Club* readers are introduced to thirteen-year-old Rilla Harmony Earth, who is without the company of other children because her New Age-y single mom home-schools her while running a small country inn. One cold day in January a mysterious box arrives from the Monster of the Month Club containing a small, seven-eyed creature named Icicle along with specific instructions as to its care and feeding. The next month, Icicle is joined by Sweetie Pie, a fluffy, pink, far-more-loveable monster that, like its companion, becomes active only when the stars are in a particular alignment. Despite the compan-

Regan takes readers to an energetic farmyard in **Barnyard Slam,** *a picture book featuring art by Paul Meisel.* (Holiday House, 2009. Illustration copyright © 2009 by Paul Meisel. Reproduced by permission of Holiday House, Inc.)

ionship they provide Rilla, keeping these monsters fed, happy, and hidden is the ultimate challenge. Rilla's quandary grows in subsequent novels as more monsters are added to the mix. In *Monsters in the Attic* not only monsters but a budding romance occupy the teen's time, creating what *Booklist* contributor Lauren Peterson praised as a "quirky coming-of-age story that is often funny, sometimes sad, and always on target." In *Monsters and My One True Love* twelve monsters now inhabit Rilla's room, and amid the stress of meeting her long-absent father and preparing for a relative's wedding, she worries that a freak shift in the heavens—an eclipse AND a comet are scheduled for Christmas Eve—will spark all manner of monster mischief. "Regan is particularly adept at mixing fantasy with realistic concerns," noted *School Library Journal* contributor Connie Tyrrell Burns in reviewing the concluding "Monster of the Month" volume. Burns went on to note in particular the interjection of "lots of tongue-in-cheek humor about Rilla's politically correct family."

A spunky fourth grader is the protagonist of Regan's chapter books *The World according to Kaley* and *Cyberpals according to Kaley*. The former work introduces readers to Kaley Bluster, an imaginative youngster who offers her somewhat skewed views on a variety of topics—both academic and personal—in a journal kept for her history class. According to a *Publishers Weekly* critic, "readers won't find many reliable historical facts here, but they will discover a scribe with a lively sense of humor." In the latter, Kaley embarks on a mission to find the perfect online pen pal, entering correspondence with a number of students around the world that are enlivened by amusing misunderstandings. "The plot is humorous," wrote Elaine Lesh Morgan in a review of *Cyberpals according to Kaley* for *School Library Journal*, "and dramatic tension is created by the conflict between Kaley and her class rival."

Regan is also the creator of the eight-volume "Ghost Twins" series. In the first installment, *The Mystery at Kickingbird Lake*, twins Robbie and Rebeka Zuffel become ghostly sleuths after drowning in a boating accident in the summer of 1942, along with their equally ghostly St. Bernard, Thatch. Haunting the lakeside house where they grew up, the twins eventually find themselves sharing space with the Shooks, a family on vacation who are the first to rent the Zuffel house in half a century. While at first occupying themselves by playing pranks on the Shook children, the twins ultimately become involved in a mystery in a story that a *Publishers Weekly* contributor praised for "humorous details, spry dialogue and characters that are, well, spirited." The saga of the ghostly twins continues in the novels *The Missing Moose Mystery* and *The Mystery of the Haunted Castle*, among others.

In *Princess Nevermore* Princess Quinn of Mandria wants to escape from her humdrum life as a king's daughter. She believes she will find more excitement by traveling up through the magical wishing pool and reaching the place known by the Mandrians as "outer Earth"—the above-ground Earth familiar to Regan's readers. Cam, a wizard's apprentice whom Quinn befriends, accidentally grants her wish, and the regal teen suddenly finds herself in a strange new world. Befriended by an old man and his grandchildren, Quinn learns about this new world—and falls in love—yet she must choose whether to stay on outer Earth or return to her own world. Reviewing *Princess Nevermore* for *Bulletin of the Center for Children's Books*, Susan Dove Lempke praised the princess's "puzzlement with the foreign Earth customs," and added that Quinn's "contemplation of the freedoms of Earth versus the traditions of Mandria provide most of the novel's interest." Calling the book both "suspenseful and poignant," a *Publishers Weekly* contributor added that Regan "has some sly fun" weaving a fairy-tale aura around twentieth-century life by "using courtly language to describe modern goings-on."

Twelve years after the publication of *Princess Nevermore*, Regan produced the sequel *Cam's Quest: The Continuing Story of Princess Nevermore and the Wizard's Apprentice*. Replaced as Melikar's apprentice, Cam ventures to the outer Earth to discover the truth about his mysterious origins. Meanwhile, Princess Quinn, facing pressure to choose a suitor before her sixteenth birthday, also flees the kingdom and embarks on a journey of her own. Speaking of the work with *Cynsations* online interviewer Cynthia Leitich Smith, Regan commented: "I admit that I left the reader hanging at the end of *Princess Nevermore*. I'd always intended to continue the story, but I never meant to wait so long." She further noted, "I love stories with twists and turns and surprises, so I promise that [Cam's] (multiple) quests are fraught with all of the above. And, just when the reader thinks Cam is home free—well, he isn't."

Regan is also the author of several picture books, including *Chance*, a tall tale about a strong-willed baby of the same name. Chance narrates the story with a cowboy's drawl, describing how he becomes fed up with being treated like a baby by his Ma and Pa soon after he is born and toddles off into the world and for nearly a year lives with different animals, including a bear, monkeys, and sea lions. Chance stays in touch with his human family through letters, and as his first birthday approaches, he becomes homesick. Once his Ma promises to stop feeding him "gooky mush" and to bake him a cake with peppermint sprinkles, he agrees to come back. Regan's "clever language reads aloud well," Donna Cardon wrote in *School Library Journal*, and a *Publishers Weekly* contributor deemed *Chance* an "offbeat tale" that readers will "delight to chance upon."

A group of farm animals gather for a night of entertainment in *Barnyard Slam*, a "good read-aloud for inspiring young poets of all species," as Laura Butler remarked in *School Library Journal*. Hosted by Yo Mama Goose, the clandestine poetry slam features performances by Charley Horse, who rants about his diet of hay, and Lamb, who offers a Dr. Seuss-ian rhyme. "The puns fly thick and fast," a critic observed of the book in *Publishers Weekly,* and a contributor in *Kirkus Reviews* noted that the "action [in *Barnyard Slam*] rapidly builds through targeted one-liners." In *Monster Baby,* a couple adopts the furry, horned creature that is left at their doorstep. Olly, as the newborn is named, grows so rapidly that he can no longer fit in the house; meanwhile, he displays impressive learning skills, moving from kindergarten to college in a matter of weeks. Although he takes care to treat his playmates gently, Olly is both pleased and surprised to meet a friend who shares his peculiar characteristics. "With his lavender horns, gap-fanged smile and fluffy golden mane, Olly's more lovable than formidable," a *Kirkus Reviews* contributor wrote, commending Doug Cushman's art for Regan's story.

"Letting my imagination run wild in the course of everyday living probably accounts for my being a writer of children's books," Regan once explained, acknowledging her imaginative plots and the fantasy elements she interjects into her fiction. "Being caught daydreaming is embarrassing when one is an adult, but it makes for good story ideas." When asked if she has plans to "'grow up' and write for adults," she responds: "I think I've already found the best audience. If writing for children means I'll never grow up, then so be it."

Biographical and Critical Sources

PERIODICALS

Booklist, March 15, 1992, Karen Hutt, review of *The Curse of the Trouble Dolls,* p. 1379; November 15, 1994, Hazel Rochman, review of *The Peppermint Race,* p. 110; January 1, 1995, Carolyn Phelan, review of *Monster of the Month Club,* p. 822; October 15, 1995, Lauren Peterson, review of *Monsters in the Attic,* p. 404; June 1, 1996, Hazel Rochman, reviews of *Daddies* and *Mommies,* both p. 1736; June 1, 1997, Lauren Peterson, review of *Monsters in Cyberspace,* p. 1706; April 15, 1998, John Peters, review of *Monsters and My One True Love,* p. 152; November 1, 2005, Carolyn Phelan, review of *The World according to Kaley,* p. 48.

Bulletin of the Center for Children's Books, January, 1995, Susan Dove Lempke, review of *Monster of the Month Club,* p. 175; November, 1995, Susan Dove Lempke, review of *Princess Nevermore,* p. 103; July, 1997, Susan S. Verner, review of *Monsters in Cyberspace,* p. 408.

Children's Digest, September, 1995, Jane Raver, review of *Monster of the Month Club,* p. 9.

Horn Book, July-August, 2003, Susan Dove Lempke, review of *Chance,* pp. 447-448.

Kirkus Reviews, May 1, 2003, review of *Chance,* p. 682; September 1, 2006, review of *Cyberpals according to Kaley,* p. 911; May 1, 2009, review of *Monster Baby;* June 15, 2009, review of *Barnyard Slam.*

Publishers Weekly, June 9, 1989, review of *Game of Survival,* p. 70; September 14, 1990, review of *Jilly's Ghost,* p. 128; September 20, 1993, review of *The Thirteen Hours of Halloween,* p. 29; September 5, 1994, review of *The Mystery of Kickingbird Lake,* p. 111; August 14, 1995, review of *Princess Nevermore,* p. 85; May 6, 1996, reviews of *Daddies* and *Mommies,* both p. 79; May 5, 2003, review of *Chance,* p. 220; December 12, 2005, review of *The World according to Kaley,* p. 66; August 17, 2009, review of *Barnyard Slam,* p. 61.

School Library Journal, April, 1991, Pamela K. Bomboy, review of *The Class with the Summer Birthdays,* p. 122; August, 1992, Lisa Dennis, review of *The Curse of the Trouble Dolls,* p. 158; February, 1994, Lisa S. Murphy, review of *The Thirteen Hours of Halloween,* p. 98; January, 1995, Margaret C. Howell, review of *The Peppermint Race,* p. 110; March, 1995, Elaine E. Knight, review of *Monster of the Month Club,* p. 206; September, 1995, Bruce Anne Shook, review of *Princess Nevermore,* p. 202; November, 1995, John Sigwald, review of *Monsters in the Attic,* p. 106; July, 1996, Blair Christolon, reviews of *Daddies* and *Mommies,* both p. 70; September, 1997, Anne Parker, review of *Dear Dr. Sillybear,* p. 191, and Leigh Ann Jones, review of *Monsters in Cyberspace,* p. 224; June, 1998, Connie Tyrrell Burns, review of *Monsters and My One True Love,* p. 152; July, 1999, Amy Lilien, review of *The Friendship of Milly and Tug,* p. 61; September, 2003, Donna Cardon, review of *Chance,* pp. 188-189; January, 2007, Elaine Lesh Morgan, review of *Cyberpals according to Kaley,* p. 107; August, 2007, Christi Voth, review of *Cam's Quest: The Continuing Story of Princess Nevermore and the Wizard's Apprentice,* p. 124; July, 2009, Rachel G. Payne, review of *Monster Baby,* p. 67; August, 2009, Laura Butler, review of *Barnyard Slam,* p. 83.

Voice of Youth Advocates, February, 1996, Sally Kotarsky, review of *Monsters in the Attic,* pp. 375-376.

ONLINE

Cynsations Web log, http://cynthialeitichsmith.blogspot. com/ (September 19, 2005), Cynthia Leitich Smith, interview with Regan; (June 4, 2007) Cynthia Leitich Smith, interview with Regan.

Dian Curtis Regan Web Site, http://www.diancurtisregan. com (January 1, 2011).

Kids Bookshelf, http://www.kidsbookshelf.com/ (October 24, 2007), "Dian Curtis Regan."*

*   *   *

RENNERT, Laura Joy

Personal

Married Barry Eisler (an author); children: Emma. *Education:* Cornell University, B.A. (magna cum laude); University of Virginia, Ph.D.

Addresses

Home—CA. *Office*—Andrea Brown Literary Agency, 2225 E. Bayshore Rd., Ste. 200, Palo Alto, CA 94303. *E-mail*—ljrennert@mac.com.

Career

Literary agent and author. Teacher at University of Virginia; Osaka University of Foreign Studies, Osaka, Japan, visiting professor, 1995-97; Santa Clara University, Santa Clara, CA, lecturer, 1997-99; Andrea Brown Literary Agency, Palo Alto, CA, senior agent, 1998—.

Member

Society of Children's Book Writers and Illustrators, Association of Authors' Representatives, Women's National Book Association.

Writings

Buying, Training, and Caring for Your Dinosaur, illustrated by Marc Brown, Knopf (New York, NY), 2009.
Emma, the Extra Ordinary Princess, illustrated by Melanie Florian, Dutton Children's Books (New York, NY), 2012.

Sidelights

A literary agent who specializes in children's books, Laura Joy Rennert also found success as a writer with the release of *Buying, Training, and Caring for Your Dinosaur,* her debut work for young readers featuring illustrations by award-winning author and artist Marc Brown. Discussing that literary adventure with *Cynsations* online interviewer Jenny Desmond Walters, Rennert noted that, although she was familiar with the editorial process, "it was still an illuminating experience for me to see how things work from the author-side of publication. I have a newfound respect for authors because now I know, first-hand, what it feels like to wait for reviews and to hold your breath as you try to gauge a book's reception. The suspense!"

A self-described "literary omnivore," Rennert developed an early love of reading and writing and by the age of ten she had decided to pursue a career that would involve books. After college she spent a number of years teaching English at the University of Virginia, Osaka University of Foreign Studies, and Santa Clara University before joining the Andrea Brown Literary Agency, where she represents such acclaimed authors as Ellen Hopkins, Jay Asher, and Maggie Stiefvater. Now on "the other side of the desk," Rennert has discovered an interest in bringing her work before the public at book signings and other presentations. As she remarked to Smith, "I love connecting with kids over my book and our shared love of pets and dinosaurs. Kids are so open and responsive at the picture book age. What a high!"

In *Buying, Training, and Caring for Your Dinosaur* Rennert draws on her childhood fascination with prehistoric creatures, offering sage advice to youngsters wishing for a triceratops, diplodocus, or spinosaurus of their own. Rennert points out, for example, that a ptera-

Laura Joy Rennert teams up with artist Marc Brown to create the handy dinoguide Buying, Training, and Caring for Your Dinosaur. (Illustration copyright © 2009 by Marc Brown. Reproduced by permission of Alfred A. Knopf, an imprint of Random House Children's Books, a division of Random House, Inc.)

nodon makes a great outfielder during baseball games, a leathery-skinned ankylosaurus can be difficult to groom, and a pea-brained stegosaurus requires extra patience during training sessions. "Youngsters will quickly become absorbed in this enjoyable mix of facts, fantasy, and fossils," remarked *Booklist* critic Andrew Medlar. *School Library Journal* contributor Susan Weitz also praised Rennert's "tongue-in-cheek guide," adding that illustrator Brown's "overly enthusiastic, sweet-faced, humongous patterned dinosaurs are—in defiance of natural history—irresistibly delicious."

Biographical and Critical Sources

PERIODICALS

Booklist, October 1, 2009, Andrew Medlar, review of *Buying, Training, and Caring for Your Dinosaur,* p. 49.
Bulletin of the Center for Children's Books, November, 2009, Kate Quealy-Gainer, review of *Buying, Training, and Caring for Your Dinosaur,* p. 125.
Kirkus Reviews, September 1, 2009, review of *Buying, Training, and Caring for Your Dinosaur.*
Publishers Weekly, October 12, 2009, review of *Buying, Training, and Caring for Your Dinosaur,* p. 49.
School Library Journal, October, 2009, Susan Weitz, review of *Buying, Training, and Caring for Your Dinosaur,* p. 102.

ONLINE

Andrea Brown Literary Agency Web site, http://andreabrownlit.com/ (January 1, 2011), "Laura Rennert."
Cynsations Web log, http://cynthialeitichsmith.blogspot.com/ (January 29, 2010), Jenny Desmond Walters, interview with Rennert.
Laura Rennert Home Page, http://www.laurajoyrennert.com (January 1, 2011).

*   *   *

RIVERA, Guadalupe
See RIVERA MARIN, Guadalupe

*   *   *

RIVERA MARIN, Guadalupe 1924-
(Guadalupe Rivera)

Personal

Born 1924, in Mexico City, Mexico; daughter of Diego Rivera (an artist and muralist) and Guadalupe Marin (a model and novelist). *Education:* Earned baccalaureate degree and J.D.

Addresses

Home—Cuernavaca, Mexico.

Career

Author and educator. Elected to Mexican congress; professor of law. Lecturer at schools in North and South America and in Europe.

Awards, Honors

Rockefeller Foundation fellow, 1993.

Writings

El contrato de reaseguro, Editorial Cultura (Mexico), 1947.
El mercado de trabajo; relaciones obrero-patronales, Fondo de Cultura Economica (Mexico), 1955.
La propiedad territorial en México, 1301-1810, Siglo Veintiuno Editores (Mexico City, Mexico), 1983.
Un río, dos Riveras: vida de Diego Rivera, 1886-1929, Alianza Editorial Mexicana (Mexico), 1989.
Encuentros con Diego Rivera, Siglo Veintiuno Editores (Mexico City, Mexico), 1993.
(With Marie-Pierre Colle; as Guadalupe Rivera) *Fiestas de Frida y Diego,* photographs by Ignacio Urquiza, translated as *Frida's Fiestas: Recipes and Reminiscences of Life with Frida Kahlo,* Clarkson Potter/Publishers (New York, NY), 1994.
(With Carol Miller; as Guadalupe Rivera) *The Winged Prophet from Hermes to Quetzalcoatl: An Introduction to the MesoAmerican Deities through the Tarot,* S. Weiser (York Beach, ME), 1994.
Diego el rojo, Nueva Imagen (Mexico), 1997, translated by Dick Gerdes as *Diego Rivera the Red,* Arte Público Press (Houston, TX), 2004.
My Papá Diego and Me/mi papá Diego y yo: Memories of My Father and His Art, illustrations by Diego Rivera, Children's Book Press (San Francisco, CA), 2009.

Sidelights

The daughter of noted Mexican muralist and sculptor Diego Rivera and his second wife, model and writer Guadalupe Marin, Guadalupe Rivera Marin grew up to become a professor of law. In addition to writing several books in her field, Rivera Marin has also shared her memories of her famous family, which included Rivera's second wife, painter Frida Kahlo, in the books *Un río, dos Riveras: vida de Diego Rivera, 1886-1929, Encuentros con Diego Rivera, Diego el Rojo,* the picture book *My Papá Diego and Me/mi papá Diego y yo: Memories of My Father and His Art,* and *Fiestas de Frida y Diego,* the last a cookbook and memoir published in English as *Frida's Fiestas: Recipes and Reminiscences of Life with Frida Kahlo.*

In 1942 Rivera Marin stayed with her father and Kahlo at their home in Coyoacan, Mexico, and her time there inspired her cookbook/memoir *Frida's Fiestas.* The book is organized in twelve chapters centering on special occasions ranging from the creative couple's wedding anniversary to the traditional Dia de los Muertos feast. In *Diego el rojo—Diego Rivera the Red* in translation—she also chronicles her father's childhood and adolescence as he discovered, first avant garde art and then the Marxism that would guide his eventual politics.

Illustrated with Diego Rivera's own paintings and murals, such as "Sueño de una tarde dominical en la Almeda," *My Papá Diego and Me* pairs thirteen child-centered images with Rivera Marin's memories regarding the creation of each work. Several of the works were painted using the author as a model, and Rivera would give young Guadalupe an orange to keep her quiet. Rivera Marin shares such memories of her early life with a famous father in her bilingual text, creating what *Booklist* contributor Andrew Medlar described as a "personal introduction to Rivera's art and some of Mexico's cultural traditions." Calling *My Papá Diego and Me* an "insightful" picture book highlighting "the vibrancy of Mexican culture," a *Publishers Weekly* critic added that "the personalities of father and daughter alike . . . shine brightly" in Rivera Marin's book. The author's "personal insight is conveyed in both languages without distracting flourishes," noted Chelsey Philpot in her *Horn Book* review, and a *Kirkus Reviews* writer recommended *My Papá Diego and Me* as "a wonderfully unexpected and delightfully accessible personal appreciation of a famous, larger-than-life man."

Biographical and Critical Sources

PERIODICALS

Booklist, November 1, 2009, Andrew Medlar, review of *My Papá Diego and Me/mi papá Diego y yo: Memories of My Father and His Art,* p. 59.

Horn Book, November-December, 2009, Chelsey Philpot, review of *My Papá Diego and Me,* p. 697.

Kirkus Reviews, September 1, 2009, review of *My Papá Diego and Me.*

Newsweek, July 19, 1999, Guadalupe Rivera Marin, "The Painting on the Wall," p. 50.

Publishers Weekly, August 24, 2009, review of *My Papá Diego and Me,* p. 61.

School Library Journal, October, 2009, Angelica G. Fortin, review of *My Papá Diego and Me,* p. 117.*

* * *

ROCKLIFF, Mara
(Lewis B. Montgomery)

Personal

Female.

Addresses

Home—Kutztown, PA. *Agent*—Jennifer Laughran, Andrea Brown Literary Agency, 2225 E. Bayshore Rd., Ste. 200, Palo Alto, CA 94303; jennL@andreabrownlit.com. *E-mail*—mararockliff@mararockliff.com.

Career

Writer.

Member

Society of Children's Book Writers and Illustrators.

Awards, Honors

Agatha Award nomination, Mystery Writers of America, 2009, for *The Case of the Poisoned Pig;* Excellence in Nonfiction for Young Adults Award nomination, YALSA/American Library Association, and Green Earth Book Award Honor Book designation, both 2011, both for *Get Real.*

Writings

Next to an Ant, illustrated by Pascale Constantin, Children's Press (New York, NY), 2004.

Pieces of Another World, illustrated by Salima Alikhan, Sylvan Dell Publishing (Mt. Pleasant, SC), 2005.

The Busiest Street in Town, illustrated by Sarah McMenemy, Knopf (New York, NY), 2009.

Get Real: What Kind of World Are You Buying?, Running Press Teens (Philadelphia, PA), 2010.

My Heart Will Not Sit Down, illustrated by Ann Tanksley, Knopf (New York, NY), 2012.

Me and Momma and Big John, illustrated by William Low, Candlewick Press (Somerville, MA), 2012.

"MILO AND JAZZ MYSTERIES" SERIES; UNDER NAME LEWIS B. MONTGOMERY

The Case of the Stinky Socks, illustrated by Amy Wummer, Kane Press (New York, NY), 2009.

The Case of the Poisoned Pig, illustrated by Amy Wummer, Kane Press (New York, NY), 2009.

The Case of the Haunted Haunted House, illustrated by Amy Wummer, Kane Press (New York, NY), 2009.

The Case of the Amazing Zelda, illustrated by Amy Wummer, Kane Press (New York, NY), 2009.

The Case of the July Fourth Jinx, illustrated by Amy Wummer, Kane Press (New York, NY), 2010.

The Case of the Missing Moose, illustrated by Amy Wummer, Kane Press (New York, NY), 2011.

The Case of the Purple Pool, illustrated by Amy Wummer, Kane Press (New York, NY), 2011.

Adaptations

"Comet Crumbs," a planetarium show staged at the Fernbank Science Center, Atlanta, GA, in 2007, was based on *Pieces of Another World. The Case of the Poisoned Pig* was produced as an animated television program by Creating4Kids.

Sidelights

A versatile author, Mara Rockliff has found success in a variety of genres, including picture books, nonfiction, and mysteries published under the pen names Lewis B. Montgomery. Rockliff frequently weaves science facts into her fictional stories, which include *The Busiest Street in Town,* About her most recent work, Rockliff told *SATA* that she "write[s] books for kids and teens who want to change the world."

In *The Busiest Street in Town* Rockliff tells a "gentle and sweet-spirited story of urban transformation," according to *Booklist* critic Michael Cart. When lifelong friends Agatha May Walker and Eulalie Scruggs find it impossible to cross congested Rushmore Boulevard to visit each other, Agatha plants herself in the middle of the road, where Eulalie soon joins her for a game of Parcheesi. As traffic slows and various neighbors stop by to join in the fun, the street metamorphoses into a pedestrian wonderland. *School Library Journal* contributor Ieva Bates praised Rockliff's picture book, noting that "the slow-down-your-life sentiment is sweet," and Rich Cohen commented in the *New York Times Book Review* that the work "reads like the last chapter in the long struggle between man and his machines, a simple act of defiance being enough to end the terrible reign of the Dinotrux."

Get Real: What Kind of World Are You Buying? was described by *Booklist* reviewer Carolyn Phelan as a "clearly written guide for readers who want to translate social and environmental awareness into action." Delving into items that teens typically use and buy—fast food, cell phones, a pair of jeans—the book covers problems such as overconsumption, commercialism, factory farming, sweatshops, and e-waste. She also presents solutions ranging from organic growing methods to fair trade and green design. In *School Library Journal,* Lisa Crandall lauded the work's "impressive bibliography" and predicted that the knowledge gained in Rockliff's book "just might make some teens think twice about their buying habits." A *Publishers Weekly* critic also cited the value of *Get Real,* concluding that "this savvy guide encourages teens to be knowledgeable and media-literate consumers."

Rockliff garnered an Agatha Award nomination from the Mystery Writers of America for *The Case of the Poisoned Pig,* one of the books in her "Milo and Jazz Mysteries" series. Released under her Montgomery pseudonym, the series concerns classmates Milo and Jasmyne (known as Jazz), who investigate strange goings-on with an assist from their detective-in-training lessons, courtesy of master detective Dash Marlowe. In the first volume, *The Case of the Stinky Socks,* the duo searches for a pair of lucky socks belong to Jazz's older

Mara Rockliff's picture book **The Busiest Street in Town** *features artwork by Sarah McMenemy.* (Illustration copyright © 2009 by Sarah McMenemy. Reproduced by permission of Alfred A. Knopf, an imprint of Random House Children's Books, a division of Random House, Inc.)

brother, a star pitcher for the local baseball team. In *The Case of the Poisoned Pig* the pair attempts to discover the cause of the mysterious illness affecting Jazz's new pet. "The stories are quick and satisfying," Bethany A. Lafferty wrote in her *School Library Journal* review of the series.

Biographical and Critical Sources

PERIODICALS

Booklist, May 1, 2009, Ilene Cooper, review of *The Case of the Stinky Socks,* p. 42; October 1, 2009, Michael Cart, review of *The Busiest Street in Town,* p. 49; August, 2010, Carolyn Phelan, review of *Get Real: What Kind of World Are You Buying?,* p. 45.

Kirkus Reviews, September 1, 2009, review of *The Busiest Street in Town.*

New York Times Book Review, November 8, 2009, Rich Cohen, review of *The Busiest Street in Town,* p. 24.

Publishers Weekly, October 19, 2009, review of *The Busiest Street in Town,* p. 51; June 21, 2010, review of *Get Real?,* p. 48.

School Library Journal, July, 2009, Bethany A. Lafferty, review of *The Case of the Poisoned Pig,* p. 66; October, 2009, Ieva Bates, review of *The Busiest Street in Town,* p. 104; October, 2010, Lisa Crandall, review of *Get Real,* p. 132.

ONLINE

Mara Rockliff Home Page, http://www.mararockliff.com (January 1, 2011).

*   *   *

ROOT, Phyllis 1949-

Personal

Born February 14, 1949, in Fort Wayne, IN; daughter of John Howard and Esther Root; married James Elliot Hansa (a mason); children: Amelia Christin, Ellen Rose. *Education:* Valparaiso University, B.A., 1971. *Hobbies and other interests:* Canoeing, sailing, gardening, reading.

Addresses

Home—Minneapolis, MN. *Office*—Hamline University, 1536 Hewitt Ave., St. Paul, MN 55104-1284. *E-mail*—phyllisiroot@gmail.com.

Career

Writer. Worked variously as an architectural drafter, costume seamstress, bicycle repair person, and administrative assistant. Vermont College, instructor in M.F.A. in Writing for Children Program for eight years; Hamline University, St. Paul, MN, instructor in M.F.A. in Writing for Children and Young Adults.

Member

Society of Children's Book Writers and Illustrators.

Awards, Honors

Children's Books of the Year citation, Child Study Association of America, and Bologna International Children's Book Fair selection, both 1985, both for *Moon Tiger;* Minnesota Picture Book Award, 1997, for *Aunt Nancy and Old Man Trouble;* Best Books of the Year selection, *School Library Journal,* 1998, for *What Baby Wants;* Oppenheim Toy Portfolio Gold Award, and Notable Children's Book in the Language Arts selection, National Council of Teachers of English, both 2001, both for *Rattletrap Car;* Oppenheim Toy Portfolio Platinum Award, 2002, for *Oliver Finds His Way;* Top-Ten Easy Readers selection, *Booklist,* 2002, for *Mouse Has Fun,* and 2003, for *Mouse Goes Out;* Best Children's Book of the Year selection, Bank Street College of Education, 2003, for *The Name Quilt; Boston Globe/Horn Book* Picture Book Award, 2003, for *Big Momma Makes the World;* McKnight fellowship, 2006, for *Lucia and the Light;* Best Children's Book of the Year selection, Bank Street College of Education, 2007, for *Aunt Nancy and the Bothersome Visitors;* Oppenheim Toy Portfolio Gold Award, 2009, for both *Thirsty Thursday* and *Toot Toot Zoom!*

Writings

FOR CHILDREN

Hidden Places, illustrated by Daniel San Souci, Carnival Press (Milwaukee, WI), 1983.

(With Carol A. Marron) *Gretchen's Grandma,* illustrated by Deborah K. Ray, Carnival Press (Milwaukee, WI), 1983.

(With Carol A. Marron) *Just One of the Family,* illustrated by George Karn, Carnival Press (Milwaukee, WI), 1984.

(With Carol A. Marron) *No Place for a Pig,* illustrated by Nathan Y. Jarvis, Carnival Press (Milwaukee, WI), 1984.

My Cousin Charlie, illustrated by Pia Marella, Carnival Press (Milwaukee, WI), 1984.

Moon Tiger, illustrated by Ed Young, Holt (New York, NY), 1985.

Soup for Supper, illustrated by Sue Truesdell, Harper (New York, NY), 1986.

Great Basin, Carnival/Crestwood (Mankato, MN), 1988.

Glacier, Carnival/Crestwood (Mankato, MN), 1989.

Galapagos, Carnival/Crestwood (Mankato, MN), 1989.

The Old Red Rocking Chair, illustrated by John Sanford, Arcade (New York, NY), 1992.

The Listening Silence, illustrated by Dennis McDermott, Harper (New York, NY), 1992.

Coyote and the Magic Words, illustrated by Sandra Speidel, Lothrop (New York, NY), 1993.

Sam Who Was Swallowed by a Shark, illustrated by Axel Scheffler, Candlewick Press (Cambridge, MA), 1994.

Aunt Nancy and Old Man Trouble, illustrated by David Parkins, Candlewick Press (Cambridge, MA), 1996.

Mrs. Potter's Pig, illustrated by Russell Ayto, Candlewick Press (Cambridge, MA), 1996.

Contrary Bear, illustrated by Laura Cornell, HarperCollins/ Laura Geringer Books (New York, NY), 1996.

One Windy Wednesday, illustrated by Helen Craig, Candlewick Press (Cambridge, MA), 1996.

Rosie's Fiddle, illustrated by Kevin O'Malley, Lothrop (New York, NY), 1997.

The Hungry Monster, illustrated by Sue Heap, Candlewick Press (Cambridge, MA), 1997.

Turnover Tuesday, illustrated by Helen Craig, Candlewick Press (Cambridge, MA), 1998.

What Baby Wants, illustrated by Jill Barton, Candlewick Press (Cambridge, MA), 1998.

One Duck Stuck: A Mucky Ducky Counting Book, illustrated by Jane Chapman, Candlewick Press (Cambridge, MA), 1998.

Aunt Nancy and Cousin Lazybones, illustrated by David Parkins, Candlewick Press (Cambridge, MA), 1998.

Grandmother Winter, illustrated by Beth Krommes, Houghton Mifflin (Boston, MA), 1999.

Hey, Tabby Cat!, illustrated by Katherine McEwen, Candlewick Press (Cambridge, MA), 2000.

All for the Newborn Baby, illustrated by Nicola Bayley, Candlewick Press (Cambridge, MA), 2000.

Kiss the Cow!, illustrated by Will Hillenbrand, Candlewick Press (Cambridge, MA), 2000.

Here Comes Tabby Cat, illustrated by Katherine McEwen, Candlewick Press (Cambridge, MA), 2000.

Meow Monday, illustrated by Helen Craig, Candlewick Press (Cambridge, MA), 2000.

Foggy Friday, illustrated by Helen Craig, Candlewick Press (Cambridge, MA), 2000.

Soggy Saturday, illustrated by Helen Craig, Candlewick Press (Cambridge, MA), 2001.

Rattletrap Car, illustrated by Jill Barton, Candlewick Press (Cambridge, MA), 2001.

(With Michelle Edwards) *What's That Noise?,* illustrated by Paul Meisel, Candlewick Press (Cambridge, MA), 2002.

Mouse Goes Out, illustrated by James Croft, Candlewick Press (Cambridge, MA), 2002.

Mouse Has Fun, illustrated by James Croft, Candlewick Press (Cambridge, MA), 2002.

Big Momma Makes the World, illustrated by Helen Oxenbury, Candlewick Press (Cambridge, MA), 2002.

Oliver Finds His Way, illustrated by Christopher Denise, Walker (New York, NY), 2002.

The Name Quilt, illustrated by Margot Apple, Farrar, Straus & Giroux (New York, NY), 2003.

Ten Sleepy Sheep, illustrated by Susan Gaber, Candlewick Press (Cambridge, MA), 2004.

Baby Ducklings, illustrated by Petra Mathers, Candlewick Press (Cambridge, MA), 2004.

Baby Bunnies, illustrated by Petra Mathers, Candlewick Press (Cambridge, MA), 2004.

If You Want to See a Caribou, illustrated by Jim Meyer, Houghton Mifflin (Boston, MA), 2004.

Hop!, illustrated by Holly Meade, Candlewick Press (Cambridge, MA), 2005.

The House That Jill Built (pop-up book), illustrated by Delphine Durand, Candlewick Press (Cambridge, MA), 2005.

Quack!, illustrated by Holly Meade, Candlewick Press (Cambridge, MA), 2005.

Who Said Boo?, illustrated by Ana Martín Larraífaga, Little Simon (New York, NY), 2005.

Looking for a Moose, illustrated by Randy Cecil, Candlewick Press (Cambridge, MA), 2006.

Lucia and the Light, illustrated by Mary GrandPré, Candlewick Press (Cambridge, MA), 2006.

Aunt Nancy and the Bothersome Visitors, illustrated by David Parkins, Candlewick Press (Cambridge, MA), 2007.

Flip, Flap, Fly!: A Book for Babies Everywhere, illustrated by David Walker, Candlewick Press (Somerville, MA), 2009.

Paula Bunyan, illustrated by Kevin O'Malley, Farrar, Straus & Giroux (New York, NY), 2009.

Thirsty Thursday, illustrated by Helen Craig, Candlewick Press (Somerville, MA), 2009.

Toot Toot Zoom!, illustrated by Matthew Cordell, Candlewick Press (Somerville, MA), 2009.

Big Belching Bog, illustrated by Betsy Bowen, University of Minnesota Press (Minneapolis, MN), 2010.

Creak! Said the Bed, illustrated by Regan Dunnick, Candlewick Press (Somerville, MA), 2010.

Lilly and the Pirates, illustrated by Bob Shepperson, Front Street (Honesdale, PA), 2010.

FOR ADULTS

Gladys on the Go, photographs by Kelly Povo, Conari Press (York Beach, ME), 2004.

Hot Flash Gal, photographs by Kelly Povo, Conari Press (York Beach, ME), 2004.

Ask Gladys: Household Hits for Gals on the Go, photographs by Kelly Povo, Conari Press (Boston, MA), 2005.

Dear Hot Flash Gal: Every Answer to a Gal's Every Question, photographs by Kelly Povo, Conari Press (Boston, MA), 2005.

Sidelights

A versatile writer, Phyllis Root has garnered critical and popular acclaim for creating picture books that range from retellings of Native-American stories and tall tales to celebrations of intergenerational relationships and the small, intimate moments of childhood. As Kelly Milner Halls noted in *Booklist,* Root "has carved a niche for herself by using homespun observations and the playful use of rural undertones." Working with illustrators such as Helen Craig, Paul Meisel, Jill Barton, Will Hillenbrand, Susan Gaber, Mary GrandPré, and Helen Oxenbury, the award-winning author has produced such popular titles as *Ten Sleepy Sheep, Rattletrap Car, Big Momma Makes the World,* and *Paula Bunyan.* "Picture books are performances," Root remarked on the *Candlewick Press* Web site. "They're performances that involve a child—something both of you do. And once I started thinking of them that way, I started getting much looser about making up words and playing around with rhythm."

Although Root became a professional author in the late 1970s, she has been writing for fun as long as she can remember. "I made up stories, poems, and songs," she once told *SATA.* "In first grade, I wrote a poem about love and a dove, and in second grade, I won a class essay contest for my four-sentence story about the Sahara desert. In fifth grade, I had a remarkable and wonderful teacher, Mrs. Keller, who encouraged me to write. It was in her class that I decided I would be an 'authoress' when I grew up."

Root went on to attend Valparaiso University, earning a bachelor's degree in 1971; she did not begin writing professionally for another eight years, after taking a course in writing for children and young adults where she learned important skills such as creating plots, settings, tension, and characters. The instructor, award-winning author and anthologist Marion Dane Bauer, "told us we could all learn the tools of writing a story, but all we had to do after we had learned the tools was to write from our hearts," Root noted in a *Cynsations* online interview with Cynthia Leitich Smith. "I'm still

Phyllis Root takes readers on an exciting ride in her picture book **Rattletrap Car,** *featuring artwork by Jill Barton.* (Illustration copyright © 2001 by Jill Barton. Reproduced by permission of Candlewick Press, Somerville, MA.)

learning what that last part means, but I did start writing in her class, and I have never really stopped. I don't claim to know what I'm doing, but I'm grateful to still be doing it."

One of Root's earliest published works, *Gretchen's Grandma,* was co-written with colleague Carol A. Marron. The 1983 picture book tells the story of Gretchen and her "Oma," or grandmother, who is visiting from Germany. At the beginning of the visit, the language barrier is troublesome, but eventually grandmother and grandchild overcome their verbal problems by creating a language of pantomime and mutual affection. Ilene Cooper, writing in *Booklist,* described *Gretchen's Grandma* as "a gentle story that could be used as [a] starting point for some preschool discussion."

Another early picture book, *Moon Tiger,* follows a young girl's imaginative journey as she dreams of being rescued from the task of babysitting her pesky younger brother by a magical tiger. When the tiger offers to eat the boy, however, the sister declines, admitting that she might actually miss her brother after all. *Moon Tiger* was described by a *Bulletin of the Center for Children's Books* writer as "the stuff of which dreams are made," and Nancy Schmidtmann dubbed it a "heavenly treat" in her *School Library Journal* review.

Root's whimsical humor shines through in picture books such as *The Old Red Rocking Chair, Contrary Bear,* and *Looking for a Moose.* In *The Old Red Rocking Chair* a discarded rocking chair is rescued time and time again from the garbage by various eagle-eyed dump-pickers. Each new owner takes from the chair different pieces and discards the remains, until what was once a chair evolves into a blue footstool which is sold back to its original—and oblivious—owner at a garage sale. In *The Hungry Monster* a hungry little alien finds that its hunger cannot be satisfied until a little Earthling offers it a banana, peel and all. "While the premise is hardly new . . . Root's cheerfulness and lucid logic" animate the text of *The Old Red Rocking Chair,* in the opinion of a *Publishers Weekly* critic, and a *Kirkus Reviews* writer praised *The Hungry Monster* as a "silly story that includes a dash of suspense" as well as "a just-right read-aloud for board-book graduates."

A "cheery tale of compromise," according to a *Publishers Weekly* writer, *Mrs. Potter's Pig* focuses on a neat freak who learns to appreciate the joy of mud when she has to rescue her dirt-loving daughter from a pigpen. Another story by Root, *Contrary Bear,* finds a toy blamed for its owner's obstinate behavior. Contrary Bear takes the rap for making loud train whistles during naptime and wanting a bigger piece of cake, but the last straw for Dad is when the stuffed toy supposedly splashes water all over the bathroom. Finally relegated to the clothesline to dry out, Contrary Bear watches its penitent owner promise to help the toy be better behaved in the future.

Jill Barton creates the humorous artwork that brings to life Root's story in **What Baby Wants.** (Illustration © copyright 2001 by Jill Barton. Reproduced by permission of Candlewick Press, Somerville, MA.)

Brought to life in humorous illustrations by Randy Cecil, *Looking for a Moose* takes story-hour participants on "an engaging romp," according to *Booklist* contributor Connie Fletcher. In Root's story, listeners follow four children on a hunt through the forest. When they reach their goal and stumble upon the moose that have been following THEM all along, the author's "infectious" onomatopoeic rhyming text comes full circle, according to a *Publishers Weekly* critic. A *Kirkus Reviews* writer also praised *Looking for a Moose*, concluding that the book's "buoyant, rhymed text makes for a stellar read-aloud." Similar in theme, *If You Want to See a Caribou* also features a poetic text, this time transporting readers into a balsam forest in search of a caribou mother and calf. Gentler in tone than *Looking for a Moose*, the book pairs Root's "subtle" poetry with illustrator Jim Meyer's "serene, expansive" block-printed illustrations, according to *Booklist* reviewer Gillian Engberg.

The author collaborates with artist Jill Barton on *What Baby Wants,* a "farmyard tale of an implacable baby," according to a contributor to *Publishers Weekly.* In Root's tale, an entire family tries to help when Mother has difficulty getting her crying infant to sleep. Each family member thinks that the fussy baby needs something different, but ultimately it is the younger brother who knows the trick: all Baby wants is a big cuddle. In *Booklist* Stephanie Zvirin deemed *What Baby Wants* a "sweet, simple charmer." Author and illustrator team up again for *Rattletrap Car,* a cumulative story about the humorous mini-disasters that befall a family during a summertime outing to the lake. As a *Publishers Weekly* reviewer commented, "Root and Barton prove that they know how to convey mounting comic mayhem" in the humorous picture book, and Ilene Cooper concluded in *Booklist* that *Rattletrap Car* "passes the fun test with flying fizz."

Root addresses some universal childhood fears in *What's That Noise?* and *Oliver Finds His Way.* In the first title,

a "story of how imagination can run amok," according to *School Library Journal* critic Susan Marie Pitard, two little brothers hear noises in the night. While at first frightened, they learn to calm their fears by making up a silly song that classifies each of the scary sounds. Similarly, *Oliver Finds His Way* explores the fear of getting lost and the consequent relief in finding one's way home again. Baby bear Oliver loses his way one warm day while his parents are busy. He follows a leaf as eddies of air carry it farther and farther away from his home, finally leading the cub into the shadowy woods. Eventually, the resilient Oliver is able to find his way back again by calling out to his parents and then following the sound of their returning calls. A critic for *Publishers Weekly* praised both Root and illustrator Christopher Denise for bringing "a fresh poignancy to the familiar theme," and Kathleen Simonetta predicted in *School Library Journal* that the "happy ending" in *Oliver Finds His Way* "will leave readers smiling."

Like many authors, Root has mined her own family experiences for many picture-book ideas. For example, *Soup for Supper* was inspired by a sudden nighttime thunderstorm. "I had gotten up to comfort my daughter Amelia," she once recalled to *SATA,* "and remembered how, when I was a child, my sister and I had sat on the bed with our parents, watching the lightning and rain. 'Don't let the thunder scare you,' they reassured us. 'It's just the noise potatoes make spilling out of the giant's cart.' Listening to the thunder with my own daughter, I suddenly saw the giant with his cart of vegetables and a wee small woman chasing after him. The next morning I wrote down the first draft of *Soup for Supper.*" The result is "an original story with a folkloric ring," wrote a *Bulletin of the Center for Children's Books* writer, the critic recommending *Soup for Supper* as "dandy [for] reading aloud because of the simple rhymes, name-calling, and sound effects." The wee small woman of Root's tale vigorously defends her garden against the Giant Rumbleton's attempts to plunder it. After an energetic confrontation, the two enemies discover a common culinary goal and become friends as together they make vegetable soup. Root even includes music for the giant's song at the end of the book.

Root called on her then-ten-year-old daughter for help with *One Windy Wednesday,* part of a series of books illustrated by Helen Craig that detail various days of the week. In the humorous tale, a day comes when the wind is so strong that it blows the sound right out of some farm animals and into others. When the wind subsides, the lamb are left quacking, the ducks start mooing, and the cow just oinks, leaving Bonnie Bumble to re-hitch the right critter to the right call. Hazel Rochman, writing in *Booklist,* described *One Windy Wednesday* as a "simple, funny story." Other books in the series include *Turnover Tuesday,* which finds Bonnie Bumble literally turning over after making plum turnovers; and *Meow Monday,* in which Bonnie's garden of pussy willows sprout some real pussycats that are hungry for milk

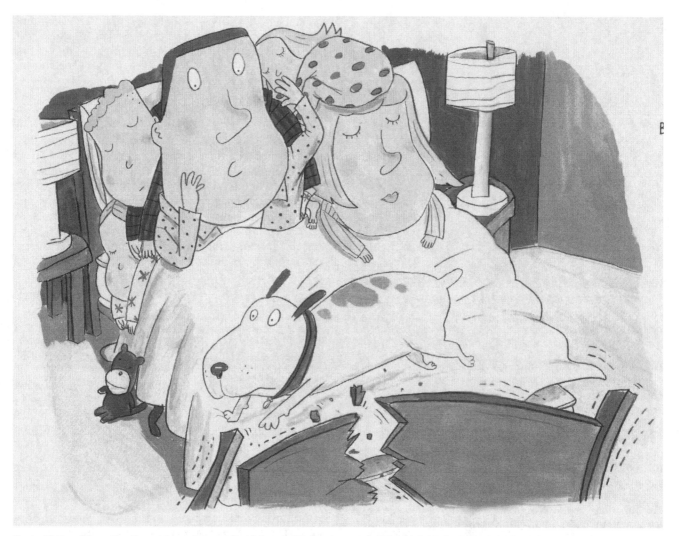

Reginald Dunnick creates the quirky cartoon art that brings to life Root's story in "Creak! Said the Bed. (Illustration copyright © 2010 by Regan Dunnick. Reproduced by permission of Candlewick Press, Somerville, MA.)

from the milkweed plant. *Foggy Friday* catches Bonnie napping when her faithful rooster forgets to crow, and in *Soggy Saturday* a heavy rain has washed the blue from the sky onto the animals on Bonnie's farm. Lynda Ritterman, writing in *School Library Journal,* cited the "winning combination of spare, well-chosen words and lively, crisp pacing" in *Meow Monday,* and a *Kirkus Reviews* critic praised the "beguiling simplicity" of *Soggy Saturday.*

More rural settings are served up in the concept books *One Duck Stuck: A Mucky Ducky Counting Book* and *Ten Sleepy Sheep.* In the first book, when a poor fowl gets stuck in the mud, it is helped in turn by varying numbers of fish, crickets, and frogs. Shirley Lewis, writing in *Teacher Librarian,* called it a "delightful picture book," and in *Booklist* Helen Rosenberg predicted that *One Duck Stuck* is "great fun and sure to become an instant favorite among the toddler crowd." Another counting book, *Ten Sleepy Sheep,* shows readers that counting sheep in order to fall asleep can sometimes be challenging, especially when the sheep are not sleepy

themselves. Fortunately, one by one, the frisky lambs nod off to sleep amid the cozy setting created by illustrator Susan Gaber.

In *Kiss the Cow!,* illustrated by Will Hillenbrand, Root returns again to the farm, this time to find little Annalisa watching her mother milk the family's cow. Without a kiss on the nose, Luella the cow refuses to give milk, but when Annalisa attempts to perform the milking herself, she needs some convincing before she can bring herself to touch Luella's damp cow nose with her lips. In *Booklist* Carolyn Phelan commented on the "satisfying folksy sound" of Root's narrative and commended Hillenbrand's artwork for its "style and panache." Anne Knickerbocker wrote in *School Library Journal* that the book's "flowing language makes it a fun read-aloud," while a reviewer for *Horn Book* called *Kiss the Cow!* "an original story of magic and mischief."

In *The Listening Silence* Root draws on Native-American traditions to create a "strong, believable" heroine, according to Ruth S. Vose in *School Library Journal.* Kiri is a young, orphaned girl who is raised in a tribe whose healer recognizes her ability to send her spirit inside of both people and animals. Reluctant to use this power, Kiri goes on a vision quest to discover her true calling and eventually uses her gift to heal a young man she encounters. While Vose praised the "smooth, lyrical, language" in *The Listening Silence,* a *Kirkus Reviews* writer hailed Root's "spare, carefully honed narration." Much like J.R.R. Tolkien did in his classic *Lord of the Rings,* Root invents names for the woodland plants and animals in *The Listening Silence,* creating what Kathryn Pierson Jennings described in the *Bulletin of the Center for Children's Books* as "a fantasy culture . . . [that] is orderly and compelling and may inspire young creative writing students who need a more modest fantasy world than Tolkien."

In *Coyote and the Magic Words* Root employs elements of Native-American folklore, including the use of a coyote as a trickster. As she once explained, the book is "a story about storytelling, about how to create worlds with nothing more than our words." In the tale, Maker-of-All-Things uses words to speak her creations into existence and grants her creatures the power to meet their own needs simply by speaking into existence what they want. Coyote grows bored with this easy way of life, however, and begins to incite mischief using the magic words. To punish him, Maker-of-All-Things takes away the magic of the words, except the ones Coyote uses in storytelling. Karen Hutt, writing for *Booklist,* characterized *Coyote and the Magic Words* as "simple but satisfying," and a *Kirkus Reviews* critic observed

***Will Hillenbrand brings to life Root's folksy story about a beautiful bovine in* Kiss the Cow!** (Illustration copyright © 2000 by Will Hillenbrand. Reproduced by permission of Candlewick Press, Somerville, MA.)

that "Root's Coyote is appropriately childlike; her lively narration is well-honed and agreeably informal, just right for oral sharing."

The homespun character of Aunt Nancy is introduced by Root in *Aunt Nancy and Old Man Trouble,* featuring artwork by David Parkins. Aunt Nancy returns in *Aunt Nancy and Cousin Lazybones.* In this episode, she is not looking forward to a visit from her Cousin Lazybones, whose laziness is legendary. Instead of going to get water from the well, Lazybones simply sets a bucket outside the door and then hopes for rain. Fed up with the slacker, Aunt Nancy decides to fight fire with fire; she becomes as lazy as her cousin. When more and more housework falls to him, Cousin Lazybones decides to cut his visit short. In *Publishers Weekly* a reviewer noted of *Aunt Nancy and Cousin Lazybones* that "Root brings generous dollops of humor and homespun flavor to her folktale." Similar praise came from *Booklist* contributor John Peters, who predicted that "youngsters will delight in this battle of wits and look forward to Aunt Nancy's next visitor." In *Horn Book* Lolly Robinson also enjoyed the book, commenting that Root and Parkins "have created another original tall tale that sounds as though it's been told for years." Robinson also praised Root's "rhythmic" text, noting that it "begs to be read aloud."

Root's third work featuring the colorful protagonist, *Aunt Nancy and the Bothersome Visitors,* contains her previous two offerings in the series as well as a pair of new trickster-type tales. In "Aunt Nancy and Old Woeful" the clever woman outsmarts an extraordinarily pessimistic creature, and "Aunt Nancy and Mister Death" centers on the heroine's confrontation with the Grim Reaper himself. "All in all, it's a nifty package that'll have readers back again and again to visit Aunt Nancy themselves," Vicky Smith noted in *Horn Book.*

Root's adaptation of an American folk tale in *Rosie's Fiddle* "bursts with vitality and spunk," according to a *Kirkus Reviews* critic. In her story the Devil enters a fiddling contest with Rosie after he hears of her stellar fiddling reputation. After three rounds, Rosie fiddles the Devil into a puff of smoke, wins his golden instrument, and saves her own soul from falling into devilish hands. A *Publishers Weekly* critic commented that "the folksy prose and stormy spreads convey the tale's intensity— the only thing missing is a bluegrass soundtrack." Janice M. Del Negro, writing in the *Bulletin of the Center for Children's Books,* also offered a favorable estimation of *Rosie's Fiddle,* asserting that "Root's adaptation of this traditional motif has a fine readaloud rhythm and a thoroughly satisfying progression as the devil gets his musical due."

Inspired by a traditional Norwegian legend about Saint Lucia Day, *Lucia and the Light* explains what must happen in order for the days to begin to lengthen in the dead of winter. In her adaptation, Root brings readers to a cabin in the mountains, where Lucia lives with her mother and younger brother, as well as Cow and White Cat. All is well until one winter, when the sun appears less and less frequently before disappearing altogether and leaving no way for Lucia to mark night from day. Determined to restore the sun, the brave girl and her cat ski off up the mountain, where she ultimately frees the sun from a band of evil trolls. Noting the tale's underlying message about loyalty and cooperation, *Booklist* contributor of Gillian Engberg added that "Root's rich language and well-paced story are sure to capture a young crowd of eager listeners." In *Publishers Weekly* a contributor noted how award-winning illustrator Mary GrandPré's "incandescent pastel art" evokes the story's Nordic setting, and *School Library Journal* reviewer Tamara E. Root predicted that, "with its terrifying trolls and triumphant travails," *Lucia and the Light* will spark the imagination of young listeners.

Again taking inspiration from traditional sources, Root adapts a German fairy-tale character in *Grandmother Winter* and provides a new take on the creation story in *Big Momma Makes the World,* two picture books featuring strong female protagonists. The eponymous heroine of *Grandmother Winter* proves to be the harbinger of the cold season. All summer long she gathers the fallen feathers from her white geese and when autumn comes she uses them to stuff a feather comforter. While fluffing up the comforter feathers are released and transformed into snowflakes as they fall from the sky. A reviewer for *Horn Book* commended Root's "cadenced" and "lyrical" text in this folktale remake. Kay Weisman, writing in *Booklist,* also recommended *Grandmother Winter* as "a wonderful choice for primary units on seasons or winter," and a *Publishers Weekly* critic called the book "a cozy mood-setter."

Big Momma Makes the World, illustrated by Helen Oxenbury, is a "sassy creation myth that tweaks the first chapter of Genesis," according to a contributor for *Publishers Weekly.* In Root's rendition, Big Momma creates the world and surveys her creation with satisfied, folksy expressions. "Root infuses her tale with a joyful spirit, and her lyrical vernacular trips off the tongue," a *Publishers Weekly* critic further commented. In *Booklist,* Cooper dubbed the tale "a raucous, joyous version of the creation story," while a *Kirkus Reviews* critic called *Big Momma Makes the World* a "paean to the Earth and to motherhood."

In another feminist take on a classic tale, *Paula Bunyan* introduces the younger sister of the famed lumberjack. When her powerful singing voice shatters windows and destroys stone walls, Paula leaves the civilized world behind and heads for the North Woods, where she befriends a seven-foot-tall bear, entices a pair of wolves to join her in song, and concocts a plan to prevent the desecration of the forest. Writing in *Booklist,* Carolyn Phelan declared that "it's good to have another tall-tale heroine," and Marianne Saccardi noted in *School Library Journal* that Root's "timely environmental message is an added plus."

Root crafts an animal-centered porquoi story in* Big Momma Makes the World, *featuring colorful illustrations by Helen Oxenbury. (Illustration copyright

A grandmother full of memories and traditional stories of her own is at the center of *The Name Quilt,* in which a little girl elicits family tales from her grandmother each night by picking a name embroidered on the patchwork quilt on her bed. When the quilt is swept away by a fierce wind, the young girl is disconsolate. Finally her grandmother suggests that they make a new quilt together, and this time the young girl's name is in the center of it. Mary Elam, writing in *School Library Journal,* noted that Root "stitches together generations, memories, and traditions in this tale of a much-loved family treasure."

A story told in verse, *Flip, Flap, Fly!: A Book for Babies Everywhere* follows six tiny animals as they enter the larger world for the first time, wriggling through the woods and splashing through the pond under their mothers' watchful eyes. "The text flows easily from scene to scene," Kate Neff remarked in *School Library Journal,* and Claire E. Gross, writing in *Horn Book,* observed that the story's "generous doses of onomatopoeia and alliteration add to the fun." In *Creak! Said the Bed,* a cumulative tale featuring Reginald Dunnick's cartoon art, Momma and Poppa's peaceful night of slumber is disturbed by their three children—each of whom crawls under the covers with them—as well as the family dog, whose entrance proves too much for the furniture to handle. Although Root treads on familiar ground with her storyline, Karen Cruze noted in *Booklist* that the author enlivens the work "by punctuating the story with the sounds of impending disaster." In the words of *School Library Journal* critic May Jean Smith, "Frequent repetition and rhyming words make [*Creak! Said the Bed*] . . . a good choice for emergent readers."

A dry spell causes tempers to flare in Root's *Thirsty Thursday.* With no rain in sight, Bonnie's snapdragons, tiger lilies, and black-eyed Susans become increasingly irritable, and her pigs, cows, and chickens also begin to wilt in the heat. Fortunately, Bonnie devises a clever solution to the problem, using the barnyard animals to help her reach to the sky. "Short, sweet and unabashedly darling, Root's text employs just the right amount of repetition" for young readers, noted a contributor in *Kirkus Reviews.* In *Toot Toot Zoom!,* a lonely fox named Pierre takes off in his convertible, hoping to find a new companion on the other side of the mountain he calls home. Along the way, Pierre encounters a friendly goat, sheep, and bear, who all agree to aid the fox in his search. In *School Library Journal,* Blair Christolon observed of *Toot Toot Zoom!* that "a satisfying conclusion marks several successful friendships" in the fox's journey.

With dozens of books for children to her credit, Root shows no signs of slowing down. As she remarked in a *Seven Impossible Things before Breakfast* online interview, "I love picture books! There's something so amazing about the text and art creating something more than either one. There's magic in the turn of the page—what happens next?—right up to the last page and a satisfying ending. Plus, in writing for young children I'm free to play with language and with sounds, with rhythm, rhyme, and repetition in a way that is almost unique to picture books."

Biographical and Critical Sources

PERIODICALS

Booklist, January 1, 1984, Ilene Cooper, review of *Gretchen's Grandma,* p. 684; November 15, 1993, Karen Hutt, review of *Coyote and the Magic Words,* p. 633; October 15, 1996, Hazel Rochman, review of *One Windy Wednesday,* p. 437; April, 1998, Helen Rosenberg, review of *One Duck Stuck: A Mucky Ducky Counting Book,* p. 1333; September 15, 1998, Stephanie Zvirin, review of *What Baby Wants,* p. 240; October 15, 1998, Ilene Cooper, review of *Turnover Tuesday,* p. 429; November 15, 1998, John Peters, review of *Aunt Nancy and Cousin Lazybones,* p. 597; November 15, 1999, Kay Weisman, review of *Grandmother Winter,* p. 637; September 1, 2000, Gillian Engberg, review of *All for the Newborn Baby,* p. 134; November 15, 2000, Kelly Milner Halls, reviews of *Meow Monday* and *Foggy Friday,* and Carolyn Phelan, review of *Kiss the Cow!,* all p. 650; December 1, 2001, Ilene Cooper, review of *Soggy Saturday,* pp. 650-651; January 1, 2002, review of *Rattletrap Car,* p. 768; January 1, 2003, Ilene Cooper, review of *Big Momma Makes the World,* p. 88; March 15, 2003, Carolyn Phelan, review of *The Name Quilt,* p. 1333; April 15, 2004, Gillian Engberg, review of *If You Want to See a Caribou,* p. 1449; September 1, 2006, Gillian Engberg, review of *Lucia and the Light,* p. 45; October 1, 2006, Connie Fletcher, review of *Looking for a Moose,* p. 60; March 1, 2009, Carolyn Phelan, review of *Paula Bunyan,* p. 53; April 15, 2009, Julie Cummins, review of *Flip, Flap, Fly!: A Book for Babies Everywhere,* p. 46; March 1, 2010, Karen Cruze, review of *Creak! Said the Bed,* p. 76.

Bulletin of the Center for Children's Books, January, 1986, review of *Moon Tiger,* p. 95; July-August, 1986, review of *Soup for Supper,* p. 216; March, 1992, Kathryn Pierson Jennings, review of *The Listening Silence,* p. 191; March, 1996, Deborah Stevenson, review of *Aunt Nancy and Old Man Trouble,* p. 240; April, 1997, Janice M. DelNegro, review of *Rosie's Fiddle,* p. 293; December, 1998, Betsy Hearne, review of *Aunt Nancy and Cousin Lazybones,* p. 144; October, 1999, Fern Kory, review of *Grandmother Winter,* p. 66; February, 2001, Kate McDowell, review of *Foggy Friday* and *Meow Monday,* pp. 235-236.

Horn Book, January-February, 1999, Lolly Robinson, review of *Aunt Nancy and Cousin Lazybones,* p. 55; September-October, 1999, review of *Grandmother Winter,* p. 599; January-February, 2001, review of *Kiss the Cow!,* p. 85; May-June, 2004, Lauren Adams, review of *Ten Sleepy Sheep,* p. 319; September-October, 2007, Vicky Smith, review of *Aunt Nancy and the Bothersome Visitors,* p. 588; May-June, 2009, Claire E. Gross, review of *Flip, Flap, Fly!,* p. 286.

Kirkus Reviews, May 1, 1992, review of *The Listening Silence,* p. 616; September 1, 1993, review of *Coyote and the Magic Words,* p. 1151; January 1, 1997, review of *The Hungry Monster,* p. 63; February 1, 1997, review of *Rosie's Fiddle,* p. 227; September 15, 2001, review of *Soggy Saturday,* p. 1366; July 1, 2002, review of *What's That Noise?,* p. 953; August 1, 2002, review of *Oliver Finds His Way,* p. 1141; January 15, 2003, review of *Big Momma Makes the World,* p. 146; March 1, 2003, review of *The Name Quilt,* p. 397; August 1, 2005, review of *The House That Jill Built,* p. 857; July 15, 2006, review of *Looking for a Moose,* p. 729; October 15, 2006, review of *Lucia and the Light,* p. 1079; July 1, 2007, review of *Aunt Nancy and the Bothersome Visitors;* February 15, 2009, review of *Flip, Flap, Fly!;* July 1, 2009, review of *Thirsty Thursday.*

Language Arts, March, 2003, review of *Rattletrap Car,* p. 317.

Publishers Weekly, May 18, 1992, review of *The Old Red Rocking Chair,* p. 68; May 30, 1994, review of *Sam Who Was Swallowed by a Shark,* pp. 55-56; May 13, 1996, review of *Contrary Bear,* p. 75; June 10, 1996, review of *Mrs. Potter's Pig,* p. 99; January 13, 1997, review of *Rosie's Fiddle,* pp. 75-76; May 4, 1998, review of *One Duck Stuck,* p. 211; September 14, 1998, review of *What Baby Wants,* p. 67; October 26, 1998, review of *Aunt Nancy and Cousin Lazybones,* p. 66; August 30, 1999, review of *Grandmother Winter,* p. 82; April 30, 2001, review of *Rattletrap Car,* p. 77; June 17, 2002, review of *What's That Noise?,* p. 64; August 19, 2002, review of *Oliver Finds His Way,* p. 87; November 25, 2002, review of *Big Momma Makes the World,* p. 66; January 13, 2003, review of *The Name Quilt,* p. 59; September 18, 2006, review of *Looking for a Moose,* p. 53; November 27, 2006, review of *Lucia and the Light,* p. 50; March 22, 2010, review of *Creak! Said the Bed,* p. 67.

School Library Journal, December, 1985, Nancy Schmidtmann, review of *Moon Tiger,* p. 81; June, 1992, Ruth S. Vose, review of *The Listening Silence,* p. 125; June, 1998, Heide Piehler, review of *One Duck Stuck,* pp. 118-119; September, 1998, Kathy M. Newby, review of *What Baby Wants,* p. 180; November 1, 1998, Gale W. Sherman, review of *Turnover Tuesday,* p. 94, and Barbara Elleman, review of *Aunt Nancy and Cousin Lazybones,* p. 94; September, 1999, Maryann H. Owens, review of *Grandmother Winter,* p. 201; August, 2000, Anne Knickerbocker, review of *Here Comes Tabby Cat,* p. 164; October, 2000, review of *All for the Newborn Baby,* p. 62; November, 2000, Lynda Ritterman, review of *Meow Monday,* p. 130; December, 2000, Anne Knickerbocker, review of *Kiss the Cow!,* p. 124; June, 2001, Adele Greenlee, review of *Rattletrap Car,* p. 128; December, 2001, Ann Cook, review of *Soggy Saturday,* p. 110; October, 2002, Kathleen Simonetta, review of *Oliver Finds His Way,* p. 126; December, 2002, Susan Marie Pitard, review of *What's That Noise?,* p. 94; March, 2003, Laurie von Mehren, review of *Big Momma Makes the World,* p. 206; May, 2003, Mary Elam, review of *The Name Quilt,* p. 129; October, 2006, Kara Schaff Dean, review of *Looking for a Moose,* p. 124; December, 2006, Tamara E. Richman, review of *Lucia and the Light,* p. 114; August, 2007, Mary Jean Smith, review of *Aunt Nancy and the Bothersome Visitors,* p. 90; March, 2009, Marianne Saccardi, review of *Paula Bunyan,* p. 126; May, 2009, Kate Neff, review of *Flip, Flap, Fly!,* p. 87, and Blair Christolon, review of *Toot Toot Zoom!,* p. 88; March, 2010, Mary Jean Smith, review of *Creak! Said the Bed,* p. 129.

Teacher Librarian, September, 1998, Shirley Lewis, review of *One Duck Stuck,* p. 47.

Times Educational Supplement, March 26, 1999, Ted Dewan, review of *What Baby Wants,* p. 23; February 23, 2001, Ted Dewan, review of *Kiss the Cow!,* pp. 19-20.

ONLINE

Candlewick Press Web site, http://www.candlewick.com/ (January 15, 2011), "Phyllis Root."

Children's Literature Network, http://www.childrens literaturenetwork.org/ (January 15, 2011), "Phyllis Root."

Cynsations Web log, http://cynthialeitichsmith.blogspot. com/ (March 23, 2006), Cynthia Leitich Smith, interview with Root.

Seven Impossible Things before Breakfast Web log, http:// blaine.org/sevenimpossiblethings/ (November 5, 2006), interview with Root.*

S

SANDERSON, Ruth 1951-
(Ruth L. Sanderson)

Personal

Born November 24, 1951, in Ware, MA; daughter of C. Kenneth and Victoria Sanderson; married Kenneth Robinson; children: Whitney, one other daughter. *Education:* Attended Paier School of Art, 1970-74. *Hobbies and other interests:* Horseback riding.

Addresses

Home—P.O. Box 638, Ware, MA 01082. *E-mail*—Ruth@RuthSanderson.com.

Career

Illustrator of books for children. Hollins University, Roanoke, VA, instructor in graduate-level illustration and M.F.A. writing program in children's literature. *Exhibitions:* Work exhibited at Norman Rockwell Museum, 2004.

Member

Society of Children's Book Writers and Illustrators, Society of Illustrators, Western Massachusetts Illustrators Group.

Awards, Honors

Outstanding Science Book Award, National Association of Science Teachers, 1980, for *Five Nests* by Caroline Arnold; Notable Children's Trade Book in the Field of Social Studies, National Council for Social Studies/Children's Book Council, 1982, for *A Different Kind of Gold* by Cecily Stern; *School Library Journal* Best Books designation, 1982, for *The Animal, the Vegetable, and John D. Jones* by Betsy Byars; Irma S. Black Award, Bank Street College of Education, 1992, and Young Hoosier Award, Association for Indiana Media Educators, 1995, both for *The Enchanted Wood;* Texas Bluebonnet Award, 2003, for *The Golden Mare, the Firebird, and the Magic Ring.*

Writings

SELF-ILLUSTRATED

(Reteller) *The Twelve Dancing Princesses,* Little, Brown (Boston, MA), 1990.
The Enchanted Wood, Little, Brown (Boston, MA), 1991.
The Nativity: From the Gospels of Matthew and Luke, Little, Brown (Boston, MA), 1993, reprinted, Eerdmans Books for Young Readers (Grand Rapids, MI), 2010.
(Reteller) *Papa Gatto: An Italian Fairy Tale,* Little, Brown (Boston, MA), 1995.
(Reteller) *Rose Red and Snow White: A Grimms Fairy Tale,* Little, Brown (Boston, MA), 1996.
(Reteller) *Tapestries: Stories of Women in the Bible,* Little, Brown (Boston, MA), 1998.
(Reteller) *The Crystal Mountain,* Little, Brown (Boston, MA), 1999.
(Reteller) *The Golden Mare, the Firebird, and the Magic Ring,* Little, Brown (Boston, MA), 2001.
(Reteller) *Cinderella,* Little, Brown (Boston, MA), 2002.
(Selector) *Mother Goose and Friends,* Little, Brown (Boston, MA), 2003.
Saints: Lives and Illuminations, Eerdmans Books for Young Readers (Grand Rapids, MI), 2003.
The Snow Princess, Little, Brown (Boston, MA), 2004.
More Saints: Lives and Illuminations, Eerdmans Books for Young Readers (Grand Rapids, MI), 2006.
(Reteller) *Goldilocks,* Little, Brown (New York, NY), 2008.

ILLUSTRATOR; FOR CHILDREN

Ilka List, *Grandma's Beach Surprise,* Putnam (New York, NY), 1975.
Glenn Balch, *Buck, Wild,* Crowell (New York, NY), 1976.
Watty Piper (pseudonym of Mabel Caroline Bragg), reteller, *The Little Engine That Could,* new edition, Platt & Munk, 1976.
Mary Francis Shura, *The Season of Silence,* Atheneum (New York, NY), 1976.

Mary Towne, *First Serve,* Atheneum (New York, NY), 1976.

Clyde Robert Bulla, *The Beast of Lor,* Crowell (New York, NY), 1977.

Charles E. Mercer, *Jimmy Carter* (biography), Putnam (New York, NY), 1977.

Willo Davis Roberts, *Don't Hurt Laurie!,* Atheneum (New York, NY), 1977.

Robert Louis Stevenson, *A Child's Garden of Verses,* Platt & Munk, 1977.

Charlene Joy Talbot, *The Great Rat Island Adventure,* Atheneum (New York, NY), 1977.

Greta Walker, *Walt Disney* (biography), Putnam (New York, NY), 1977.

Lynn Hall, *The Mystery of Pony Hollow,* Garrard (Champlain, IL), 1978, reprinted, Random House (New York, NY), 1992.

Beverly Hollett Renner, *The Hideaway Summer,* Harper (New York, NY), 1978.

Miriam Schlein, *On the Track of the Mystery Animal: The Story of the Discovery of the Okapi* (nonfiction), Four Winds (New York, NY), 1978.

William Cole, compiler, *The Poetry of Horses,* Scribner (New York, NY), 1979.

Susan Clement Farrar, *Samantha on Stage,* Dial (New York, NY), 1979.

Norma Simon, *We Remember Philip,* Albert Whitman (Morton Grove, IL), 1979.

William Sleator, *Into the Dream,* Dutton (New York, NY), 1979.

Caroline Arnold, *Five Nests* (nonfiction), Dutton (New York, NY), 1980.

Margaret Chittenden, *The Mystery of the Missing Pony,* Garrard (Champlain, IL), 1980.

Nikki Amdur, *One of Us,* Dial (New York, NY), 1981.

William Cole, compiler, *Good Dog Poems,* Scribner (New York, NY), 1981.

Lynn Hall, *The Mysterious Moortown Bridge,* Follett (Chicago, IL), 1981.

Lynn Hall, *The Mystery of the Caramel Cat,* Garrard (Champlain, IL), 1981.

Cecily Stern, *A Different Kind of Gold,* Harper (New York, NY), 1981.

Betsy Byars, *The Animal, the Vegetable, and John D. Jones,* Delacorte (New York, NY), 1982.

Linda Hayward, *When You Were a Baby,* Golden Press (New York, NY), 1982.

Edward Lear, *The Owl and the Pussycat,* Golden Press (New York, NY), 1982.

Peggy Archer, *One of the Family,* Golden Press (New York, NY), 1983.

Judith Gorog, *Caught in the Turtle,* Philomel (New York, NY), 1983.

Lois Meyer, *The Store-bought Doll,* Golden Press (New York, NY), 1983.

Joan Webb, *Poochie and the Four Seasons Fair,* Western Publishing (Racine, WI), 1983.

Johanna Spyri, *Heidi,* Knopf (New York, NY), 1984.

The Pudgy Bunny Book, Grosset (New York, NY), 1984.

Linda Hayward, *Five Little Bunnies,* Golden Press (New York, NY), 1984.

Jane Yolen, reteller, *The Sleeping Beauty,* Knopf (New York, NY), 1986.

Phyllis Krasilovsky, *The Happy Times Storybook,* Western Publishing (Racine, WI), 1987.

Frances Hodgson Burnett, *The Secret Garden,* Knopf (New York, NY), 1988.

Fran Manushkin, *Puppies and Kittens,* Western Publishing (Racine, WI), 1989.

Samantha Easton, reteller, *Beauty and the Beast,* Andrews McMeel (Kansas City, MO), 1992.

Bruce Coville, reteller, *William Shakespeare's "The Tempest,"* Delacorte (New York, NY), 1994.

Clement Clarke Moore, *The Night before Christmas,* Turner, 1994.

The Story of the First Christmas: A Carousel Book, Turner, 1994.

Shirley Climo, *A Treasury of Princesses: Princess Tales from around the World,* HarperCollins (New York, NY), 1996.

Cats, Andrews McMeel (Kansas City, MO), 1997.

Jane Yolen, *Where Have the Unicorns Gone?,* Simon & Schuster (New York, NY), 2000.

Jean Slaughter Doty, *Winter Pony,* Random House (New York, NY), 2008.

Jane Yolen, *Hush, Little Horsie,* Random House (New York, NY), 2010.

Also illustrator of revised editions of "Black Stallion" books by Walter Farley.

ILLUSTRATOR; "NANCY DREW" SERIES BY CAROLYN KEENE

The Triple Hoax, Wanderer Books (New York, NY), 1979.

The Flying Saucer Mystery, Wanderer Books (New York, NY), 1980.

The Secret in the Old Lace, Wanderer Books (New York, NY), 1980.

The Greek Symbol Mystery, Wanderer Books (New York, NY), 1981.

ILLUSTRATOR; "BOBBSEY TWINS" SERIES BY LAURA LEE HOPE

Secret in the Pirate's Cave, Wanderer Books (New York, NY), 1980.

The Dune Buggy Mystery, Wanderer Books (New York, NY), 1981.

The Missing Pony Mystery, Wanderer Books (New York, NY), 1981.

The Rose Parade Mystery, Wanderer Books (New York, NY), 1981.

ILLUSTRATOR; "HORSE DIARIES" SERIES

Catherine Hapka, *Elska,* Random House (New York, NY), 2009.

Alison Hart, *Bell's Star,* Random House (New York, NY), 2009.

Patricia Hermes, *Koda,* Random House (New York, NY), 2009.

Whitney Sanderson, *Golden Sun,* Random House (New York, NY), 2010.

Jane Kendall, *Maestoso Petra,* Random House (New York, NY), 2010.

Catherine Hapka, *Yatimah,* Random House (New York, NY), 2010.

Alison Hart, *Risky Chance,* Random House (New York, NY), 2011.

Adaptations

Sanderson's illustrated version of *The Little Engine That Could* was adapted as a filmstrip with cassette or book, 1976. Sanderson's artwork for *The Night before Christmas* was adapted for holiday housewares by Pottery Barn Kids, 2009. *Cinderella* and *Mother Goose* were adapted as puzzle books by White Mountain Puzzles, 2010.

Sidelights

An illustrator and author, Ruth Sanderson creates sumptuous illustrations that she pairs with original retelling of classic fairy tales as well as crafting artwork for stories by popular authors such as William Sleator, Fran Manushkin, Bruce Coville, Jane Yolen, and Clyde Robert Bulla. As an artist, Sanderson has been applauded by critics and readers alike for her attention to detail and her ability to evoke what *Booklist* contributor Phyl-

Sanderson's detailed art brings to life traditional tales for a new generation in her retellings for **Mother Goose and Friends.** (Illustration copyright © 2008 by Ruth Sanderson. Reproduced by permission of Little, Brown & Company.)

lis Wilson characterized as a "sun-dappled, old-master-landscape feeling." Calling her *Mother Goose and Friends* "an invitation to an old-fashioned world of enchantment," a *Publishers Weekly* contributor added that the illustrations Sanderson pairs with these beloved rhymes "teem with Victorian elves and fairies" and contribute to a volume that is both "luminous and elegant." In addition to illustrating her own fairy-tale adaptations of such stories as "Sleeping Beauty," "Cinderella," and "Goldilocks and the Three Bears," Sanderson has also illustrated books in the "Bobbsey Twins," "Nancy Drew," and "Horse Diaries" series and has created an original fairy story, the self-illustrated *The Enchanted Wood.* One book in the "Horse Diaries" series, *Golden Sun,* is authored by Sanderson's daughter, Whitney Sanderson.

Born in 1951, Sanderson was raised in the small town of Monson, Massachusetts, which she later recalled as "a magical place." As a child she spent the majority of her time in the woods and in the library; it was at the library that Sanderson's grandmother introduced her to Grimms' fairy tales. Sanderson also began drawing during childhood and shared her enthusiasm for her hobby with her friends. "I held an art class for my second-grade friends and taught them all how to draw horses. When my mother bought me *How to Draw Horses* by Walter Foster, I spent hours copying horses, trying to get them right." In addition to drawing horses, she also spent many years riding and caring for her favorite animal; in fact, Sanderson credits her love of horses with fueling her desire to become an illustrator.

Sanderson attended Paier School of Art in Hamden, Connecticut, where she studied anatomy, figure drawing, and painting and majored in illustration. "I gravitated toward illustration because I liked having problems to solve," she later explained. "I preferred developing concepts and pictorial impressions of a manuscript to initiating my own ideas. As an exercise, we were asked to find a book in the library, read the story and come up with new ideas for the cover illustration. During my senior year, I studied with illustrator Michael Eagle. He made us think in new and different ways, stretching our imagination. Every teacher at Paier contributed something to our training. Thus our development was a group effort."

During her senior year at Paier, Sanderson accepted an apprenticeship with a corporate editorial illustrator for six months. Her mentor passed her portfolio on to a children's book agent who was looking for new artists, and "within six months she had given me so much freelance work that I had to decide whether to follow in [my mentor's] footsteps and work in commercial adult magazine illustration or strike out on my own and try children's books. I opted for children's books. I started doing textbook illustration and then slowly worked my way up to trade books and then jacket illustration." As an illustrator, Sanderson has worked in varied media, including watercolor, oils, acrylic, air brush, colored pencil, and alkyd.

Sanderson's detailed paintings bring to life Ruth Sorenson's fairy-tale retelling **Papa Gatto,** *featuring a story from Italy.* (Little, Brown & Company, 1995. Copyright © 1995 by Ruth Sanderson. Reproduced by permission of the illustrator.)

Beginning with book covers, Sanderson graduated to picture-book illustration with Ilka List's *Grandma's Beach Surprise,* published in 1975. Since then, she has amassed numerous illustration credits, most notably in the fairy-tale genre because the medieval overtones of such stories complement Sanderson's own style. In the Grimm Brothers' *The Twelve Dancing Princesses,* which she both retells and illustrates, her oil paintings, rendered "in a realistic yet romantic style, . . . have the dark, rich texture of old velvet," in the opinion of *School Library Journal* contributor Linda Boyles. Boyles went on to praise Sanderson's text as "coherent and fully fleshed out," adding that it reads "with a straightforward formality that is complemented by the classic nature of the illustrations."

Similar accolades were bestowed upon Sanderson's original version of *Rose Red and Snow White: A Grimms Fairy Tale,* a *Publishers Weekly* contributor lauding the illustrator's use of "rusty tones" to create "heroines whose warm coloring blends perfectly with the woods they roam in and with the firelit domesticity of their mother's neat cottage." Another fairy-tale retelling, *Cinderella,* incorporates elements from time-honored versions by both the Brothers Grimm and folklorist Charles Perrault, while *Goldilocks* transports readers to a rural home in the Austrian Alps where the titular character is taught tidiness by a methodical Mother Bear. According to *School Library Journal* contributor Grace Oliff, Sanderson's text features "a graceful style that flows quite nicely," while her sepia-toned oil paintings, set in the eighteenth century, "depict lush landscapes and stately ballrooms with equal precision and artistry." In *Booklist,* Ellen Mandel maintained in her review of Sanderson's *Cinderella* that the author/illustrator is "as gifted with the turn of a phrase as she is with the stroke of a pen," while Patricia Austin predicted in the same periodical that the "incredibly expressive, friendly-looking bears" in *Goldilocks* will "delight" young storytime audiences.

In addition to well-known fairy tales, Sanderson has also given new life to several lesser-known (to English-speaking readers) tales. She turns to Italian folklore in *Papa Gatto: An Italian Fairy Tale,* in which a father cat in service to the king hires two stepsisters—one beautiful but selfish and the other plain but giving—to care for his bewhiskered and motherless offspring. Sanderson's "elegant, richly descriptive language" enhances this charming story, according to *Booklist* reviewer Janice Del Negro, and her oil paintings "are as beautifully handled as the narrative." "Familiar elements in combination with new twists, the perennial appeal of intelligent animals interacting with people on equal terms, and the drama of treachery and romance" all combine to make *Papa Gatto* "an especially good story," concluded a contributor to *Quill & Quire.*

Based on a Chinese fairytale titled "The Magic Brocade" and interwoven with details from the Norwegian tale "Princess on the Glass Hill," Sanderson's *The Crystal Mountain* is an adventurous tale that centers on Anna, a weaver who creates ornate brocades for the nobility. One night Anna has a dream that revolves around a paradise that includes a marble mansion, rolling hills, and beautiful orchards. When Anna awakens she is determined to replicate her dream by creating a tapestry based on her vision. After three years she completes this inspired embroidery, but upon completion the tapestry is stolen by the fairies of Crystal Mountain. Anna then sends her three sons to rescue her beloved tapestry, but the two elder sons fail. Ultimately, it is Anna's youngest son, Perrin, who succeeds in climbing and conquering Crystal Mountain and recovering his mother's handiwork. *Booklist* reviewer GraceAnne A. DeCandido commented that the book's "beautiful oil paintings are rich with medieval allusion and full of flora, fauna, and details," while a *Publishers Weekly* contributor remarked that in *The Crystal Mountain* Sanderson "weaves a story as intricate and pleasant as the tapestry at the heart of this folktale."

Pairing a text with oil paintings that are characteristically rich in detail and color, Sanderson retells a classic Russian fairytale in *The Golden Mare, the Firebird, and the Magic Ring.* In the story—described by *Booklist* reviewer Carolyn Phelan as a "romantic adventure . . . [that] will hold readers' attention"—young Alexi, a huntsman, leaves his home in search of adventure and fortune. During his quest Alexi encounters a magical mare that can talk. When he spares the mare's life, she vows to remain his loyal servant. With the mare's help, Alexi soon becomes a successful hunter under the servitude of the local tzar. Seeing the magical powers of the mare, the tzar covets the creature and orders Alexi to complete several impossible tasks or face death. The story follows Alexi and his mare as they strive to complete the tzar's tasks and also attempt to overthrow the unreasonable monarch. In *Publishers Weekly* a contributor commented that Sanderson's "sumptuous oil paintings take immediate command of the double-page spreads," while Margaret A. Chang noted in *School Li-*

brary Journal that the art in *The Golden Mare, the Firebird, and the Magic Ring* recalls "the painterly style of the old masters" while also "revel[ing] in the rich decoration of traditional Russian architecture and costume."

The Snow Princess, inspired by a famous Russian ballet, is another self-illustrated title that includes Sanderson's characteristic lush oil illustrations. The princess born of Father Frost and Mother Spring longs to explore the world outside of her home. Ultimately, she leaves, counselled by her parents not to fall in love with a mortal lest she die. Upon entering the world of the mortals the princess falls in love with Sergei, but she hopes to disarm her feelings of love by creating a snow storm so that she can escape from her affection. When Sergei pursues his beloved, he becomes trapped in the snow storm and the princess realizes that she cannot escape her romantic destiny. In appraising *The Snow Princess* for *Kirkus Reviews,* a contributor acknowledged Sanderson's "exquisite oil paintings, with their glowing textures and near-perfect detail."

Christianity and the bible have inspired several books that pair Sanderson's art with her original retellings. In *Tapestries: Stories of Women in the Bible* she recounts tales featuring the Bible's most prominent females—

Sanderson's paintings capture the magical setting of her original story in **The Enchanted Wood.** (Little, Brown & Company, 1991. Copyright © 1991 by Ruth Sanderson. Reproduced by permission of the illustrator.)

Eve, Sarah, Mary of Nazareth, Rahab, Jael, and the Witch of Endor—and intertwines those from the old and new testaments. Each intricate portrait also reveals the weaving techniques used by the women of ancient times by incorporating these well-researched details about the craft. "Sanderson's colorfully detailed sketches are so convincing that readers may well mistake them for genuine tapestry weavings," acknowledged a *Publishers Weekly* writer, the critic adding that *Tapestries* is enhanced by "involving storytelling." While Ilene Cooper claimed in *Booklist* that Sanderson's text has "little emotional range," she nonetheless concluded that "the artwork is more full-bodied" and "conveys an impression of strength, durability, and beauty."

Sanderson adopts a Renaissance style in *Saints: Lives and Illuminations* and *More Saints: Lives and Illuminations,* two books that contain short, illustrated biographies detailing the lives, patronage, and feast days of well-known religious from both Roman and Eastern Orthodox Catholic tradition. In *Saints* she assembles forty saints, among them the martyred Christopher, patron saint of travelers, Nicholas, patron saint of children, and Patrick, patron saint of Ireland. Three dozen additional saints are included in *More Saints,* which focuses on those who achieved sainthood in the second thousand years of church history. In addition to Joan of Arc and Saint Francis, Sanderson also includes Mother Teresa, whose future sainthood is assumed by many. Although the author "shows no aversion to relating experiences that may seem odd to modern readers," her paintings of the saints are "soft and gentle" and do not reflect the violence that often ended their lives, according to Cooper. For a *Kirkus Reviews* writer, Sanderson's biographies "of these splendid and colorful figures read almost like folktales," and *School Library Journal* contributor Lucinda Snyder Whitehurst recommended *Saints* to adults "interested in sharing inspiring stories of Christian devotion with children." *More Saints* "strikes a truly compelling tone," asserted a *Publishers Weekly* critic, the reviewer noting that Sanderson's second millennial "holy figures intrigue as much as they inspire."

Sanderson brings to life a Christmas favorite in her illustrated version of *The Night before Christmas* by Clement Clarke Moore. Among the detailed oil paintings that she creates for this book are images of Christmas stockings hanging over a fireplace, children snuggled up and sound asleep in their beds, and Santa traveling through the night sky aboard a well-laden sleigh. In *Booklist* Shelley Townsend-Hudson commented that "Sanderson's old-fashioned renderings" in her version of Moore's holiday classic "have a lovely twilight a glow that helps evoke the excitement of the season." Likewise, a writer for *Publishers Weekly* noted that "Old Saint Nick has rarely looked jollier than in Sanderson's edition of the traditional poem."

Sanderson spends an average of forty hours a week in her studio, and often alternates work on three or four

paintings. "That way, I always have the choice of a different subject to paint," she once told *SATA.* "Some days I am in the mood to paint a portrait, some days a moody background, and some days if I am not in the mood to paint at all I will do the detailed pencil underdrawing for the next painting." Depending on the complexity of the piece, Sanderson spends from three days to three weeks on each illustration. Her medium is oils and she paints on canvas, board, and sometimes primed watercolor paper, depending on the finished look she is trying to achieve.

Discussing her inspiration, Sanderson cites as her favorite illustrators N.C. Wyeth, Norman Rockwell, and Maxfield Parrish. "I'm also influenced by the artists of the English Pre-Raphaelite period whose work is illustrative and tells a story, as well as by the Hudson River School," she added. "Though my own style is representational, I love symbolic art, particularly the work of Magritte."

Symbolism in stories inspires Sanderson as well. As she once told *SATA:* "The archetypal characters and the universal symbolism that are inherent in fairy tales can be as meaningful for children today as they have been for centuries past. I am drawn to 'rites of passage' stories, where the hero (child) leaves home to seek adventure or to go on an impossible quest, learning in the process how to become independent and form new relationships outside of parental influence. For instance, in *The Twelve Dancing Princesses* the three magical woods that the princesses pass through symbolize their rite of passage into adulthood."

In addition to illustrating and writing, Sanderson devotes much of her time to speaking at school assemblies, "so that children will have an opportunity to see that it is a real person creating art and not a machine." Her advice to aspiring young artists: "Practice. The love of drawing is enough to keep you going until high school If you decide to pursue a career in art, apply to a good art school. And remember, an artist can always improve: I still try new techniques after being a professional for over thirty years."

Biographical and Critical Sources

BOOKS

Kingman, Lee, and others, compilers, *Illustrators of Children's Books: 1967-1976,* Horn Book (Boston, MA), 1978.

PERIODICALS

Booklist, September 15, 1997, Shelley Townsend-Hudson, review of *The Night before Christmas,* p. 238; October 1, 1998, Ilene Cooper, review of *Tapestries: Sto-*

ries of Women in the Bible, p. 340; September 1, 1999, GraceAnne A. DeCandido, review of *The Crystal Mountain,* p. 129; April 1, 2001, Carolyn Phelan, review of *The Golden Mare, the Firebird, and the Magic Ring,* p. 1463; April 15, 2002, Ellen Mandel, review of *Cinderella,* p. 1399; February 1, 2003, Ilene Cooper, review of *Saints: Lives and Illuminations,* p. 992; February 1, 2007, Ilene Cooper, review of *More Saints: Lives and Illuminations,* p. 44; August, 2007, Hazel Rochman, review of *Mother Goose and Friends,* p. 80; February 15, 2009, Hazel Rochman, review of *Elska,* p. 82; October 1, 2009, Patricia Austin, review of *Goldilocks,* p. 48.

Children's Bookwatch, May, 2007, review of *More Saints.*

Horn Book, July-August, 2009, Robin L. Smith, review of *Elska,* p. 425.

Kirkus Reviews, March 1, 2002, review of *Cinderella,* p. 344; January 15, 2003, review of *Saints,* p. 146; October 15, 2004, review of *The Snow Princess,* p. 1013; September 1, 2009, review of *Goldilocks.*

Publishers Weekly, October 6, 1997, review of *The Night before Christmas,* p. 56; July 27, 1998, review of *Tapestries,* p. 70; September 13, 1999, review of *The Crystal Mountain,* p. 84; April 9, 2001, review of *The Golden Mare, the Firebird, and the Magic Ring,* p. 74; December 18, 2006, review of *More Saints,* p. 66; February 25, 2008, review of *Mother Goose and Friends,* p. 77.

School Library Journal, April, 2001, Margaret A. Chang, review of *The Golden Mare, the Firebird, and the Magic Ring,* p. 135; June, 2002, Grace Oliff, review of *Cinderella,* p. 125; May, 2003, Lucinda Snyder Whitehurst, review of *Saints,* p. 140; December, 2004, Susan Scheps, review of *The Snow Princess,* p. 120; January, 2008, Kathy Krasniewicz, review of *Mother Goose and Friends,* p. 111; October, 2009, Barbara Elleman, review of *Goldilocks,* p. 114.

ONLINE

Ruth Sanderson Home Page, http://www.ruthsanderson. com (December 27, 2010).

*   *   *

SANDERSON, Ruth L.
See SANDERSON, Ruth

*   *   *

SANTAT, Dan

Personal

Married; wife's name Leah; children: two. *Education:* University of California, San Diego, B.S. (biology); Art Center College of Design, degree, 2001.

Addresses

Home—Southern CA. *Agent*—Jodi Reamer, Writers House, 21 W. 26th St., New York, NY 10010; jreamer writershouse.com. *E-mail*—dsantat@yahoo.com.

Career

Children's book author and commercial illustrator. Worked as a texture artist and 3-D modeler, 2001-04; creator of animated cartoon *The Replacements,* Disney Channel, 2006-08; currently freelance illustrator. *Exhibitions:* Work included in Original Art Show, Society of Illustrators, New York, NY, 2004, 2007, 2010.

Member

Society of Children's Book Writers and Illustrators.

Awards, Honors

Don Freeman Memorial Grant-in-Aid finalist, Society of Children's Book Writers and Illustrators (SCBWI); first prize, juried art portfolio display, SCBWI Los Angeles Conference, 2002; Marion Vannett Ridgeway Honor Award, 2005, for *The Guild of Geniuses;* 100 Titles for Reading and Sharing inclusion, New York Public Library, 2008, or *The Ghosts of Luckless Gulch* by Anne Isaacs; Best Children's Books of the Year selection, Bank Street College of Education, 2009, for *The Christmas Genie* by Dan Gutman; silver medal, Society of Illustrators, 2010, for *Oh No!; or, How My Science Project Destroyed the World* by Mac Barnett.

Writings

SELF-ILLUSTRATED

The Guild of Geniuses, Arthur A. Levine Books (New York, NY), 2004.

Author of comic strip "The Contender."

ILLUSTRATOR

Rhea Perlman, *Born to Drive* ("Otto Undercover" series), Katherine Tegan Books (New York, NY), 2006.

Rhea Perlman, *Water Balloon Doom* ("Otto Undercover" series), Katherine Tegan Books (New York, NY), 2006.

Rhea Perlman, *Canyon Catastrophe* ("Otto Undercover" series), Katherine Tegan Books (New York, NY), 2006.

Rhea Perlman, *Toxic Taffy Takeover* ("Otto Undercover" series), Katherine Tegan Books (New York, NY), 2006.

Rhea Perlman, *The Brink of Ex-Stink-tion* ("Otto Undercover" series), Katherine Tegan Books (New York, NY), 2006.

Rhea Perlman, *Brain Freeze* ("Otto Undercover" series), Katherine Tegan Books (New York, NY), 2007.

Barbara Jean Hicks, *The Secret Life of Walter Kitty,* Alfred A. Knopf (New York, NY), 2007.

Phyllis Shalant, *The Society of Super Secret Heroes: The Great Cape Rescue,* Dutton (New York, NY), 2007.

Anne Isaacs, *The Ghosts of Luckless Gulch,* Atheneum Books for Young Readers (New York, NY), 2008.

Ayun Halliday, *Always Lots of Heinies at the Zoo,* Disney/Hyperion Books (New York, NY), 2009.

Lisa Yee, *Bobby vs. Girls (Accidentally),* Arthur A. Levine Books (New York, NY), 2009.

Tammi Sauer, *Chicken Dance,* Sterling Publishing (New York, NY), 2009.

Dan Gutman, *The Christmas Genie,* Simon & Schuster Books for Young Readers (New York, NY), 2009.

Andrea Beaty, *Attack of the Fluffy Bunnies,* Amulet Books (New York, NY), 2010.

Lisa Yee, *Bobby the Brave (Sometimes),* Arthur A. Levine Books (New York, NY), 2010.

Mac Barnett, *Oh No!; or, How My Science Project Destroyed the World,* Disney/Hyperion Books (New York, NY), 2010.

R.A. Spratt, *The Adventures of Nanny Piggins,* Little, Brown (New York, NY), 2010.

Jenn Berman and Cynthia Weil, *Rockin' Babies,* Sterling Publishing (New York, NY), 2011.

Contributor to periodicals, including *Wall Street Journal, Esquire, Time for Kids,* and *Village Voice.*

Sidelights

Based in Southern California, Dan Santat is a commercial illustrator and cartoonist who has become well known for his dynamic and often droll contributions to children's books. Some readers already know Santat as the creator of *The Replacements,* an animated series that aired on the Disney Channel in which a brother and sister are able to replace any adult in their life with a simple phone call. In his book illustrations, Santat uses a mixture of acrylics, pen and ink, and digital imaging. As a commercial artist, his cartoon-style art has appeared in video games, film animation, and magazines as well as in galleries throughout the United States.

Through the illustrations he created for actress Rhea Pearlman's five-book "Otto Undercover" series, Santat established his reputation in the world of children's publishing; in *Publishers Weekly* a reviewer remarked of series opener *Born to Drive* that the artist's "brash cartoons add to" the humorous tone of Pearlman's high-action story. Santat takes on the role of both author and illustrator in *The Guild of Geniuses,* a picture book that transports young readers into a futuristic 'fifties-inspired fantasy world. In his story, a monkey named Mr. Pip finds what he thinks is the perfect gift for his best friend, Frederick Lipton. Lipton is a famous actor, however, and is used to the finer things in life. As Mr. Pip watches a succession of lavish gifts being presented to his friend during the birthday celebration, he goes glum with worry that his own gift does not reflect the depth of his friendship. Meanwhile, Lipton does not understand his monkey friend's down mood, so he takes Mr. Pip to the Guild of Geniuses in order to find out what is wrong. "Inventive is the word here, especially for the artwork,"

Santat's quirky art is a good match with Andrea Beatty's story in **Attack of the Fluffy Bunnies.** (Amulet Books, 2010. Illustration copyright © 2010 by Dan Santat. Reproduced by permission.)

wrote Ilene Cooper in her *Booklist* review of *The Guild of Geniuses.* While Blair Christolon noted in *School Library Journal* that Santat's story features an ending that children might anticipate, she nonetheless noted that his artwork, with its "varying perspectives and bold colors, keep the action moving quickly." Praising the "kitschy fifties design and appealingly drawn characters" in *The Guild of Geniuses,* a contributor to *Publishers Weekly* dubbed Santat's picture book "a promising debut."

In Barbara Jean Hicks's *The Secret Life of Walter Kitty,* a picture-book nod to James Thurber's short story "The Secret Life of Walter Mitty," a mild-mannered but wildly imaginative housecat pictures itself as a fearless adventurer, then a razor-toothed wildcat, a swashbuckling pirate, and other extraordinary characters. Santat's cartoon-like art "juxtaposes these energetic caricatures with prosaic images of Walter grooming or tracking mud across the linoleum," according to a *Publishers Weekly* reviewer. In *The Ghosts of Luckless Gulch,* a tall tale by Anne Isaacs, a youngster with both amazing speed and incredible healing powers must rescue her pets, which have been kidnapped by sinister gold miners. Santat's acrylic paintings for the story "capture the flavor of the Wild West and are appropriately exaggerated to complement the extraordinary events," a critic in *Kirkus Reviews* observed, and Barbara Elleman

Dan Santat's illustration projects include Barbara Jean Hicks's engaging picture book **The Secret Life of Walter Kitty.** (Illustration copyright © 2007 by Dan Santat. All rights reserved. Used by permission of Alfred A. Knopf, an imprint of Random House Children's Books, a division of Random House, Inc.)

noted in *School Library Journal* that his depictions of "the ghosts are particularly, and delightfully, ghoulish." Ayun Halliday offers a look at a host of animal rear ends in *Always Lots of Heinies at the Zoo.* "Santat's detailed, full-page illustrations carry the story along, injecting subtle humor into the scenes," remarked a *Kirkus Reviews* contributor in appraising Halliday's quirky picture book.

Santat has also provided the artwork for Lisa Yee's humorous chapter books *Bobby vs. Girls (Accidentally)* and *Bobby the Brave (Sometimes).* The former work introduces best friends Bobby and Holly, fourth graders whose relationship is tested when they became rivals for ano opening on the student council. "Santat's expressive [black-and-white] illustrations evoke the energy of Saturday morning cartoons," a critic declared in *Publishers Weekly,* and a contributor in *Kirkus Reviews* noted that his pictures "add dimension to the events."

A barnyard talent show offers excitement aplenty in *Chicken Dance,* a story by Tammi Sauer. With tickets to an Elvis Poultry concert on the line, coop-mates Marge and Lola bravely take the stage, despite the fact that these hens lacki any semblance of talent. In the words of *Booklist* reviewer Kay Weisman, "Santat's computer-enhanced acrylic-and-ink artwork comically extends Sauer's droll text" for *Chicken Dance,* and a *Publishers Weekly* critic wrote that the pictures "exude an old-fashioned, theatrical drama that lifts the many jokes—visual and textual—into sublime silliness."

Silliness continues to reign supreme in Santat's illustration projects. In Andrea Beaty's *Attack of the Fluffy Bunnies* twins Joules and Kevin Rockman help their fellow summer campers combat a band of floppy-eared alien invaders. A reviewer in *Publishers Weekly* applauded Santat's "kinetic comic book-style panel art" in this "wholly fun read." A pigtailed youngster's robotic creation—designed, unfortunately, with superclaws but no ears—rampages through town in Mac Barnett's *Oh No!: (or, How My Science Project Destroyed the World).* In *School Library Journal,* Kathleen Kelly MacMillan wrote that Santat's "graphic style bring[s] a true comic-book sensibility," to the tale, and a *Publishers Weekly* reviewer observed that the artist's "skylines pay homage to old monster movies."

Biographical and Critical Sources

PERIODICALS

Booklist, November 15, 2004, Ilene Cooper, review of *The Guild of Geniuses,* p. 592; October 15, 2008, Thom Barthelmess, review of *The Ghosts of Luckless Gulch,* p. 45; August 1, 2009, Kay Weisman, review of *Chicken Dance,* p. 77; October 15, 2009, Hazel Rochman, review of *Bobby vs. Girls (Accidentally),* p. 52; May 1, 2010, Ian Chipman, review of *Attack of the Fluffy Bunnies,* p. 86.

Tammi Sauer's rambunctious story in **Chicken Dance** *allows Santat's humorous cartoon art full rein.* (Illustration copyright © 2009 by Dan Santat. Reproduced by permission of Sterling Publishing Co., Inc.)

Horn Book, September-October, 2009, Jennifer M. Brabander, review of *Bobby vs. Girls (Accidentally),* p. 577.

Kirkus Reviews, November 15, 2004, review of *The Guild of Geniuses,* p. 1093; April 1, 2007, review of *The Secret Life of Walter Kitty;* October 15, 2008, review of *The Ghosts of Luckless Gulch;* April 1, 2009, review of *Always Lots of Heinies at the Zoo;* July 1, 2009, review of *Chicken Dance;* August 15, 2009, review of *Bobby vs. Girls (Accidentally).*

Publishers Weekly, January 10, 2005, review of *The Guild of Geniuses,* p. 55; December 19, 2005, review of *Born to Drive,* p. 65; April 23, 2007, review of *The Secret Life of Walter Kitty,* p. 50; November 10, 2008, review of *The Ghosts of Luckless Gulch,* p. 50; April 27, 2009, review of *Always Lots of Heinies at the Zoo,* p. 130; July 20, 2009, review of *Chicken Dance,* p. 139; August 31, 2009, review of *Bobby vs. Girls (Accidentally),* p. 58; October 26, 2009, review of *The Christmas Genie,* p. 57; April 26, 2010, review of *Attack of the Fluffy Bunnies,* p. 109; May 10, 2010, review of *Oh, No!: (or, How My Science Project Destroyed the World),* p. 44.

School Library Journal, December, 2004, Blair Christolon, review of *The Guild of Geniuses,* p. 120; July, 2006, Walter Minkel, review of *Born to Drive,* p. 109; January, 2007, H.H. Henderson, review of *Water Balloon Doom,* p. 100; June, 2007, Elaine E. Knight, review of *The Society of Super Secret Heroes: The Great*

Cape Rescue, p. 123; November, 2008, Barbara Elleman, review of *The Ghosts of Luckless Gulch,* p. 90; April, 2009, Blair Christolon, review of *Always Lots of Heinies at the Zoo,* p. 106; September, 2009, Barbara Elleman, review of *Chicken Dance,* p. 133; October, 2009, Linda Israelson, review of *The Christmas Genie,* p. 80; November, 2009, Tina Martin, review of *Bobby vs. Girls (Accidentally),* p. 91; July, 2010, Kathleen Kelly MacMillan, review of *Oh No!,* p. 55, and Elaine E. Knight, review of *Attack of the Fluffy Bunnies,* p. 55; August, 2010, Nicole Waskie, review of *Bobby the Brave (Sometimes),* p. 89, and Kira Moody, review of *The Adventures of Nanny Piggins,* p. 113.

ONLINE

Dan Santat Web log, http://dantat.typepad.com (January 1, 2011).*

*   *   *

SCALORA, Suza

Personal

Female. *Education:* Art Center College of Design, B.F.A., 1987.

Addresses

Home—New York, NY. *Agent*—Utopia, 601 W. 26th St., No. 1223, New York, NY 10001; carolynutopianyc.com. *E-mail*—suza@myth.com.

Career

Photographer and author. Has also taught at International Center for Photography and Omega Center.

Awards, Honors

Ten Best Picture Books designation, *Newsweek,* for *The Fairies;* named Hasselblad Master, 2005; *Booklist* Top-ten Spirituality Book selection, 2009, for *Evidence of Angels.*

Writings

(And photographer) *The Fairies: Photographic Evidence of the Existence of Another World,* Joanna Cotler Books (New York, NY), 1999.

(And photographer) *The Witches and Wizards of Oberin,* Joanna Cotler Books (New York, NY), 2001.

(With Francesca Lia Block; and photographer) *Evidence of Angels,* Harper (New York, NY), 2009.

Sidelights

Suza Scalora has gained recognition for her haunting and evocative photographs, which are seen to great effect in books such as *The Fairies: Photographic Evi-*

dence of the Existence of Another World and *Evidence of Angels.* A highly regarded commercial photographer based in New York City, Scalora chooses to explore her interest in the supernatural, especially the presence of angels, in her written works. "I am fascinated by the energies in the Universe, which are difficult to see through human eyes," she remarked on *Myth.com.* "I imagine this is the reason why I am so attracted to creating artwork in which the 'Unseen World' is depicted."

In *The Fairies* Scalora presents the results of her global quest to capture and catalog the denizens of the faerie world on film, including such mysterious creatures as Eugenie, a guardian of the forest whom the photographer spotted in Mexico. *Booklist* reviewer Ilene Cooper applauded "Scalora's striking, ethereal photo work," and Charles de Lint, writing in the *Magazine of Fantasy and Science Fiction,* similarly noted that "the photographs are quite stunning."

In *The Witches and Wizards of Oberin* a French anthropologist discovers a secret cave used as a gathering place by a group of powerful mages, including Orella, Enchantress of the Dawn. In *School Library Journal* John Peters complimented Scalora's alluring, saturated photo-collages, noting that "fans of romantic high fantasy and readers who enjoy creating entire imaginary worlds will linger over these mysterious, evocative portraits." *Evidence of Angels,* coauthored with young-adult novelist Francesca Lia Block, centers on a grief-

Photographer Suza Scalora collaborates with novelist Francesca Lia Block to create the colorfully illustrated Evidence of Angels. (Copyright © 2009 by Suza Scalora. Used by permission of HarperCollins Children's Books, a division of HarperCollins Publishers.)

stricken woman who finds solace through her encounters with a host of ethereal creatures. A contributor in *Kirkus Reviews* offered praise for the "luminous mixtures of photography, swirling color and pulsating digital enhancement" that are featured throughout. In *Booklist,* Daniel Kraus also cited Scalora's photographs as a strength of the work, characterizing them as angelic "forms made abstract by lush sunbursts and vivid smudges, as if each were seen through a crystal."

Biographical and Critical Sources

PERIODICALS

Booklist, November 1, 1999, Ilene Cooper, review of *The Fairies: Photographic Evidence of the Existence of Another World,* p. 520; August 1, 2009, Daniel Kraus, review of *Evidence of Angels,* p. 55.
Kirkus Reviews, September 1, 2009, review of *Evidence of Angels.*
Magazine of Fantasy and Science Fiction, March, 2000, Charles de Lint, review of *The Fairies,* p. 29.
Publishers Weekly, December 6, 1999, review of *The Fairies,* p. 79; December 17, 2001, review of *The Witches and Wizards of Oberin,* p. 94.
School Library Journal, October, 2001, John Peters, review of *The Witches and Wizards of Oberin,* p. 169.

ONLINE

Hasselblad Web site, http://www.hasselblad.com/ (February, 2005), "Suza Scalora."
Myth.com, http://www.myth.com/ (January 1, 2011), "Suza Scalora."
Suza Scalora Home Page, http://www.suzascaloraphotography.com (January 1, 2011).*

*   *   *

SEAGRAVES, D.B.
See SEAGRAVES, Donny Bailey

*   *   *

SEAGRAVES, Donny
See SEAGRAVES, Donny Bailey

*   *   *

SEAGRAVES, Donny Bailey 1951-
(D.B. Seagraves, Donny Seagraves)

Personal

Born December 29, 1951, in Athens, GA; daughter of H.D. and M.F. Bailey; married Phillip Seagraves; children: Jennifer, Gregory (twins). *Education:* University

**Donny Bailey Seagraves** (Photograph by Lorin Sinn-Clark. Reproduced by permission.)

of Georgia, bachelor's degree (journalism). _Hobbies and other interests:_ Reading, collecting books, many by Georgia authors.

Addresses

Home—P.O. Box 556, Winterville, GA 30683. _Agent_— Andrea Brown, Andrea Brown Literary Agency, andrea@andreabrownlit.com. _E-mail_—donnyseagraves @gmail.com.

Career

Journalist and author. Former newspaper columnist; freelance writer; Junebug Books (online used and rare book dealer), owner and operator. Presenter at schools, festivals, and conferences.

Member

Author's Guild, Society of Children's Book Writers and Illustrators (Southern Breeze region), Georgia Writers Association.

Writings

Gone from These Woods, Delacorte Press (New York, NY), 2009.

Contributor to periodicals, including _Athens_ magazine and _Chicago Tribune,_ sometimes under names Donny Seagraves and D.B. Seagraves.

Sidelights

"L. Frank Baum's _The Wizard of Oz_ gave me the gift of becoming an avid reader at the age of eight," Donny Bailey Seagraves told _SATA._ "In the books of others, I found comfort, knowledge, and a world far beyond my Athens, Georgia home. My fifth-grade teacher, Mrs. Clara Doster, encouraged me to write my own stories and I've been doing so ever since.

"My books usually start with a character, either imagined or created from people I've known or read about. Sometimes I find inspiration for plot in a real life event, as I did in my debut children's middle grade novel, _Gone from These Woods._ My settings come from the rural North Georgia area where I grew up and still live.

"I believe there will always be a love, a hunger, and a place for original stories in our world, whether they're published in physical books or in digital format. I write for young readers because they need the power of words most of all."

Biographical and Critical Sources

PERIODICALS

Bulletin of the Center for Children's Books, review of _Gone from These Woods,_ p. 40.
Kirkus Reviews, July 1, 2009, review of _Gone from These Woods._
School Library Journal, September, 2009, Carol A. Edwards, review of _Gone from These Woods,_ p. 172.

ONLINE

Donny Bailey Seagraves Home Page, http://www.donny seagraves.com/ (December 27, 2010).
Donny Bailey Seagraves Web log, http://www.dbseagraves. com (December 27, 2010).

*　　*　　*

SIMS, Rudine
See BISHOP, Rudine Sims

*　　*　　*

SMITH, Lane 1959-

Personal

Born August 25, 1959, in Tulsa, OK; son of Lewis (an accountant) and Mildred Annette (a homemaker) Smith; married Molly Leach (a designer), 1996. _Education:_ Art Center College of Design (Pasadena, CA), B.F.A. (illustration), 1983.

Lane Smith (Photograph by Brian Smale. Reproduced by permission.)

Addresses

Home and office—Washington Depot, CT. *Agent*—Steven Malk, Writers House, 21 W. 26th St., New York, NY 10010; smalkwritershouse.com. *E-mail*—lane smithbooks@gmail.com.

Career

Illustrator and author. Freelance illustrator, 1983—. Art director for film adaptation of *James and the Giant Peach,* Disney, 1996; contributed design work to *Monsters, Inc.,* Pixar, 2000. *Exhibitions:* Works exhibited at Master Eagle Gallery, New York, NY; Brockton Children's Museum, Brockton, MA; Joseloff Gallery, Hartford, CT; Bruce Museum; American Institute of Graphic Artists touring show; and Original Art Show, Society of Illustrators, New York, NY, 2009.

Awards, Honors

New York Times Ten Best Illustrated Books of the Year selection, *School Library Journal* Best Book of the Year citation, *Horn Book* Honor List inclusion, *Booklist* Editor's Choice selection, and Silver Buckeye Award, all 1987, all for *Halloween ABC* by Eve Merriam; Silver Medal, Society of Illustrators, *New York Times* Best Books of the Year citation, American Library Association (ALA) Notable Children's Book citation, Maryland Black-eyed Susan Picture-Book Award, and *Parenting* Reading Magic Award, all 1989, all for *The True Story of the Three Little Pigs!* by Jon Scieszka; Golden Apple Award, Bratislava International Biennial of Illustrations, 1990, Society of Illustrators Silver Medal, 1991, and first-place award, New York Book Show, all for *The*

Big Pets; Parent's Choice Award for Illustration, *New York Times* Best Books of the Year citation, and ALA Notable Children's Book citation, all 1991, all for *Glasses—Who Needs 'Em?;* ALA Caldecott Honor Book designation *New York Times* Best Illustrated Books of the Year citation and Notable Children's Book citation, and *School Library Journal* Best Books of the Year citation, all 1992, all for *The Stinky Cheese Man, and Other Fairly Stupid Tales* by Scieszka; *Publishers Weekly* Best Children's Book citation, and *Booklist* Editors' Choice citation, both 1995, and ALA Best Book for Young Adults citation, 1996, all for *Math Curse* by Scieszka; *New York Times* Best Illustrated Book of the Year and Notable Book designations, National Parenting Publication Gold Award, Oppenheim Toy Portfolio Platinum Award, Quills Award nomination, *School Library Journal, Horn Book, Publishers Weekly, Parenting,* and *Child* magazine Best Book of the Year designations, and Bookbinder's Guild New York Book Show Merit Award, all 2006, all for *John, Paul, George, and Ben;* Cooperative Children's Book Center (CCBC) Choices selection, 2008, for *Cowboy and Octopus* by Scieszka, 2009, for *Madame President,* 2010, for *Princess Hyacinth (The Surprising Tale of a Girl Who Floated)* by Florence Parry Heide.

Writings

SELF-ILLUSTRATED

Flying Jake, Macmillan (New York, NY), 1989.
The Big Pets, Viking (New York, NY), 1990.
Glasses—Who Needs 'Em?, Viking (New York, NY), 1991.
The Happy Hocky Family!, Viking (New York, NY), 1993.
Pinocchio: The Boy, Viking (New York, NY), 2002.
The Happy Hocky Family Moves to the Country!, Viking (New York, NY), 2003.
John, Paul, George, and Ben, Hyperion (New York, NY), 2006.
Madam President, Hyperion Books for Children (New York, NY), 2008.
The Big Elephant in the Room, Disney/Hyperion Books (New York, NY), 2009.

ILLUSTRATOR

Eve Merriam, *Halloween ABC,* Macmillan (New York, NY), 1987, revised as *Spooky ABC,* Simon & Schuster (New York, NY), 2002.
Jon Scieszka, *The True Story of the Three Little Pigs!,* Viking (New York, NY), 1989.
Jon Scieszka, *The Stinky Cheese Man, and Other Fairly Stupid Tales,* Viking (New York, NY), 1992.
Jon Scieszka, *Math Curse,* Viking (New York, NY), 1995.
Roald Dahl, *James and the Giant Peach: A Children's Story,* adapted by Karey Kirkpatrick, Knopf (New York, NY), 1996.

Dr. Seuss and Jack Prelutsky, *Hooray for Diffendoofer Day!,* Knopf (New York, NY), 1998.

Jon Scieszka, *Squids Will Be Squids: Fresh Morals, Beastly Fables,* Viking (New York, NY), 1998.

George Saunders, *The Very Persistent Gappers of Frip* (for adults), Villard (New York, NY), 2000.

Jon Scieszka, *Baloney, (Henry P.),* Viking (New York, NY), 2001.

Jon Scieszka, *Science Verse,* Viking (New York, NY), 2004.

Jon Scieszka, *Seen Art?,* Viking/Museum of Modern Art (New York, NY), 2005.

Jon Scieszka, *Cowboy and Octopus,* Viking (New York, NY), 2007.

Bob Shea, *Big Plans,* Hyperion Books for Children (New York, NY), 2008.

Florence Parry Heide, *Princess Hyacinth (The Surprising Tale of a Girl Who Floated),* Schwartz & Wade Books (New York, NY), 2009.

Judith Viorst, *Lulu and the Brontosaurus,* Atheneum Books for Young Readers (New York, NY), 2010.

Contributor of illustrations to periodicals, including *Rolling Stone, Time, Ms., Newsweek, New York Times, Atlantic Monthly,* and *Esquire.*

ILLUSTRATOR; "TIME WARP TRIO" SERIES BY JON SCIESZKA

Knights of the Kitchen Table, Viking (New York, NY), 1991.

The Not-So-Jolly Roger, Viking (New York, NY), 1991.

The Good, the Bad, and the Goofy, Viking (New York, NY), 1992.

Your Mother Was a Neanderthal, Viking (New York, NY), 1993.

2095, Viking (New York, NY), 1995.

Jon Scieszka, *Tut, Tut,* Viking (New York, NY), 1996.

Summer Reading Is Killing Me!, Viking (New York, NY), 1998.

It's All Greek to Me, Viking (New York, NY), 1999.

Adaptations

The "Tim Warp Trio" books were adapted as a television series, which itself has been novelized.

Sidelights

Children's book aficionados of all ages are likely acquainted with the work of Lane Smith, whose satirical illustrations range from the downright goofy to the more-than-a-bit-unsettling. The winner of numerous awards, including a Caldecott Honor, and the author of several original self-illustrated picture books, Smith is best known for his long-time collaboration with writer Jon Scieszka (pronounced "shes-ka"), which has produced such popular children's books as *The True Story of the Three Little Pigs!, The Stinky Cheese Man, and Other Fairly Stupid Tales, Cowboy and Octopus,* and the multi-volume "Time Warp Trio" series. Smith's illustrations have also appeared in magazines such as *Rolling Stone, Time,* and *Ms.,* and he designed the characters for the Disney film adaptation of Roald Dahl's classic children's book *James and the Giant Peach.*

Smith is noted for his textured, mixed-media illustrations, often featuring oddly shaped figures with large heads and small bodies, and in his picture-book worlds the laws of physics often do not apply. He frequently worked in oils and acrylics, using dark pigments to give his figures a distinctively strange, otherworldly quality, although he has also incorporated digital techniques into his repertoire. Smith's work has drawn praise for its irreverence, eccentricity, and innovative palette of colors. "While not conventionally beautiful, [his illustrations] do what all good art must—create an alternate and believable universe," remarked *New York Times Book Review* contributor Signe Wilkinson.

Born in Oklahoma, Smith grew up in Corona, California, with his parents and brother Shane. Influenced by the humor in his household, he developed an early fascination for the offbeat and the absurd. During summer trips back to Oklahoma along Route 66, he enjoyed discovering unusual sights along the way. "I think that's where my bizarre sense of design comes from," he once revealed. "Once you've seen a 100-foot cement buffalo on top of a doughnut stand in the middle of nowhere, you're never the same."

Smith's artistic talent became evident during grade school and junior high school. As he admitted in an essay for *Talking with Artists,* his career was determined by his lack of mathematical ability: "I guess I really knew I wanted to be an artist when my fourth-grade math test came back with a big 'D' on it." While Smith spent his time drawing and writing stories, he also read extensively. "I think one of my fondest memories is of lying stretched out on the library floor at Parkridge Elementary, reading Eleanor Cameron's *Wonderful Flight to the Mushroom Planet,*" he recalled in the same essay. "I loved the story and the art. To this day, whenever I smell hard-boiled eggs I think of how Chuck and David saved the planet with the sulfur-smelling eggs. From then on I drew only space stuff."

After high school Smith enrolled at the prestigious Art Center College of Design in Pasadena, California, where he studied illustration. To earn money for tuition, he worked as a night janitor at nearby Disneyland, maintaining park attractions such as the Haunted Mansion and the Revolving Teacup. When he developed an interest in pop art and European illustration, one of his teachers warned Smith that, with those influences, he would never find a job in the United States. In 1984, the year after he earned his degree, Smith moved to New York City and, contrary to his teacher's prediction, was soon selling his illustrations to some of the nation's most popular magazines. As the artist later admitted in *Horn Book,* although he was initially worried about employment prospects in New York City, "the punk/new-wave movement came, and my work seemed to fit acceptably into that category."

Smith's artwork for **Hooray for Diffendoofer Day!** ***brings to life the animated text by popular writers Dr. Seuss and Jack Prelutsky.*** (Illustration in body of
work copyright © 1998 by Lane Smith. Representations in Lane Smith's Illustration of original and modified Dr. Seuss characters Trademark and © Dr. Seuss Enterprises, L.P. Reproduced
by permission of Random House Children's Books, a division of Random house, Inc.)

While working on assignments for *Ms., Time, Rolling Stone,* and other magazines by day, Smith developed his oil-painting technique at night. In college he had concentrated on drawing, so oils were a new medium for him. His first substantial project was a series of thirty Halloween-themed paintings that illustrated the letters of the alphabet. He submitted the finished work to the children's book department at Macmillan. Impressed by his work, the publisher hired children's author Eve Merriam to compose poems for each of the thirty illustrations. Smith enjoyed this first experience in collaboration, finding that Merriam's poetry gave him new ideas. For instance, as he commented in his *Horn Book* essay, "I had *V* for 'Vampire,' and she came up with 'Viper,' which I liked a lot because I could use the *V* for the viper's open mouth." When *Halloween ABC* was published in 1987, reviewers responded positively; although the book was actually banned in some places because it was considered "Satanic," it received several awards.

In the mid-1980s Smith met Scieszka, a teacher and aspiring children's author. Sharing the same wacky sense of humor—they both enjoyed "Monty Python" films and *Mad* magazine—they collaborated on the book *The True Story of the Three Little Pigs!* In this version of the traditional tale, Alexander T. Wolf is jailed in the Pig Pen and charged with killing the three pigs. Claiming that he has been misunderstood and victimized by the media, Alexander maintains that he called on the pigs only to borrow a cup of sugar to make a birthday cake for his grandmother. At the time he had a bad cold, and his sneeze blew their houses down. Alexander is quick to add that if the houses had not been so poorly constructed they would not have collapsed. In *Horn Book* Smith explained his approach to illustrating Scieszka's story: "I think Jon thought of the wolf as a con artist trying to talk his way out of a situation. But I really believed the wolf, so I portrayed him with glasses and a little bow tie and tried to make him a victim of circumstance."

When *The True Story of the Three Little Pigs!* was published, it sold out within a few weeks, and children, teachers, and librarians all praised its contemporary twist on an old story. While a *Publishers Weekly* reviewer predicted that Smith's pictures might seem "mystifyingly adult," other critics delighted in his quirky style. In their review of the book for the *Wilson Library Bulletin,* Donnarae MacCann and Olga Richard observed that by "using minimal but subtly changing browns and ochres, he combines a great variety of creative modes: fanciful, realist, surreal, cartoonish."

The Stinky Cheese Man, and Other Fairly Stupid Tales, another of Smith's collaborations with Scieszka, contains "updated" versions of such classic stories as "Chicken Little," "The Ugly Duckling," "The Princess and the Frog," and "The Princess and the Pea." As part of Scieszka's updating, however, Chicken Little becomes Chicken Licken, and while the animals the

chicken warns are indeed crushed, the crusher is the book's table of contents rather than a falling sky. In another updated retelling, the ugly duckling grows up to be an ugly duck, not a lovely swan, and the frog prince is revealed to be . . . just a frog. Sustaining the ironic theme, "The Princess and the Pea" is retitled "The Princess and the Bowling Ball."

The Stinky Cheese Man, and Other Fairly Stupid Tales was an immediate hit, receiving praise from readers and reviewers alike. Smith received a 1993 Caldecott Honor Book award as well as several other citations for his illustrations, and Mary M. Burns, writing in *Horn Book,* lauded it as "another masterpiece from the team that created *The True Story of the Three Little Pigs!*" Wilkinson predicted that the book will appeal not only to children but to readers of all ages: "Kids, who rejoice in anything stinky, will no doubt enjoy the blithe, mean-spirited anarchy of these wildly spinning stories," while "for those who are studying fairy tales at the college level, 'The Stinky Cheese Man' would be a perfect key to the genre."

In *The Stinky Cheese Man, and Other Fairly Stupid Tales* Smith and Scieszka turned the tables on Mother Goose; with *Squids Will Be Squids: Fresh Morals, Beastly Fables* they take Aesop to task in eighteen contemporary wacky fables and tales. A reviewer for *Publishers Weekly* praised Smith's illustrations for *Squids Will Be Squids,* writing that his artwork "ardently keeps pace with Scieszka's leaps of fancy."

Concidered among the most popular of Smith and Scieszka's many collaborations, the "Time Warp Trio" novel series includes *Knights of the Kitchen Table, Your Mother Was a Neanderthal,* and *It's All Greek to Me.* In the series, Joe, Sam, and Fred travel back in time and, with the aid of a magical book, encounter fantastic adventures. When they are transported to medieval England in *Knights of the Kitchen Table,* they save King Arthur's Camelot. Using their magic power to read, the three friends are able to defeat an evil knight, a giant, and a dragon. In *The Not-So-Jolly Roger* the boys meet Blackbeard and his band of pirates, who threaten to kill Joe, Sam, and Fred and make them walk the plank. The trio's good fortune fades in *Your Mother Was a Neanderthal,* which finds the boys blasting back to the Stone Age. Once there, they discover that, not only are they naked, they also do not have their magic book. After Sam fashions suitable garments, the boys embark on a series of escapades as they try to flee cave-girls, ultimately escaping to a happy ending. In *2095* Joe, Fred, and Sam are launched into the future, courtesy of their magic book. Starting out in the 1920s room of the Natural History Museum, their move forward in time lands them in the equally dated 1990s exhibition room, where they meet their great-grandchildren and try to return to their own present. A 266-pound chicken presents a substantial threat to the trio in *Summer Reading Is Killing Me!,* after Joe thoughlessly puts his summer reading list in The Book and summons forth a host of famous picture-book characters.

The "Time Warp Trio" series received positive responses from reviewers who, like Smith-Scieszka fans, have looked forward to each new installment. In the *New York Times Book Review* Elizabeth-Ann Sachs dubbed *Knights of the Kitchen Table* a "rollicking good story," and a *Publishers Weekly* critic predicted that fans would "gobble up" *The Good, the Bad, and the Goofy* "as they eagerly await the next" "Time Warp Trio" adventure. In her *Booklist* review, Janice Del Negro praised *Your Mother Was a Neanderthal,* noting that Smith's illustrations "add a rollicking, somewhat riotous air to the proceedings." "This is the kind of book that kids tell one another to read," Gale W. Sherman asserted of the same book in her review for *School Library Journal.* Julie Yates Walton, in a review of *2095* for *Booklist,* praised Smith's black-pencil illustrations, which are "brimming with zany, adolescent hyperbole." "The farce is as furious and silly as ever," announced *Booklist* contributor Hazel Rochman in a review of Scieszka and Smith's *Summer Reading Is Killing Me!*

In another humorous collaboration, *Math Curse,* a girl wakes up one morning to find that every event during the day—from getting dressed to eating breakfast and going to school—has been transformed into a math problem that must be solved. She decides her teacher, Mrs. Fibonacci, has put a math curse on her, but that night she dreams of a way to get rid of the curse. Reviewing the work in *Booklist,* Carolyn Phelan wrote that, both "bold in design and often bizarre in expression, Smith's paintings clearly express the child's feelings of bemusement, frustration, and panic as well as her eventual joy when she overcomes the math curse."

With a story similar to that in *Math Curse, Science Verse* assembles what a *Kirkus Reviews* contributor described as a "madcap collection of science poetry that lampoons familiar songs" as technoterminology infiltrates a child's everyday world. Also featuring a story by Scieczka, *Cowboy and Octopus* offers seven vignettes that illuminate the unlikely but intensely loyal friendship between amazingly disparate paper cut-outs. "Attractive, clever illustrations are executed in mixed media collages," observed *Booklist* critic Randall Enos, and Tanya D. Auger commented in *Horn Book* that the mini-tales are "simply told, surprisingly fresh, and genuinely funny—with Smith's artfully weathered mixed-media orchestrations pushing the humor level up and up and up."

In addition to his work with Scieszka, Smith has also provided illustrations for *Hooray for Diffendoofer Day!,* a book begun by Dr. Seuss (Theodore Geisel) and completed following Geisel's death by poet Jack Prelutsky. Describing the artist's contribution to the work, *Horn Book* critic Joanna Rudge Long wrote that Smith's "satirical renditions, in his own distinctive, sophisticated style," contain "such zany folk and weirdly expressive settings as" the late pseudonymous author "might have dreamed up" himself.

Another of Smith's illustration projects, Bob Shea's *Big Plans* finds an ambitious youngster loudly announcing his intentions to blaze a trail in the boardroom, the political arena, and even in outer space. According to a contributor in *Publishers Weekly,* here Smith's "punchy collages and grainy wallpaper patterns, along with emphatic typefaces, reinforce the speaker's unquenchable spirit." Smith joins forces with one of his literary idols, Florence Parry Heide, in *Princess Hyacinth (The Surprising Tale of a Girl Who Floated),* "a goofy romp that maintains a gentle feel throughout," according to Daniel Kraus in *Booklist.* The work follows the misadventures of a young royal who defies gravity, centering on her growing awareness of the benefits of weightlessness. "The quirky oil and watercolor illustrations seamlessly match Heide's wry, understated text," a reviewer declared in *Publishers Weekly.* "Understated yet witty," as Martha V. Parravano concluded in *Horn Book,* "Smith's pictures [in *Princess Hyacinth*] communicate the ennui of the princess's encumbered existence . . . and her stratospheric delight in her newfound freedom."

Working with short-story writer George Saunders, Smith also provided illustrations for *The Very Persistent Gappers of Frip,* "a delightful story, lavishly illustrated," as Susan Salpini described the book in *School Library Journal.* Something of a departure for Smith, *The Very Persistent Gappers of Frip* is geared mainly for adult readers. Caitlin Dover, reviewing the book in *Print* magazine, applauded Smith's "perceptive, eclectic paintings" and concluded of the sophisticated offering: "This may be Smith's first foray into adult fiction, but we doubt it will be his last."

In 1989 Smith both wrote and illustrated *Flying Jake,* the first of several solo picture books he has produced. He dedicated the work to his high-school art teacher, Mr. Baughman, who taught him to experiment with different media when expressing various moods. He described his second original work, *The Big Pets,* in *Children's Books and Their Creators* as "a surreal nighttime journey of a little girl and her giant cat." In Smith's story, the girl and her cat travel to the Milk Pool, where children swim and other cats happily drink along the pool's edge, then also encounter the Bone Garden and the Hamster Hole. In *Children's Books and Their Creators* Smith recalled that, "when I wrote *Big Pets* . . . I was expanding on my own childhood fantasies of slipping out into the night for fantastic adventures while knowing there was a home base of security to come back to." Reviewers were charmed by the book's illustrations, finding them to be less threatening than those in *The True Story of the Three Little Pigs!* As a *Publishers Weekly* reviewer noted, Smith's "enticing illustrations . . . provide the perfect landscape for this nocturnal romp."

Another original work, *Glasses—Who Needs 'Em?,* describes a boy's visit to the eye doctor to be fitted for his first pair of eyeglasses and is based on Smith's own experience getting glasses in the fifth grade. As he told

Publishers Weekly interviewer Amanda Smith, he wanted the book's young protagonist to be "a little reluctant about [getting glasses] but still be kind of cool, so kids who wear glasses empathize and get some laughs out of the book, too." Writing in *Children's Books and Their Creators,* he also credited his wife, book designer Molly Leach, with giving *Glasses—Who Needs 'Em?* the right visual effect by creating the opening lines of the story in the form of an eye examination chart. The words in the first line are in large letters, then they shrink down to the type size used in the rest of the book. "Not only did this device draw the reader into the story and establish the proper framework," Smith observed, "it also looked smashing!" Leach has also designed several of Smith's other books.

Both *The Happy Hocky Family!* and *The Happy Hocky Family Moves to the Country!* are playful spoofs on the beginner-level schoolbooks of the 1950s. The seventeen-episode plot in *The Happy Hocky Family!* is designed to help young readers understand the disappointments, mistakes, and accidents—as well as the positive experiences—that occur in life. In his illustrations, Smith uses stick figures, basic outline shapes, and primary colors. In reviewing the book for the *New York Times Book Review,* Edward Koren noted that "Smith's draftsmanship, wonderfully expressive, still manages to create a family that is general and unspecific, one that could be of any racial or ethnic group." Moving from primary to brown tones for *The Happy Hocky Family Moves to the Country!,* Smith contrasts the city amenities with their country counterparts through visual images; for example, "Milk" is shown as a cow rather than a supermarket container, and "garbage collector" is a raccoon rather than a city employee. Noting the retro-appeal of the work, *School Library Journal* contributor Barbara Auerbach dubbed *The Happy Hocky Family Moves to the Country!* "an irreverent look at country life."

With *John, Paul, George, and Ben* Smith attracted both the attention of educators and numerous picture-book honors. With a title that plays on popular culture, the book focuses on the Founding Fathers, who achieved America's independence from England despite an amusing collection of personal foibles are illustrated by Smith in a somewhat shaky historical framework. For example, George Washington's legendary admission to chopping down cherry trees prompted the establishment of the nation's capital in New York, where few cherry trees would tempt the president's axe. "While children will love the off-the-wall humor" in *John, Paul, George, and Ben, School Library Journal* contributor Marianne Saccardi added that "there is plenty for adult readers to enjoy" as well. While Carolyn Phelan wrote in *Booklist* that Smith's un-history might "confuse children unfamiliar with the period," the book's illustrations are "deftly drawn, witty, and instantly appealing." "Humor, both broad . . . and sly . . . reminds readers that books hold many discoveries, and quite a bit of ye olde fun," wrote *Horn Book* reviewer Betty Carter in praise of Smith's patriotic picture-book effort.

Another politically tinged work written and illustrated by Smith, *Madam President* focuses on a ponytailed youngster's fanciful musings about the duties of the nation's most important elected official. Whether she is negotiating a peace treaty between angry pets, appointing her Mr. Potato Head to a cabinet post, or vetoing a meal of tuna casserole, the grade schooler confidently navigates the day's activities while Smith, according to a *Publishers Weekly* critic, "ably skewers the pitfalls of political office." Smith's offbeat, mixed-media illustrations for this book drew praise from several critics. Cooper, writing in *Booklist,* cited *Madam President* for its "amazing artwork," noting in particular the "disparate uses of materials and images that often give the look of collage." In *School Library Journal* Wendy Lukehart wrote that the author/illustrator's "understated text is accompanied by clean, cleverly designed compositions."

A series of embarrassing misunderstandings is at the heart of *The Big Elephant in the Room,* a "laugh-out-loud opus from the master of kid-companionable humor," declared Joy Fleishhacker in *School Library Journal.* When a bespectacled donkey asks its friend if they can discuss the proverbial "elephant in the room," the companion begins reciting a litany of their most discomfiting encounters, which include a mishap involving super glue and a nearly-naked talent show performance. Little does he realize, however, that the question was meant to be taken literally. "Frenetic illustrations in muted neutrals show the various situations," a critic in *Kirkus Reviews* stated, and Fleishhacker observed that Smith's "droll artwork tells much of the story through lively layouts and funny details"

Smith casts a satirical eye at society's fascination with technology in *It's a Book,* in which a pixel-addicted donkey discovers the joys of the paginated version of Robert Louis Stevenson's *Treasure Island.* Reviewing the self-illustrated work in *School Library Journal,* Sara Lissa Paulson complimented especially a wordless spread showing the donkey engrossed in the classic novel, which "offer[s] a priceless visual testimony to the focused interaction between readers' imaginations and a narrative." *New York Times Book Review* critic Adam Gopnick applauded the theme of Smith's tale: "not that screens are bad and books are good, that what books do depends on the totality of what they are—their turning pages, their sturdy self-sufficiency, above all the way they invite a child to withdraw from this world into a world alongside ours in an activity at once mentally strenuous and physically still."

Biographical and Critical Sources

BOOKS

Cummings, Pat, compiler and editor, *Talking with Artists,* Bradbury Press (New York, NY), 1992, pp. 72-75.

Silvey, Anita, editor, *Children's Books and Their Creators*, Houghton (Boston, MA), 1995.

PERIODICALS

Booklist, October 1, 1993, Janice Del Negro, review of *Your Mother Was a Neanderthal,* p. 346; July 1 & 15, 1995, Julie Yates Walton, review of *2095,* p. 1773; November 1, 1995, Carolyn Phelan, review of *Math Curse,* p. 472; May 1, 1996, Ilene Cooper, reviews of *Disney's James and the Giant Peach* and *James and the Giant Peach,* both p. 1511; June 1, 1998, Hazel Rochman, review of *Summer Reading Is Killing Me!,* p. 1769; April 15, 2005, Gillian Engberg, review of *Seen Art?,* p. 1456; February 15, 2006, Carolyn Phelan, review of *John, Paul, George, and Ben,* p. 104; July 1, 2007, Randall Enos, review of *Cowboy and Octopus,* p. 64; May 1, 2008, Ilene Cooper, review of *Madam President,* p. 89; September 1, 2009, Daniel Kraus, review of *Princess Hyacinth (The Surprising Tale of a Girl Who Floated),* p. 102; July 1, 2010, Andrew Medlar, review of *It's a Book,* p. 66.

Bulletin of the Center for Children's Books, May, 2006, Elizabeth Bush, review of *John, Paul, George, and Ben,* p. 424.

Horn Book, November-December, 1992, Mary M. Burns, review of *The Stinky Cheese Man, and Other Fairly Stupid Tales,* p. 720; January-February, 1993, Lane Smith, "The Artist at Work," pp. 64-70; July-August, 1998, Joanna Rudge Long, review of *Hooray for Diffendoofer Day!,* pp. 479-481; May-June, 2006, Betty Carter, review of *John, Paul, George, and Ben,* p. 349; September-October, 2007, Tanya D. Auger, review of *Cowboy and Octopus,* p. 562; November-December, 2009, Martha V. Parravano, review of *Princess Hyacinth,* p. 653.

Kirkus Reviews, August 15, 2004, review of *Science Verse,* p. 813; April 15, 2005, review of *Seen Art?,* p. 481; March 15, 2006, review of *John, Paul, George, and Ben,* p. 301; August 1, 2007, review of *Cowboy and Octopus;* April 1, 2008, review of *Big Plans;* June 15, 2008, review of *Madam President;* June 1, 2009, review of *The Big Elephant in the Room.*

New York Times Book Review, October 6, 1991, Elizabeth-Ann Sachs, reviews of *Knights of the Kitchen Table* and *The Not-So-Jolly Roger,* both p. 23; November 8, 1992, Signe Wilkinson, "No Princes, No White Horses, No Happy Endings," pp. 29, 59; November 14, 1993, Edward Koren, review of *The Happy Hocky Family!,* p. 44; October 15, 2010, Adam Gopnick, review of *It's a Book.*

Print, November, 2000, Caitlin Dover, review of *The Very Persistent Gappers of Frip,* p. 16.

Publishers Weekly, July 28, 1989, review of *The True Story of the Three Little Pigs!,* p. 218; December 21, 1990, review of *The Big Pets,* p. 55; July 26, 1991, Amanda Smith, "Jon Scieszka and Lane Smith," pp. 220-221; May 11, 1992, review of *The Good, the Bad, and the Goofy,* p. 72; May 18, 1998, review of *Squids Will Be Squids: Fresh Morals, Beastly Fables,* p. 78; May 2, 2005, review of *Seen Art?,* p. 198; January 23, 2006, review of *John, Paul, George, and Ben,* p. 207; July 16, 2007, review of *Cowboy and Octopus,* p. 162; March 31, 2008, review of *Big Plans,* p. 61; June 23, 2008, review of *Madam President,* p. 54; July 13, 2009, review of *The Big Elephant in the Room,* p. 56; August 17, 2009, review of *Princess Hyacinth,* p. 60; July 19, 2010, review of *It's a Book,* p. 127.

School Library Journal, October, 1993, Gale W. Sherman, review of *Your Mother Was a Neanderthal,* p. 130; September, 1995, Lucinda Snyder Whitehurst, review of *Math Curse,* p. 215; January, 2001, Susan Salpini, review of *The Very Persistent Gappers of Frip,* p. 160; May, 2001, Mary Ann Carich, review of *Baloney (Henry P.),* p. 134; June, 2004, Steven Engelfried, review of *Baloney (Henry P.),* p. 58; May, 2005, Carol Ann Wilson, review of *Seen Art?,* p. 96; June, 2005, Steven Engelfried, review of *Science Verse,* p. 56; March, 2006, Marianne Saccardi, review of *John, Paul, George, and Ben,* p. 214; July, 2008, Wendy Lukehart, review of *Madam President,* p. 82; September, 2009, Joy Fleishhacker, review of *The Big Elephant in the Room,* p. 134; August, 2010, Sara Lissa Paulson, review of *It's a Book,* p. 86.

Time, December 21, 1992, "Kid-Lit Capers," pp. 69-70.

Wilson Library Bulletin, June, 1992, Donnarae MacCann, and Olga Richard, review of *The True Story of the Three Little Pigs!,* p. 118.

ONLINE

Kidsreads.com, http://www.kidsreads.com/ (September, 2010), "Author Talk: Lane Smith."

Lane Smith Home Page, http://www.lanesmithbooks.com (January 1, 2011).

Lane Smith Web log, http://lanesart.blogspot.com/ (January 1, 2011).

Seven Impossible Things before Breakfast Web log, http://blaine.org/sevenimpossiblethings/ (August 25, 2008), "Seven Questions over Breakfast with Lane Smith."

*   *   *

STEPHENSON, Kristina

Personal

Born in England; married; husband a musician; children: one son, one daughter. *Education:* Central School of Art and Design, degree (set and costume design).

Addresses

Home—Salisbury, Wiltshire, England.

Career

Author and illustrator of children's books, animator, and creative director. Set and costume designer for stage productions; animator and producer of animated television programming for British Broadcasting Corporation and Channel 4.

Writings

SELF-ILLUSTRATED

The Christmas Story, Zonderkidz (Grand Rapids, MI), 2001.

Sir Charlie Stinky Socks and the Really Big Adventure, Egmont (Oxford, England), 2007, Egmont USA (New York, NY), 2009.

Sir Charlie Stinky Socks and the Really Frightful Night, Egmont (Oxford, England), 2008.

Sir Charlie Stinky Socks and the Really Dreadful Spell, Egmont (Oxford, England), 2010.

ILLUSTRATOR

Cecile Schoberle, *The Thanksgiving Parade Surprise,* Little Simon (New York, NY), 2000.

Barrie Wade, *Goldilocks and the Three Bears,* Franklin Watts (London, England), 2001, Picture Window Books (Minneapolis, MN), 2003.

Susan Hood, *Meet Trouble,* Grosset & Dunlap (New York, NY), 2001.

Allia Zobel-Nolan, *Something Yummy for Sunny,* Reader's Digest, 2002.

Gloria Gaither, *I Am a Promise,* Zonderkidz (Grand Rapids, MI), 2002.

Jillian Harker, *I Love You, Daddy,* Marks & Spencer (Chester, England), 2004.

Jillian Harker, *I Love You, Mummy,* Marks & Spencer (Chester, England), 2004.

Miriam Schlein, *The Story about Me,* Albert Whitman (Morton Grove, IL), 2004.

Heather Maisner, *Time to See the Doctor,* Kingfisher (Boston, MA), 2004.

Heather Maisner, *We're Moving!,* Kingfisher (Boston, MA), 2004, published as *We're Moving House,* Kingfisher (London, England), 2004.

Sarah Toulmin, *Baby Boy Bible,* Lion Children's (Oxford, England), 2004, Good Books (Intercourse, PA), 2007.

Heather Maisner, *It's My Turn!,* Kingfisher (London, England), 2004, Kingfisher (Boston, MA), 2005.

Heather Maisner, *Our New Baby,* Kingfisher (London, England), 2004, Kingfisher (Boston, MA), 2005.

Teresa Bateman, *Will You Be My Valenswine?,* Albert Whitman (Morton Grove, IL), 2005.

Sarah Toulmin, reteller, *Baby Bible,* Lion Children's (Oxford, England), 2006, Good Books (Intercourse, PA), 2007.

Claire Freedman, *New Kid in Town,* Good Books (Intercourse, PA), 2006.

Sophie Piper, *When You Were Very Small,* Good Books (Intercourse, PA), 2006.

Sarah Toulmin, *Baby Girl Bible,* Lion Children's (Oxford, England), 2006, Good Books (Intercourse, PA), 2007.

Jillian Harker, *I Love You, Grandma,* Parragon (Bath, England), 2006.

Sarah Toulmin, *Baby Prayers,* Lion Children's (Oxford, England), 2007, Good Books (Intercourse, PA), 2008.

Ronica Stromberg, *The Time-for-Bed Angel,* Lion Children's (Oxford, England), 2008.

Sophie Piper, *The Angel and the Lamb,* Lion Children's (Oxford, England), 2008.

Sophie Piper, *The Angel and the Dove,* Lion Children's (Oxford, England), 2009.

Marion Dane Bauer, *Thank You for Me!,* Simon & Schuster Books for Young Readers (New York, NY), 2010.

Adaptations

The "Sir Charlie Stinky Socks" books were released with audio CD's narrated by Michale Maloney.

Sidelights

Before she turned her creative focus to children's picture books, British author and illustrator Kristina Stephenson worked in the theatre, where she designed both sets and costumes. From there she moved to television, designing, writing, and producing children's programs for the British Broadcasting Corporation and Channel 4. Once she started her family, however, Stephenson decided to find a career that would allow her to stay at home with her children. Beginning in 2000, her illustrations have brought to life stories by authors such as Sophie Piper, Heather Maisner, Teresa Bateman, Jillian Harker, and Marion Dane Bauer, as well as being featured in such in original, self-illustrated stories as *The Christmas Story* and Stephenson's "Sir Charlie Stinky Socks" books. In reviewing her illustrations for Bauer's *Thank You for Me!, School Library*

Kristina Stephenson's illustration projects include Marion Dane Bauer's upbeat and toddler-friendly picture book **Thank You for Me!** (Illustration copyright © 2010 by Kristina Stephenson. Reproduced by permission of Simon & Schuster Books for Young Readers, an imprint of Simon & Schuster Macmillan.)

Journal contributor James K. Irwin cited the "jubilant energy in Stephenson's watercolor rainbow palette," and a *Kirkus Reviews* writer praised the book as "a simple celebration of self" in which the artwork "follow[s] the gentle mood of the text with soft colors, rounded shapes and smiling children."

Stephenson introduces a spunky young hero in *Sir Charlie Stinky Socks and the Really Big Adventure,* which finds an imaginative young boy headed off to a world of exciting challenges. Together with his cat Envelope, Sir Charlie Stinky Socks packs up his sandwich, takes up his sword, and toddles off into a dark and spooky forest where a host of fairy-tale characters—including a beautiful princess—figure in his exciting day. Charlie's adventures continue in *Sir Charlie Stinky Socks and the Really Frightful Night* and *Sir Charlie Stinky Socks and the Really Dreadful Spell,* as Stephenson's hero weaves through tangled forests, braves hidden creatures, and thwarts the magic spells of evil witches. Featuring the artist/illustrator's characteristic "brightly colored cartoon" art inhabited by round-eyed children, *Sir Charlie Stinky Stocks and the Really Big Adventure* also treats readers to "plenty of comic twists and crude details" that will appeal particularly to young boys, according to a *Kirkus Reviews* writer.

Biographical and Critical Sources

PERIODICALS

Booklist, May 1, 2004, Lauren Peterson, review of *The Story about Me,* p. 1564; December 1, 2004, Hazel Rochman, review of *We're Moving,* p. 661; January 1, 2010, Carolyn Phelan, review of *Thank You for Me!,* p. 100.

Kirkus Reviews, February 15, 2004, review of *The Story about Me*; October 1, 2006, review of *New Kid in Town,* p. 1013; August 15, 2009, review of *Sir Charlie Stinky Socks and the Really Big Adventure;* February 15, 2010, review of *Thank You for Me!*

Publishers Weekly, September 24, 2001, review of *The Christmas Story,* p. 54; December 24, 2001, reviews of *Something Yummy for Sunny* and *Let's Play, Lily,* both p. 66.

School Library Journal, December, 2001, Louie Lahana, review of *Meet Trouble,* p. 104; May, 2004, Deborah Rothaug, review of *The Story about Me,* p. 123; February, 2010, James K. Irvin, review of *Thank You for Me!,* p. 74.

ONLINE

Egmont Web site, http://www.egmont.co.uk/ (December 27, 2010), "Kristina Stephenson."*

T

TAYLOR, Carrie-Jo
See TAYLOR, C.J.

*   *   *

TAYLOR, C.J. 1952-
(Carrie-Jo Taylor)

Personal

Born Carrie-Jo Taylor, August 31, 1952, in Montreal, Québec, Canada; mother a teacher; married; children: three. *Education:* Attended school in Glen Sutton and Matsonville, Quebec, Canada.

Addresses

Home—Vancouver Island, British Columbia, Canada.

Career

Artist, storyteller, and writer. KRK Radio, host of "Earth Songs" program for four years; Canadian Broadcasting Corporation, animator for "Legends of the Land" series. *Exhibitions:* Work included in private collections in Canada and the United States.

Awards, Honors

Notable Canadian Illustrated Book selection, *Canadian Review of Materials,* 1990, and Our Choice selection, Canadian Children's Book Centre (CCBC), 1991, both for *How Two-Feather Was Saved;* Ruth Schwartz Children's Book Award finalist, 1991, Our Choice selection, CCBC, 1992, and Best 100 Books for Children and Teens listee, Toronto Public Library, 2003, all for *The Ghost and the Lone Warrior;* Our Choice selection, CCBC, 1993, for *Little Water and the Gift of the Animals,* 1994, for both *How We Saw the World* and *The Secret of the White Buffalo,* and 1995-96, for *Bones in the Basket;* Red Cedar Book Award for Nonfiction shortlist, 1995, Our Choice selection, CCBC, 1996-97,

and Hackmatack Children's Choice Book Award, 2000, all for *The Monster from the Swamp;* Our Choice selection, CCBC, 1998-99, for *The Messenger of Spring;* McNally Robinson Aboriginal Book of the Year shortlist, 2004, for *Peace Walker;* Amelia Frances Howard-Gibbon Illustrator's Award nominee, 2007, for *All the Stars in the Sky.*

Writings

SELF-ILLUSTRATED

How Two-Feather Was Saved from Loneliness: An Abenaki Legend, Tundra Books of Northern New York (Plattsburgh, NY), 1990.
The Ghost and Lone Warrior: An Arapaho Legend, Tundra Books of Northern New York (Plattsburgh, NY), 1991.
How We Saw the World: Nine Native Stories of the Way Things Began, Tundra Books of Northern New York (Plattsburgh, NY), 1993.
The Secret of the White Buffalo, Tundra Books of Northern New York (Plattsburgh, NY), 1993.
Bones in the Basket, Tundra Books of Northern New York (Plattsburgh, NY), 1994.
The Monster from the Swamp: Native Legends about Demons, Monsters, and Other Creatures, Tundra Books of Northern New York (Plattsburgh, NY), 1995.
Little Water and the Gift of Animals, Tundra Books of Northern New York (Plattsburgh, NY), 1997.
The Messenger of Spring, Tundra Books of Northern New York (Plattsburgh, NY), 1997.
Peace Walker: The Legend of Hiawatha and Tekanawita, Tundra Books of Northern New York (Plattsburgh, NY), 2004.
All the Stars in the Sky: Native Stories from the Heavens, Tundra Books of Northern New York (Plattsburgh, NY), 2006.
Spirits, Fairies, and Merpeople: Native Stories of Other Worlds, Tundra Books of Northern New York (Plattsburgh, NY), 2009.

Several of Taylor's books have been published in French.

ILLUSTRATOR

Jan Bourdeau Waboose, *Firedancers*, Stoddart Kids (New York, NY), 2000.

Sidelights

An internationally renowned Canadian painter and author, C.J. Taylor often focuses on her Mohawk heritage in her children's books, which include *Peace Walker: The Legend of Hiawatha and Tekanawita* and *Spirits, Fairies, and Merpeople: Native Stories of Other Worlds.* "I want my books to enlighten people, make them think," Taylor told *Canadian Review of Materials* interviewer Dave Jenkinson. "I want them to have a respect for the Native people, and I think that's something that's been lacking since 1492. I think that 'we've' got a bad rap down through history. We've been portrayed as being without religion, without spirituality, that we were stupid and without a sense of humour. We have a wonderful sense of humour. It's very simple humour. There's nothing complex about it. It's just good down home laughter."

Taylor was born in 1952 in Montreal and raised in the small town of Glen Sutton. Her mother, who was British and German, worked as a schoolteacher; her father was Mohawk. "I was about six when I discovered my culture," Taylor related to Jenkinson. "I remember being fascinated all the time by the old westerns on television. I would look at them and look at my father and see that there was some similarity there. I kept asking my mother, and she told me that my father was native." Taylor's father encountered racism throughout his life and was also greatly affected by issues facing the Native peoples of North America, issue that came to a head during 1990's Oka Crisis, an armed conflict between the Mohawk people, officials from the town of Oka, Quebec, Canada, and the Canadian army. "I suddenly realized what my father had gone through, and it just clicked in my mind," she recalled. "The tears that rolled down my face that day were not mine but my father's, and I promised myself, my children and my father that I would make a difference. From that day forward, I've been doing books and touring and talking about it and learning and sharing. I write for one race—the human race so we can all live in harmony."

In her works for young readers, Taylor often retells stories from Native communities across North America. In *How We Saw the World: Nine Native Stories of the Way Things Began* she includes tales from the Kiowa, Algonquin, and Micmac tribes, among others. "Taylor's staccato storytelling style lends crispness and verve," remarked a *Publishers Weekly* critic, who also applauded the author's "surreal" illustrations. *The Secret of the White Buffalo*, a story of harmony that is based on an Oglala Sioux legend, showcases "Taylor's unique way of presenting Native People against vast landscapes, unforgettable individual faces in relationship to nature," according to Patricia Fry, writing in the *Canadian Review of Materials.*

Taylor collects eight tales from such tribal groups as the Tlingit and the Comanche in her self-illustrated *The Monster from the Swamp: Native Legends about Demons, Monsters and Other Creatures.* "The stories are spare but well written," remarked *Canadian Review of Materials* critic Harriet Zaidman, and a contributor in *Emergency Librarian* praised Taylor's illustrations as "full of motion and emotion." A Ojibwa and Chippewa legend that explores the changing of the seasons, *The Messenger of Spring* was described as a "simple and gentle-toned story" by *Quill & Quire* reviewer Bridget Donald, the critic going on to note that Taylor's "paintings are dynamic as well as detailed: there is energy in the gestures of the human figures and movement in the swirling lines of wind in the skies."

In her self-illustrated *Peace Walker* Taylor explores the origins of the Iroquois Confederacy through the relationship of Onondaga chieftain Hiawatha and Huron leader Tekanawita. "Taylor's artist's sensibility is very evident in the writing of *Peace Walker*," Corey Coates remarked in the *Canadian Ethnic Studies Journal,* "for her image-laden descriptions of meetings, natural settings, and individuals have the qualities of static yet fluid word-pictures." In *Spirits, Fairies, and Merpeople* she presents seven legends from the Dakota, Coos, Cree, and other First Nations groups. "The language of the stories is rich and descriptive," Moira Kirkpatrick stated in her *Resource Links* review and in *School Library Journal* Marilyn Taniguchi observed of *Spirits, Fairies, and Merpeople* that Taylor's "powerful images featuring fearsome creatures and tiny human figures balance the taut economy of the text."

Biographical and Critical Sources

PERIODICALS

Booklist, January 1, 1994, Janice Del Negro, review of *The Secret of the White Buffalo,* p. 831; July, 2000, Karen Hutt, review of *Firedancers,* p. 2044; February 15, 2005, Karen Hutt, review of *Peace Walker: The Legend of Hiawatha and Tekanawita,* p. 1072; December 1, 2006, Karen Hutt, review of *All the Stars in the Sky: Native Stories from the Heavens,* p. 55.

Canadian Ethnic Studies Journal, summer, 2005, Corey Coates, review of *Peace Walker,* p. 135.

Canadian Review of Materials, March-April, 1994, Patricia Fry, review of *The Secret of the White Buffalo;* June 14, 1996, Harriet Zaidman, review of *The Monster from the Swamp: Native Legends about Demons, Monsters, and Other Creatures;* October 27, 1998, Dave Jenkinson, "C.J. Taylor."

Emergency Librarian, March-April, 1998, reviews of *The Messenger of Spring* and *The Monster from the Swamp,* both p. 48.

Kirkus Reviews, August 1, 2009, *Spirits, Fairies, and Merpeople: Native Stories of Other Worlds.*

Publishers Weekly, August 9, 1993, review of *How We Saw the World: Nine Native Stories of Beginnings,* p. 479.

Quill & Quire, November, 1997, Bridget Donald, review of *The Messenger of Spring;* December, 1999, Arlene Perly-Rae, review of *Firedancers;* October, 2004, Patty Lawlor, review of *Peace Walker.*

Resource Links, April, 2000, review of *Firedancers,* p. 8; December, 2004, Maria Forte, review of *Peace Walker,* p. 23; October, 2009, Moira Kirkpatrick, review of *Spirits, Fairies, and Merpeople,* p. 8.

School Library Journal, April, 2005, Cris Riedel, review of *Peace Walker,* p. 158; October, 2009, Marilyn Taniguchi, review of *Spirits, Fairies, and Merpeople,* p. 154.

ONLINE

PaperTigers Web site, http://www.papertigers.org/ (April, 2010), interview with Taylor.*

*   *   *

THOMPSON, Alicia 1984-

Personal

Born 1984, in FL; married Ryan Guy (a musician); has children. *Education:* New College of Florida, B.S. (psychology and history), 2006; University of South Florida, MA. (creative writing), c. 2010.

Addresses

Home—Riverview, FL.

Career

Author. Worked as a legal assistant, 2006-08.

Writings

Psych Major Syndrome, Disney/Hyperion (New York, NY), 2009.

Contributor to periodicals, including *Girl's Life.*

Sidelights

While studying for her major in psychology, Alicia Thompson found the time to write a teen novel, and her determination to find a publisher proved successful even after she received several rejections. Only a few years after earning her degree, Thompson's manuscript was published and this accomplishment prompted her to shift her career course to writing. Thompson's college studies were not for naught, however; her novel *Psych*

Major Syndrome is based on her experience as an undergraduate at a small, liberal-arts college and follows her own realization that sitting back and studying the lives of others is far easier that living out one's own. Remarking on why she chooses to write for adolescent readers, Thompson told *St. Petersburt Times* interviewer Colette Bancroft: "What I like is how consuming it is, that time of life. Everything is just so important, every decision you make is so critical."

In *Psych Major Syndrome* Leigh Nolan is a freshman at California's Stiles College, where psychology is one of her scheduled classes. Once she is introduced to the field's basic theory and jargon, Leigh begins to interpret the people around her, finding signs of troubled pasts, passive-aggressive behavior, and cognitive dissonance everywhere. Turning her lens on herself, she starts to question her own actions and habits, decisions, and relationships, including her sexless romance with her year-long boyfriend Andrew. As the semester unfolds, the young woman begins to pull meaning from her choices and uses the competitive environment within

Cover of Alicia Thompson's young-adult novel **Psych Major Syndrome,** *which finds a college freshman taking her college studies to heart.* (Jacket photography copyright © 2009 by Greg Weiner. Reproduced by permission of Hyperion Books for Children.)

her psychology class as well as her experiences mentoring a combative young teen to figure out what she really wants in life.

Reviewing *Psych Major Syndrome* in *Publishers Weekly,* a critic noted that "ironies abound," citing the "supporting cast of offbeat characters" in Thompson's first novel. Maggie Knapp cited the "healthy dose of quirky, introspective humor" that peppers the author's narrative, adding in her *School Library Journal* review that *Psych Major Syndrome* is "heavily laced with brand and celebrity names, music references, and esoteric comments." "Leigh's concern with sexual readiness will leave readers . . . doing a little self-analysis," predicted a *Kirkus Reviews* writer, referencing the mature subject matter that makes Thompson's story particularly appropriate for older teens who are "anticipating their time away from home."

Biographical and Critical Sources

PERIODICALS

Kirkus Reviews, July 1, 2009, review of *Psych Major Syndrome.*
Publishers Weekly, July 27, 2009, review of *Psych Major Syndrome,* p. 64.
St. Petersburg Times (St. Petersburg, FL), September 20, 2009, Colette Bancroft, "Young Writer Makes It Look Easy," p. L8.
School Library Journal, September, 2009, Maggie Knapp, review of *Psych Major Syndrome,* p. 174.

ONLINE

Alicia Thompson Web log, http://alicia-thompson.com/ (December 7, 2010).*

*   *   *

TILLOTSON, Katherine

Personal

Born in Minneapolis, MN; married. *Education:* University of Colorado, degree.

Addresses

Home—San Francisco, CA. *E-mail*—katherinetillotson@ att.net.

Career

Illustrator and designer.

Member

Society of Children's Book Writers and Illustrators.

Awards, Honors

Notable Children's Books designation, American Library Association, 1996, for *Songs of Papa's Island* by Barbara Kerley; Best Children's Books of the Year designation, Bank Street College of Education, and Honors designation, National Parenting Publications Awards, both 2009, both for *It's Picture Day Today!* by Megan McDonald.

Illustrator

Barbara Kerley, *Songs of Papa's Island,* Houghton Mifflin (Boston, MA), 1995.
Mary W. Olson, *Nice Try, Tooth Fairy,* Simon & Schuster Books for Young Readers (New York, NY), 2000.
Caroline Stutson, *Night Train,* Roaring Brook Press (Brookfield, CT), 2002.
Megan McDonald, *Penguin and Little Blue,* Atheneum Books for Young Readers (New York, NY), 2003.
Megan McDonald, *When the Library Lights Go Out,* Atheneum Books for Young Readers (New York, NY), 2005.
Megan McDonald, *It's Picture Day Today!,* Atheneum Books for Young Readers (New York, NY), 2009.
George Ella Lyon, *All the Water in the World,* Atheneum Books for Young Readers (New York, NY), 2011.

Sidelights

Katherine Tillotson's evocative and richly colored illustrations have graced the pages of such children's books as *Night Train* by Caroline Stutson and *When the Library Lights Go Out* by Megan McDonald. An artist and designer who is based in the San Francisco Bay area, Tillotson remarked on her home page that "picture books fill many of the bookcases in our house and have always held a special place in my heart."

A series of humorous mishaps propel the narrative of *Nice Try, Tooth Fairy,* a story by Mary W. Olson. When a little girl asks to show her first baby tooth to her grandfather, the Tooth Fairy, who has already collected the goods, attempts to oblige her. Unfortunately, the wingéd benefactor brings a hippo's tooth instead, the first of several unsuccessful attempts to help the amiable—and patient—youngster. "The perspective of [Tillotson's] jewel-toned oil paintings is slightly askew, giving them a sense of liveliness," Donna L. Scanlon observed in *School Library Journal.* In *Night Train,* a tale told in verse, Stutson depicts the experiences of a young boy and his father traveling through the night aboard a locomotive. Tillotson, wrote a contributor in *Kirkus Reviews,* "works with shades of blue, lavender, and gold to convey the gigantic size and power of the train," while a *Publishers Weekly* critic observed that the story's "spare tone acts as counterpoint to the glowing lighting and dramatic angles of Tillotson's full-bleed pastels."

Tillotson has enjoyed a particularly successful collaboration with McDonald. In their joint project *Penguin and Little Blue* a pair of stunt performers for a traveling

Katherine Tillotson captures the excitement of a special part of elementary school in her art for Megan McDonald's **It's Picture Day Today!** (Illustration copyright © 2009 by Katherine Tillotson. Reproduced by permission of Atheneum Books for Young Readers, an imprint of Simon & Schuster Macmillan.)

aquatic show miss their animal friends back at home in Antarctica. Spending night after night in hotel rooms, the duo attempts to recreate the comforts of home by filling hotel bathtubs with ice-cold water and ordering krill from room service. Their fortunes change, however, when Penguin spots a cruise ship headed to the South Pole. "In pictures rich in blues and purples, Tillotson depicts the portly performers as avian celebrities," a critic stated in *Kirkus Reviews,* and Catherine Threadgill maintained in *School Library Journal* that Tillotson's paintings "flesh out the comical aspects of the animals' predicament." Two story-time puppets embark on a nighttime journey to locate their missing friend in *When the Library Lights Go Out,* another story pairing McDonald's text with Tillotson's art. "Amiable and amusing full-page illustrations, done in oils on paper, capture a sense of being alone in a big space," Kathie Meizner wrote of this book in *School Library Journal.*

Tillotson alters her artistic methods for another work by McDonald, using cut-paper illustrations to enliven *It's Picture Day Today!,* a whimsical tale about a most unusual group of students. According to Mary Jean Smith in *School Library Journal,* Tillotson's "artwork is presented on brightly colored spreads, and the dynamic layouts are varied and filled with action." Daniel Kraus, writing in *Booklist,* predicted that the book's collages, "both creative and endearingly clunky, will awaken the inner cutter-and-paster in almost any young child."

Biographical and Critical Sources

PERIODICALS

Booklist, May 1, 2002, Gillian Engberg, review of *Night Train,* p. 1536; November 1, 2003, Lauren Peterson, review of *Penguin and Little Blue,* p. 502; November 1, 2005, Karen Hutt, review of *When the Library Lights Go Out,* p. 53; May 1, 2009, Daniel Kraus, review of *It's Picture Day Today!,* p. 86.

Kirkus Reviews, March 1, 2002, review of *Night Train,* p. 346; September 1, 2003, review of *Penguin and Little Blue,* p. 1128; October 1, 2005, review of *When the Library Lights Go Out,* p. 1084; June 15, 2009, review of *It's Picture Day Today!*

Horn Book, July-August, 2009, Susan Dove Lempke, review of *It's Picture Day Today!,* p. 411.

New York Times Book Review, October 23, 2005, Jan Benzel, review of *When the Library Lights Go Out,* p. 21.

Publishers Weekly, March 18, 2002, review of *Night Train,* p. 102; August 25, 2003, review of *Penguin and Little Blue,* p. 63.

School Library Journal, November, 2000, Donna L. Scanlon, review of *Nice Try, Tooth Fairy,* p. 129; May, 2002, Wanda Meyers-Hines, review of *Night Train,* p. 128; November, 2003, Catherine Threadgill, review of *Penguin and Little Blue,* p. 107; November, 2005, Kathie Meizner, review of *When the Library Lights Go Out,* p. 98; June, 2009, Mary Jean Smith, review of *It's Picture Day Today!,* p. 95.

ONLINE

Katherine Tillotson Home Page, http://www.katherine tillotson.com (January 1, 2011).

Seven Impossible Things before Breakfast Web log, http://blaine.org/sevenimpossiblethings/ (May 31, 2009), interview with Tillotson.

U-Z

UDOVIC, Jane Morris 1947-

Personal

Born 1947, in OH; married Terry Udovic (a scientist); children: Andrew. *Education:* George Washington University, B.S. (international affairs); Case Western Reserve University, J.D.

Addresses

Home—Washington, DC. *E-mail*—jmu@janemorris udovic.com.

Career

Attorney and author. Attorney in private practice for one year; attorney for U.S. government for twenty years.

Member

Society of Children's Book Writers and Illustrators, Writer's Center (Bethesda, MD).

Awards, Honors

Letter of Merit, Society of Children's Book Writers and Illustrators Magazine Merit Competition, 2009.

Writings

Aunt Matilda's Almost-Boring Party, illustrated by David Udovic, Front Street (Honesdale, PA), 2009.

Contributor of poetry to periodicals, including *Hop-scotch* and *Ladybug.*

Sidelights

"While I followed in my father's footsteps to become a lawyer, my passion for poetry goes back to my childhood," Jane Morris Udovic told *SATA.* "As a writer, I am grateful to both of my parents for the belief instilled in me that I can make any dreams come true."

Jane Morris Udovic (Reproduced by permission.)

Biographical and Critical Sources

PERIODICALS

Booklist, September 15, 2009, Abby Nolan, review of *Aunt Matilda's Almost-Boring Party,* p. 62.

Children's Bookwatch, October, 2009, review of *Aunt Matilda's Almost-Boring Party.*

Kirkus Reviews, August 15, 2009, review of *Aunt Matilda's Almost-Boring Party.*

School Library Journal, October, 2009, Rachel Kamin, review of *Aunt Matilda's Almost-Boring Party,* p. 106.

Washington Parent, October, 2009, Mary Quattlebaum, review of *Aunt Matilda's Almost-Boring Party.*

ONLINE

Jane Morris Udovic Home Page, http://www.janemorris udovic.com (December 7, 2010).

* * *

UMANSKY, Kaye 1946-

Personal

Born December 6, 1946, in Devon, England; father a music teacher; married; husband's name Mo (an engineer); children: Ella; (stepchildren) Dave, Dan, Zoë. *Education:* Attended teachers' training college. *Hobbies and other interests:* Travel, reading, music.

Addresses

Home—Crouch End, North London, England. *Agent*—Caroline Sheldon, Caroline Sheldon Literary Agency, 71 Hillgate Pl., London W8 7SS, England.

Career

Writer, actor, musician, and educator. Teacher of music and drama in London, England.

Awards, Honors

Nottinghamshire Book Award, 1993, for *Pongwiffy and the Spell of the Year; Times Educational Supplement* Junior Music Book Award, 1999, for *Three Rapping Rats.*

Writings

Bandybones, illustrated by Maggie Read, Macmillan Education (Basingstoke, England), 1986.

Little Sister, illustrated by David Dowland and Joyce Smith, Macmillan Education (Basingstoke, England), 1986.

The Toymaker's Birthday, illustrated by Ken Morton, Macmillan Educational (Basingstoke, England), 1986.

Big Iggy, illustrated by Katie Thomas, A. & C. Black (London, England), 1987, reprinted, 2004.

Litterbugs (play), Macmillan Educational (Basingstoke, England), 1987.

Phantasmagoria: Thirty-three Songs, Story Lines, and Sound Adventures (song book), music by Andy Jackson, A. & C. Black (London, England), 1988.

Witches in Stitches, illustrated by Judy Brown, Puffin (London, England), 1988.

The Fwog Pwince, illustrated by Gwyneth Williamson, A. & C. Black (London, England), 1989.

King Keith and the Nasty Case of Dragonitis, illustrated by Ainslie Macleod, Viking (London, England), 1990.

Tin Can Hero, illustrated by John Dyke, Hodder & Stoughton (London, England), 1990.

Tiger and Me, illustrated by Susie Jenkin-Pearce, Red Fox (London, England), 1991.

Trash Hits, illustrated by Judy Brown, Puffin (London, England), 1991.

King Keith and the Jolly Lodger, illustrated by Ainslie Macleod, Viking (London, England), 1991.

Sir Quinton Quest Hunts the Yeti, illustrated by Judy Brown, A. & C. Black (London, England), 1992.

The Misfortunes of Captain Cadaverous, illustrated by Judy Brown, BBC Books (London, England), 1992.

Pass the Jam, Jim, illustrated by Margaret Chamberlain, Red Fox (London, England), 1993.

Do Not Open before Christmas Day!, illustrated by Garry Davies, Puffin (London, England), 1993.

Sir Quinton Quest Hunts the Jewel, illustrated by Judy Brown, Young Lions (London, England), 1994.

Three Singing Pigs: Making Music with Traditional Stories, illustrated by Michael Evans, A. & C. Black (London, England), 1994.

(Author of text) Annabel Collis, *Dobbin,* Bodley Head (London, England), 1994.

Sophie and Abigail, illustrated by Anna Currey, Gollancz (London, England), 1995, Good Books (Intercourse, PA), 2004.

A Ruby, a Rug, and a Prince Called Doug, illustrated by Chris Fisher, Young Lions (London, England), 1995.

The Empty Suit of Armour, illustrated by Keren Ludlow, Orion (London, England), 1995.

Sophie in Charge, illustrated by Anna Currey, Gollancz (London, England), 1995, Good Books (Intercourse, PA), 2005.

Sophie and the Mother's Day Card, illustrated by Anna Currey, Gollancz (London, England), 1995, Good Books (Intercourse, PA), 2005.

Sophie and the Wonderful Picture, illustrated by Anna Currey, Gollancz (London, England), 1995, Good Books (Intercourse, PA), 2004.

The Night I Was Chased by a Vampire, illustrated by Keren Ludlow, Orion (London, England), 1995.

Cinderella (play), illustrated by Caroline Crossland, A. & C. Black (London, England), 1996.

The Jealous Giant, illustrated by Doffy Weir, Hamish Hamilton (London, England), 1997.

Noah's Ark (play), illustrated by Tessa Richardson-Jones, A. & C. Black (London, England), 1997.

The Emperor's New Clothes (play), illustrated by Caroline Crossland, A. & C. Black (London, England), 1997.

The Romantic Giant, illustrated by Doffy Weir, Puffin (London, England), 1997.

The Spooks Step Out, illustrated by Keren Ludlow, Orion (London, England), 1997.

The Bogey Men and the Trolls Next Door, illustrated by Keren Ludlow, Orion (London, England), 1997.

Beyond the Beanstalk, illustrated by Chris Fisher, Hodder Children's (London, England), 1997.

Hammy House of Horror, illustrated by Chris Fisher, Hodder Children's (London, England), 1998.

You Can Swim, Jim, illustrated by Margaret Chamberlain, Bodley Head (London, England), 1998.

Three Rapping Rats: Making Music with Traditional Stories, illustrated by Stephen Chadwick and Katie Buchanan, A. & C. Black (London, England), 1998.

Never Meddle with Magic Mirrors, illustrated by Stella Voce, Cambridge University Press (Cambridge, England), 1998.

Tickle My Nose, and Other Action Rhymes, illustrated by Nick Sharratt, Puffin (New York, NY), 1999.

Donkey Ride to Disaster, illustrated by Chris Fisher, Hodder Children's (London, England), 1999.

Madness in the Mountains, illustrated by Chris Fisher, Hodder Children's (London, England), 1999.

Nonsense Counting Rhymes, illustrated by Chris Fisher, Oxford University Press (Oxford, England), 1999.

Need a Trim, Jim, illustrated by Margaret Chamberlain, Bodley Head (London, England), 1999.

Moon Adventure, illustrated by Steve Smallman, Longman (Harlow, England), 2000.

Strange Days at Sea, illustrated by Chris Fisher, Hodder Children's (London, England), 2000.

Sleeping Beauty (play), illustrated by Caroline Crossland, A. & C. Black (London, England), 2000.

Three Tapping Teddies: Musical Stories and Chants for the Very Young, A. & C. Black (London, England), 2000.

The Rubbish Monster, illustrated by Ken Stott, Pearson Education (Harlow, England), 2000.

I Am Miss Cherry, illustrated by Steve Smallman, Pearson Education (Harlow, England), 2000.

The Carnival, illustrated by Steve Smallman, Pearson Education (Harlow, England), 2000.

Rope That Cow!, illustrated by Steve Smallman, Pearson Education (Harlow, England), 2000.

What a Mess! (play), illustrated by Tom Clayton and Steve Smallman, Pearson Education (Harlow, England), 2000.

Poor Sam (play), illustrated by Tom Clayton, Pearson Education (Harlow, England), 2000.

Pirates Ahoy!, illustrated by Steve Smallman, Pearson Education (Harlow, England), 2000.

Wilma's Wicked Revenge, illustrated by Tony Blundell, Puffin (London, England), 2000.

No More Master Niceguy, illustrated by Chris Fisher, Hodder Children's (London, England), 2000.

Beyond Strange Street, illustrated by Steve Smallman, Pearson Education (Harlow, England), 2001.

Soup with Obby, illustrated by Steve Smallman, Pearson Education (Harlow, England), 2001.

Down the Rushing River, illustrated by Steve Smallman, Pearson Education (Harlow, England), 2001.

Wizard Wagoo, illustrated by Steve Smallman, Pearson Education (Harlow, England), 2001.

Up the Dizzy Mountain, illustrated by Steve Smallman, Pearson Education (Harlow, England), 2001.

Gong!, illustrated by Steve Smallman, Pearson Education (Harlow, England), 2001.

Nonsense Animal Rhymes, illustrated by Chris Fisher, Oxford University Press (Oxford, England), 2001.

Big Iggy, A. & C. Black (London, England), 2001.

The Dressed-up Giant, illustrated by Doffy Weir, Penguin (London, England), 2001.

Three Days with Jim, illustrated by Judy Brown, Red Fox (London, England), 2001.

Prince Dandypants and the Masked Avenger, illustrated by Trevor Dunton, Puffin (London, England), 2001.

Cruel Times: A Victorian Play, illustrated by Martin Ursell, Hodder Wayland (London, England), 2002.

Goblinz!, illustrated by Andi Good, Puffin (London, England), 2002.

This Is Jane, Jim, illustrated by Margaret Chamberlain, Red Fox (London, England), 2002.

Wiggle My Toes, illustrated by Nick Sharratt, Puffin (London, England), 2002.

Wilma's Wicked Spell, illustrated by Tony Blundell, Penguin (London, England), 2002.

Humble Tom's Big Trip (play), illustrated by Chris Mould, Hodder Wayland (London, England), 2003.

Meet the Weirds, illustrated by Chris Mould, Barrington Stoke (Edinburgh, Scotland), 2003.

Buster's Big Surprise, illustrated by Leo Broadley, Scholastic (London, England), 2003.

The Big Mix up, Scholastic (London, England), 2003.

The Snow Queen (musical), A. & C. Black (London, England), 2003.

Mick McMenace, Ghost Detective, illustrated by Ian Cunliffe, Puffin (London, England), 2003.

The Romantic Giant, illustrated by Doffy Weir, Barn Owl Books (London, England), 2004.

The Jealous Giant, illustrated by Doffy Weir, Barn Owl Books (London, England), 2004.

The Night I Was Chased by a Vampire, and Other Stories, illustrated by Chris Mould, Orion (London, England), 2004.

A Chair for Baby Bear, illustrated by Chris Fisher, Barrons Educational (Hauppauge, NY), 2004.

The Time the Play Went Wrong, illustrated by Kelly Waldek, Pearson Education (Harlow, England), 2004.

My Very First Joke Book, Puffin (London, England), 2004.

The Silver Spoon of Solomon Snow, Puffin (London, England), 2004, Candlewick Press (Cambridge, MA), 2005.

Goblinz: Detectives, Inc., illustrated by Andi Good, Puffin (London, England), 2004.

Solomon Snow and the Stolen Jewel, Puffin (London, England), 2004, Candlewick Press (Cambridge, MA), 2006.

Weird Happenings, illustrated by Chris Mould, Barrington Stoke (London, England), 2004.

Horses' Holiday, illustrated by Ainslie Macleod, Collins (London, England), 2005.

I Want a Pet!, illustrated by Sarah Horne, Collins (London, England), 2005.

Goblinz and the Witch, illustrated by Andi Good, Puffin (London, England), 2005.

Wildly Weird, illustrated by Chris Mould, Barrington Stoke (Edinburgh, Scotland), 2006.

I Am a Tree, illustrated by Kate Sheppard, A. & C. Black (London, England), 2006.

I Don't Like Gloria!, illustrated by Margaret Chamberlain, Candlewick Press (Cambridge, MA), 2007.

I Live in a Mad House, illustrated by Kate Sheppard, A. & C. Black (London, England), 2007.

The Stepsisters' Story, illustrated by Mike Phillips, Barrington Stoke (Edinburgh, Scotland), 2007.

Let's Go to London!, illustrated by Adrienne Salgado, A. & C. Black (London, England), 2007.

Clover Twig and the Incredible Flying Cottage, illustrated by Johanna Wright, Bloomsbury (London, England), 2008, published as *Clover Twig and the Magical Cottage,* Roaring Brook Press (New York, NY), 2009.

Yo Ho Ho, a Pirating We'll Go, illustrated by Nick Sharratt, Puffin (London, England), 2008.

Contributor to books, including *Bingo Lingo: Supporting Language Development through Songs,* by Helen MacGregor, A. & C. Black (London, England), 1999.

Author's works have been translated into numerous languages, including Danish, German, Greek, Italian, Polish, Romanian, and Spanish.

"PONGWIFFY" SERIES; FOR CHILDREN

Pongwiffy: A Witch of Dirty Habits, illustrated by Chris Smedley, A. & C. Black (London, England), 1988, Pocket Books (New York, NY), 2001, illustrated by Nick Price, Bloomsbury (London, England), 2009.

Broomnapped, illustrated by Chris Smedley, A. & C. Black (London, England), 1991, published as *Pongwiffy and the Goblins' Revenge,* illustrated by Chris Smedley, Puffin (London, England), 1992, illustrated by Nick Price, Bloomsbury (London, England), 2009.

Pongwiffy and the Spell of the Year, illustrated by Chris Smedley, Viking (London, England), 1992, illustrated by Nick Price, Bloomsbury (London, England), 2009.

Pongwiffy and the Holiday of Doom, illustrated by David Roberts, Puffin (London, England), 1996, illustrated by Nick Price, Bloomsbury (London, England), 2009.

Pongwiffy and the Pantomime, illustrated by Chris Smedley, Puffin (London, England), 1997, illustrated by Nick Price, Bloomsbury (London, England), 2009.

The Spellovision Song Contest, illustrated by David Roberts, Puffin (London, England), 2003.

Pongwiffy: Back on Track, illustrated by Nick Price, Puffin (London, England), 2009.

Adaptations

The "Pongwiffy" books were adapted by Telemagination as television programs airing on British and Australian television, c. 2004. Many of Umansky's books were adapted as audiobooks by Chivers Children's Audio, including the "Pongwiffy" books, which are narrated by Prunella Scales. *I Live in a Mad House* was adapted as an audiobook, narrated by Tom Lawrence, Chivers Audio, 2009

Sidelights

A music teacher and actress, Kaye Umansky is also a popular author who has channeled her creativity and quirky humor into a long list of books for younger readers. Her creation of the unkempt witch Pongwiffy, who made her introduction to readers in 1988's *Pongwiffy: A Witch of Dirty Habits,* has made Umansky well known in her native United Kingdom as well as in Australia, while her other humor-filled works have gained

her a large following as far away as North America, where many have been published. "I have always been a daydreamer, right from when I was a child," Umansky told a interviewer for Bristol, England's *Western Daily Press.* "I've never been interested in writing for adults and I don't think I'd be any good at it. I write funny books for children because that's where my heart lies."

Born in Devon, England, in 1946, Umansky started her writing career in the mid-1980s, after she left teaching to stay home and raise her just-about-to-be-born daughter. "I always thought authors must be special people—not ordinary, like me," she explained on the Penguin UK Web site. "In fact, there is no magic to it. You just need to enjoy it and be prepared to work hard." Her advice to beginning writers includes keeping a paper and pencil handy to write down ideas, as well as her number-one suggestion: "Read, read and read again. It is by reading that you learn how to become a good writer."

Since her introduction, the witch called Pongwiffy has reappeared in several books by Umansky, and has proved so popular with British readers that the "Pongwiffy" books were adapted for television. In *Pongwiffy and the Spell of the Year* the witch is keen to enter a local Spell of the Year contest, and when she locates a highly touted recipe by spellmeister Granny Malodour, Pongwiffy assumes that the win will be hers. However a search for the necessary ingredients—the spell includes wild cat whiskers, quicksand, a vulture's feather, and the hair of a princess cut during a full moon to ensure maximum potency—proves problematic. *Pongwiffy and the Pantomime* finds the resilient sorceress penning a play for members of her local coven to perform. However, in typical Umansky fashion, things quickly degenerate into humorous chaos. In 2009 all six of the original "Pongwiffy" books were reprinted, and Umansky also added to the series with a seventh book, *Pongwiffy: Back on Track.*

As she does in the "Pongwiffy" books, Umansky enjoys creating stories that feature supernatural and ghostly elements, and she makes scary characters comical—and far less scary—in the process. In *Goblinz!,* for example, a lone goblin named Shy has aspirations of being part of a gaggle. Unfortunately, coming up with the six other members to make the seven goblins required for official gaggle status is hard when you do not have any friends. Once Shy decides to take action and find a way to attract members, Tuf, Wheels, and Oggy sign up for his group and thus form the core of the Goblinz.

Having assembled her cast of quirky ghouls, Umansky continues their story in *Goblinz: Detectives, Inc.,* which finds the gaggle all outfitted in super-spy gear and ready to go sleuthing, and *Goblinz and the Witch,* in which the gruesome gang hits a rough spot with a local witch when members attempt to take a new go-cart for a trial run down Gaspup Hill. Umansky balances such fantastic fictions with down-to-earth stories such as *The Carnival* and *Sophie and the Wonderful Picture,* the latter in which a frog and rabbit attempt to create an impressive work of art for presentation at their school. In a *School Arts* review, Ken Marantz predicted that beginning readers will get a "smiling boost" from *Sophie and the Wonderful Picture* and praised the "light-hearted illustrations" created for the book by Anna Currey.

Umansky turns to fantasy in the mock-Victorian melodrama *The Silver Spoon of Solomon Snow.* Solomon is the quintessential foundling: he was discovered abandoned on the doorstep of laundress Ma Stubbins while teething on the proverbial silver spoon. Raised in the rough-and-tumble Stubbins household, where Mr. Stubbins' drinking keeps life on an uneven keel, Solomon exhibits unusually good manners. When the boy turns ten, he goes in search of his actual parents, helped by loyal friends Prudence Pidy, Freddy the chimney sweep's son, a pet rabbit named Mr. Skippy, and Rosabella, a young prodigy who has escaped from a traveling circus. Readers reunite with the troupe in *Solomon Snow and the Stolen Jewel,* as Solomon and Prudence

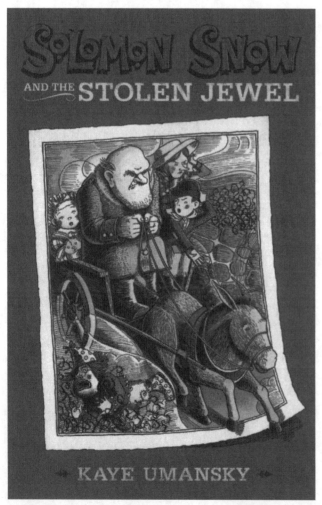

Cover of Kay Umansky's middle-grade mystery novel Solomon Snow and the Stolen Jewel, *featuring artwork by Scott Nash.* (Illustration copyright © by Scott Nash. Reproduced by permission of Candlewick Press, Somerville, MA.)

attempt to save Prudence's poacher father from being imprisoned on a convict ship. Divided into short chapters, Umansky's fast-moving plot thickens when the evil Dr. Casimir Calimari enters the picture, involving the travelers in his theft of a huge but cursed ruby. Reviewing *The Silver Spoon of Solomon Snow,* Ilene Cooper wrote in *Booklist* that the novel features "enough Dickensian moments and clever characters" to capture children's imaginations, and *School Library Journal* contributor Steven Engelfried cited the story's "quirky characters and funny moments." A *Kirkus Reviews* writer dubbed Umansky's "over-the-top parody of Oliver Twist-type adventures" as "a good giggle." In her *Booklist* review of *Solomon Snow and the Stolen Jewel* Kathleen Isaacs praised the sequel's "gently humorous third-person narrative" and "satisfying end." Commending both books as attractive to reluctant readers, Carly B. Wiskoff wrote of *Solomon Snow and the Stolen Jewel* that Umansky's "fast-paced read" trades "character development . . . for some Victorian-tinted atmosphere and humor."

A fanciful story illustrated by Johanna Wright, Umansky's *Clover Twig and the Magical Cottage* finds a hardworking eleven year old taking on work as a cottage-cleaner for kindly witch Mrs. Eckles. After the witch leaves home for several days, her evil sister, Mesmeranza, whisks the cottage away to Coldiron Castle, taking Clover, housecat Neville, and young neighbor Wilf along with it. From the castle's dark and dusty dungeon, the girl must now find a way to restore the flying cottage in an upper-elementary-grade fantasy that "moves quickly to an unanticipated resolution and a final, surprising authorial trick," according to *Booklist* contributor Kathleen Isaacs. In *School Library Journal* Amanda Raklovits described Clover as "a plucky and capable protagonist" and predicted that *Clover Twig and the Magical Cottage* will appeal to "fans of Roald Dahl or Eva Ibbotson," and in *Kirkus Reviews* a critic maintained that "Umansky's giggle-worthy characterizations and dialogue make this winsome read-aloud stand out from the pack." *Clover Twig and the Magical Cottage* was published in the United Kingdom as *Clover Twig and the Incredible Flying Cottage.*

Reviewing the picture book *A Chair for Baby Bear,* Umansky's sequel to the well-known story of Goldilocks and the three bears in which the young cub goes shopping for a new chair, *School Library Journal* critic Catherine Callegari described the author's "lighhearted" story as "just right for . . . one-on-one sharing." Youngsters left with questions at the close of the traditional tale will find that Umansky and illustrator Chris Fisher do "a nifty job of tying up the loose ends," according to a *Publishers Weekly* contributor. Umansky also shares her unique humor in *I Don't Like Gloria!,* a tale about a disgruntled bulldog whose family has adopted a fluffy Persian cat. Humorously brought to life in Margaret Chamberlain's cartoon art, *I Don't Like Gloria!* benefits from a "deadpan prose" that even "nascent readers may well be able to tackle," according to a *Publishers Weekly*

Umansky's entertaining picture book I Don't Like Gloria *features entertaining art by Margaret Chamberlain.* (Illustration copyright © 2007 by Margaret Chamberlain. Reproduced by permission of Candlewick Press, Somerville, MA.)

contributor. In *School Library Journal* Maryann H. Owen dubbed the same book "a humorous look at a familiar situation."

Biographical and Critical Sources

PERIODICALS

Booklist, November 1, 2005, Ilene Cooper, review of *The Silver Spoon of Solomon Snow,* p. 48; April 15, 2007, Kathleen Isaacs, review of *Solomon Snow and the Stolen Jewel,* p. 45; August 1, 2009, Kathleen Isaacs, review of *Clover Twig and the Magical Cottage,* p. 65.

Horn Book, January-February, 2006, Joanna Rudge Long, review of *The Silver Spoon of Solomon Snow,* p. 90; May-June, 2007, Joanna Rudge Long, review of *Solomon Snow and the Stolen Jewel,* p. 292; September-October, 2009, Sarah Ellis, review of *Clover Twig and the Magical Cottage,* p. 577.

Kirkus Reviews, March 15, 2005, review of *Sophie and the Mother's Day Card,* p. 360; October 1, 2005, review of *The Silver Spoon of Solomon Snow,* p. 1091; April 1, 2007, review of *Solomon Snow and the Stolen Jewel;* July 1, 2009, review of *Clover Twig and the Magical Cottage.*

Publishers Weekly, July 5, 1999, review of *Tickle My Nose, and Other Action Rhymes,* p. 73; November 15, 2004, review of *A Chair for Baby Bear,* p. 58; February 12, 2007, review of *I Don't Like Gloria!,* p. 84.

School Arts, October, 2004, Ken Marantz, review of *Sophie and the Wonderful Picture,* p. 66.

School Library Journal, August, 2002, Ronni Krasnow, review of *Sleeping Beauty,* p. 179; February, 2005, Catherine Callegari, review of *A Chair for Baby Bear,* p. 110; December, 2005, Steven Engelfried, review of *The Silver Spoon of Solomon Snow,* p. 156; May, 2007, Maryann H. Owen, review of *I Don't Like Gloria!,* p. 109; July, 2007, Carly B. Wiskoff, review of *Solomon Snow and the Stolen Jewel,* p. 86; September, 2009, Amanda Raklovits, review of *Clover Twig and the Magical Cottage,* p. 175.

Western Daily Press (Bristol, England), May 30, 2009, "Fun Is the Key to Kaye's Success."

ONLINE

Kaye Umansky Home Page, http://kayeumansky.com (December 27, 2010).

Puffin UK Web site, http://www.penguin.co.uk/ (March 26, 2008), "Kaye Umansky."

Story Street Web site, http://www.storystreet.co.uk/ (March 14, 2005), "Kaye Umansky."*

*   *   *

WHELAN, Gloria 1923-
(Gloria Ann Whelan)

Personal

Born November 23, 1923, in Detroit, MI; daughter of William Joseph (a contractor) and Hildegarde Rewoldt; married Joseph L. Whelan (a physician), June 12, 1948; children: Joseph William, Jennifer Nolan. *Education:* University of Michigan, B.S., 1945, M.S.W., 1948.

Addresses

Home—Grosse Pointe, MI. *Agent*—Liza Vogues, 866 United Nations Plaza, New York, NY 10017. *E-mail*—gloriawhelan@comcast.net.

Career

Writer. Minneapolis Family and Children's Service, Minneapolis, MN, social worker, 1948-49; Children's Center of Wayne County, Detroit, MI, supervisor of group services and day-care program, 1963-68; Spring Arbor College, Spring Arbor, MI, instructor in American literature, beginning 1979. Writer-in-residence, Interlochen Academy for the Arts; instructor in writing workshops.

Awards, Honors

Juvenile Book Merit Award (older), Friends of American Writers, 1979, for *A Clearing in the Forest;* Juvenile Fiction Award, Society of Midland Authors, 1994; Great Lakes Book Award, 1996, for *Once on This Island;* named Michigan Author of the Year, Michigan Library Association/Michigan Center for the Book,

Gloria Whelan (Reproduced by permission.)

1998; National Book Award, 2000, and New York Public Library Books for the Teen Age designation, 2001, both for *Homeless Bird;* National Parenting Publications Honor Book designation, Great Lakes Booksellers Award finalist, National Outdoor Book Award, and Midwest Independent Publishers Association Merit Award, all 2003, all for *Jams and Jellies by Holly and Nelly;* Jefferson Cup Honor Book designation, 2004, for *Friend on Freedom River;* Michigan Notable Book selection, Library of Michigan, 2007, for both *Summer of the War* and *Mackinac Bridge;* Amelia Bloomer listee, American Library Association, and *U.S.A. Book News* Honor designation, both 2007, both for *Yatandou;* Society of Illustrators Gold Medal, 2008, and Teachers' Choice selection, International Reading Association, 2009, for *Yuki and the One Thousand Carriers* illustrated by Yan Nascimbene; Best Books of the Year citation, Bank Street College of Education; Edgar Award nomination, Mystery Writers of America; four Pushcart Prize nominations; Creative Artist Award, Michigan Council for the Arts; citations for Texas Lone Star Reading List and International Reading Association (IRA) Children's Choice List; nominations for Dorothy Canfield Fisher Award, Georgia Children's Book Award, and Mark Twain Award.

Writings

FOR CHILDREN

A Clearing in the Forest, Putnam (New York, NY), 1978.

A Time to Keep Silent, Putnam (New York, NY), 1979, reprinted, 1993.

The Pathless Woods, illustrated by Walter Kessell, Lippincott (New York, NY), 1981, published as *The Pathless Woods: Ernest Hemingway's Sixteenth Summer in Northern Michigan,* illustrated by Glenn Wolff, Thunder Bay Press, 1999.

Silver, illustrated by Stephen Marchesi, Random House (New York, NY), 1988.

A Week of Raccoons, illustrated by Lynn Munsinger, Knopf (New York, NY), 1988.

The Secret Keeper, Knopf (New York, NY), 1990.

Hannah, illustrated by Leslie Bowman, Knopf (New York, NY), 1991.

Bringing the Farmhouse Home, illustrated by Jada Rowland, Simon & Schuster (New York, NY), 1992.

Goodbye, Vietnam, Knopf (New York, NY), 1992.

That Wild Berries Should Grow: The Diary of a Summer, Eerdmans (Grand Rapids, MI), 1994.

Once on This Island, HarperCollins (New York, NY), 1995.

The Indian School, illustrated by Gabriella Dellosso, HarperCollins (New York, NY), 1996.

The Miracle of Saint Nicholas (picture book), illustrated by Judith Brown, Ignatius (San Francisco, CA), 1997.

Forgive the River, Forgive the Sky, Eerdmans (Grand Rapids, MI), 1998.

Farewell to the Island (sequel to *Once on This Island*), HarperCollins (New York, NY), 1998.

Miranda's Last Stand, HarperCollins (New York, NY), 1999.

Homeless Bird, HarperCollins (New York, NY), 2000.

Welcome to Starvation Lake (chapter book), illustrated by Lynne Cravath, Golden (New York, NY), 2000.

Return to the Island (sequel to *Farewell to the Island*), HarperCollins (New York, NY), 2000.

Rich and Famous in Starvation Lake, illustrated by Lynne Cravath, Golden (New York, NY), 2001.

The Wanigan: A Life on the River, illustrated by Emily Martindale, Knopf (New York, NY), 2002.

Are There Bears in Starvation Lake?, illustrated by Lynne Cravath, Golden (New York, NY), 2002.

Fruitlands: Louisa May Alcott Made Perfect, HarperCollins (New York, NY), 2002.

A Haunted House in Starvation Lake, illustrated by Lynne Cravath, Random House (New York, NY), 2003.

Chu Ju's House, HarperCollins (New York, NY), 2004.

Listening for Lions, HarperCollins (New York, NY), 2005.

Summer of the War, HarperCollins (New York, NY), 2006.

Parade of Shadows, HarperCollins (New York, NY), 2007.

After the Train, HarperCollins (New York, NY), 2009.

The Locked Garden, HarperCollins (New York, NY), 2009.

See What I See, HarperTeen (New York, NY), 2011.

Small Acts of Amazing Courage, Simon & Schuster Books for Young Readers (New York, NY), 2011.

"ST. PETERSBURG" NOVEL SERIES

Angel on the Square, HarperCollins (New York, NY), 2001.
The Impossible Journey (sequel to *Angel on the Square*), HarperCollins (New York, NY), 2003.
Burying the Sun, HarperCollins (New York, NY), 2004.
The Turning, HarperCollins (New York, NY), 2006.

"ORIOLE" NOVEL SERIES

Next Spring an Oriole, illustrated by Pamela Johnson, Random House (New York, NY), 1987.
Night of the Full Moon, illustrated by Leslie Bowman, Knopf (New York, NY), 1993.
The Shadow of the Wolf, illustrated by Tony Meers, Random House (New York, NY), 1997.

"TALES OF YOUNG AMERICANS" SERIES

Friend on Freedom River, illustrated by Gijsbert van Frankenhuyzen, Sleeping Bear Press (Chelsea, MI), 2004.
Mackinac Bridge: The Five-Mile Poem, illustrated by Gijsbert van Frankenhuyzen, Sleeping Bear Press (Chelsea, MI), 2006.
The Listeners, illustrated by Mike Benny, Sleeping Bear Press (Chelsea, MI), 2009.

"TALES OF THE WORLD" SERIES

Yatandou, illustrated by Peter Sylvada, Sleeping Bear Press (Chelsea, MI), 2007.
The Disappeared, Dial Books (New York, NY), 2008.
Yuki and the One Thousand Carriers, illustrated by Yan Nascimbene, Sleeping Bear Press (Chelsea, MI), 2008.
Waiting for the Owl's Call, illustrated by Pascal Milelli, Sleeping Bear Press (Chelsea, MI), 2009.

PICTURE BOOKS

Jam and Jelly by Holly and Nellie, illustrated by Gijsbert van Frankenhuyzen, Sleeping Bear Press (Chelsea, MI), 2002.
(With Jennifer Nolan) *K Is for Kabuki: A Japan Alphabet,* illustrated by Oki S. Han, Sleeping Bear Press (Chelsea, MI), 2009.

OTHER

Playing with Shadows (short-story collection; for adults), University of Illinois Press (Champaign, IL), 1988.
The President's Mother (adult novel), Servant Publications, 1996.
The Ambassador's Wife (adult novel), Servant Publications, 1997.

Short fiction anthologized in *O. Henry Prize Stories.* Contributor of adult fiction to periodicals, including *Michigan Quarterly, Virginia Quarterly, Story Quar-* *terly, Missouri Review, Gettysburg Review, Detroit Monthly,* and *Ontario Review.* Contributor of poetry to periodicals, including *Ontario Review* and *Country Life.*

Adaptations
Many of Whelan's novels have been adapted as audiobooks.

Sidelights
A National Book Award-winning writer for young people, Gloria Whelan is the author of a number of novels featuring young characters who weather challenging periods in history while holding fast to traditional values and family. In her mid-fifties when her first novel, *A Clearing in the Forest,* was published, Whelan has made up for lost time by producing a steady stream of historical and contemporary fiction for children and teens since the mid-1970s. In addition to novels such as *Homeless Bird, Goodbye, Vietnam, The Turning,* and *After the Train,* she has also authored the

Whelan's humorous elementary-grade chapter book Welcome to Starvation Lake *comes to life in Lynne Cravath's lighthearted art.* (Illustration copyright © 2000 by Golden Books. Reproduced by permission of Golden Books, an imprint of Random House Children's Books, a division of Random House, Inc.)

award-winning picture book *Jams and Jellies by Holly and Nelly* as well as chapter books, short fiction, and poetry for adults. Reviewing Whelan's work in the *Chicago Tribune*, Liz Rosenberg dubbed her "an accomplished, graceful, and intelligent writer," while *Booklist* contributor Kay Weisman cited Whelan's "reputation for [creating] insightful prose."

Born an only child in Detroit, Michigan, in 1923, Whelan has been writing stories "as long as I can remember," as she told Kathleen T. Isaacs in a *School Library Journal* interview. As she noted in her speech to the National Book Award committee (as posted on the National Book Foundation Web site), books served as both friends and solace when things were difficult or frightening. One of Whelan's role models while growing up was Jo March from Louisa May Alcott's novel *Little Women,* and *Fruitlands: Louisa May Alcott Made Perfect* draws on that affection in its story about the writer's unusual childhood as the daughter of a nineteenth-century utopian and free spirit.

Whelan's love of books and writing continued through high school and her years as a student at the University of Michigan. While she focused on the novel form, she also dabbled in short stories and poetry, but life eventually put her writing ambitions on the back burner. Married to a physician and raising her two children, Whelan eventually worked as a social worker and a supervisor of group services at a day-care program in Detroit. Finally, in 1977 she and her husband decided to leave the city life behind and moved to a house near a small lake in northern Michigan. "Our family had been coming up here for years in the summertime," Whelan explained of the move to Isaacs, adding that she also visited the area during her own childhood due to her father's love of fishing.

The Whelans' idyllic rural retreat was soon disrupted, however, when the oil drilling company that owned their property's mineral rights announced their intent to drill for oil. Although the workers bulldozed three acres, erected a derrick, and began drilling, the Whelans were lucky: the well came in dry and the drilling was discontinued. The experience was upsetting, it jump-started Whelan's desire to write, however, and *A Clearing in the Forest* was the result. This young-adult novel, about a boy who works on an oil rig, was also her first book to be set in northern Michigan.

Whelan's second novel, *A Time to Keep Silent,* also takes a contemporary setting and focuses on thirteen-year-old Clair, who has reacted to her mother's death by refusing to speak to anyone. To make matters worse, Clair's widowed father, a minister in an affluent suburban community, now decides to uproot the family in order to build a mission church in a poor, rural area. After moving to their new home, Clair meets independent and adventurous Dorrie, a runaway who is trying to make it on her own while living in a ramshackle house in the woods. When Dorrie's abusive father comes look-

Cover of Whelan's middle-grade novel Forgive the River, Forgive the Sky, *featuring artwork by Gayle Brown.* (William B. Eerdmans, 1998. Reproduced by permission.)

ing for her after his release from prison, Clair must speak out in order to help her friend. Writing in *Kliatt*, Claire Rosser called *A Time to Keep Silent* "strong and life-affirming" and noted that "there is suspense amidst the story of emotional healing."

Whelan ventures further into the suspense genre with *The Secret Keeper.* This story is told from the perspective of Annie, a young teen who is hired to take care of ten-year-old Matt during a summer at the Beaches, a private Lake Michigan resort. Annie finds it odd that Matt's grandparents refuse to let him see his father, Bryce, and seem unwilling to discuss his mother's death. When Bryce kidnaps Matt, Annie discovers the terrible family secret that the entire resort community has conspired to conceal, thus putting herself in danger. In a *School Library Journal* review, Kathryn Havris commented of *The Secret Keeper* that "the element of lurking evil is there, making this a book that will hold readers' interest and provoke discussions on vigilante justice and just who is above the law." A reviewer for *Publishers Weekly* also cited *The Secret Keeper* as a novel of merit. "Containing many elements of a modern-day Gothic, Whelan's thoroughly satisfying novel is sure to produce shivers," the critic maintained.

The novels *Once on This Island, Farewell to the Island,* and *Return to the Island* comprise a trilogy focusing on a young woman living on Mackinac Island during the early 1800s. When readers meet Mary in *Once on This Island,* she is twelve years old and living on her family's small island farm between Lake Michigan and Lake Huron. The year is 1812, and when the invading British troops capture the island, Mary's widowed father leaves home to fight on the side of the Americans. Left behind, Mary and her two siblings must survive the vicissitudes of the next three years on their own. The local fort is taken by the British, Mary's sister Angelique flirts with a British lieutenant, and her brother Jacques must escape from British troops. Through it all, Mary worries that her father will never return from the war. In "Mary's narration, the everyday details of life in 1812 intertwine with larger events," wrote *Booklist* contributor Susan Dove Lempke, the critic also praising "Whelan's smooth writing, vivid characters, and strong sense of place" in *Once on This Island.*

Farewell to the Island finds Mary leaving her island home to visit Angelique, who is now married and living in London. Hotheaded Jacques is left behind with his new wife, Little Cloud, as is White Hawk, a Native American to whom Mary has grown close. Mary's father has given the farm to his son rather than to oldest child Mary, despite the fact that she worked so hard to keep it safe during the war. On the voyage to England, Mary meets a handsome young sailor who turns out to be the son of a duke, Lord Lindsay. England, proves to be a disappointment, however, for the plucky young American is a bit too outspoken for the locals. Although Lempke viewed *Farewell to the Island* as less historically grounded than *Once on This Island,* she predicted that "it will satisfy young readers with a taste for romance." Mary is back on her beloved farm in *Return to the Island,* working with Jacques and the gentle White Hawk when James, an English artist she met in England, arrives with his canvasses, intending to paint on the island and also to woo Mary. "Readers of the first two books will want this one," wrote *Booklist* critic GraceAnne A. DeCandido, while Carrie Lynn Cooper commented in *School Library Journal* that Whelan's "convincing third novel . . . deftly integrates history into" an engaging story.

As she does in her "Mackinac Island" trilogy, Whelan frequently spins a story around a fascinating historical incident or era, interweaving fact with fiction. In her middle-grade novel *Miranda's Last Stand,* for example, a girl learns what it means to be a Native American when her mother takes a job with William Cody's Wild West Show. Miranda, whose father was killed at Custer's Last Stand, has always been taught that Indians are bad, but when she comes into contact with a group of Lakota Sioux children firsthand—and even with Sitting Bull when the famed Lakota chief joins the show—she is forced to reassess her attitudes. Whelan's novel was described by *School Library Journal* contributor Carol A. Edwards as a compelling account of

"one young girl's gradual coming to terms with the loss of her father and understanding the plight of the Sioux." "Miranda's story, filled with characters from the American West, will fascinate middle readers," predicted Karen Hutt in *Booklist,* while a contributor for *Publishers Weekly* wrote that in *Miranda's Last Stand* Whelan "uses an accessible first-person narrative and polished, easy prose filled with behind-the-scenes detail."

Phelan returns to the islands of Michigan's upper peninsula in *Summer of the War,* which takes place in 1942, following the Japanese bombardment of Pearl Harbor. In the story, fourteen-year-old Belle and her siblings are on vacation at their grandparents' cottage on Turtle Island when they are joined by their Paris-born-and-bred cousin Caroline. The daughter of an overseas diplomat, Caroline has been sent to safety in the United States. Her spoiled nature and distain for rural life causes upheaval in the formerly placid family dynamic, especially when tragedy strikes. "While the family is deeply affected by Carrie, . . . the island's flora and fauna, its storms and calm, mitigate and soothe everyone's distress," wrote a *Publishers Weekly.* reviewer, while Engberg deemed *Summer of the War* "a moving story" about

Cover of Whelan's young-adult novel **Summer of the War,** *featuring artwork by Chris Sheban.* (Illustration copyright © 2006 by Chris Sheban. Used by permission of HarperCollins Children's Books, a division of HarperCollins Publishers.)

a young girl's coming of age. In *Kirkus Reviews,* a reviewer praised Whelan's novel as "an exceptional portrayal of how war becomes personal."

Returning to northern Michigan history in *The Indian School,* Whelan depicts, with "eloquent if predictable precision, . . . the tensions of early 19th-century Michigan," according to a writer for *Publishers Weekly.* When both her parents are killed in a wagon accident, eleven-year-old Lucy is sent north from Detroit to live with her aunt and uncle at a mission school for Indian children. While Lucy works hard to earn her keep, she also learns about Native-American culture from the students who have not yet been Americanized by her diligent Aunt Emma. One of the children, Raven, refuses to adapt to Western ways and runs away, leaving Lucy with a secret. Whelan is able to "transport the reader into a believable and complex past" despite a climax that is "frustrating in its patness," according to the *Publishers Weekly* reviewer, and Lauren Peterson wrote in *Booklist* that teachers "in search of fiction tie-ins to Native American units will welcome" *The Indian School.*

Cover of Whelan's evocative middle-grade novel The Locked Garden, *featuring artwork by Brett Helquist.* (Jacket art copyright © 2009 by Brett Helquist. Used by permission of HarperCollins Children's Books, a division of HarperCollins Publishers.)

Set at the turn of the twentieth century, *The Locked Garden* also takes place in Michigan as Verna and younger sister Carlie move with their widowed psychiatrist father to an asylum for the mentally ill. While their father deals with his troubled patients, the girls stay with Aunt Maude, a suspicious woman who tolerates little. The imaginative Verna refuses to be oppressed by her dismal surroundings, however, and her optimism is buoyed by her friendship with Maude's young maid Eleanor and her discovery of a locked garden on the hospital grounds. Reviewing *The Locked Garden* in *Booklist,* Gillian Engberg described the novel as both a "sensitive, sometimes comedic family story filled with character lessons" and a "compassionate" depiction of the care of the mentally ill circa 1900. A *Kirkus Reviews* writer remarked in particular upon Whelan's ability to "establish . . . a strong sense of time, unusual setting and characters" in her Michigan-based fiction. The novelist "adds authentic period flavor and crafts affecting moments" in her "straightforward and thoughtful story," observed a *Publishers Weekly* critic, and in *School Library Journal* Debra Banna dubbed *The Locked Garden* "a thoroughly enjoyable read."

Whelan was known primarily as a regional author early in her career because she set her stories in northern Michigan, where she grew up. Her 1992 novel *Goodbye, Vietnam* marked a change, however, and in the years since she has increasingly set her stories amid the historical epochs of other nations. In *Goodbye, Vietnam* thirteen-year-old Mai and her family are forced to leave their village after Mai's grandmother is accused of practicing folk medicine and following the old religion. The family endures a dangerous journey on a small, crowded boat to seek freedom in Hong Kong and eventually in the United States. Diane S. Marton noted in *School Library Journal* that Whelan "describes well the hardships many of America's newest refugees have endured," while Roger Sutton stated in a *Bulletin of the Center for Children's Books* review that *Goodbye, Vietnam* has "a rare simplicity and sharp focus." Reviewing the same title in *Horn Book,* Carolyn K. Jenks noted that "Mai's stark, straightforward narration" lets the reader make his or her own judgment regarding the plight of the Vietnamese boat people. Jenks also felt that, while the conclusion of the book "ties together a few too many loose ends to be completely realistic, . . . the people and the journey are compelling." "Mai is the perfect narrator through whom to introduce a large cast of unusual, sympathetic characters," commented a contributor for *Publishers Weekly,* the critic further observing that the teen's "emotional control and keen observations prove to be a source of calm in the storm that swirls around her."

Inspired by a newspaper article about an Indian city where widows as young as age thirteen are abandoned by their in-laws, Whelan's National Book Award-winning *Homeless Bird* also features an exotic setting. Koly is considered simply an extra mouth to feed in her parent's household and, as it is with many daughters in contemporary India plans are underway to marry her off as early as possible. However, Koly's arranged marriage with Hari does not go as planned; it is discovered that the groom is younger than promised, and also sickly. In fact, Koly is desired mainly for her dowry, which Hari's family uses in a vain attempt to procure medical treatment for the dying young man. Soon widowed, Koly finds herself penniless and homeless, abandoned by her in-laws as well as by her own family. Forced to survive on her own in the city, she does so partly through the intercession of a mysterious and handsome young man, but mainly through her own will and drive.

Alice Stern, reviewing *Homeless Bird* for *Voice of Youth Advocates,* called Whelan's novel "beautifully written" and containing all the elements of a great read: "a strong, empathic heroine, a fascinating culture, triumph over adversity . . . romance, and hope for the future." Other reviewers agreed, Shelle Rosenfeld writing in *Booklist* that the novel is a "beautifully told, inspiring story" that takes readers on "a fascinating journey through modern India." Rosenfeld also commended Whelan's "lyrical, poetic prose, interwoven with Hindi words and terms," and noted that the book's accompanying glossary is another sign of the prodigious amount of research Whelan did for the book. "Whelan has enhanced a simple but satisfying story with loving detail," noted Isaacs in her *School Library Journal* review of *Homeless Bird.* "Readers with a curiosity about other worlds and other ways will find Koly's story fascinating," the critic concluded.

Whelan turns her focus to Russia during the Communist revolution in *Angel on the Square,* the first novel in her "St. Petersburg" series. *Angel on the Square* opens in 1914, as the Russian aristocracy under Tsar Nicholas II is still in power and enjoying a lavish life despite the rumblings of World War I. Katya Ivanova, the twelve-year-old daughter of a Russian countess, lives in the palace at St. Petersburg, where she enjoys a lavish life and is friends with the four tsarinas. As Russia is pulled relentlessly into war with Germany, the country's vast poor begin to revolt. Katya now begins to understand the concerns of her political-minded friend Misha, and ultimately she is forced to confront an uncertain future in a world where all traditions are threatened in the face of a brutal communist regime.

The year is 1934 and Josef Stalin has taken the reigns of power in Russia when Whelan resumes Katya's story in *The Impossible Journey.* Now married to Misha and the mother of Marya and Georgi, Katya bravely speaks out against Stalin's decrees. Because she is considered an enemy of the Soviet government due to her aristocratic heritage, she and her husband are arrested by the Soviet police. With their father confined to a Stalinist gulag, or labor camp, thirteen-year-old Marya decides to locate her mother, who she has been told is living in exile in northern Siberia. Together with seven-year-old Georgi, the resilient young teen undertakes the

thousand-mile journey into the Russian wilderness, where the true danger may come when and if she locates Katya. While noting that the children's "lucky breaks may be hard to believe," *Horn Book* contributor Lauren Adams added that "the desperate plight of Russians under Stalin is only too real" and praised *The Impossible Journey* as "a bold adventure in exotic territory." Calling the novel an "evocative sequel" to *Angel in the Square,* a *Publishers Weekly* critic concluded that "Whelan once again brings to life the beauty, sadness and rich culture of Russia's past."

The family's saga continues in *Burying the Sun* as Georgi takes over the narrative. Now fifteen, the boy is living in Leningrad and poised to join the Soviet Army. The year is 1941, and German bombs are falling on the city while a blockade causes other hardships. Marya, with her love of art, is helping to relocate the treasures of the Hermitage to safety, while Katya nurses Russian soldiers at the front. The saga moves half a century into the future in *The Turning,* which finds Georgi's seventeen-year-old granddaughter, Tanya, dancing with the Kirov ballet as the USSR faces its final days. Despite her reserved tone, in *Burying the Sun* "Whelan creates a memorable, perhaps indelible, picture of a particular time and place," according to *Booklist* contributor Carolyn Phelan, the critic noting the continued references to the symphony written by Dimitri Shostakovich in honor of "his imperiled city." In *School Library Journal* Kristen Oravec commended *Burying the Sun* for its "haunting images and elegant prose," while *Kliatt* contributor Claire Rosser maintained that Katya, Marya, and Georgi "once again show . . . their ability to cope in impossible circumstances with grace and courage." Commending the young protagonist in *The Turning* for similar characteristics, *School Library Journal* critic Carol Shene wrote that "Tanya is an appealing, thoughtful heroine whose political awareness and integrity will encourage readers to" consider the events underlying their own decisions.

Life under communism as it was enacted during China's Cultural Revolution is the focus of *Chu Ju's House,* a novel that a *Kirkus Reviews* writer dubbed "well-done and convincing." Here Whelan introduces fourteen-year-old narrator Chu Ju as she faces a terrible choice. Due to the government's decree that no family can have more than two children and the prevailing social view that girl children are an economic detriment to a family, Chu Ju's pregnant mother prays that her next child will be a boy. When a daughter is born, Chu Ju's grandmother makes plans to sell the infant, thereby giving the parents another chance at a boy before the two-child quota is reached. Seeing her mother's sadness at this plan, the compassionate teen runs away from home. While her action allows her sister to remain part of the family, it also results in hardships as the wandering Chu Ju must perform difficult manual labor in order to stay alive. Writing that the author "skillfully shows the perspectives of both sides" of Mao's Cultural Revolution, a *Publishers Weekly* contributor added that the novel's protagonist "emerges as a heroine worthy of the rare and coveted rewards she ultimately receives."

Whelan spins what *Horn Book* contributor Robin Smith dubbed "a satisfying, old-fashioned tale" in *Listening for Lions.* Set in British East Africa in 1919, immediately following World War I, the novel finds thirteen-year-old Rachel Sheridan living among the Kikuyu tribe with her missionary family. After her parents perish in an influenza outbreak, the girl escapes life in a local orphanage but winds up in an even more unbearable situation: she is taken in by British neighbors and shipped to the home of their elderly relative in England in the hope that they can use the teen to gain control of the inheritance intended for their own recently deceased daughter. In addition to its intriguing and unusual heroine, *Listening for Lions* rewards readers with "rich details of the natural world on two continents" as well as "melodramatic twists and turns of plot," according to Smith. *Booklist* reviewer Gillian Engberg praised the young narrator's "straightforward, sympathetic voice," while in *Publishers Weekly* a critic explained that the homesick "Rachel's lack of choices and her sensitive nature make her complicity [in the unscrupulous scheme] wholly believable."

Set in West Germany during the years following World War II, *After the Train* introduces Peter Liebig. An eighth grader, Peter lives in a town where most vestiges of the war have been eliminated by chastened residents; only Peter's teacher brings up the horrors of the Nazi regime and its anti-Semitism. Peter is looking forward to a summer of soccer-playing and working with his father, but then he finds a letter that contains a life-changing family secret: one that causes him to look differently at the war, the Holocaust, and his family legacy. "The intensity of the issues" in *After the Train* combines with "personal conflict and historical facts, and the young teen's present-tense narrative will hold readers," according to *Booklist* critic Hazel Rochman, while in *School Library Journal* Rita Soltan wrote that "Whelan's well-developed story line and characterization" bring to life "a boy struggling to come to terms with his past."

Whelan transports readers to the Middle East in *Parade of Shadows,* which is set in 1907. Having grown up with tutors and in relative isolation, sixteen-year-old Julia Hamilton gains a sense of the world when she joins her diplomat father on a trip to the Middle East. Accompanied by an idealistic college student, father and daughter plan to stop in several historic cities. As they journey, Julia becomes aware of the political turmoil in that region, as a movement of young Turks are pushing to end the overarching government of the Ottoman Empire. She also learns to see the region the way many Mid-Easterners did in the era of colonization: as a land ripe for pillage of its art, its natural resources, and its land. In a story that mixes adventure, travel, and history, Whelan creates a heroine whose "experiences

Cover of Whelan's post-World War II-era novel After the Train, *featuring artwork by Richard Tuschman.* (Jacket art copyright © 2009 by Richard Tuschman. Used by permission of HarperCollins Children's Books, a division of HarperCollins Publishers.)

illuminate the region's convulsive history," in the opinion of *Booklist* critic Jennifer Mattson. "Once again" the author "whisks readers to another time and place to experience history in the making," wrote a *Publishers Weekly* critic, citing the thought-provoking nature of Whelan's "meticulously researched" story. A "satisfying read," according to *School Library Journal* contributor Kathleen Isaacs, *Parade of Shadows* is also "a romantic adventure in the best tradition by a master of such stories," while a *Kirkus Reviews* writer recommended the novel as a "fine work of historical fiction with a likable and strong-willed heroine."

Many of Whelan's books are geared for younger readers, among them *Next Spring an Oriole, Silver, Friend on Freedom River,* and her series of humorous chapter books following the antics of students at Starvation Lake Elementary School. Set in 1837, *Next Spring an Oriole* is narrated by ten-year-old Libby, who describes her family's difficult move from Virginia to Michigan on a wagon train. After Libby's parents help Fawn, a Potawatomi Indian girl, survive an outbreak of measles, Fawn's family returns the favor by providing food during a long winter. Betsy Hearne, reviewing Whelan's story in the *Bulletin of the Center for Children's Books,* described *Next Spring an Oriole* as "smoothly written and appealing," and a *Kirkus Reviews* writer remarked that it seems "historically authentic."

In a sequel, *Night of the Full Moon,* Libby is disappointed that her father cannot take her to visit Fawn's village and so she sneaks away by herself. While she is there, however, the U.S. Army arrives at the village to forcibly relocate the Potawatomi, and Libby is included in the forced march by mistake. Noting that "Whelan packs quite a story into this brief sequel," a *Publishers Weekly* critic added that *Night of the Full Moon,* told in "simple, well-chosen language," is as "captivating" as any of the "Little House" series, but "far more insightful and thought-provoking" with regard to historical events and the history of the tribes that once flourished in northern Michigan.

In *Silver* Whelan introduces nine-year-old Rachel, who lives in rural Alaska. Rachel's father, an avid dogsled racer, allows her to raise the runt of the litter produced by his best lead dog. Rescuing the pup from wolves, Rachel names it Silver and raises it to be a champion. A *Kirkus Reviews* contributor praised the story as "a charming, unassuming narrative that authentically conveys its setting." Likewise, *School Library Journal* reviewer Hayden E. Atwood called *Silver* "a lively, thoroughly credible story emphasizing the loneliness and excitement of Alaskan living for a young girl."

Part of Whelan's "Tales of Young Americans" series, *Friend on Freedom River* is set in the mid-1800s and introduces a young boy who must help his mother survive the long winter while her husband leaves the family to work in a Michigan logging camp. Louis gains a first-hand appreciation for the abolitionist battles coming to a head in the southern states when he comes upon a family of runaway slaves in need of help crossing the frozen Detroit River into Canada. In *School Library Journal,* Wanda Meyers-Hines praised the illustrations by Gijsbert van Frankenhuyzen, noting that they enhance Whelan's "compelling text," while a *Kirkus Reviews* contributor cited *Friend on Freedom River* for its "complex, believable characters."

Other books in Whelan's "Tales of Young Americans" series include *Mackinac Bridge: The Story of the Five-Mile Poem* and *The Listeners.* In the first book the author focuses on the building of the Mackinac Bridge in the late 1950s through a story about the son of a ferryboat captain whose livelihood is now threatened. *The Listeners* takes readers back almost a century in its story of Ella May, a young slave whose days are spent in the cotton fields and whose nights are spent eavesdripping outside the windows of the plantation house in the hopes of learning the fate of family and friends planned to be sold at the whim of the master. Praising *The Listeners* as a "powerful picture book," Hazel Rochman added in her *Booklist* review that Whelan's

"spare, lyrical narrative" pairs well with Mike Benny's "moving" paintings featuring their "dusk-toned" images of plantation life.

In the nostalgic *Bringing the Farmhouse Home* a family of five adult siblings and their children gathers to divide up the treasured belongings of a deceased grandmother. They share their memories of the grandmother and the farm, and then devise a fair method of allocating the contents of the farmhouse. In the end, seven-year-old Sarah's mother trades a beautiful platter for the quilt that Sarah hoped to keep. A *Kirkus Reviews* contributor claimed that people dividing up possessions "are faced with an experience that's in some ways like preschoolers' first bouts with sharing," and Whelan's successful conclusion provides a positive example for children. A writer for *Publishers Weekly* called the picture book "unusually atmospheric" as well as one that "celebrates the passage of traditions from one generation to the next."

Whelan's "Tales of the World" series includes *Yatandou, Waiting for the Owl's Call,* and *Yuki and the One Thousand Carriers,* each of which takes readers to a different part of the world. In *Yatandou* readers meet an eight-year-old girl who works grinding millet with the women of her Mali village. Although the work is arduous, the women work hard, hoping that their industriousness will earn them the funds needed to purchase a grinding machine and free their time from the lengthy task. Set in Afghanistan, *Waiting for the Owl's Call* finds three cousins following in the rug-weaving tradition of both their mother and grandmother. For eight-year-old Zulviya, the long days and pain of knotting the rough-spun wool are lightened by imagining the world around her in stylized pictures and patterns as intricate as those in her rugs. The girl's "sad, poignant story . . . portrays the stolen childhoods of youngsters involved in illegal child labor," observed *School Library Journal* contributor Mary N. Oluonye in a review of *Waiting for the Owl's Call,* and in *Booklist* Gillian Engberg wrote that Peter Sylvada's "sensitive" earth-toned paintings for *Yatandou* "skillfully mimic the . . . impressionistic, poetic style" of Whelan's text.

Another international-themed picture book, *Yuki and the One Thousand Carriers* reveals its story in haiku that are brought to life in Japanese-inspired art by award-winning illustrator Yan Nascimbene. Reflecting the thoughts of the young daughter of a seventeenth-century governor, the book captures the momentous journey of Yuki's family as they and their many attendants travel over 300 miles along the Tokaido road from Kyoto to Tokyo. Inspired by the woodcuts of noted printmaker Hiroshige, Nascimbene's "handsome, well-composed watercolor illustrations" pair well with Whelan's spare but evocative text, according to *School Library Journal* contributor Margaret A. Chang, and Rochman praised the "simple prose narrative" that captures a young girl's "longing" for home "and then her joy" at the end of her long journey. *Yuki and the One Thousand Carriers* inspires readers with the beauty of an exotic art form, according to a *Kirkus Reviews* writer, the critic describing the work as "an excellent introduction to the art of haiku and the world of old Japan."

A prolific writer, Whelan sums up her ambition in the Latin phrase "nulla dies sine linea"—"no day without a line." "The Greek Pythagoras could draw a perfect line," she explained during her interview with Isaacs, "but he said if he didn't draw it every day, he would lose the skill. So on my computer I have 'no day without a line,' and I really make myself write every day. It's what I like best to do, and it's what I do."

Biographical and Critical Sources

PERIODICALS

Booklist, October 15, 1992, review of *Goodbye, Vietnam,* p. 443; May 1, 1994, Carolyn Phelan, review of *That Wild Berries Should Grow: The Diary of a Summer,* p. 1602; October 1, 1995, Susan Dove Lempke, review of *Once on This Island,* p. 321; December 1, 1995, Susan Dove Lempke, review of *Farewell to the Island,* p. 667; October 15, 1996, Lauren Peterson, review of *The Indian School,* p. 425; November 1, 1999, Karen Hutt, review of *Miranda's Last Stand,* p. 531; March 1, 2000, Shelle Rosenfeld, review of *Homeless Bird,* p. 1243; January 1, 2001, Renee Olson, "Of Satin and Surprises: The 2000 National Book Awards," p. 874, and GraceAnne A. DeCandido, review of *Return to the Island,* p. 961; August, 2001, GraceAnne A. DeCandido, review of *Rich and Famous in Starvation Lake,* p. 2123; September 15, 2001, Gillian Engberg, review of *Angel on the Square,* p. 215; November 1, 2002, Kay Weisman, review of *Fruitlands: Louisa May Alcott Made Perfect,* p. 500; December 15, 2002, Kay Weisman, review of *The Impossible Journey,* p. 761; March 15, 2003, Carolyn Phelan, review of *Are There Bears in Starvation Lake?,* p. 1328; March 15, 2004, Gillian Engberg, review of *Chu Ju's House,* p. 1301; October 15, 2004, Carolyn Phelan, review of *Burying the Sun,* p. 405; May 15, 2005, Gillian Engberg, review of *Listening for Lions,* p. 1672; February 1, 2006, Carolyn Phelan, review of *The Turning,* p. 51; April 15, 2006, Gillian Engberg, review of *Summer of the War,* p. 57; October 1, 2007, Gillian Engberg, review of *Yatandou,* p. 61; November 15, 2007, Jennifer Mattson, review of *Parade of Shadows,* p. 38; April 15, 2008, Hazel Rochman, review of *The Disappeared,* p. 52; December 1, 2008, Hazel Rochman, review of *After the Train,* p. 41; April 15, 2009, Hazel Rochman, review of *Yuki and the One Thousand Carriers,* p. 50, and Gillian Engberg, review of *The Locked Garden,* p. 51; October 1, 2009, Hazel Rochman, review of *The Listeners,* p. 51.

Book Report, January-February, 1993, review of *Goodbye, Vietnam,* pp. 49-50.

Bulletin of the Center for Children's Books, October, 1987, Betsy Hearne, review of *Next Spring an Oriole,* p. 39; October, 1992, Roger Sutton, review of *Goodbye, Viet-*nam, p. 57; September, 2005, Timnah Card, review of *Listening for Lions,* p. 52; February, 2006, Deborah Stevenson, review of *The Turning,* p. 291; July-August, 2006, Cindy Welch, review of *Summer of the War,* p. 523.

Chicago Tribune, January 15, 1989, Liz Rosenberg, "Consistent Strength: Four New Volumes in the University of Illinois' Short Fiction Series," sec. 14, p. 3.

Horn Book, January-February, 1993, Carolyn K. Jenks, review of *Goodbye, Vietnam,* p. 87; September-October, 2002, Christine M. Heppermann, review of *Fruitlands,* p. 585; March-April, 2003, Lauren Adams, review of *The Impossible Journey,* p. 218; September-October, 2005, Robin Smith, review of *Listening for Lions,* p. 590.

Kirkus Reviews, November 1, 1987, review of *Next Spring an Oriole,* p. 1682; May 15, 1988, review of *Silver,* p. 768; July 1, 1992, review of *Bringing the Farmhouse Home,* p. 856; March 15, 2002, review of *The Wanigan: A Life on the River,* p. 429; November 15, 2002, reviews of *The Impossible Journey* and *Fruitlands,* both p. 1703; April 1, 2004, review of *Chu Ju's House,* p. 339; September 15, 2004, review of *Burying the Sun,* p. 923; February 1, 2005, review of *Friends on Freedom River,* p. 183; June 15, 2005, review of *Listening for Lions,* p. 692; February 1, 2006, review of *The Turning,* p. 138; June 1, 2006, review of *Summer of the War,* p. 583; September 15, 2007, review of *Parade of Shadows;* April 1, 2008, review of *Yuki and the One Thousand Carriers;* May 1, 2008, review of *The Disappeared;* January 1, 2009, review of *After the Train;* May 1, 2009, review of *The Locked Garden.*

Kliatt, November, 1993, Claire Rosser, review of *A Time to Keep Silent,* p. 12; July, 2002, Claire Rosser, review of *Return to the Island,* p. 25; March, 2003, Claire Rosser, review of *Angel on the Square,* p. 238; March, 2004, Claire Rosser, review of *Chu Ju's House,* p. 17; May, 2004, Claire Rosser, review of *The Impossible Journey,* p. 24; September, 2004, Claire Rosser, review of *Burying the Sun,* p. 17; July, 2005, Claire Rosser, review of *Listening for Lions,* p. 17; July, 2006, Claire Rosser, review of *Summer of the War,* p. 15.

Publishers Weekly, February 9, 1990, review of *The Secret Keeper,* p. 64; July 10, 1992, review of *Bringing the Farmhouse Home,* p. 247; July 27, 1992, review of *Goodbye, Vietnam,* p. 63; November 8, 1993, review of *Night of the Full Moon,* p. 77; September 23, 1996, review of *The Indian School,* p. 77; October 11, 1999, review of *Miranda's Last Stand,* p. 76; July 16, 2001, review of *Angel on the Square,* p. 182; December 2, 2002, review of *Fruitlands,* p. 52; December 16, 2002, review of *The Impossible Journey,* p. 68; December 15, 2003, review of *The Wanigan,* p. 76; March 1, 2004, review of *Chu Ju's House,* p. 70; August 22, 2005, review of *Listening for Lions,* p. 65; August 28, 2006, review of *Summer of the War,* p. 55; October 15, 2007, reviews of *Yatandou,* p. 60, and *Parade of Shadows,* p. 61; December 22, 2008, review of *After the Train,* p. 52; June 15, 2009, review of *The Locked Garden,* p. 49.

School Library Journal, October, 1988, Hayden E. Atwood, review of *Silver,* p. 129; December, 1988, Margaret Bush, review of *A Week of Raccoons,* p. 95; May, 1990, Kathryn Havris, review of *The Secret Keeper,* pp. 128-129; June, 1991, Margaret C. Howell, review of *Hannah,* p. 113; September, 1992, Diane S. Marton, review of *Goodbye, Vietnam,* p. 262; July, 1994, Sally Bates Goodroe, review of *That Wild Berries Should Grow,* pp. 104-105; November, 1999, Carol A. Edwards, review of *Miranda's Last Stand,* p. 166; February, 2000, Kathleen Isaacs, review of *Homeless Bird,* p. 127; December, 2000, Carrie Lynn Cooper, review of *Return to the Island,* p. 150; January, 2001, Rick Margolis, "The Bird Is the Word," p. 17; March, 2001, Kathleen T. Isaacs, "Flying High," pp. 52-56; October, 2001, Lisa Prolman, review of *Angel on the Square,* p. 175; November, 2001, Blair Christolon, review of *Rich and Famous in Starvation Lake,* p. 123; January, 2003, Susan Marie Pitard, review of *Jam and Jelly by Holly and Nellie,* p. 115, and Connie Tyrrell Burns, review of *The Impossible Journey,* p. 146; May, 2004, Barbara Scotto, review of *Chu Ju's House,* p. 159; November, 2004, Kristen Oravec, review of *Burying the Sun,* p. 156; June, 2005, Wanda Meyers-Hines, review of *Friend on Freedom River,* p. 131; August, 2005, Kathleen Isaacs, review of *Listening for Lions,* p. 138; February, 2006, Carol Schene, review of *The Turning,* p. 139; August, 2006, Rita Soltan, review of *Summer of the War,* p. 132; October, 2007, Kathleen Isaacs, review of *Parade of Shadows,* p. 166; July, 2008, Margaret A. Chang, review of *Yuki and the One Thousand Carriers,* p. 83, and Alison Follos, review of *The Disappeared,* p. 109; March, 2009, Rita Soltan, review of *After the Train,* p. 158; July, 2009, Debra Banna, review of *The Locked Garden,* p. 95; January, 2010, Mary N. Oluonye, review of *Waiting for the Owl's Call,* p. 91.

Voice of Youth Advocates, February, 2001, Alice Stern, review of *Homeless Bird,* pp. 428-429; April, 2001, Leslie Carter, review of *Return to the Island,* p. 47; October, 2004, Angela Carstensen, review of *Goodbye, Vietnam* and *Chu Ju's House,* p. 310; February, 2006, Elaine J. O'Quinn, review of *The Turning,* p. 494; February, 2007, Lucy Schall, review of *Summer of the War,* p. 536.

ONLINE

Gloria Whelan Home Page, http://www.gloriawhelan.com (December 27, 2010).

National Book Foundation Web site, http://www.nationalbook.org/ (May 25, 2007), transcript of Whelan's acceptance speech.

News Hour Online, http://www.pbs.org/newshour/ (November 23, 2000), transcript of interview with Whelan.*

*   *   *

WHELAN, Gloria Ann
See WHELAN, Gloria

WHINNEM, Reade Scott

Personal

Born in CT; married; wife a teacher. *Education:* M.F.A. *Hobbies and other interests:* Gardening, cooking, photography.

Addresses

Home—Cape Cod, MA. *E-mail*—rscottwhinnem@ comcast.net.

Career

Teacher and author.

Writings

Utten and Plumley, Hampton Roads (Charlottesville, VA), 2003.
The Pricker Boy, Random House (New York, NY), 2009.

Sidelights

A teacher and writer who is based in Cape Cod, Massachusetts, Reade Scott Whinnem has produced two very different novels for young readers. His time-travel fan-

Reade Scott Whinnem (Photograph by John Sykes. Reproduced by permission.)

Cover of Whinnem's middle-grade suspense novel The Pricker Boy, *which features artwork by Angus Hall.* (Illustration copyright © 2009 by August Hall. Reproduced by permission of Random House, an imprint of Random House Children's Books, a division of Random House, Inc.)

tasy novel *Utten and Plumley* finds a magical creature traveling back in time to change the life course of a boy who will otherwise grow up to be a cantankerous old man feared by everyone in his town, while *The Pricker Boy* is designed to send shivers up the spine of middle-grade readers. Reviewing Whinnem's debut in *School Library Journal,* Mara Alpert described the author's humorous prose for *Utten and Plumley* as "cozy and readable" and "brimming with imaginative detail," while in *Kliatt* Phyllis LaMontagne praised the book as a "highly imaginative" and "simply written" tale that "resonates with the importance of living one's life to the fullest."

Whinnem draws on the rich supernatural tradition of his native New England in his middle-grade novel *The Pricker Boy,* which a *Kirkus Reviews* writer described as "part horror, [and] part ghost story." Set during Stucks Cumberland's fourteenth summer, the novel revolves around the teen and his friends as they pass summer evenings telling stories around a crackling fire. When Ronnie recounts a well-known local legend about the violent and vengeful spirit of a boy who disappeared into a thicket of prickly hawthorn trees after being cruelly tricked by a group of local children, it in-

spires the teens to remember their childhood fear of the "Pricker Boy." Then a box is discovered that contains the offerings that they made as children, each one thrown into the woods in the hopes of keeping the fearsome Pricker Boy at bay. Their offerings seemingly rejected and their curiosity now piqued, Stucks, Ronnie, and their friends now decide to go further into the woods than ever before. In the event, their friendship and bravery are tested in a novel that "will carry many readers to consider their own nightmares . . . and have empathy for these characters dealing with their own bogeymen," according to *School Library Journal* contributor Joel Shoemaker. While noting that Whinnem's story would benefit from more fully developed characters, Michael Cart concluded that *The Pricker Boy* treats readers to "enough tantalizing imponderables . . . to hold young horror readers' attention."

Biographical and Critical Sources

PERIODICALS

Booklist, August 1, 2009, Michael Cart, review of *The Pricker Boy,* p. 61.
Bulletin of the Center for Children's Books, November, 2009, Kate McDowell, review of *The Pricker Boy,* p. 133.
Kirkus Reviews, September 15, 2009, review of *The Pricker Boy.*
Kliatt, November, 2003, Phyllis LaMontagne, review of *Utten and Plumley,* p. 26.
School Library Journal, August, 2003, Mara Alpert, review of *Utten and Plumley,* p. 169; December, 2009, Joel Shoemaker, review of *The Pricker Boy,* p. 136.

ONLINE

Reade Scott Whinnem Home Page, http://readescottwhin nem.com/ (December 7, 2010).

*   *   *

WILKS, Mike 1947-

Personal

Born 1947, in London, England. *Education:* Art college.

Addresses

Home—London, England. *Agent*—Kate Shaw, The Viney Agency, 8, Goodrich Rd., East Dulwich, London SE22 9EH, England. *E-mail*—feedback@mike-wilks. com.

Career

Artist, author, illustrator, and designer. TWD (design firm), London, England), founder and designer, 1970-75; freelance writer and illustrator. *Exhibitions:* Work exhibited in solo and group exhibitions in the United Kingdom, United States, and Europe; included in permanent collections, including at Museum of Modern Art, New York, NY, and Victoria & Albert Museum, London, England.

Writings

SELF-ILLUSTRATED

The Weather Works, Holt, Rinehart & Winston (New York, NY), 1983.
The Ultimate Alphabet, Henry Holt (New York, NY), 1986.
The Annotated Ultimate Alphabet, Henry Holt (New York, NY), 1988.
BBC Drawing Course, BBC Books (London, England), 1990, Parkwest (New York, NY), 1991.
The Ultimate Noah's Ark, Henry Holt (New York, NY), 1993.
Metamorphosis: The Ultimate Spot-the-Difference Book, Penguin Studio (New York, NY), 1997.

Author's works have been translated into several languages, including Japanese.

NOVELS

Mirrorscape, Egmont (London, England), 2007, Egmont USA (New York, NY), 2009.
Mirrorstorm, Egmont USA (New York, NY), 2010.

ILLUSTRATOR

Alan Sillitoe, *The Incredible Fencing Fleas,* Robson (London, England), 1978.
Brian W. Aldiss, *Pile: Petals from St. Klaed's Computer,* Holt, Rinehart & Winston (New York, NY), 1979.
Sarah Harrison, *In Granny's Garden,* Holt, Rinehart & Winston (New York, NY), 1980.
Lionel Davidson, *Under Plum Lake,* J. Cape (London, England), 1980.

Adaptations

Mirrorscape was adapted as an audiobook, read by Paul English, Brilliance Audio, 2009.

Sidelights

Mike Wilks is a British author, artist, and designer whose surreal and detailed paintings have been exhibited in galleries through out the world as well as in original picture books such as *The Ultimate Alphabet, The Weather Works,* and *The Ultimate Noah's Ark.* "I is for imaginative, ingenious and inventive," wrote a *Time* contributor in a laudatory review of *The Ultimate Alphabet.* On each of the book's twenty-six pages Wilks includes hundreds of objects that begin with the letter

in question; on the page for the letter T, for example, determined viewers can discover over 425 things. Expanding his creative vision from pictures to words, Wilks also draws readers into a visionary fantasy world in *Mirrorscape,* the first novel in his "Mirrorscape Trilogy."

Exhibiting a talent for art at a young age, Wilks won a scholarship to art school at age thirteen. In *Mirrorscape* he shares this early history with his fictional alter ego, twelve-year-old Melkin Womper, who lives in the parallel world of Nem. Mel's talent gets him apprenticed to master artist Ambrosius Blenk, a master of lushly colored paintings. In Nem color is rare and its use is overseen by the Fifth Mystery, one of five guilds that control the senses. As Mel and his friends Wren and Ludo learn the secret of Blenk's paintings and are able to pass into them and explore a bizarre and illogical world known as the Mirrorscape, the members of the Fifth Mystery are alerted and guild leader Adolfus Sprute marshals an army of evil to end Blenk's creative power. *Mirrorstorm,* the second book in the trilogy, follows Mel and his friends as they once again enter the Mirrorscape, this time forced by a new threat to Nem. The boy's fantastical adventures conclude in *Mirrorshade.*

Cover of Mike Wilks' middle-grade fantasy **Mirrorscape,** *featuring Wilks' own cover illustration.* (Egmont, 2009. Illustration copyright © 2005 by Mike Wilks. Reproduced by permission.)

Describing the first installment in the "Mirrorscape Trilogy" as "a no-holds-barred battle of the brushes" that features everything from buildings that can walk and talk to supernatural creatures, a *Publishers Weekly* critic recommended Wilks' debut novel as "a chaotic, whimsical romp that will appeal to the mind's eye." In *Booklist* Kimberly Garnick recommended *Mirrorscape* as an "innovative debut" that is "devoid of typical wizardry," and Melissa Moore wrote in *School Library Journal* that the story's "textures . . . all blend together to create a fascinating world of color and magic." "Positively riddled with captures, rescues and hair's-breadth escapes," *Mirrorscape* "makes a refreshing change of pace from . . . high-toned sword-and-sorcery epics," concluded a *Kirkus Reviews* writer. In the London *Guardian*, Philip Ardagh cited the influence of C.S. Lewis's "Narnia" books on the "Mirrorscape" fantasies. "The special thing that Wilks brings to his tale is the artist's eye," Ardagh added, noting that the author "play[s] . . . with everything from perspective to the different inspirations and styles of the artists whose works his characters inhabit."

Discussing his perspective on writing versus painting, Wilks told Anna Richardson in a *Bookseller* interview that writing is "not like a painting, where you go out and you only have to find one person who likes it for it to be successful. With a book, you have to find thousands who like it. But writing is such a joyous thing, to get up and to make your imagination come alive. It's wonderful."

Biographical and Critical Sources

PERIODICALS

Booklist, October 1, 2009, Kimberly Garnick, review of *Mirrorscape,* p. 37.
Bookseller, June 29, 2007, Anna Richardson, interview with Wilks, p. 26.
Guardian (London, England), November 17, 2007, Philip Ardagh, review of *Mirrorscape.*
Kirkus Reviews, September 15, 2009, review of *Mirrorscape.*
New York Times, December 4, 1986, Christopher Lehmann-Haupt, review of *The Ultimate Alphabet,* p. 25.
Publishers Weekly, October 19, 2009, review of *Mirrorscape,* p. 55.
School Library Journal, December, 2009, Melissa Moore, review of *Mirrorscape,* p. 136.
Time, December 15, 1986, review of *The Ultimate Alphabet,* p. 90.

ONLINE

Mike Wilks Home Page, http://www.mike-wilks.com (December 7, 2010).

OTHER

Mike Wilks: Making His Mark (television documentary), BBC-TV, 1990.*

* * *

WILLIAMS, Karen Lynn 1952-

Personal

Born March 22, 1952, in New Haven, CT; daughter of Russell Drake (an optometrist) and Lenora Mary (a homemaker) Howard; married Steven Cranston Williams (a physician), June 18, 1978; children: Peter, Christopher, Rachel, Jonathan. *Education:* University of Connecticut, B.S. (speech pathology), 1974; Southern Connecticut State University, M.S. (deaf education), 1977. *Hobbies and other interests:* Reading, quilting, hiking, biking, photography, painting, Navajo weaving, cross-country skiing.

Addresses

Home—Chinle, AZ. *Agent*—Lynn Bennett, Transatlantic Literary Agency, Inc., 2 Bloor St. E., Ste. 3500, Toronto, Ontario M4W 1A8, Canada. *E-mail*—karen@karenlynnwilliams.com.

Career

Educator and author. Teacher of the deaf in North Haven, CT, 1977-80; U.S. Peace Corps, Washington, DC, teacher of English in Malawi, 1980-83; writer in Haiti, 1991-93; instructor for Institute for Children's Literature, c. late 1990s, and for graduate programs in writing at Seaton Hill University and Chatham University. Presenter at schools and libraries. Volunteer for Pittsburgh Refugee Center.

Writings

PICTURE BOOKS

Galimoto, illustrated by Catherine Stock, Lothrop, Lee & Shepard (New York, NY), 1990.
When Africa Was Home, illustrated by Floyd Cooper, Orchard (New York, NY), 1991.
Tap-Tap, illustrated by Catherine Stock, Clarion (New York, NY), 1994.
Painted Dreams, illustrated by Catherine Stock, Lothrop, Lee & Shepard (New York, NY), 1998.
Circles of Hope, illustrated by Linda Saport, Eerdmans Books for Young Readers (Grand Rapids, MI), 2005.
(With Khandra Mohammed) *Four Feet, Two Sandals,* illustrated by Doug Chayka, Eerdmans Books for Young Readers (Grand Rapids, MI), 2007.
(With Khandra Mohammed) *My Name Is Sangoel,* illustrated by Catherine Stock, Eerdmans Books for Young Readers (Grand Rapids, MI), 2009.

A Beach Tail, illustrated by Floyd Cooper, Boyds Mills Press (Honesdale, PA), 2010.

Lubuto Means Light, Boyds Mills Press (Honesdale, PA), 2010.

Beatrice's Dream: A Story of Kuberia Slum, photographs by Wendy Stone, Boyds Mills Press (Honesdale, PA), 2011.

JUVENILE NOVELS

Baseball and Butterflies, illustrated by Linda Storm, Lothrop, Lee & Shepard (New York, NY), 1990.

First Grade King, illustrated by Lena Shiffman, Clarion (New York, NY), 1992.

Applebaum's Garage, Clarion (New York, NY), 1993.

A Real Christmas This Year, Clarion (New York, NY), 1995.

One Thing I'm Good At, Lothrop, Lee & Shepard (New York, NY), 1999.

Contributor of articles and stories to adult and children's magazines.

Sidelights

Karen Lynn Williams captures a variety of childhood experiences in her writing, much of which has been inspired by her travels. Williams taught deaf children in North Haven, Connecticut, for several years before working as a teacher of English in Malawi with the U.S. Peace Corps. She also spent a few years in Haiti, while her husband worked there as a physician. In addition to picture-book stories that are set as close to her home as the seaside or as far away as Africa or Haiti, she has also produced novels for young readers that are based on her own experiences as well as those of her children. Reviewing her picture book *A Beach Tail,* which features light-filled paintings by award-winning artist Floyd Cooper, Karen Cruze noted in *Booklist* that "Williams . . . always takes readers on a worthwhile journey," while a *Publishers Weekly* contributor wrote that her "even pacing and soothing text" in *A Beach Tail,* highlights the "resourcefulness" of her story's young hero.

Williams began her writing career with the picture book *Galimoto,* one of several stories she has set in Africa. Illustrated by Catherine Stock, *Galimoto* tells how seven-year-old Kondi creates a galimoto (a moving push toy) despite a lack of wire and his brother's warning that the project is too difficult. Determined to make the toy, Kondi seeks the materials to construct it for it in his Malawi village. His uncle, the village miller, and a little girl all give him wire, and Kondi constructs the galimoto. According to Patricia C. McKissack in the *New York Times Book Review,* Williams's text is "smooth and lyrical—a joy to read aloud," while *Booklist* critic Julie Corsaro called *Galimoto* an "enlightening" story with "universal appeal."

In *When Africa Was Home* Peter, a white child born to American parents is sad at the prospect of leaving Africa because he loves life in his village. After Peter moves to America he feels homesick for the cool shade and the warm rain of his African birthplace, but happiness returns when he goes back to the village for a visit. Throughout her text, Williams introduces words in Chichewa, a language used in Malawi. *When Africa Was Home* "evokes Africa as . . . a place of warmth, belonging, and freedom," wrote Susan Giffard in a *School Library Journal* review of the book. "Peter's viewpoint is refreshingly Afrocentric," commented Ruth Ann Smith in *Bulletin of the Center for Children's Books.*

Set in a middle-eastern refugee camp at the border between Pakistan and Afghanistan, Williams' picture book *Four Feet, Two Sandals* was inspired by Somali coauthor Khandra Mohammed's volunteer work in both Pakistan and the United States, where a young Afghani requested books that contained stories she could relate to. In the book, ten-year-old Lina lives at a Afghani refugee camp and has little that she can call her own. When she finds a sandal that fits her, Lina is happy. When she discovers the matching sandal on the foot of another Muslim girl, Faroza, she is initially possessive of her shoe's mate. However, the girls soon work out a plan to share the precious shoes, and by working together they also forge a close friendship. Captured in the simple, thick lines of Doug Chayka's large-format acrylic paintings, *Four Feet, Two Sandals* "uses simple words to tell the facts," according to *Booklist* critic Hazel Rochman, and a *Kirkus Reviews* writer lauded the book's lack of either "preaching or pontificating." In *School Library Journal* Margaret R. Tassia also praised Williams and Mohammed's picture book, writing that their "poignant story of loss, friendship, and sharing introduces readers to the realities of children growing up in refugee camps."

Also coauthored by Mohammed, *My Name Is Sangoel* focuses on a young Sudanese boy who, now living with his mother in the United States, feels even more displaced than he had as a homeless refugee in his native Africa. Determined to keep the name of his deceased father and grandfather, even though no one in his new school can pronounce it, Sangoel finds a creative way to teach others his name and also forge new friendships. Reviewing *My Name Is Sangoel* for *Booklist,* Rochman commented on the "bright watercolor" illustrations by Stock while praising the "strong child focus" in Mohammed and Williams' "moving" story. In *Publishers Weekly* a contributor cited the coauthors inclusion of an afterword to their "uplifting story" that "succinctly explains the plight of todays refugees," and a *Kirkus Reviews* writer praised the book's young hero as "such a picture of quiet dignity that readers will come away admiring his courage and self-possession."

In *Painted Dreams, Circles of Hope,* and *Tap-Tap* Williams introduces readers to life in Haiti. *Tap-Tap* features eight-year-old Sasifi, a girl who is just old enough to help her mother at the market. Although Sasifi would rather ride in a tap-tap, or truck, Sasifi and her mother

Karen Lynn Williams captures life in an African village in her picture book Galimoto, *featuring artwork by Catherine Stock.* (Illustration copyright © 1990 by Catherine Stock. Used by permission of HarperCollins Children's Books, a division of HarperCollins Publishers.)

carry their oranges to market. (The truck is called a tap-tap because riders tap the side of the truck to let the driver know they want to get off.) Sasifi earns enough money at the market to buy them a seat on the colorful, crowded tap-tap for the trip home.When her new hat flies away, Sasifi must tap-tap the side of the truck so she can disembark and retrieve it. In *Painted Dreams* eight-year-old Ti Marie joyfully expresses herself by creating art with whatever she can find at hand, while *Circles of Hope* focuses on Facile's effort to grow a mango tree large enough to bear fruit for his infant sister, Lucia. While hungry goats and heavy rains uproot the first two saplings the boy plants, he finds a way to protect the third and soon it is firmly rooted in the earth. Calling *Circles of Hope* a "hopeful, gentle" story that embodies Haiti's struggle against dire poverty, a *Publishers Weekly* contributor added that Williams' "uplifting tale suggests that one child can make a difference—a powerful message for readers." In *Booklist* Carolyn Phelan praised Stock's expressive watercolor illustrations as "full of life" and Williams' story for its "distinctive and well-defined locale."

Baseball and Butterflies, the author's first novel, introduces Daniel. Daniel is not looking forward to baseball season; even his younger brother Joey is better at it than he is. Daniel really wants to spend the summer tending to his butterfly collection. "Williams provides enough information about Daniel's favorite insect to help us understand . . . his fascination," wrote Ruth Ann Smith in *Bulletin of the Center for Children's Books*. Pamela K. Bomboy remarked that the book would be useful for instructors in "discussions intended to develop a conservation ethic" in *School Library Journal. First Grade King,* a chapter book, features Joey, Daniel's little brother. Readers follow Joey as he makes his way through the first grade, learning to read and also learning to deal with a bully. A *Publishers Weekly* critic found the book "reminiscent of the classic Ramona series" by Beverly Cleary

Applebaum's Garage, a novel for older children, is about a boy whose best friend becomes interested in a new group of playmates. Jeremy responds by visiting the handyman who lives next door. Mr. Applebaum is elderly, and his garage and yard are full of things that fascinate Jeremy. He works next to Mr. Applebaum creating things, and he even builds a fort on Mr. Applebaum's property. However, when a girl breaks her arm in the fort, her father demands a clean-up. Mr. Applebaum grows depressed, and Jeremy feels guilty. Meanwhile, Jeremy's friend Randy is in trouble for his delinquent activities. Jeremy finds a way to make things right, and, as a *Kirkus Reviews* critic noted, Jeremy and Mr. Applebaum "demonstrate that a good friendship is based on loyalty and respect."

In *A Real Christmas This Year* Williams introduces a female protagonist with a disabled brother. Twelve-year-old Megan is adjusting to seventh grade and new friends when Kevin destroys his glasses and hearing aid. Without them, the boy acts out in a destructive fashion. To budget the money needed to replace the expensive equipment, the family decides to do without a Christmas tree. Megan does what she can to help the family, from trying to earn money to making creative, meaningful gifts. According to *Bulletin of the Center for Children's Books* critic Deborah Stevenson, *A Real Christmas This Year* treats readers to "a cozy Christmas finale that the characters have earned and readers will appreciate," while in *Booklist* Leone McDermott predicted that "young readers will be pulling for Megan to succeed."

One Thing I'm Good At was inspired by Williams' own daughter, who was hampered during her childhood by her difficulty in learning to read. In the novel, Julie Dorinsky feels that nothing is working out for her now that she has reached fourth grade. While her best friend Abby has the good grades needed to win acceptance by the popular students, Julie struggles with reading and dreads each spelling test. With all the stresses at home now that her father has become disabled and her mom has had to go back to work, the girl worries that her dismal report card will only make things worse. Older sister Alexia uses Julie's reading problems as the subject of continued sarcasm, especially when praising little brother Bean's mastery of letter sounds. Fortunately, Julie has her own success on the playground,

Williams teams up with artist Catherine Stock to create the picture book **My Name Is Sangoel.** (Eerdmans Books for Young Readers, 2009. Illustration copyright © 2009 by Catherine Stock. Reproduced by permission.)

Cover of Williams' holiday-themed story **A Real Christmas This Year,** *featuring artwork by Gail Owens.* (Illustration copyright © 1995 by Gail Owens. All rights reserved. Reproduced by permission of Clarion Books, an imprint of Houghton Mifflin Harcourt Publishing Company.)

where she is tops at shooting marbles. She also discovers another, even more important skill when her father has a heart attack and receives the medical care he needs because of Julie's success in teaching Bean to dial 9-1-1. In her *Booklist* review of *One Thing I'm Good At,* Shelly Townsend-Hudson praised Williams' "thoughtful, sensitive" elementary-grade novel and added that the story's "terrific conclusion resonates [with] hope." Although a *Publishers Weekly* contributor wondered whether Julie's "ineptitude is overblown," she nonetheless enjoyed the novel, writing that *One Thing I'm Good At* "delivers an encouraging message" to readers "short on confidence and self-esteem."

Biographical and Critical Sources

PERIODICALS

Booklist, March 15, 1990, Julie Corsaro, review of *Galimoto,* pp. 1460-1462; April 15, 1994, Julie Corsaro, review of *Tap-Tap,* p. 1541.

Bulletin of the Center for Children's Books, October, 1990, Ruth Ann Smith, review of *Baseball and Butterflies,*

p. 49; February, 1991, Ruth Ann Smith, review of *When Africa Was Home,* pp. 155-156; September 15, 1996, Donna Miller, review of *Tap-Tap,* p. 263; September 15, 1998, Carolyn Phelan, review of *Painted Dreams,* p. 242; October 15, 1999, Shelley Townsend-Hudson, review of *One Thing I'm Good At,* p. 447; May 15, 2005, Hazel Rochman, review of *Circles of Hope,* p. 1667; September 15, 2007, Hazel Rochman, review of *Four Feet, Two Sandals,* p. 72; August 1, 2009, Hazel Rochman, review of *My Name Is Sangoe,* p. 80; April 15, 2010, Karen Cruze, review of *A Beach Tail,* p. 49.

Horn Book, November-December, 1995, Elizabeth S. Watson, review of *A Real Christmas This Year,* p. 731.

Kirkus Reviews, October 15, 1993, review of *Applebaum's Garage,* p. 1340; January 15, 2005, review of *Circles of Hope,* p. 127; August 1, 2007, review of *Four Feet, Two Sandals*; June 15, 2009, review of *My Name Is Sangoel.*

New York Times Book Review, May 20, 1990, Patricia C. McKissack, review of *Galimoto,* p. 42.

Publishers Weekly, March 2, 1992, review of *First Grade King,* p. 66; August 3, 1998, review of *Painted Dreams,* p. 85; December 13, 1999, review of *One Thing I'm Good At,* p. 82; February 28, 2005, review of *Circles of Hope,* p. 66; October 29, 2007, review of *Four Feet, Two Sandals,* p. 55; June 29, 2009, review of *My Name Is Sangoel,* p. 128; January 11, 2010, review of *A Beach Tail,* p. 46.

School Library Journal, December, 1990, Pamela K. Bomboy, review of *Baseball and Butterflies,* pp. 90-91; April, 1991, Susan Giffard, review of *When Africa Was Home,* p. 106; November, 1995, Deborah Stevenson, review of *A Real Christmas This Year,* p. 110; April, 2005, Linda L. Walkins, review of *Circles of Hope,* p. 116; October, 2007, Margaret R. Tassia, review of *Four Feet, Two Sandals,* p. 130; August, 2009, Kathleen Isaacs, review of *My Name Is Sangoel,* p. 87; March, 2010, Anne Beier, review of *A Beach Tail,* p. 136.

ONLINE

Eerdmans Web site, http://www.eerdmans.com/ (December, 2007), interview with Williams and Khandra Mohammed.

Karen Lynn Williams Home Page, http://www.karen lynnwilliams.com (December 15, 2010).

Karen Lynn Williams Web log, http://karenlynnwilliams. blogspot.com (December 15, 2010).

*   *   *

WILSON, Anne 1974-

Personal

Born 1974; married; children: Ella. *Education:* Bath College, B.A., 1996; Central Saint Martins College of Art & Design, M.A. (with distinction). *Hobbies and other interests:* Going to the gym, visiting friends.

Addresses

Home—England. *Agent*—Illustration Ltd., 23 Ohio St., Maplewood NJ 07040; howdy@illustrationweb.com.

Career

Artist and illustrator.

Writings

SELF-ILLUSTRATED

Noah's Ark, Chronicle Books (San Francisco, CA), 2002.

ILLUSTRATOR

Lois Rock, *I Wish Tonight,* Lion (Oxford, England), 1999, Good Books (Intercourse, PA), 2000.

Margaret Bateson Hill, *Masha and the Firebird,* Zero to Ten (Slough, England), 1999.

Michael Morpurgo, *Snakes and Ladders,* Crabtree Publishing (New York, NY), 2000, published in *Three for Tea: Tasty Tales for You and Me,* Egmont (London, England), 2006.

Bernard Ashley, *Growing Good,* Bloomsbury (London, England), 2000.

Linda Schlafer, *A Gift for the Christ Child: A Christmas Folktale,* Loyola Press (Chicago, IL), 2000.

Rhonda Growler Greene, *The Beautiful World That God Made,* Eerdmans Books for Young Readers (Grand Rapids, MI), 2002.

The Lord Is My Shepherd, Eerdmans Books for Young Readers (Grand Rapids, MI), 2003.

Edward Lear, *The Owl and the Pussycat,* new edition, Chronicle Books (San Francisco, CA), 2003.

Lyra Edmonds, *An African Princess,* Candlewick Press (Cambridge, MA), 2004.

Stella Blackstone, *Storytime: First Tales for Sharing,* Barefoot Books (Cambridge, MA), 2005.

Elizabeth Swados, *The Animal Rescue Store,* Arthur A. Levine Books (New York, NY), 2005.

Dawn Casey, *The Great Race: The Story of the Chinese Zodiac,* Barefoot Books (Cambridge, MA), 2006.

Laurie Krebs, *We're Sailing down the Nile: A Journey through Egypt,* Barefoot Books (Cambridge, MA), 2007.

Sophie Piper, *Prayers for Each and Every Day,* Lion (Oxford, England), 2008.

Dawn Casey, reteller, *The Barefoot Book of Earth Tales,* Barefoot Books (Bath, England), 2008, Barefoot Books (Cambridge, MA), 2009.

Laurie Krebs, *We're Roaming in the Rainforest: An Amazon Adventure,* Barefoot Books (Cambridge, MA), 2010.

Sidelights

British illustrator Anne Wilson has earned recognition for the brightly colored mixed-media images she creates for the pages of such children's books as *The Beau-*

tiful World That God Made, The Animal Rescue Store, and *We're Sailing down the Nile: A Journey through Egypt.* In addition to her works for other authors, Wilson has produced the self-illustrated *Noah's Ark,* an original retelling in which she uses "flat perspective, simple patterns, and vibrant colors" to introduce readers to the Biblical tale, as Kathy Piehl noted in *School Library Journal.*

Wilson made her literary debut in 1999 with *I Wish Tonight,* a bedtime story written by Lois Rock. According to *School Library Journal* critic Meghan R. Malone, Wilson's illustrations "display bold, brilliant colors and create a sense of movement." *Masha and the Firebird,* an original fairy tale by Margaret Bateson Hill, concerns a young Russian girl who comes to the aid of a magical creature when a witch steals its egg. "Wilson's illustrations are wildly imaginative and richly hued," stated Gillian Engberg in her *Booklist* review of this book.

Wilson has provided the artwork for a number of texts with religious themes. In *The Beautiful World That God Made,* for example, Rhonda Growler Greene offers her version of the Creation story, augmented by Wilson's "bold, streamlined compositions," as a *Publishers Weekly* contributor observed. Patricia Pearl, writing in

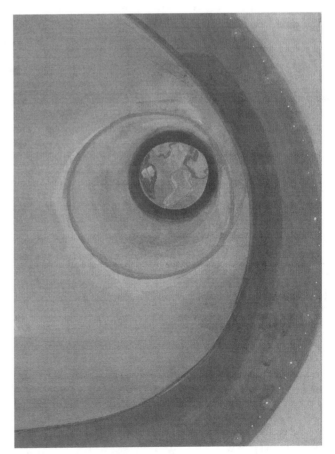

Anne Wilson's illustration projects include creating artwork for Rhonda Gowler Greene's The Beautiful World That God Made. (Eerdmans Books for Young Readers, 2002. Illustration copyright © 2002 by Anne Wilson. All rights reserved. Reproduced by permission.)

School Library Journal, also complimented the pictures in *The Beautiful World That God Made,* stating that the artist's "swirling, whirling patterns of form, color, and intricate detailing are arresting and sophisticated." *The Lord Is My Shepherd,* a visual presentation of the Twenty-third Psalm, features Wilson's "sophisticated printmaking techniques," as a contributor reported in *Publishers Weekly.*

Wilson presents a contemporary take on a classic poem in *The Owl and the Pussycat* by Edward Lear. The artist's blend of colors and patterns "creates a feeling of dreamlike spontaneity," Carolyn Phelan remarked in *Booklist.* A *Publishers Weekly* reviewer complimented the intricacy of Wilson's art for Lear's classic poem, stating that, "however elaborate the components, the illustrations are remarkably harmonious, unified by subtly geometric motifs." In *The Animal Rescue Store,* a collection of verse written by Elizabeth Swados, a young narrator humorously describes the inhabitants of a pet store for abandoned creatures. A critic in *Publishers Weekly* noted that the artist's "equally whimsical illustrations playfully portray the human and animal characters with an energetic mix of pencil outlines, swirling brushstrokes and collage elements."

Dawn Casey recounts an ancient legend in *The Great Race: The Story of the Chinese Zodiac,* a story that centers on a magnificent contest hosted by the Jade Emperor. "The book is a visual treat," Grace Oliff noted

Wilson's art is a feature of Dawn Casey's nature-themed anthology The Barefoot Book of Earth Tales. (Barefoot Books, 2009. Illustration copyright © 2009 by Anne Wilson. Reproduced by permission.)

in *Booklist,* and a contributor in *Publishers Weekly* asserted that Wilson's "creatively stylized folk art gives this retelling of an ancient legend a distinctive look." Myths and folk tales from Nigeria, Australia, and other nations are at the heart of Casey's *The Barefoot Book of Earth Tales,* another of the artist's illustration projects. C.J. Connor, writing in *School Library Journal,* noted that Wilson's "illustrations and colorful decorative borders reflect the spirit and origins of each offering."

Wilson has collaborated with Laurie Krebs on a pair of travelogues for young readers: *We're Sailing down the Nile* and *We're Roaming in the Rainforest: An Amazon Adventure.* In the former title, six children visit the wonders of Egypt, including the Valley of the Kings, and the spectacular sights "come alive in the printed collaged papers on painted backgrounds," acccordiing to *School Library Journal* critic Julie Ranelli. In the latter, a young trio explores the flora and fauna found along the banks of the great South American river. *Booklist* reviewer Patricia Austin maintained that Wilson's artwork for *We're Sailing down the Nile* "reflects the richness and diversity of the Amazon, teeming with life."

Biographical and Critical Sources

PERIODICALS

Booklist, January 1, 2001, Gillian Engberg, review of *Masha and the Firebird,* p. 963; February 1, 2002, Shelley Townsend-Hudson, review of *The Beautiful World That God Made,* p. 946; October 1, 2002, Shelley Townsend-Hudson, review of *Noah's Ark,* p. 346; February 1, 2003, Ilene Cooper, review of *The Lord Is My Shepherd,* p. 998; May 15, 2003, Carolyn Phelan, review of *The Owl and the Pussycat,* p. 1668; August, 2004, Hazel Rochman, review of *An African Princess,* p. 1941; April 1, 2005, Gillian Engberg, review of *The Animal Rescue Store,* p. 1368; January 1, 2006, Julie Cummins, review of *Storytime: First Tales for Sharing,* p. 103; May 1, 2010, Patricia Austin, review of *We're Roaming in the Rainforest: An Amazon Adventure,* p. 92.

Kirkus Reviews, February 1, 2003, review of *The Lord Is My Shepherd,* p. 243; March 15, 2003, review of *The Owl and the Pussycat,* p. 471; August 1, 2004, review of *An African Princess,* p. 740; March 1, 2005, review of *The Animal Rescue Store,* p. 296.

New York Times Book Review, November 14, 2004, Linda Villarosa, review of *An African Princess,* p. 44.

Publishers Weekly, April 1, 2002, review of *The Beautiful World That God Made,* p. 79; March 10, 2003, review of *The Owl and the Pussycat,* p. 70; March 31, 2003, review of *The Lord Is My Shepherd,* p. 63; April 4, 2005, review of *The Animal Rescue Store,* p. 58; September 4, 2006, review of *The Great Race: The Story of the Chinese Zodiac,* p. 66; January 29, 2007, review of *We're Sailing down the Nile: A Journey through Egypt,* p. 71; March 16, 2009, review of *The Barefoot Book of Earth Tales,* p. 63.

School Library Journal, December, 2000, Meghan R. Malone, review of *I Wish Tonight,* p. 124; September, 2002, Patricia Pearl, review of *The Beautiful World That God Made,* p. 212; October, 2002, Kathy Piehl, review of *Noah's Ark,* p. 152; July, 2003, Linda L. Walkins, review of *The Lord Is My Shepherd,* p. 111; November, 2004, Mary N. Oluonye, review of *An African Princess,* p. 97; March, 2005, Be Astengo, review of *The Animal Rescue Store,* p. 203; November, 2005, Judith Constantinides, review of *Storytime,* p. 112; November, 2006, Grace Oliff, review of *The Great Race,* p. 118; July, 2007, Julie Ranelli, review of *We're Sailing down the Nile,* p. 79; July, 2009, C.J. Connor, review of *The Barefoot Book of Earth Tales,* p. 70; June, 2010, Kathy Piehl, review of *We're Roaming in the Rainforest,* p. 76.

ONLINE

Childrensillustrators.com, http://www.childrensillustrators. com/ (January 15, 2011), "Anne Wilson."

Illustration Ltd. Web site, http://www.illustrationweb.com/ (January 15, 2011), "Anne Wilson."*

*   *   *

ZADOFF, Allen 1967-

Personal

Born 1967, in Boston, MA. *Education:* Cornell University, bachelor's degree; Harvard University Institute for Advanced Theatre Training, graduate degree.

Addresses

Home—Los Angeles, CA. *E-mail*—allenzadoff@gmail. com.

Career

Author, writing coach, and motivational speaker. Former stage director; presenter at schools and community groups; presenter at conferences; instructor at writing workshops.

Member

Society of Children's Book Writers and Illustrators.

Awards, Honors

Sid Fleischman Humor award, 2010, for *Food, Girls, and Other Things I Can't Have.*

Writings

Hungry: Lessons Learned on the Journey from Fat to Thin (memoir), Da Capo Press (Cambridge, MA), 2007.

Allen Zadoff (Photograph by Douglas Hill. Reproduced by permission.)

Food, Girls, and Other Things I Can't Have, Egmont USA (New York, NY), 2009.
My Life, the Theatre, and Other Tragedies, Egmont USA (New York, NY), 2011.

Author's work has been translated into Italian.

Sidelights

Born and raised in New England, Allen Zadoff now lives on the West Coast, where he writes and coaches others in the writer's trade. His experiences in the theatre—Zadoff has also worked as a stage director—have also made him an engaging speaker, and he shares his advice as a writer and memoirist with groups at schools, workshops, and conferences. In addition to recounting his experiences as an overweight child and adult in *Hungry: Lessons Learned on the Journey from Fat to Thin,* Zadoff also shares his humorous and upbeat perspective in the young-adult novel *Food, Girls, and Other Things I Can't Have,* which earned the author the Sid Fleischman Humor Award.

By the time Zadoff reached his late twenties, he topped the bathroom scale at 350 pounds, and he shares the story of his struggle with his weight in *Hungry.* Determined to reach a healthier size, he attempted several unsuccessful diets, each followed by a period of discouragement in which he binged on favorite foods. After several years of this, he decided to take a different tack to getting healthy. Viewing overeating as an addiction that was fueled by both emotional and physical elements, Zadoff was able to get help with controlling his food intake and also gain a greater contentment with his life. A *Publishers Weekly* contributor dubbed *Hungry* "encouraging reading for problem eaters," and Susan Salter Reynolds wrote in the *Los Angeles Times* that Zadoff's "gentle, non-preachy, funny and forgiving tone is uncommonly appealing."

Zadoff's problems with weight inspired his teen novel *Food, Girls, and Other Things I Can't Have.* Andrew Zansky has the distinction of being the second heaviest student in his high school, and the sophomore has dealt with the teasing by spending his time with geeky and equally unpopular students. Keeping away from the football field has a down side, however: although it keeps him away from the school's bullies, it also limits the time Andrew can spend with April, a new student who has earned a spot on the cheerleading squad. When the school's star quarterback asks the overweight teen to join the team as a center fielder, Andrew sees it as an

opportunity to change his life for the better. "Watching Andy's transformation . . . is both entertaining and moving," wrote a *Publishers Weekly* critic in praising *Food, Girls, and Other Things I Can't Have,* the reviewer adding that Zadoff's unique story of a "boy makeover . . . is a gem." In *School Library Journal* Sue Lloyd described Andrew as a "thoughtful and refreshing" teen character, adding that "readers will relate to . . . his desire to be popular" as well as "his insecurities." Zadoff's "warm, witty prose" brings to life Andrew's life-changing years, according to a *Kirkus Reviews* writer, and in *Horn Book* Jonathan Hunt recommended *Food, Girls, and Other Things I Can't Have* for its "combination of humor, romance, and sports" and its "fresh spin on the high school clique story."

Biographical and Critical Sources

PERIODICALS

Los Angeles Times, December 2, 2007, Susan Salter Reynolds, review of *Hungry: Lessons Learned on the Journey from Fat to Thin.*
Horn Book, November-December, 2009, Jonathan Hunt, review of *Food, Girls, and Other Things I Can't Have,* p. 690.
Kirkus Reviews, August 15, 2009, review of *Food, Girls, and Other Things I Can't Have.*
Publishers Weekly, September 11, 2006, Matthew Thornton, review of *Hungry;* September 14, 2009, review of *Food, Girls, and Other Things I Can't Have,* p. 47.
School Library Journal, September, 2009, Sue Lloyd, review of *Food, Girls, and Other Things I Can't Have,* p. 177.

ONLINE

Allen Zadoff Home Page, http://www.allenzadoff.com (December 7, 2010).*

* * *

ZUCKERMAN, Andrew 1977-

Personal

Born 1977, in Washington, DC. *Education:* School of the Visual Arts, B.F.A. (photography and film), 1999.

Addresses

Home—New York, NY.

Career

Photographer, filmmaker, and author of children's books. Films include *High Falls,* 2007. Executive producer of documentary *Still Bill. Exhibitions:* Work ex-

Cover of Zadoff's semi-autobiographical teen novel Food, Girls, and Other Things I Can't Have. *(Egmont, 2009. Reproduced by permission.)*

hibited at SUNY Ulster Muroff Kotler Gallery, Stone Ridge, NY, 2007, and Carrousel du Louvre, Paris, France, 2008. Solo exhibits at Forma International Center of Photography, Milan Italy, 2007, State Library of New South Wales, Sydney, Australia, 2008, Colette Center, Paris, 2009, World Financial Center, New York, NY, 2010, and Siamsa Tire Gallery, Dingle, Ireland, 2010. Touring exhibits include "Wisdom," 2010.

Awards, Honors

Young Guns award, Art Directors Club, 2003; Broadcast Design Award, 2005; Yellow Pencil Award for Photography, Design & Art Direction, 2006; Best Short Narrative award, Woodstock Film Festival, and Sundance Film Festival Official Selection, both 2007, both for *High Falls;* The One Show honor.

Writings

Creature, Chronicle Books (San Francisco, CA), 2007.
Wisdom, edited by Alex Vlack, Abrams (New York, NY), 2008.
Bird, Chronicle Books (San Francisco, CA), 2009.
Creature ABC, Chronicle Books (San Francisco, CA), 2009.
Wisdom: Life, edited by Alex Vlack, Abrams (New York, NY), 2009.
Music, Abrams (New York, NY), 2010.
Wisdom: Three New Interviews, Abrams (New York, NY), 2011.

Photographs included in photography annuals, including *American Photography, Communication Arts, Graphis,* and *PDN Photography.* Contributor of articles to periodicals, including *Wired;* contributor of photographs to numerous periodicals, including *Vogue.*

Sidelights

Andrew Zuckerman is a photographer and filmmaker who has gained renown for creating still photographs that allow readers to perceive his subjects in a new way: in isolation. Since his first book, *Creature,* introduced his unique technique through its images of dozens of the world's animals, Zuckerman has narrowed his focus to capture the many varieties within a species in his colorful photographs for *Birds.* He also celebrates the insights of world's most influential older adults in a multi-volume project that begins with *Wisdom: Three New Interviews.* "I tend to elevate my subjects by reducing the elements around them," Zuckerman explained to *Fstop* online interviewer Zack Seckler in discussing his photography technique. "I'm interested in the bare essence of the subject."

While growing up in Maryland, Zuckerman was drawn to photography, and as a teenager he used his camera to photograph and document the lifestyle of local rock bands. Summers spent in New York City with his sister also fueled his interest; he worked cleaning darkrooms at the International Center of Photography in exchange for the opportunity to develop and print his photographs there. Although Zuckerman widened his interests to include short films and sculpture while studying at the city's School of Visual Arts, he refocused on the still image after graduation, eventually establishing a New York studio where he did fashion shoots. In his work for one client, athletic footwear manufacturer Puma, Zuckerman was given the chance to direct several television commercials, and this opportunity widened his exposure among both audiences and potential clients.

Apart from his commercial work, Zuckerman was also developing his unique style, inspired by a summer shortly after graduation that he had spent unemployed and wandering through the exhibits at the city's Museum of Natural History as a way of avoiding the heat. The dioramas at the museum fascinated the young photographer, who realized that by removing the creature from its natural setting it was transformed into something akin to sculpture. "When a subject is stripped from its context," explained Zuckerman in an article for *Wired,* "its behavior, rather than its purpose, is all that remains." The use of a pure white background and directed lighting to minimize shadows allowed the photographer to visually simulate the effect of a museum diorama. "The resulting portraits explore not just the forms, textures, and movements of the creatures but, more important, their characters," he explained. "These images are an attempt to reveal an underlying consciousness that all living things share."

In the process of creating *Creature* a parade of live animals—a toad, a brown hare, and an armadillo; a pair of tiger cubs and a kangaroo; a school of fish; a lean gray wolf and a long-nosed brown bear; and even a giraffe, a zebra, and an elephant—visited Zuckerman's studio and were photographed against a white ground. An ultra-fast camera and the use of multiple Speedotron lights allowed Zuckerman to capture the finest details of fur, feather, skin, and scale. In addition to appearing in *Creature,* which *New York Times Book Review* contributor Leonard S. Marcus described as "sumptuous," Zuckerman's photos are also the star of *Creature ABC,* which pairs each letter of the alphabet with an animal image sure to captivate young children. Noting that "animal alphabets have long been a mainstay of children's books," Marcus added that "Zuckerman's signature white backdrops and minimal captions . . . suit the format well, leaving the way clear for readers to lock eyes, largely undistracted, not only with a lion but also with a mandrill, hippopotamus, black bear, kangaroo and screech owl, to name a few." In *School Library Journal* Julie Roach also hailed the "breathtaking photography" in *Creature ABC,* while a *Kirkus Reviews* contributor asserted that "elephant freckles, mandrill stripes and porcupine quills appear in such startling clarity that the animals seem to breathe on the page."

To capture, on film, the seventy-four species depicted in *Bird* Zuckerman spent a year traveling the world. As with *Creature,* he created temporary studios filled with light, but here he also required a cage to prevent flight. Aided by a team of bird handlers, cranes, buzzards, macaws and magpies, kestrels, eagles, and dozens of other varieties of bird were placed inside the confined studio space, which was then illuminated by high-speed strobe lights that would freeze each bird's movements. The birds' short flight from one side of the cage to the other to reach a feeding dish allowed Zuckerman to capture the grace of flight with his sophisticated Leaf Aptus digital camera.

In *Wisdom* and *Music* Zuckerman captures the images and ideas of notable individuals, in the first older men and women such as actors Clint Eastwood and Dame Judi Dench, South African politician Nelson Mandela, religious leaders the Dalai lama and Archbishop Benjamin Tutu, athlete Billie Jean King, and painter Andrew Wyeth among many others. Also featuring detailed black-and-white photographs paired with quotations and personal essays from each of the photographer's subjects, *Music* focuses on fifty influential musicians who range across the stylistic spectrum, from Ozzie Osborne to Philip Glass. Both *Wisdom* and *Music* reflect Zuckerman's interest in "the human experience as a theme," as he told Seckler. Having explored that theme with his camera, however, he has no interest in pursuing it indefinitely. "The world is a mysterious place," Zuckerman noted, "and I find that curiosity is driven by the urge to demystify things. When a project is completed it's demystified and I go on to the next thing. I think it's unhealthy to think of achievement as arriving somewhere. I don't think there is anywhere to arrive at. You're constantly moving."

Biographical and Critical Sources

PERIODICALS

Kirkus Reviews, August 1, 2009, review of *Creature ABC.*

New York Times Book Review, December 6, 2009, Leonard S. Marcus, review of *Creature ABC,* p. 53.

Publishers Weekly, August 24, 2009, review of *Creature ABC,* p. 60.

School Library Journal, November, 2009, Julie Roach, review of *Creature ABC,* p. 92.

Shoot, May 26, 2006, "New Directors Showcase."

Wired, October 23, 2007, Andrew Zuckerman, "Creature from the Artist and Filmmaker's Perspective."

ONLINE

Andrew Zuckerman Home Page, http://www.andrew zuckerman.com (December 7, 2010).

FStop Web site, http://www.thefstopmag.com/ (December 27, 2009), Zack Seckler, interview with Zuckerman.*